THE OLD NORTH TRAIL

THE SENTINEL   By Walter McClintock

THE
OLD NORTH TRAIL

OR

Life, Legends and Religion of the Blackfeet Indians

BY

WALTER McCLINTOCK

Introduction to the Bison Book Edition
by Sidner J. Larson

UNIVERSITY OF NEBRASKA PRESS
LINCOLN AND LONDON

TO

MY FATHER

WHOSE INTEREST AND ENCOURAGEMENT HAVE BEEN UNFAILING,

THIS BOOK IS AFFECTIONATELY DEDICATED

Introduction copyright © 1992 by the
University of Nebraska Press
All rights reserved
Manufactured in the United States of America

Reprinted from the original 1910 edition
published by Macmillan and Co., London

First Bison Book printing: March 1968
First printing of this Bison Book edition: 1992
Most recent printing shown by the first digit below:
10   9   8   7   6   5   4   3   2   1

Library of Congress Cataloging-in-Publication Data
McClintock, Walter, 1870–1949.
The old North trail, or, Life, legends, and religion of the
Blackfeet Indians / by Walter McClintock; introduction by
Sidner J. Larson.
p.   cm.
Originally published: London: Macmillan, 1910.
"A Bison book."
ISBN 0-8032-8188-9 (pbk.)
1. Siksika Indians. 2. Northwestern States—Description and travel.
I. Title. II. Title: Old North trail. III. Title: Life, legends, and religion
of the Blackfeet Indians.
E99.S54M2   1993
978.6'004973—dc20   92-16001
CIP

∞

INTRODUCTION

By Sidner J. Larson

It was with considerable pleasure that I learned recently of the University of Nebraska Press decision to issue a new Bison Book edition of Walter McClintock's *The Old North Trail*. It is a work of enduring merit that brings us as near as we can now get to the world of the Blackfeet Indians before the intrusion of the white people.

Published in England in 1910, *The Old North Trail* contains a mixture of stories, legends, and descriptions of religious rituals, all woven into McClintock's personal account of his life with the Blackfeet. He tells of being inducted into the tribe, participating in ceremonies, and living with his adoptive family, balanced with serious anthropological descriptions of social customs of the tribe and the names, uses, and preparations of various herbs and medicinal plants.

The strongest feature of the book is the fact that it contains much more personal detail about Blackfeet daily life than can be found in any other sources from that period. McClintock's detailed descriptions of medicine pipe ceremonies and other sacred rituals offer a truly rare "insider" view of native religion seldom available to the public. McClintock's photography; descriptions of daily life, hunts, and ceremonials, vignettes of warriors and medicine men; reminiscences of the famous missionary Father De Smet; legends and mythical stories recorded in the words of the narrators; and much information on such subjects as warrior societies, proper names, songs, and beliefs add considerably to our knowledge of a nearly lost way of life.

McClintock (1870–1949) the scion of a wealthy Pittsburgh family, is known as an ethnologist who lectured on the Blackfeet Indians of Montana and Canada. His audiences included European nobility, among them the crown prince of Germany. He was also an accomplished photographer who produced quality hand-colored studies of the Blackfeet people and their environment. His papers are preserved in a collection at Yale University, his alma mater. A collection of his manuscripts can be found at the Southwest Museum.

In his 1910 preface to *The Old North Trail* McClintock indicated that he had chosen to present a narrative of his experiences, rather than a more formal treatise, as a means of creating a portrait of the environment, family life, and personal character of the Blackfeet as he experienced them. McClintock's narrative begins in the Flathead Valley of northwestern Montana. In the spring of 1896 he visited the area as a member of a government expedition appointed by President Cleveland to recommend a national policy for the United States Forest Reserves and to advise the secretary of the interior as to the reserving of certain other forests.

McClintock's expedition, which went in advance of the main commission, was composed of Gifford Pinchot, chief of the Forest Service, and Henry S. Graves, later chief forester and dean of the Yale School of Forestry. McClintock went as photographer and to help in the forest surveys. There were two guides, William Jackson, or Siksikakoan (Blackfoot-Man), an Indian guide of the Blackfeet tribe, and Jack Munroe, a white man who was married into that tribe.

The party examined the forests in northwestern Montana, on both the eastern and western slopes of the Rocky Mountains, including the Flathead Forest Reserve and Glacier National Park. After concluding the survey in the heavy forest on the western side of the Rocky Mountains, Graves set out for Kalispell and civilization; Pinchot, with Jack Munroe and the expedition's bear dogs, started south for Fort Missoula; McClintock stayed with Siksikakoan.

The two men crossed the Continental Divide to the east by Cutbank Pass, entering Blackfeet country on an old war trail, and joined the tribal camp of the Blackfeet Indians on the plains. There McClintock met many of their leading men, among them Chief Mad Wolf, who adopted him as his son and made him a member of the tribe.

This east-west route intersects the old north-south trail by which Indians traveled into the far distant North Land, and southward as far as Mexico, from perhaps as far back in time as the fabled Bering land bridge. McClintock organizes his narrative spatially around a trip north on the trail to the Blood reserve in Alberta, Canada. Along the way he meets Blackfeet and Blood chiefs Mad Wolf and Brings Down the Sun, who inform him about tribal customs as a means of pleading their case to someone capable of passing the information on to the proper authorities. This organizational pattern then incorporates elements of a Euro-american rhetorical device, the "as told to" autobiography.

Of the four modes of Euro-american narrative (tragedy, romance, comedy, irony), tragedy appears to be the primary one that McClintock imposes on the Blackfeet stories contained in *The Old North Trail*. In this context tragedy represents the stories of Indian people who were not enthusiastic about the white way of life, but who could not bring back their old ways, however much they wanted to. These modes, derived from the Euro-american literary tradition, have practically been elevated to the position of literary statutes in opposition to non-European forms that are constructed differently. One effect can be the repression of other forms of narrative, which get reflected as alien, or truly "other." This is a consideration that needs to be made when placing a book such as *The Old North Trail* in the modern context. One of the strengths of the book is that it resists recasting the Indian stories completely, instead effecting a reasonable compromise of European narrative form and Indian storytelling, which was oral, communal in nature, ongoing without closure.

One instance of McClintock's adherence to the Indian way of storytelling is his consistent reflection of their idea of conservation of animals. For example, in the story "Old Man and the Ground Squirrels," Old Man tricks the squirrels into roasting themselves so he can eat them: "[H]e covered them all over with hot ashes, excepting one mother squirrel, who was afraid. He warned her to run away, so that there might be other squirrels, but left the others in the ashes, until they were well roasted" (339). The idea of taking care to ensure the survival of species is consistent with stories I have heard among the White Clay people on the Fort Belknap Reservation where I was raised, and with Percy Bullchild's native rendition of Blackfeet tales in his book *The Sun Came Down* (Harper & Row, 1985).

The Indian form of narrative was to indicate as many of the circumstances of the narration as possible, or to tell the story of how the story was told. It included internal breaks in the narration to reflect such things as pauses, hesitations, tones of voice, and gestures. This was a distinct departure from the Euro-american approach of author as complete authority and was derived from the communal nature of oral tradition. The form insisted upon the performed quality of the story, rather than a process of editing intended to produce a text that would read smoothly. A primary feature was to not let the audience forget that the text was a recitation, with all the characteristics of spoken conversation. Although McClintock probably cannot be said to have adhered to this type of approach religiously, he does so much more effectively than many writers. For example, during his rendition of the Beaver Medicine Ceremonial, he describes audience activities incidental to the actual praying going on: "During this prayer, Mad Wolf and the entire assembly reverently bowed their heads, joining in an ejaculatory assent (Amen) when he had finished" (85).

In permitting others to speak, the oral style provided perhaps as much objectivity as is possible in the recreation of events. When put in written form, this dialogic presentation can include notes, appendices, and extensive quotation from any source in an effort to provide as much context as possible. This is similar to storytelling techniques of the Nez Perce, whose custom it was, for example, to include witnesses to the telling of coup stories. These witnesses were encouraged to interject, to authenticate, or to correct if they felt it was necessary. Once again, although McClintock did not always incorporate notes, appendices and quotation into the actual storytelling, he did provide rather extensive detail in the form of commentary and in appendices placed at the end of the book. Evidence of McClintock's observation of authenticity is found in the Beaver Medicine Ceremonial:

At this point, O-mis-tai-po-kah raised his hand and stopped the service. The medicine women were astonished. Everyone in the lodge was silent. The chief announced that the ceremonial had not been conducted correctly. The rhythmic drumming and singing began again, as the old chief took the tail. He represented the lynx as making several feints, and then ran suddenly to the tree, just as the women had done. But O-mis-tai-po-kah made it climb more slowly and held it for some time on top, where it had a dance, keeping time with the singing. He then brought it slowly down the other side, clambering little by little as a lynx would do, pausing frequently to look around and listen, making sure that all was well. It finally reached the ground, and, scampering away, was returned to the medicine bundle. (95)

It is important to note that coup stories were not self-centered. Because of this, white biographers often had a difficult time getting Indians to tell things the way they wanted them to. The Indians always attempted to adhere to the Plains sense of the coup story, the story of actions performed in war, as the central meaning of the request to tell their stories. But the biographers were usually true to the Western conception of autobiography as the story of a whole life, and it is that conception that prevails.

It seems fair to say this conception prevails in *The Old North Trail* as well. In the last chapter of the book, "Future of the Blackfeet," McClintock says, "Dispossessed of their ancestral domains, their armed resistance overcome, their sources of subsistence destroyed, they had become the helpless dependents of the American nation, requiring immediate action and the highest statesmanship and constructive philanthropy for their redemption" (510). The meaning of the story of a "whole life," then, usually translates into the fact that when an Indian speaks for himself, about himself, it is not fiction, but autobiography—the "true account" of a "real" Indian's life. With notable exceptions Indian autobiographies perpetuate the image of the defeated "noble savage"; such accounts of Indian lives, while purportedly "true stories," speak more to the white need to believe that all real Indians are safely vanishing. Although McClintock tempers this considerably, it is the responsibility of the readers of *The Old North Trail* to be aware of the idiosyncrasies of "as told to" auto-biography and make their own judgments accordingly.

Although *The Old North Trail* exhibits to a certain degree the tendency to change the form of Indian stories to conform to written tradition; and the content of those stories to reflect a "sepia-romantic" tragic story, there is a wealth of material that overcomes these shortcomings. The book can be compared to James Willard Schultz's *Blackfeet and Buffalo: Memories of Life among the Indians* (University of Oklahoma Press, 1981), and George Bird Grinnell's *Blackfoot Lodge Tales: The Story of a Prairie People* (1892; reprint University of Nebraska Press, 1962). Schultz's book contains folksy, highly entertaining stories that consistently feature the Blackfeet as heroes. Grinnell's work is a more serious yet readable study of the Blackfeet people. *The Old North Trail* stands about midway between Schultz and Grinnell in its treatment of the Blackfeet.

The Old North Trail was written when the Blackfeet were barely into their first generation of reservation life, affording a valuable look at a culture still steeped in tribal kinship traditions. In the words of Walter McClintock, "[The Indians'] unselfish and patriotic lives, devoted to the welfare of their tribe, rise before me in strange and painful contrast with the selfish and sordid lives of many of the rich and powerful of my race. The latter's wealth and power, notwithstanding the advantages of education and Christianity, are not devoted to the amelioration, but tend rather to increase the suffering and degradation of their fellow men" (509). Kinship-based societies have much to offer to help balance technology and capitalism; it could be that the Blackfeet tribal way of life contains valuable clues for modern survival. In addition to the fact the book is good reading, this is a compelling reason it has enduring value for readers of today.

PREFACE

AFTER becoming acquainted with the Blackfeet Indians, I realised that there were locked up in the breasts of the old chiefs and medicine men rich treasures of folk-lore, religious beliefs and ceremonials. I saw that the younger generation was indifferent to their tribal customs, traditions and religion. I also observed that they had no written language, and it seemed inevitable that, with the passing of the old chiefs and medicine men, their ancient religion and folk-lore would fall into oblivion. When I discovered that I could obtain the unbosoming of their secrets and that the door was open to me for study and investigation, I resolved that I would do my best to preserve all the knowledge available.

Having kept accurate records of my experiences and investigations, I have been encouraged to believe that information has been secured worthy of publication. This book has accordingly been published with the hope that its narrative of experiences among the Blackfeet would interest the general reader, and its records of investigation would be of some value to the science of ethnology. The narrative form has been chosen in the belief that this method would furnish a more faithful portraiture of the environment, family life and personal character of this tribe of Indians, and would enable the reader to form a better conception of their religion, tribal customs and social organisation, than if a more formal treatise on these subjects had been attempted.

I gratefully acknowledge my indebtedness to Professor Doctor Karl von den Steinen, President of the Berlin Anthropological Society; Mr. George A. Macmillan of London; Doctor J. G. Frazer, Fellow of Trinity College, Cambridge, England; and Professor William Ridgeway, President of the Royal Anthropological Institute of Great Britain and Ireland, for their interest and encouragement in my work:

To Mr. Francis E. Leupp, former United States Commissioner of Indian Affairs; Mr. Gifford Pinchot, former Chief of the Forest Service, and the resident government agents of the Blackfeet Indians, for their cordial support, during my various visits at the reservations:

To Dr. J. A. Brashear of Pittsburg for his astronomical notes:

To Dr. Clark Wissler of the American Museum of Natural History for sending me his anthropological papers:

To Mr. O. E. Jennings, assistant curator of Botany in Carnegie Institute, Pittsburg, for his identification of my collection of herbs and plants:

To Mr. and Mrs. Thomas B. Magee of Browning, Montana, for their assistance and friendship during many years:

And to my brother Norman McClintock for his valuable assistance in photographic matters and identification of birds.

WALTER McCLINTOCK

PITTSBURG, PA., U.S.A.,
June, 1910.

CONTENTS

CHAPTER I.

CHAPTER II.

CHAPTER III.

CONTENTS

CONTENTS

CONTENTS

CONTENTS

CONTENTS

CONTENTS

CONTENTS

CHAPTER XXVII.

CHAPTER XXVIII.

CHAPTER XXIX.

CHAPTER XXX.

CONTENTS

CONTENTS

CONTENTS

HERD OF BUFFALO ON THE PRAIRIE.

THE OLD NORTH TRAIL

INTRODUCTION

THE once powerful confederation of the Blackfeet or
Siksikaua Indians comprising the North Blackfeet,
Bloods and Piegans, is of Algonquin origin. Although they speak the same language, have similar
customs, and are closely intermarried, these three
divisions are independent of each other, each having
its own Sun-dance, council and head chief. When the
dominant white race, both in Canada and the United
States, restricted the Blackfeet from their nomadic life,
which had covered the vast region stretching, from the
North Saskatchewan River in Alberta, to the Yellowstone River in Montana, and from longitude 105 degrees
west from Greenwich to the Rocky Mountains, their
fixed settlements were made in the localities where
their permanent camps were formerly located. Thus
the present reservations of the Bloods (Kainau), and
North Blackfeet, in the Province of Alberta, Canada,
are along the same rivers, where their ancestors camped.
The Piegans became subdivided into North and South
Piegans, the former in Alberta, and the latter in North-
western Montana.

The most reliable authorities that I could consult
among the Blackfeet, as to the origin of their tribal

name, stated that, ages ago, their people lived far to the north of their present country, where the dark fertile soil so constantly discoloured their moccasins that they were called Siksikaua, or Black Moccasins.

They were the most aggressive and warlike of all the Plains tribes. They were constantly at war with the Crows, Sioux, Cheyennes, Assinniboines, Snakes, Kutenai and Flatheads. Their war-parties frequently met in conflict along the Old North Trail. The Blackfeet say that the Crows once roamed along the eastern slopes of the Rocky Mountains, but were driven by them to the south-east, where the Crow reservation is now situated. The Lewis and Clark Journals mention the Blackfeet as the only tribe against which their expedition was compelled to use firearms.

In 1832 Catlin wrote about the Plains Indians : " The several tribes of Indians, inhabiting the Upper Missouri, are undoubtedly the finest looking, best equipped and most beautifully costumed. . . . They live in a country well stocked with buffaloes and wild horses, which furnish them an excellent and easy living ; their atmos-phere is pure, which produces good health and long life, and they are the most independent and happiest race of Indians I have met with : they are all entirely in a state of primitive rudeness and wildness, and con-sequently are picturesque and handsome, almost beyond description. Nothing in the world, of its kind, can possibly surpass in beauty and grace some of their games, amusements and parades. In my travels I have more than realised my former predictions that those Indians, who could be found almost entirely in a state of nature, with the least knowledge of civilised society, would be found the most cleanly in their persons, elegant in their dress and manners, and enjoying life to the greatest perfection. Of such tribes perhaps the Crows and Blackfeet stand first; and no one would be able to appreciate the richness and elegance, (and even taste too), with which some of these people dress, without seeing them in their own country."

The Blackfeet traversed wide tracts of country in quest of plunder and adventure. They were the most daring and enterprising of the Plains tribes, their expeditions following the Old North Trail into the far distant North Land, and southward as far as Mexico. That they used horses, on these far-seeking expeditions, we have the testimony of Mackenzie, who says of the Blackfeet in 1800, "They are the people who deal in horses and take them upon war parties towards Mexico, from which they enter into the country to the south-east, which consists of plains." Sometimes their expeditions did not return for several years, and then would appear unexpectedly in full view of the tribal camp, bearing their spoils and singing their songs of victory, amid general rejoicing. The bravery of their chiefs and their wonderful adventures were then heralded throughout the tribe, and the young men were thus stimulated to emulate their deeds of valour.

In the former domain of the Blackfeet, lying between the Rocky Mountains and the Yellowstone and Upper Missouri Rivers, the mountain slopes abounded in beaver, wapiti, moose, mountain sheep and grizzly bears, while immense herds of antelope and buffalo roamed over the plains, furnishing them with an abundance of meat for food, and skins for clothing and shelter. But the irresistible advance of the white race was like the invasion of a hostile army in its effects upon this Indian paradise. It brought small-pox, measles and other contagious diseases and the seductive poison, alcohol, each in turn contributing to the undermining of the vigour of the Indian race. The last of several plagues of small-pox was introduced by a Missouri River steamboat in 1869, spreading rapidly among the Plains tribes. It decimated the Blackfeet and is still referred to by them as "the great sickness." The climax of their misfortunes finally came with the sudden annihilation in 1883 of the last of the great herds of buffalo, which had afforded them occupation and their chief means of subsistence. At the beginning of the following winter, the Blackfeet found themselves deprived of their usual winter stores of dried buffalo meat, with the result that, during that winter and the spring of 1884, a large number of them perished from starvation.

Greatly reduced in numbers and crippled in resources, the Blackfeet slowly retreated before the advancing tide of white settlers. Yielding to the pressure from the whites and their own dire necessities, they sold by treaty vast tracts of land to the United States, so that they now occupy only a narrow strip of country bordering upon the eastern slopes of the northern Rockies. The climate, being subject to severe storms in summer and blizzards in winter, has so far seemed unfavourable for agriculture. Their chief occupation of raising cattle and horses is handicapped by the hazards of extreme heat and cold.

They have held themselves, as much as possible, aloof from civilisation, cherishing the remembrance of their former days of comfort, freedom and power. Oft repeated wrongs by the whites have provoked individual retaliation and bloodshed, but not organised rebellion against the Government, and developed in the Indian heart a deep-seated mistrust and hatred of the white race. Early explorers estimated that the Blackfeet once numbered from 30,000 to 40,000. They have gradually dwindled, until at the present time there are about 3,500 full bloods in Canada and the United States. This constant decline of the full-blooded Blackfeet still continues, and we have the pathetic spectacle of a dying race.

CHAPTER I

MY INTRODUCTION TO THE BLACKFEET

Visit North-Western Montana as member of a Forestry Expedition under Gifford Pinchot, Chief of the Forest Service of the United States.—Meet with Siksikakoan, an Indian Scout.—He invites me to go with him to his home among the Blackfeet.—Our journey eastward through the forests up the western slope of the Rocky Mountains. —We cross the Continental Divide by the Cutbank Pass. —Flora, birds and Fauna of the mountains.—Magnificent scenery. —Many glaciers and snowcapped peaks.—Enter the Blackfeet Country by an old Indian war-trail.—First glimpse of the tribal camp of the Blackfeet on the plains. —Siksikakoan introduces me to the leaders of the Blackfeet.—Meeting with Chief Mad Wolf.—Novel experiences in the big camp.—Accompany Siksikakoan to his home on Cutbank River.—My first summer among the Blackfeet.

I FIRST visited the country of the Blackfeet as a member of a Government expedition under Gifford Pinchot, Chief of the Forest Service of the United States, which had been sent into the north-west by the National Forest Commission, to report upon the advisability of forming certain national forest reserves.

Siksikakoan (Blackfoot-Man), also known as William Jackson, was a noted Indian scout, who had served in the Indian campaigns under Generals Miles and Custer. He related to me the thrilling story of his escape through the Sioux lines, at the time of the disastrous battle of the Little Big Horn, June 25th, 1876, when General Custer and his battalion of the 7th U.S. cavalry were annihilated by the Sioux.[1]   Siksikakoan was attached

[1] The Blackfeet tribe of Montana and Alberta should not be confused with the Sioux Blackfeet of Dakota who fought against General Custer in the battle of The Little Big Horn.

as a scout to Major Reno's battalion, co-operating with
General Custer's.   During the first confusion of Major
Reno's attack and repulse in the first day's fighting,
First Lieutenant De Rudio, Interpreter Girard, Private
O'Neal and Siksikakoan were cut off.[1]   Under cover of
darkness, Siksikakoan ventured upon the battle-field
and stripped from the dead Sioux sufficient leggings,
moccasins and blankets to disguise themselves.   Then,
in the dead of night, on the 26th, he led his companions
safely through their sleeping enemies, to the bluffs north
of the river, to which Major Reno had retreated for
safety.   During the movement Siksikakoan answered
the challenges of the Sioux by giving satisfactory replies
in the Sioux language.

Siksikakoan continued his scouting service until the
close of the Indian wars on the northern plains, when
he returned to his tribe on the Blackfeet Reservation.
He erected a cabin on Cutbank River, at the foot of the
Rocky Mountains.   He gradually built up a well-
equipped ranch, and owned large herds of cattle and
horses.   He lived there till the winter of 1899, when
he died, as the final result of injuries received during
his life of adventure and hardship as a scout.

When the forestry work was completed and my
Government associates had departed, Siksikakoan and
I were camped together in the forest country of the
Flathead Indians, on the western slope of the Rocky
Mountains.   One evening, by our camp-fire, I agreed
to his proposal that we should return to the Blackfeet
Reservation on the eastern side of the range ; " for

[1] " During the night Lieutenant De Rudio, Private O'Neal, Mr. Girard,
the interpreter, and Jackson, a scout, came to our line.   They had been
left in the river bottom when Major Reno made his retreat."   (Extract
from Capt. E. S. Godfrey's "Custer's Last Battle," *Century Magazine*,
volume 43, p. 379, Jan. 1892.)   The same incident is referred to in the
report of Gen. W. T. Sherman, Secretary of War, 1876, p. 33.

there," said he, " I have many horses and cattle. The mountains are not far distant, where the hunting is good, and the lakes and streams are full of fish. We

CAMP ON WESTERN SLOPE.

shall be in the midst of my people, and I will introduce you to the leading chiefs of the Blackfeet."

It was at the beginning of summer, when we started on our journey across the Rocky Mountains, toward the country of the Blackfeet. Our outfit was carried on the backs of pack horses. The trail was difficult and overgrown and frequently blocked by windfalls. Siksikakoan led the way with his axe, while I followed driving the pack horses. On the western slope of the Rockies the forests are very dense, because of the mild climate and abundant rainfall. The trees grow to a large size and the undergrowth is luxuriant. We rode

RIVER ON WESTERN SLOPE.

through glades, where the rank masses of weeds and grasses were shoulder high, and passed chains of beautiful lakes, hidden in the gloomy recesses of the forest, where huge tamaracks, firs and spruces grew to the water's edge, and extended high up on the sides of the mountains This was the haunt of deer, wapiti and moose, many of their tracks being visible in the soft ground along the lake shores.

A botanist would have been delighted with the

great numbers of wild flowers in full bloom. I saw
magnificent specimens of bear grass (Xerophyllum
Douglasii), growing to the height of five feet. Their
stalks were surmounted by dense caps of white flowers,
each flower on an ascending pedicel an inch or more
long. The leaves at the base of the stem were narrow
and stiff. The root is used by the Blackfeet as a

ADDERS' TONGUES.

remedy for fractures and sprains. The leaves of a
similar species are used by other Indian tribes in
making baskets. There was also a great profusion of
pink twin flowers (Linnaeus borealis), with its vine
of shiny dark green leaves, also bishop's caps, light
yellow adders' tongues and flowering dogwood (Cornus
canadensis).

During our forest journey I recognised many birds

native to my home in the east. When passing lonely lakes, I heard the wild, laughing cry of the loon, and olive-backed thrushes singing along the shores. In the lofty pines were chicadees, winter wrens, hermit thrushes, and myrtle warblers. In the open glades were robins, doves, ruffed grouse, chipping sparrows, flickers, juncos, and tree swallows. Here I first became acquainted with the Macgillivray warbler, his little gray

A MOUNTAIN LAKE.

head frequently peering out shyly from the willows along the streams. I found the nest, with four eggs, hidden away in some blackberry bushes, close to a lake. In the bushes were vireos, fly-catchers, and yellow warblers, and, in the deep woods, woodpeckers, red-breasted nuthatches, and golden-crown kinglets.

We surprised a large bear sunning himself in the trail, but he quietly and quickly disappeared into the forest. The trail led through a broad valley and along the bank of a swift mountain stream, climbing continually upwards towards the Continental Divide. When we reached a high altitude, the trees became gnarled and stunted, and we were frequently enveloped in heavy clouds. Here were many tracks of big-horn, and we saw a band of Rocky Mountain goats high

"WE ENTERED A HUGE BASIN SURROUNDED BY TOWERING PEAKS."

up on the mountain side. Hoary marmots, or whistlers greeted us from the cliffs with their shrill calls, but they were so timid that they quickly disappeared on our approach. We entered a huge basin, surrounded by towering peaks—a superb and vast amphitheatre about four miles wide from side to side. At the bottom was a sparkling lake, with wooded shores, surmounted by a circular mountain wall with a sheer height of 3,000 feet. It was fed by many streams, which had their sources in the glaciers and fell over precipitous cliffs with a constant roar, reverberating like thunder from the surrounding walls of rock.

THE PASS.

The Indians have given to the main range of the Rocky Mountains the appropriate name " Backbone-of-the-World." Standing on the summit of the Cutbank Pass (7,861 feet), we were surrounded by dazzling glaciers and stupendous mountains mantled with snow. The intense brightness of the snow-fields was relieved by the dark green covering of forests, which lined the valleys far below.   Four miles to the north lay the Triple Divide—the Crown of the Continent, where the water-shed divides between the Pacific Ocean, Hudson Bay, and the Gulf of Mexico.   Directly south was the sharply-pointed Flinch's peak, which lifted its towering mass like a cathedral spire 5,000 feet above the valley.   It is impossible from the illustration to realise the sheer precipitousness of this peak.

On the west were Mt. James (10,155 feet), Mt. Pinchot (9,332 feet), and Ram Mountain, so called because frequented by many Rocky Mountain rams. To the north-west was Mt. Blackfoot (9,591), and the magnificent Blackfoot Glacier, a vast expanse of ice and snow.   Beyond rose the summit of Mt. Jackson [1] (10,023), and under its shoulder the Harrison Glacier, with its wonderful ice cascades.   Turning farther to the north, we could see a multitude of peaks. Among them were Mt. Siyeh [2] (or Mad Wolf, 10,004); Little Chief [2] (9,542); Going-to-the-Sun (9,594); Four Bears [2]; Almost-a-Dog [2] (8,911); Mt. Grinnell (8,838), and the Grinnell Glacier; Mt. Red Eagle, [2] and the Red Eagle Glacier, which is the source of Red Eagle Creek. The Grinnell Glacier is fenced on the west by a remarkable, serrated ridge of the Continental Divide known as "The Garden Wall."

In close proximity are the Gun-sight Pass (its contour resembling a gun-sight), and the Sperry Glacier; the Sexton Glacier, with its half mile of ice front, and the Swift Current Pass.   Words fail to describe the

---

[1] Named after Wm. Jackson (Siksikakoan).
[2] Name of a Blackfoot chief.

magnificence of the glaciers and waterfalls, and the majesty and impressive beauty of the numerous high peaks and stupendous mountain ranges. Although this country is practically unknown, the difficult trails being frequented only by hunters, trappers, and Indians, its scenic wonders are probably unsurpassed by any within the United States. The region should be

FLINCH'S PEAK.

" A mass of rock towering 5,000 feet above the valley."

reserved by the Government as a National Park and Game Preserve.[1]

From the summit of the Pass, Siksikakoan pointed out the course of our trail eastward, following the Cutbank River through a long, winding valley, with high, snow-covered mountain ranges on either side. Beyond stretched the tawny plains—the country of the Blackfeet, resembling a distant ocean in its level

[1] See Appendix.

expanse, and extending eastward many hundreds of miles into the dim and hazy horizon. We descended from the summit of Cutbank Pass between two small

THE CUTBANK TRAIL.
(Ancient Indian route of travel.)

glacier lakes. In their dark and still waters, the surrounding crags and mountain walls were clearly reflected and many miniature icebergs were floating, having fallen from the fronts of the overhanging glaciers.

The travelling on the eastern side of the Rockies was much easier and in marked contrast with our difficult ascent of the western side. We now followed a trail, worn deep into the ground by generations of Blackfeet and other Indian tribes, when they crossed and recrossed the Rocky Mountains on their war and hunting expeditions. We entered a forest at the head of the canyon,

EAST CUT-BANK CANYON.

where the snow clung heavily to the balsams and pines. As we descended, the snow disappeared and the air became balmy.

The climate east of the mountains is more severe, because subject to extreme changes of temperature. Hailstorms are frequent, and snowstorms often occur in midsummer. In winter there are terrible blizzards, during which the thermometer drops to 50° below zero, (Fahrenheit).

We camped after sunset in a beautiful, natural park of luxuriant bunch-grass, fragrant with wild flowers and surrounded by forests of spruce and pine.

Early next morning—our last day in the mountains —we again took up the trail through the canyon of the Cutbank River. As the sun's rays entered the canyon, the massive walls of rock, towering overhead, became a brilliant red, while the high peaks glistened with colours as varied as the rainbow's. In crossing the summit of a high rocky ridge, we had an extended view of the forest-covered valley below, and the course of the river winding through open glades and grassy meadows, until it passed through the entrance of the canyon. Beyond were the foothills, or high, grass-covered ridges, lying in front of the canyon entrance, like a mighty barrier. Here the luxuriant vegetation of the mountains abruptly ended and the dry grass of the prairies began.

After riding through the foothills, we crossed an old trail, running north and south, now overgrown with grass. Siksikakoan explained that it was the Old North Trail. It is no longer used by the Indians, its course having been broken in many places by the fences and towns of the white man's advancing civilisation. Yet the old horse trail and travois tracks were still plainly visible, having been worn deep by many generations of travelling Indians.

We rode out over the treeless plains until, from the crest of a ridge, about twenty miles from the main range of the Rockies, we looked down upon a scene, which I will never forget because of its novel and exceeding beauty. In a luxuriant tract of meadow, and on the shore of a lake, lay the tribal camp of the Blackfeet, pitched in the form of an enormous circle.

The undulating ridges, which surrounded it were brilliant with blue lupines and velvet-leaf sun-flowers. Great herds of horses were contentedly feeding on the rich bunch grass. Smoke from the evening fires was rising from the lodges. A faint breeze, laden with a pleasant fragrance from the meadows, brought distinctly

VELVET LEAF SUNFLOWERS ON PRAIRIE.

the sounds of an Indian camp, the shouts of men and women, the crying of children, the barking of many dogs and the slow, measured beating of Indian tom-toms in dances and ceremonial gatherings.

After entering the Blackfeet camp, I accompanied Siksikakoan while he visited the lodges of the different chiefs. As we sat smoking a friendly pipe together, he explained to them that I had come from the Great Father (President of the United States), for the purpose of protecting the forests of their country, that they might be preserved for future generations. In this way I first met Chief Mad Wolf (Siyeh), their greatest orator, the high priest of their Sun-dance and the owner of the Beaver Medicine Bundle (an important ceremonial). This was the beginning of a mutual bond of sympathy and attachment, unusual between an Indian and a

TRIBAL CAMP OF THE BLACKFEET.

white man, which developed gradually into a strong and lasting friendship.

On my first night in the Blackfeet camp, I chose to sleep outside the camp circle in a meadow, not far from Mad Wolf's lodge, because the weather was clear and warm and I had no fear of being molested by the Indians. I was within hearing of any ceremonials that would take place in Mad Wolf's lodge and nothing of moment could occur in the encampment without my knowledge.

My own decorated Tipi in the Blackfeet Camp.

I placed my blanket-bed on the prairie-grass, and, instead of the lodge covering for a roof, I had the magnificent canopy of the night-sky, spangled with an innumerable multitude of stars. On account of the clearness of the atmosphere over the plains, these sparkling orbs of light shone with a rare brilliance and splendour, and appeared lower down in the horizon than I had ever seen elsewhere. Lying on my back and gazing up into the wonderful beauty of the heavens gave me an overwhelming sense of the infinity of God's universe and my own littleness by comparison.

I was not, however, to be entirely free from disturbance. While lying upon my blankets, my attention was attracted by two wandering Indian boys, who had been startled by the weird and ghostly appearance of my bed. They were standing at a short distance conversing together in awed whispers. When I gave a sudden jump and rattled the white canvas covering, they took to their heels, believing that I was a ghost. During the night, I was again aroused by the hot breath of a large animal upon my face. Being awakened from a deep slumber, I imagined that it was a grizzly bear standing over me. Jumping from my blankets with a yell, I found that it was an Indian horse, which had been standing quietly, with lowered head, over my bed. My outfit had aroused his curiosity, but my actions were so precipitate and my appearance, clad in white, so startling, that he quickly stampeded with frightened snorts.

At first I was at a loss to know how to secure suitable board and lodging in the Blackfoot camp. Their diet of dried meat and meat stews was to me neither appetising nor sufficiently nourishing. The difficult problem was, however, solved for me in a very satisfactory way by my friend Big Eyes. I had gained the good will of himself and wife through the interest I had taken in their children. To show their appreciation, his wife, Ips-e-nik-ki, who was skilled in the making of lodges, presented me with an Indian tipi, decorated with pictographs of interesting events in her husband's life. With the acquisition of a tipi, I had my own home in the camp, but it was necessary to do my own cooking and to care for my own horses and outfit, for the Blackfeet have no servants, and I had not taken a wife.

I soon discovered that my diet of bacon, cereals, and dried fruits was no more pleasing to the Blackfeet than theirs was to me. After Spotted Eagle, the medicine man, had dined with me, he said that he had never been able to understand how people could live on the food eaten by white men. He told me of a journey he had once taken with some officers of the United States Army, " with whom he could stay no longer than a week, because of the strange food they ate."

When the Sun festival was finished and the Indians separated, I accompanied Siksikakoan to live on his Blackfoot ranch, not far from Mad Wolf's home on Cutbank River. I found him to be a man of fine mind and practical common sense, resourceful and fearless in emergencies and thoroughly equipped in all that goes to make an ideal guide and companion in the wilds. Under him I learned woodcraft, the handling of the broncho, the mysteries of the " diamond hitch " and the location of the old Indian trails leading across the plains and through the mountains. He was a natural orator and had standing and influence in the councils of his tribe. He spoke English fluently as well as the Blackfoot and Sioux tongues, and was thoroughly familiar with the ancient customs and traditions of his people. It was under his influence that I became deeply interested in the Blackfeet, and through his friendship that I was gradually brought into an intimate association with their leaders.

During my first summer among the Blackfeet, I rode over the reservation, visiting them in their camps and in their homes. Many interesting subjects crowded themselves upon my mind and enlisted my energies. I carried a medicine case containing simple remedies with which I was sometimes able to relieve the sick and help the injured. I endeavoured in every way to aid their advancement towards the white man's civilisation, helping in the cultivation of the ground, herding horses and cattle, and cutting timber in the mountains for building their cabins, fences, and corrals. When the sun was hot in midsummer, I helped them to make hay in the luxuriant meadows of the river bottoms. Although that kind of work was hard, it never seemed to dull my mind to the wonderful and ever-changing beauty of prairie, river, and distant mountains. In the clear days of autumn, when the bite of frost was in the air, I joined their hunting expeditions across the broad plains and into the Rocky Mountains.

I now look back with the deepest pleasure upon the freedom of that life, the delight of living and of working in that exhilarating mountain atmosphere. Those who spend sleepless nights, because of the absorbing and nerve-racking occupations of modern civilisation, may well envy my nights of refreshing sleep, while wrapped in my blankets beside some swiftly flowing mountain stream, or on the plains under the open sky. The life of the Indian, so close to the heart of nature, the companionship with inspiring mountains, sunlit plains, lakes and rivers, the ceaseless, but ever beautiful succession of lights and colourings, while day waned into night and night gave place to day, and the wonderful colour transformations, which came and went with the changing seasons, all these fascinated and held me with an irresistible grip.

It required, however, a long period of cordial relations to overcome the natural prejudice of the Indians against a white man, but I gradually gained their confidence, which I was careful never to abuse. I lived with them, not merely for pleasure and adventure, but chiefly for the purpose of gaining as full a knowledge as possible of their characteristics and customs, their traditions and religion. I realised that I had an unusual opportunity of studying a remarkable race of people, who properly belonged to the Stone Age, whose religion and social organisation had come down from a distant past, free from contact with any other religion, or culture. The younger generation were indifferent to their ancient customs and religion and it seemed that this primitive and most interesting people must soon lose their identity and disappear for ever.

CHAPTER II

MY ADOPTION BY MAD WOLF

My meeting with Mad Wolf on the plains.—He proposes to adopt me as his son.—Mad Wolf's camp.—The ceremonial of adoption.—Mad Wolf's prayer.—He directs me to take part in the ceremonial.—Appoints a second ceremonial for giving my Indian name.

ONE afternoon in midsummer, while riding with Siksikakoan across the plains, we met Mad Wolf near Willow Creek. He was alone and signified his desire to speak with me. He was standing with his blanket drawn closely around him. His long hair tinged with gray fell loosely over his shoulders. From his neck hung a medicine whistle made from the wing-bone of an eagle. In his back hair, a single eagle feather stood erect. When I had dismounted, he warmly shook my hand. For a moment, he gazed into my face with eyes as penetrating as those of an eagle. Then, with head erect, he addressed me in a strong and earnest voice.

"The snows of two winters have now passed since you first came to live in my country. I have been watching you continually from the time when you first arrived, and my heart feels warm towards you. I have never taken a son from among the white men, but I now wish to adopt you as my son, because I believe that some day you will become a chief among your people. I am growing old, and it is probable that I will go before you to dwell with the Great Spirit, for you are still a young man. When I am gone you will then be left to help and to advise my people."

Having in a few words made known to Mad Wolf

my willingness to become his son, he waved his hand towards the North, and said :

" My lodge is out there on the plains. It is on the other side of yonder butte, and cannot be seen from here. Come to my lodge to-morrow, when the sun is high. My relatives will be there; I will hold a ceremonial, in which I will paint you with the sacred red paint, and in their presence adopt you as my son."

The developments of subsequent years have enabled me more fully to appreciate Mad Wolf's serious purpose in adopting me as his son. Prompted by the constant misrepresentation and mis-understanding of the In-dian by the whites, his purpose was to seek a white man's strong friend-ship, hoping for an alliance that would be productive of sympathy and fidelity to the welfare of his tribe. He wanted a white repre-sentative, who had lived sufficiently long among his

Copyright in United States
by Walter McClintock.
MAD WOLF (SIYEH).

people, to become familiar with their customs, religion, and manner of life, and would tell the truth about them to the white race.

Upon the day following my meeting with Mad Wolf the sky was overcast. Riding in a northerly direction, I arrived at the ridge pointed out by the chief. I paused on its crest, and looked down upon a small Indian camp. The freshening wind had begun to drive low clouds over the plains, while occasionally a furious gust shook the lodges, firmly anchored by ropes thrown around their tops. The only living thing to be seen was a coyote, slinking away over a neighbouring butte, and the only sign of human occupation was the slender wisp of blue smoke issuing from the top of Mad Wolf's tipi. During a lull in the wind I heard the subdued and measured sounds of Indians chanting and beating upon drums. As I sat still upon my horse, my mind went back many years, and I pictured to

LOOKED DOWN ON A SMALL INDIAN CAMP.

myself the days when the ancestors of Mad Wolf and his followers were the rulers of this entire region, and their lodges were numbered by thousands. When the song had ceased I rode down from the ridge and dismounting, raised the door. A small fire was burning in the center, and in the dim light I saw that a large number of Indians were assembled.

"Oki!" (come in), cried Mad Wolf. Upon entering I found myself in a large, well ordered tipi of about twenty-five feet in diameter. Mad Wolf was seated at the back,—the position of honour. His relatives and friends were on either side, the men to his left, and the women to his right. He greeted me with a warm handshake and said, " Ke-a-e-es-tsa-kos-ach-kit-satope " (spread the robe out for him to sit down). He wore beaded buckskin leggings and moccasins and from his neck was suspended a medicine whistle. He had a noble countenance, and a large and shapely head, the upper part of his body was bare, his shoulders broad and well formed, and his arms strongly developed, he was in every way a magnificent specimen of Indian manhood. From his piercing glance and the firm expression of his mouth, I knew he was accustomed to command. He had a natural dignity of manner, while conducting the ceremonial, that fascinated me, and I found myself intently watching his every movement.

Next to Mad Wolf, and assisting him in the ceremonial, was Natoya Apau (Blessed Weasel). The expression of his face and eyes told me that he had a kind heart and a good disposition. On my left was Morning Plume, who gave me a smile of welcome and was careful of my comfort, spreading a robe for my seat and watching that I should make no mistake during the ceremonial. Beyond him were Isoko-yo-kinni, Double Runner, Stock-stchi, Bear Child, and Many White Horses. The latter was so named because he made a speciality of white horses and would have no other colour in his herds.

To the right of Mad Wolf lay the sacred bundle of the Beaver Medicine.[1] Next to it sat Mad Wolf's wife, Gives-to-the-Sun. From the lodge poles over their heads hung the Medicine Pipe [1] and a raw-hide case

[1] See Appendix.

containing the Medicine Bonnet.[1] To the right of Gives-to-the-Sun were women and children completely filling the circle to the doorway of the lodge.

All sat silently gazing into the small fire, for they were about to commence a religious ceremony. Gives-to-the-Sun spoke in a low voice to a young woman, who arose and, bending over the fire, slowly stirred a

" Strikes-on-both-sides."

large kettle containing a stew of sarvis berries and tongues. Pointing to her, Mad Wolf explained that she was his daughter who would now become my sister, saying also, " When she was small, the enemy had captured her, but I followed them and, when they were preparing to kill her, I jumped among them and, striking the enemy down on both sides, rescued her. So we named her " Strikes-on-both-sides ! "

[1] See Appendix.

A large pipe of polished red stone was continually circulating, everyone smoking except the children. The pipe always started from Mad Wolf, who first blew four whiffs to the Sun and four to the Earth, then it was passed to Blessed Weasel on his left, who handed it to me, stem first. After smoking I passed it on to Morning Plume. On its return I handed it to Blessed Weasel, stem first as before, but was corrected by him, with the explanation that, in going towards Mad Wolf, the pipe should have been handed bowl first. No one else seemed to notice this infraction of one of their customs. I was often impressed, in gatherings of the Blackfeet, by the dignified courtesy and genuine nobility of manners on the part of their head men, in passing over, without remark, or notice, any unwitting breach of social or ceremonial observance.

Mad Wolf began the ceremonial by taking a hot coal from the fire with a long forked stick. He placed dried sweet grass upon it and the rising smoke soon filled the lodge with a pleasing fragrance. At this moment the clouds parted in the sky, and the sun came out. The bright rays, streaming down through the top of the lodge, shone upon the ground in front of Mad Wolf. Holding his hands in the sweet smoke of the incense, Mad Wolf passed them along his arms and upon his breast to purify himself, and then chanted :

"To-day, our father (Sun) shines into the lodge, his power is very strong.

"Last night our mother (Moon) shone into the lodge, her power is very strong.

"I pray the Morning Star (their Son) that, when he rises at daybreak, he too will shine in to bless us and to bring us long life."

Mad Wolf and Blessed Weasel together led a chorus in which all joined. The women held aloft their left hands and closely watched Mad Wolf, who with bent arms held his hands folded on a level with his head. Then passing his hands along his arms alternately, after their manner of a blessing, he finally folded them upon his breast, and chanted :

> " Mother Earth have pity on us, and give us food to eat!
> " Father, the Sun, bless all our children, and may our paths be straight ! "

Taking a sacred stick decorated with red paint, representing a cane, Mad Wolf placed it upon his right and left shoulders in turn, and prayed for long life. Blessed Weasel did likewise, handing the cane to me. I laid it upon both of my shoulders while they prayed that I might live to be old. The cane was passed around the circle, all performing the same ceremony. When the stick was returned to Mad Wolf, he and Blessed Weasel with their wives placed their hands upon it and sang a low chant.

Mad Wolf brought forth a small buckskin bag from which he took some red clay, the sacred paint which the Blackfeet believe has power to ward off sickness and to bring long life. When I saw him preparing it in his hands, I knew the moment for my adoption had arrived. There was an impressive silence as he motioned to me and said, " Here comes my white son." While kneeling before him, he painted my face on the forehead, chin and both cheeks, representing the Sun's daily course through the heavens. The forehead represented the rising, and the left cheek the setting Sun. Then taking the beaver skin, he passed it down both sides of my head, shoulders and arms to the hands, ending with an upward movement, by which he imparted his blessing and prayed :

"Before you, my father, Great Sun Chief, I now adopt this young man as my son. Let the red paint be like the sunlight to protect and bring him health and strength. May all my people be friendly and protect him that he may be happy as long as he remains among his Indian brothers and sisters. My father, the Sun, who gives us light, keep him from harm when he goes again to his home towards the East. Give him light by day, that his path may be free from danger. If he should go into the wrong trail, lead him safely back, that his path may be firm and down hill to old age. As the sweet smoke of the incense ascends towards the sky, so may our prayers arise and be acceptable to thee, O thou great Sun God!"

After the prayer Mad Wolf directed Blessed Weasel to unroll a bundle containing buffalo and elk hides, which were spread out before the men. Large rattles were also distributed among them. Mad Wolf handed me two rattles, saying "You are now my son and should take part in this ceremonial." Kneeling on the ancient buffalo hide, I joined with them in the chants and beat time on the hide with my rattles. The first chant we sang represented a porcupine sitting on a hill and watching a beaver at work. The porcupine said: "I will take my bow and arrows and kill you." But the beaver jumping into the stream swam off under the water and escaped. We also sang the song of the war eagle, describing it as soaring high in the air above the mountain peaks and at times swooping down towards the earth when seeking its prey. Mad Wolf then danced around the fire with the pipe, singing and, at intervals, blowing upon his medicine whistle. Stockstchi took the pipe from Mad Wolf. He blew four whiffs to the North, South, East and West, and then, holding the pipe towards the Sun, prayed to the Great Spirit in the Sun for the recovery of his sick child.

Mad Wolf ended the ceremonial at sunset with the prayer:

" Great Sun God ! Continue to give us your light that the leaves and grass may grow so that our cattle will increase and our children may live to be old.

" Our mother ! (the Moon), give us sleep that we may rise again like our father (the Sun). May our lives be strong, and may our hearts feel good towards our white brothers, as we are all your children."

When the wife of Blessed Weasel arose to ladle out the stew, Mad Wolf directed that she set aside for his white son some of the tongue which the Blackfeet consider a delicacy. When the stew had been passed to everyone, I was preparing to eat, when Blessed Weasel motioned to me. Then I noticed that all were waiting. To my surprise it was for a blessing upon the food , for, after a short pause, Mad Wolf said : " The berries that grow are blessed, for upon them we live." He held a sarvis berry aloft in his right hand and chanted, everyone imitating his motions and joining with him in his prayer to Mother Earth that they might live to see many summers. After each person had planted a berry in the ground, a symbolic act in recognition of the source of their sustenance, they partook of the feast. None of the food was wasted. What remained was gathered together and set aside.

When I was ready to depart for my camp, Mad Wolf said, " O-mis-tai-po-kah (White Calf), the head chief, and I are selecting for you an Indian name. I ask you to come again to my lodge in one week." I replied, that next day I would start with Siksikakoan on a hunting expedition into the Rocky Mountains. He sat in silence for a moment and then said :

" It is now the moon when the leaves are beginning to turn yellow. I have adopted you as my son, and you have met my family and relatives. On the first day of the full moon, at the time when the leaves are falling, I will be camped on the South Fork of Cutbank River. Come to my lodge on that day, for I will have there the leading chiefs and medicine men. I will hold a sacred ceremonial, and will unroll the ancient Medicine Bundle [1] of the Beavers. We will give you an Indian name, again painting you with the sacred paint, and receiving you into the tribe of the Blackfeet."

[1] See Appendix.

CHAPTER III

HUNTING IN THE ROCKY MOUNTAINS

Our ride across the plains.—Individuality of pack horses.—Difficulties of mountain travel.—A mountain camp.—Fresh grizzly bear tracks.—Siksikakoan's bear story at the camp fire.—Climbing for Rocky Mountain Sheep.—A thrilling adventure with a huge grizzly. —Siksikakoan relates the legend of A-koch-kit-ope, the Medicine Grizzly of Cutbank Canyon.—Story of Meneopka and the coyotes.

EARLY on the following morning, the herd was driven into the corral, the pack and saddle horses selected and roped. In a short time the packs were on and we started across the plains for the mountains. The sky was of the deepest blue. In the clear air the high peaks of the Rockies, white with fresh snow, appeared deceptively near. Siksikakoan led the way, while I followed driving the pack horses. From the start, instead of keeping in line and moving at their usual gait, they persistently straggled off over the plain. It is a peculiarity of most pack horses that, at the beginning of an expedition, they realise the work ahead and spend their first energies in seeking to avoid their task.

They very much resemble men in disposition. First of all, there is the ambitious horse, who is only content when leading the rest, and in that capacity is invaluable ; then the reliable hard-working horse, who attends strictly to business ; the crafty and lazy horse, whose

36

wits are devoted to shirking rather than working. Baldy, my own pack horse, was an animal of the latter kind. His ingenuity in dodging work, his cuteness in eluding capture when getting ready for an early start, his habit of puffing out his sides during the cinching of the pack-saddle, necessitating a halt in a short time to tighten, and his readiness for leadership in a stampede, made him a disturbing and exasperating element in the

SUNRISE.

outfit, requiring constant vigilance. On this occasion he was lightly packed, for he carried only my blankets and personal effects. With the intuition of an experienced veteran, he realised that there was hard work ahead and made such loud grunts that one, not familiar with his disposition, would have thought him abused and overburdened. When I took no notice of his complaints, he lay down, closed his eyes and groaned as if in great distress. But I saw through his crafty tricks. Dismounting, I seized a stick and, brandishing it with much energy, ran towards him with a shout. Baldy was so taken by surprise, that he quickly rose to his feet and, with an angry snort and toss of his head (a horse's imprecation), joined the outfit. Although he

Copyright in United States   by *Walter McClintock.*
REPACKING (BAGGAGE) BUCK.

failed to have his pack removed, no further complaints were heard from him.

No pack horse outfit is complete without its Buckskin, distinguished alike for his colour and for his endurance and tractability. Our Buckskin was no exception. The hardest drives never seemed to tire him. At the day's finish he was still fresh and generally in the lead. After his long rest, Buck was feeling in fine trim and was eager for adventure. The chance soon came. His sides were so round and yielding from his recent high living that, after we were well under way, the cinches became loose and the saddle slipped. He expressed his disapproval in one of his highest bucks, landing stiff-legged on all-fours, and giving the pack such a jar that it turned, and away he went. As the pots and kettles began to fly, his example proved instantly contagious to the other horses, for they turned at once and galloped in an opposite direction across the plain. It was a complete stampede. Siksikakoan followed the main outfit, while I started to overtake Buck, who was fast disappearing in the distance. On coming up with him, I saw that everything had been kicked off except the cinch-rope and pack-cover, which were dragging behind. Going back over Buck's trail, which was plainly marked by cooking utensils and provisions of all kinds, we gathered together, little by little, the precious contents of his pack. Such an experience brought forcibly to mind the difference between the cayuse of the Rocky Mountains and the plodding horse of the city. The wits of the former become sharpened by hard knocks, unexpected emergencies and the necessity of hustling for a living, developing both a capacity for mischief and a resourcefulness in danger that the latter, made dull and plodding by the featureless routine of daily work, is a stranger to.

Passing through the foot hills, and riding along the Cutbank River, we entered the mountains. Siksikakoan followed the old Blackfoot war-trail, used by them in the early days, when they crossed the Rockies on war expeditions against the Pend d'Oreille, Kutenai, and Flathead tribes. We passed through small parks of luxuriant bunch grass brilliant with wild flowers, and along the shores of lakes hidden away among the mountains.   Then we plunged into a dark forest of fir, spruce, and pine.   When the trail became well nigh impassable, because of fallen timber, Siksikakoan went

A BLACKFOOT WARPATH.

ahead with an axe and chopped a way through.   This trying situation again put to test the real disposition of our pack horses, bringing out the bad traits of the vicious.   The bell-mare promptly chose to turn aside and go down the mountain, while I dodged through the thick timber to head her off. The obstinate Baldy led the other horses away from the trail and, in driving them back, many of their packs were torn and loosened by the trees, and it became necessary to repack them. The Blackfoot language being deficient in curse words, Siksikakoan, suitably to express his feelings, fell back upon a picturesque and expressive assortment of English imprecations he had learned, while a scout, from army officers. Under similarly irritating conditions I have seen men, who were never known to swear, become suddenly profane, and no man, who has not himself driven a pack outfit along a steep trail and through thick, or fallen timber, is competent to sit in judgment upon such offenders.

While fording a swift stream, the horses stopped to drink. When Baldy, my pack horse, had his fill, he began pawing the water, a sign that he intended lying down for a roll. I prevented this catastrophe by jerking his neck-rope, but to my dismay, my trusty saddle-horse, catching his frolicsome impulse from Baldy, suddenly lay down in midstream and took a roll, dumping me off into the icy water.

We finally passed from the forest into an open basin surrounded by lofty peaks. I marvelled at the luxuriant growth of the grass and the variety and brilliant colouring of the flowers, caused by the abundant precipitation. There was the beautiful dark blue flower of the camass, the violet red of the wild geranium, the violet blue of the western virgin's bower, and the yellow of the wild parsley; also forget-me-nots, mountain lilies, spring daisies, and blue larkspurs.

A stream of clear water, cold as ice, flowed along one side of the meadow, the pines standing tall and

Copyright in United States   by Walter McClintock.

"AT THE UPPER END OF THE BASIN WAS A LAKE SURROUNDED BY AN UNBROKEN FOREST."

straight on the farther bank. At the upper end of
the basin was a lake surrounded by an unbroken forest,

Two Medicine Falls and Mount Rising Wolf.

which extended from the north and south shores high
up on the mountain sides. To the south, Mount Rising

Wolf and a pair of twin peaks rose abruptly, and to the west, like a massive wall, the Continental Divide, with its imposing procession of snowy peaks. This was a welcome haven of rest for our weary outfit, and we hastily prepared camp for the night. Our lodge was pitched at the edge of the forest near an old fir tree, a thick grove of spruces protecting us from the west winds.

After a warm supper, we forgot our hard day's work and sat closely together around a small fire. The Indian invariably builds a small fire. He will tell you that it is more convenient for cooking and better for warmth, and will speak with derision of the white man's fire as too large and wasteful.

The horses were quietly feeding close to camp. We felt secure in turning them loose because of the rich pasturage, their weariness, and the difficult back-trail. Suddenly we heard loud snorting, and a clatter of hoofs as they galloped madly through the valley. Hurrying to discover the cause of their fright, we found among their tracks the huge footprints of a grizzly bear. Unmindful of our presence, until discovered by the horses, he had been feasting on huckleberries, tearing up the ground, and turning over large stones for insects.

Returning again to our camp fire, Siksikakoan said : " I once had an experience with a bear in this same locality so unusual, that the bear himself can hardly have forgotten it. It was in the early spring, about the time when bears leave their winter dens. I had followed so long and eagerly the fresh trail of a large mountain ram, that nightfall overtook me unprepared. The weather luckily was warm and pleasant. Finding a depression in the ground filled with long soft grass,

HUNTING CAMP IN THE ROCKY MOUNTAINS

By Walter McClintock

I stood my rifle against a neighbouring tree and lay down in the hollow place to sleep. During the night I was aroused by the heavy breathing of a large animal, and an oppressive and disagreeable odour. At first I was dazed and only half conscious, as in a dream, of something standing over me, but I lay perfectly still. A grunting and snuffing, close by my head,

"OUR LODGE WAS PITCHED AT THE EDGE OF THE FOREST."

quickly forced me to realise that I was in the strange and horrible predicament of lying beneath a grizzly bear. A cold sweat came over me, and I was half paralysed with terror. The grizzly had been prowling about, led to my bed by his scent of the remnants of my supper, and so happened to walk over my body, partly covered by the grass and hidden in the depression. It was of course impossible to reach my rifle standing against the tree. Acting on a sudden impulse, I doubled up my knees, and with all my strength plunged my fists and feet simultaneously against the belly of the brute. It was a complete surprise for the grizzly, who was, if possible, the more frightened of the two, for he ran bellowing into the forest, while I quickly gathered up my small outfit and started away in the dark."

On the following morning, while Siksikakoan was examining the surrounding heights for game, he caught sight of a band of Rocky Mountain sheep. They were quietly feeding above timber line. While considering the best way of approaching them, the band suddenly took flight. Then a dark form appeared with awkward gait, following the sheep over the boulders. My glasses showed it to be a large grizzly bear. Siksikakoan said : " It is our old friend of last evening," and seizing his rifle called to me to follow him. We climbed the mountain facing us, crawling through thick underbrush and scaling difficult ledges. In one place we discovered the grizzly's freshly-made tracks in the soft earth beside a small stream. But the excitement over our seeming proximity to the monster was of short duration. When we reached the timber line, Siksikakoan stopped and said dejectedly, " the wind has shifted and old grizzly is gone." But I must confess that the announcement gave me great relief.

During the following two days, from early morning until sunset, Siksikakoan and I hunted in vain for sheep and goats on the surrounding mountains. We saw many tracks but no more game. On the third day we came upon a camp of two lodges, beyond a high wooded ridge to the south-east, belonging to Sis-ta-wau (Bird-Rattle), and A-po-at-sis-ipo (Looking for Smoke). Having reported that they had secured six sheep, we knew that they had frightened the game from our vicinity. Siksikakoan then resolved to go among the high peaks at the head of the canyon. There the mountains were difficult of access and he could take but one horse, so I consented to remain in camp as guard for our provisions and outfit. To increase his chances of success in hunting, I made him take my large Winchester rifle, while he left with me his inferior gun of small calibre. After he had gone, I busied myself with caring for the horses, securing a plentiful supply of trout from the stream near-by and some small game in the forest.

My active life and a Rocky Mountain appetite, with abundance of good food, the best of water and plenty of sleep gave me such a feeling of vigour and exhilaration, that I could not remain idle, but occupied myself in hunting with the camera, climbing to the summit of the Continental Divide, and to other high points in quest of new scenes. The most beautiful landscapes were along the old Indian war-trail, which skirted our camp. It was flanked by magnificent snowy mountain peaks and disappeared in a forest of firs, arching overhead, and thickly carpeted with pine-needles underfoot.

I spent my evenings completing my notes and reading, while lying in my comfortable blanket bed beside the lodge fire. It was made of small, resinous pine sticks, which gave out an abundance of light and heat. I was awakened early each morning by the shrill cries of a flock of blue jays. The leader, or chief of the flock, made himself especially obnoxious by sitting in the big fir tree, close to the lodge, as if remonstrating against my wanting to sleep after sunrise. His chatter was so incessant, and so like a challenge, that I finally took a shot at him from the doorway. But my bullet went too high and he flew away with a parting cry, very like a derisive laugh.

I prepared an out-of-door kitchen, about twenty feet distant, but stored the bulk of the provisions within the lodge, for protection from storms and invasion by wild animals. During the afternoon the sky became overcast. Dark clouds gathered along the divide. In the evening, a storm broke suddenly, the wind rushing down with a roar from the high peaks at the head of the canyon. The lodge would have been carried away, if it had not been for the protection of the small grove of gnarled and twisted balsams, through which the wind whistled as through the rigging of a ship. I lay comfortably wrapped in my blankets, gazing into the fire and listening with peaceful indifference to the howling storm. I watched the fire burn low, until there were but a few glowing embers, and then fell asleep. During the night I was awakened by the horses coming close to the lodge. I wondered at their having left their feeding grounds and went outside to drive them back. The wind had ceased, and all signs of the storm had disappeared. I stood for a moment, fascinated by the wildness of my surroundings. The deep stillness was broken only by the subdued roar of rapids in the valley below, the distant howling of wolves in the forest on the mountain side, and the hooting of a pair of owls; I could distinguish between the voice of the male and the answering call of his mate.

When I was again under my warm blankets, I fell into a doze but had a vague feeling that something was prowling about. Startled by heavy footsteps near the lodge, I sat up and listened They led in the direction of the kitchen some twenty feet away, and then followed a rattling of pans. I seized a stick and ran out to investigate. I saw a large, black-looking object near by, and thinking that one of the horses had returned, was about to hurl my club. But a sudden intuition changed my mind. This intruder could not be a horse. It stood too high in front and low behind. It looked steadily at me with head lowered and moving slowly from side to side. When I heard a vicious "woof!" the terrible reality flashed over me that I was in close quarters with a huge grizzly bear. The thought of having come so near charging upon him with a club made me shudder and my knees feel weak. A cold chill crept up my back and over my scalp, with the feeling that my hair was standing on end. I backed into the lodge and sat down, debating what could be done. I realised that, in such close quarters with a large grizzly at night, and with an inferior rifle, my large rifle having been taken by Siksikakoan, it would be madness to shoot. A bold front is the best defence, and to run from a grizzly is but to invite attack. Any further deliberation was cut short by his moving towards the lodge. He stopped for an instant a few feet away, sniffing the scent of the provisions stored inside the lodge, but fortunately turned again towards the kitchen. Believing. that the fire-light might drive him off, I cut a few shavings and soon revived my smouldering fire. Hearing him coming again, I seized the small rifle and jumped to the side farthest from him. While I stood waiting, the suspense and strain upon my nerves were terrible. He came straight to the lodge door, but again turned aside to investigate my saddles. His curiosity being satisfied, he stopped at the side of the lodge where my provisions were stored. I cocked the rifle and knelt in readiness to receive him. Rising on his hind legs, he placed his fore paws against the lodge poles. I saw the canvas pressed in with his weight, and heard his deep breathing, for I was underneath him. I had now recovered my nerve. My heart beat steadily and I held the rifle without a tremor, although I thought my end had surely come. I quickly loosened the canvas from its pegs and prepared to escape from under, for I thought his weight would break through. But he stood there sniffing the air and seemingly undecided as to his next move. Then I stood erect and gave a loud yell. He must have thought my " power " was stronger than his own, for he turned away and the next moment I heard him at the kitchen, tearing off the canvas covering from a mess of trout. Having safely passed through what I thought was the crisis of his visit, I actually began to take a friendly interest in the old grizzly's performances, and watched him from the doorway. He tore open the parfleches [1] containing flour and sugar and smelled at the heavy iron " dutch-oven " containing a small piece of butter, my greatest delicacy, although not very fresh. He turned the oven over and over, but the lid held fast. Finally he gave it a heavy blow with his big fore paw, and the lid flew off. Its contents were quickly disposed of and I heard his rough tongue licking with relish the inside of the kettle. With the hope that I might drive him away, I opened the lodge door that the fire-light might show more brightly, and stepping out fired my rifle into the air. But he only threw up his head, as if annoyed at the interruption, and dropped it quickly to finish a bowl of stewed peaches, the last of my store of provisions at the kitchen. When the first faint streaks of dawn appeared, my dangerous visitor suddenly departed into the deep forest. Having built a cheerful

[1] See Appendix.

and comfortable fire, I at once wrote in my note book the details of the grizzly's visit, and then, wrapping myself in my blankets, slept soundly until wakened by the squirrels racing over the frozen canvas above my head. The thrilling events of the night seemed like a dream and I hastened to find the grizzly's tracks and prove the reality of the adventure. Close beside the lodge, I found prints of his feet measuring thirteen inches in length, six inches broad at the heel and seven inches across the toes. When Siksikakoan returned from his hunt, and saw the tracks, he said that a grizzly of that size would weigh as much as a large horse. He brought back with him a Rocky Mountain sheep and two goats. In the evening, while seated beside our outside fire, after telling about his hunt, Siksikakoan said : " We are now camped within the range of a grizzly bear, who has been famous for many years among the Blackfeet for his size and daring. I will tell you the story, just as Mad Wolf told it to me."

The Medicine Grizzly of Cutbank Canyon.

" When Mad Wolf was a young man, he was chief of a war party, that crossed the Rocky Mountains against the Flathead Indians. Two of his brothers also started with the expedition, but turned back, before they reached the Flathead country. Mad Wolf and his party returned later by the Cutbank Pass. After crossing the summit, they entered the dense forest near the head of the canyon. Mad Wolf was in the lead, while the others followed in two separate columns along each side of the trail, as was the custom of war parties in those days. They rode in silence because the trees were so dense they could not see far in advance. Suddenly Mad Wolf stopped and signed to the others that he heard someone ahead striking his horse with a quirt (whip). The Blackfeet quickly ambushed themselves among the trees. A war party of Kutenai (Mountain Indians) were returning from an expedition into the Blackfeet country. They ran into the ambush and there was a fierce battle. Mad Wolf, as chief of the expedition, was entitled to the first shot. He singled out the leader, but the Kutenai chief was very brave. Although badly wounded, he ran into the thick woods where Mad Wolf killed him. While taking his scalp, Mad Wolf recognised on his belt the scalps of his own two brothers. He hurried back to his people, who were by this time hard pressed by the Kutenai and were retreating. Mad Wolf, now aroused to great courage and daring, rallied the Blackfeet to another attack and soon turned the rout into a victory. They killed all of the Kutenai save one old squaw. After scalping the dead, they clothed her in a soft tanned buckskin dress, ornamented with elk teeth and with leggings and moccasins decorated with porcupine quills. They painted her face black and giving her a warm blanket and a sack of dried meat, set her free, with the prayer that the Sun would take pity on themselves, just as they had pitied their helpless enemy. They then continued on their way until they came upon the camp of Running Wolf, Black Bear, Ear Rings, Stock-stchi, Ahpasis, and other well-known Blackfeet chiefs pitched in this same glade near yonder big fir tree, by which our people have ever since identified this camping ground. It was in early summer, the time when the camass is in bloom and they were engaged in cutting and peeling lodge poles. In those days the Blackfeet travelled so far in a year that their lodge poles were worn too short.[1]   Every spring they went into the mountains to cut new poles and to dig camass roots.

"It happened that in the evening, the chiefs were assembled in Stock-stchi's lodge, listening to Mad Wolf's story of his war expedition against the Flatheads.   It was a warm moonlight night and the women were sitting outside singing and talking together. Stock-stchi called to his wife to go to the stream for water.   But she was afraid, saying, 'The woods are dark down there and the water deep.'   But her husband made her go.   She soon returned, badly frightened, and said, 'I was dipping my bucket, when a man came from the forest.   He jumped across the stream and ran up the trail.   He carried a rifle and wore a war bonnet.' Just then another woman came into the lodge saying, 'We saw a stranger go to the big fir tree yonder.   He hung his war bonnet there and then stole over to the lodge. He looked in and went away. He was an enemy. We saw him plainly in the bright moonlight.'

"Mad Wolf and the other chiefs hurriedly seized their rifles and ran down to the stream just in time to see a small party of Gros Ventres emerging from the forest. The Blackfeet opened fire and killed all except their leader.   He stood his ground until his ammunition gave out, when he took refuge in the underbrush.

"Our people clipped the branches off all around him with their bullets, but could not hit him.   Finally they made a charge, but the Gros Ventre chief fought savagely with his knife, roaring all the time like a grizzly bear at bay and calling to the Blackfeet 'Come on, I am not afraid.   My name is A-koch-kit-ope and my medicine is powerful.   When day broke, our

[1] See Appendix.

people were uneasy, thinking the Gros Ventre chief might have supernatural power. They told him he was free to go, but they would scalp the others. A-koch-kit-ope replied, ' No, they are my brothers and I will not leave them.' Feeling thirsty, he walked to the river and drank, daring any of the Blackfeet to stand forth for a hand-to-hand conflict. When our people finally killed him, they discovered that the grizzly bear was his medicine. He had a grizzly claw tied in his front hair. The Blackfeet were so afraid that some of his power might escape, that they built a fire and burned A-koch-kit-ope's body. If a spark or coal flew out, they carefully threw it back into the fire, to prevent the possible escape of any of his power. They scalped the other dead Gros Ventres and had a scalp dance around the fire.

" When the fire had burned out, the Blackfeet hurriedly moved camp. But in spite of their precautions, A-koch-kit-ope transformed himself into an enormous grizzly bear and followed them. He came upon the Blackfeet when they were pitching camp, killing some, while the rest escaped by flight.

" The next spring when our people went up the canyon to cut lodge poles, they camped again near the big fir tree in the same park. Early in the night, while the horses were still picketed close to the lodges, an enormous grizzly bear came into camp. The horses were frightened and stampeded, just as ours have done. The dogs attacked him, and he killed some of them and put the others to flight. The people were afraid to shoot, because they recognised the bear as A-koch-kit-ope. He appeared beside the fir tree, where the year before the Gros Ventre medicine man had hung his war bonnet. The grizzly boldly went through camp

eating all the food he found and tearing to pieces hides
and parfleches. Whenever our people camp near the
fir tree in the canyon they see the medicine grizzly,
whom they have named A-koch-kit-ope. He comes
only at night and disappears before daybreak. The
Blackfeet know his medicine is strong and are afraid to
shoot at him. When we made peace with the Gros
Ventres, we told them about this medicine grizzly and
they said that he was A-koch-kit-ope, their great
medicine man. They declared he could not have been
killed, if all of his followers had not been slain first.
A-koch-kit-ope had predicted to them that he would be
killed, if he should ever be left alone in battle with no
one to make a ' medicine smoke.' As this happened
many years ago, A-koch-kit-ope, the medicine grizzly,
must now be very old."

After Siksikakoan had finished telling the legend of
the Medicine Grizzly I went out into the night. I
gazed with a deeper interest at the big fir tree, where
the Gros Ventre warrior hung his war bonnet, while
making the night attack upon the Blackfeet, and at the
black, wall-like line of forest, where the Blackfoot woman
first encountered A-koch-kit-ope. I felt convinced that
the huge grizzly, who had frightened me the night
before, must be the dreaded " Medicine Grizzly, A-koch-
kit-ope," who had already made this locality famous by
so many manifestations of his supernatural power.
Beyond were the massive mountains, their snowy
summits dimly lighted by the myriads of brightly
shining stars. I saw the dog star in the north-east,
rising with remarkable brilliancy over the tops of the
tall spruces and pines. I could faintly distinguish the
horses at the edge of the timber and heard Baldy give
a frightened whinny when he suddenly realised that

he was feeding alone, too near the ghostly woods, and hurriedly joined his companions. Returning to the lodge, which looked most picturesque, lighted up by the golden glow from the fire within, and showing in clear outline the weird decorations on the canvas, and the tapering poles overhead, we turned into our comfortable blanket-beds beside the fire. The deep stillness of the night was broken by the mournful howl of a wolf in the forest close by. He was answered by another and then another, until they all united in a chorus of long howls. Siksikakoan said: "When the wolves howl like that, it is a sign of coming storm. This morning when the sun rose, I saw two large sun dogs in the eastern sky, that resembled enormous crosses, and at midday there was a huge circle around the sun,—nature's warning signs of a big storm."

I asked Siksikakoan if he had ever known of a man being attacked by wolves. He said: "Wolves and coyotes are very wise, their wisdom having been given to them by Napi (Old Man). Although savage by nature, they sometimes use their wisdom to help people when in danger and distress. I recall a strange incident that happened many years ago, when we were camped far out on the plains. It was a cold winter. There had been a big storm and the snow lay deep. Menepoka, an old man, went alone and on foot from camp to look for horses. He carried a quirt and was dragging a long raw-hide lariat. He felt something tugging, and turning about, saw a large coyote biting at the other end of his lariat. He stopped and yelled at the coyote, calling him evil names to scare him away. The coyote trotted to the summit of a butte near by, and howled four times to the north, south, east and west. Before long another coyote appeared. Then another came running up to him, and they kept on coming, until Menepoka found himself surrounded by them. The terrible circle, with hideous cries, red mouths and glittering eyes, drew closer and closer. He tried to drive them away with his quirt, but without effect. He expected that, in a moment, they would rush upon him and tear him to pieces. He was old and not strong, and in his terror his legs gave way and he sank down into the snow. It happened that an Indian on horseback had ridden to the summit of a neighbouring butte looking for his horses. Hearing the coyote pack making an unusual outcry, he rode towards them, thinking they had made a kill of game they had run down in the snow. Discovering a human body lying on the ground, he gave a shrill cry and galloped towards them, shooting an arrow into their midst. The coyotes quickly scattered, and he then saw that it was Menepoka lying in the snow as if dead. Lifting him upon his horse he took him back to camp. Our medicine man tried to drive out the evil spirit, going through with the motions of pulling something from his body, explaining that, when the coyotes were closing in upon Menepoka, they were constantly shooting their hairs into him. But the incantations were of no avail, because the evil spirit was one over which the medicine man had no power. Menepoka lived for only a few days. When he died, his body was placed upon the summit of the high butte, where the famous chief Big Nose now lies. They both belonged to the Ich-poch-semo band (clan of Grease Melters)."

CHAPTER IV

A ROCKY MOUNTAIN BLIZZARD

I WAS wakened on the following morning by mournful howls from a band of coyotes at the edge of the forest near the lodge. Lifting the door-skin and looking out the sky was heavily overcast and a huge bank of clouds hung over the entrance to the canyon. After an early breakfast, we lost no time in beginning preparations for the approaching storm. We constructed an outdoor kitchen, without a roof, under the shelter of a thick grove of pines. It was made of forked poles supporting cross-pieces with green branches laid against it to form a wind-break. We placed inside of this enclosure our cooking utensils and the tripod with its heavy camp kettle.

Almost before we were in readiness, a heavy east wind, with a drenching rain, set in, but we made safe against it by anchoring the tipi on its eastern side in true Indian fashion. This was done by driving two strong stakes firmly into the ground, throwing the noose of a lariat over the tops of the tipi poles, taking a hitch around the stakes and then drawing it taut, until the ropes sang in the gale. We reset the ears for the change of wind, crossing the earpoles in front to protect the smoke-hole and to prevent the ears from being torn, and laying stones and logs around the bottom of the canvas, so that the pegs could not be loosened by the wind-strain.

The storm which Siksikakoan predicted from nature's

LODGE WITH EAR POLES CROSSED IN FRONT FOR STORM.

signs, began with snow and a high wind from the west, continuing three days and three nights. Dense masses of clouds hung low upon the mountains, but moved uncertainly about the high peaks, sometimes lifting, as if to disappear, only to lower again more dense and threatening than before. The temperature fell rapidly, and by evening, the rain had changed to snow. The horses, which we had left unpicketed, feeding in the meadow, were driven by the storm into the thick underbrush for protection. We could hear them whinnying to each other for encouragement, while trying to keep together. When the sky cleared at sunset of the third day, it seemed as if the storm was over, but Siksikakoan shook his head dubiously, saying, " When a storm breaks at sunset, the weather is still unsettled, but, if the sky clears during the night, or in the early morning, we will have settled weather."

After nightfall the wind increased. The snow and sleet beat violently against the canvas. The furious blasts rushed through the tops of the pines and firs, with a sound like that of escaping steam, and swept the exposed slopes above timber-line, with a confused and distant roar. It was a wild night and sleep was impossible. But it was just the night for story-telling while lying secure and comfortable by our small inside-fire. Siksikakoan whiled the hours away with Blackfeet legends and tales of his adventures as an army scout, during the Indian wars of the north-west. I will only take space to repeat two of his legends.

The Home of the Wind Maker.

" Many years ago, when a heavy wind swept across the plains, a chief of the Blackfeet faced the storm and made a vow to find its origin. He crossed the plains and entered the mountains. His way led through dark canyons and dense forests, where the wind rushed and roared. The terrible wind and the dark and gloomy surroundings filled him with dread, but, because of his vow, he pressed forward until, at last, he saw in the distance, close to one of the highest peaks, the shining water of a lake. During a lull in the storm, he crept

close to the shore and watched. Suddenly from the
middle of the lake, arose the huge antlers of an
enormous bull elk. His eyes were red and flames

THE SNOW-COVERED FOREST.

darted from his nostrils. When he waved his huge
ears, a wind arose, so fierce and terrible, that the waters
of the lake were whisked up into the air. When the
elk sank again beneath the waves, the wind went down.

The chief hurried back to his tribe to tell them of his wonderful discovery of the home of Medicine Elk, the Wind Maker."

Origin and Destruction of the Grizzly Bear Clan.

"Weasel Tail was a man noted for his skill in catching eagles. He lived close to the mountains with his wife and six children, far from the main camp, in a place where eagles were plentiful. He dug a pit for trapping them, covering it ingeniously with green branches, grass and stones. He sat in it every day from sunrise to sunset, watching his bait of buffalo meat, lying overhead on the covering of branches. Whenever an eagle came to the bait, he seized it firmly by the legs and, drawing it between the branches into the pit, wrung its neck.

"Weasel Tail had been having bad luck for many days. The eagles would not come to his bait, although he prayed all night in his lodge, chanting Eagle songs and rubbing himself with the smoke of sweet grass, that his body might be free from scent. He then fasted for many days and took a human skull with him into the pit, that it might make him invisible like a ghost. But it was all in vain, for the eagles continued flying high above him and avoided his bait.

"One day exhausted by his efforts and weary waiting, he fell asleep in the pit, when an eagle appeared to him in a dream and said, 'If you will kill one of your children as an offering, you will have the power to catch many eagles.' When Weasel Tail awoke, he decided to offer his dog as a substitute, which he loved next to his children. He dressed the dead body of the dog to resemble a child and, placing it on the roof of the pit, returned to his lodge. At night the Eagle again appeared to him in a dream saying, ' I did not like the dog you offered me for food and could not eat it. I told you I wanted one of your children.' Weasel Tail then went on a hunt and killed an antelope. Returning he directed his wife to bring in the meat. While she was gone he killed his youngest child. He then felt so badly that he killed all of his children. He did not offer any of their bodies to the eagle, but buried them together, and sat in his lodge, waiting for his wife to come back. When she returned, he said, ' I have killed all of our children, but we shall all be together soon in the Spirit World, for I will now kill you and then myself.' She replied, ' Be it as you say, only wait until I go to the stream for water to wash the antelope meat.' She did not return, but ran away into the mountains. Worn out and famished, she wandered into a bear's den. A large grizzly was seated inside with her family of four children. When the bears saw that the woman was starving, they took pity on her. They were so kind and hospitable, that she lived with them for many years, and became the wife of a big grizzly.

"One day, her grizzly husband asked her if she wanted to return to her own people. She replied, ' Yes! if you can change yourself and our children into people, and can also get another family of bears to go with us, so that we can protect ourselves.' He said : ' I have a relative with four children. He lives farther up on this mountain. I will get him to come down here and live with us. I can then change all of us into people.' When the big grizzly had brought the other family of bears down, he said to his relative : ' We two will go together to the Indian camp on the prairie and kill a man. We must get his heart, for with it I can doctor and change all of us into people.' The two grizzlies went to the camp and returned with the heart.

THE FROZEN STREAM.

When the big grizzly had driven the others from his den, he began his incantations. He divided the heart, cutting a portion for each bear. Calling them together, after sundown, he distributed the pieces, and said, if they would go at once to bed they would arise as people. In the morning the woman arose first. After cooking the meal, she told all the bears to get up, and when they stood upon their feet they became people.

" The two families intermarried, the big grizzly becoming the chief of the band and taking the name Red Bear. The men hunted buffalo upon the prairies, making six lodges from their hides. They joined the Blackfeet camp, where the woman was recognised. She told the story of her murdered children, and said that the people with her had come from a long distance. They dressed in bear skins and wore grizzly claws around their necks, arms, wrists, and ankles. Their arrows were wrapped with bear skin, and they also carried daggers and spears for weapons. They painted themselves with red clay mixed with bear fur and flint, which they rubbed in so hard that their faces and bodies were covered with blood. They also painted black streaks across their eyes and mouths. For robes they used the smoked tops of lodges. This band of strangers soon became so insolent and dangerous, that if any of the Blackfeet objected to their actions they were killed. Whenever one of their own number was killed, the old mother was said to be able to doctor him and bring him back to life. The people were compelled to do whatever the bears wanted. They increased in number rapidly, for their children, according to the nature of bears, grew up and became mature in one year. The strangers acted like bears in so many ways, that the Blackfeet called them the clan of Grizzly Bears.

" A young man named Owl went on the war path against the Snake Indians. He came back unsuccessful.   Disheartened and worn out from travel, he wandered aimlessly over the prairies, for he was ashamed to return to camp.   One night a small underground animal came to him in his sleep, saying, 'Near the high rocky cliff the Chief Bear wishes to see you.'   He awoke, and from the top of a butte examined the surrounding country.   Seeing near the mountains a rocky and precipitous ridge, he went towards it.   At the foot of the cliff, he found a bear's den, and lay down to sleep in front of the door.   During the night, he was awakened by a large bear dragging him into the cave.   When it became light, he saw at the back of the den a huge grizzly with his family on either side of him.   Finally the big bear spoke to Owl, saying : 'I am the head chief over all the bears.   My medicine is strong, and I cannot be killed.   I have brought you here for I have taken pity on you and your people.   I will give you power so that, like me, you cannot be killed.'   The Chief Bear then sang a medicine song, and burned sweet grass as incense, rubbing the smoke over Owl's body.   He arose and danced around the den, grunting, blowing, and snorting.   He shot an arrow at Owl ; it struck him between the shoulders, but fell harmlessly to the ground.   He thrust a spear at his side, but the point broke off.   He struck him with a tomahawk which did him no injury.   For the fourth trial the Chief Bear stabbed him in the side, but when he pulled out the dagger, there was no wound.   The Chief Bear then directed Owl to return to his people, saying : 'You cannot be hurt as long as you stand your ground and fight.   You can only be killed when you flee from an enemy.'

" As soon as Owl returned to the Blackfeet camp, he

dressed and painted himself like the tribe of Grizzly Bears who had been ruling the people.

"The old mother of the bears had an instinctive fear of Owl. She warned all of her children to make a friend of him, and said: 'I fear him, for I know his supernatural power is greater than ours.' But Red Bear, the chief, was scornful towards Owl, saying: 'There is no reason why we should fear that fellow.' He commanded that no one of the tribe should sit on top of the butte north of the camp. When Owl heard of the command, he immediately went up and sat there in sight of the people. The Grizzly Bears then went out together and shot at Owl, but could do him no harm. They next said they would kill anyone leaving camp for a hunt. To show his contempt for this order, Owl announced to his people that he was going away for a buffalo hunt. When the Grizzly Bears tried in vain to kill him, the old mother again warned her children, saying, 'I advised you to make friends with Owl; now behold, he is stronger than you. If he prevails over us, we will all be killed.'

"Owl selected for his comrade a poor boy, named Little Robe, saying to him: 'To-morrow night when the moon rises, I will doctor you so that you cannot be killed.' On the following evening, taking the boy into his lodge, he painted and dressed him after the manner of the Grizzly Bears. He said: 'When I have finished doctoring you, we will have a game of " hide the bones " with the Bear tribe.' Owl rubbed sweet grass smoke over Little Robe's body, as the Chief Bear had done. He took the tooth and claw of a grizzly bear and directed him to hide the claw, either in his mouth, or in one of his hands. He then started a song,[1] while Little Robe, swaying his body in time with the singing, hid the claw. Taking his bow and arrow, Owl shot Little Robe between the shoulders. The arrow did him no harm, for the shaft was splintered, and Little Robe said, 'You guessed wrong, for I have the tooth and not the claw in my mouth.'[2] 'I will try again,' said Owl. Grasping his spear, he thrust it at the boy's side. But the point was broken off, and the spear did not penetrate the flesh. Little Robe said: 'I have the claw in my left hand, it is not in the right.' He next plunged his dagger into the boy's side, but it left no wound. Then Owl said: 'Go now to the Grizzly Bears and tell them that Owl wants to gamble with them.' Word was sent back by Little Robe that they were willing to have the game if it could be played in their own camp. When the Blackfeet heard the news, they crowded into Owl's lodge, saying, 'Why do you want to gamble with this terrible people? They will only kill you, and probably the rest of us also.' Owl said to Little Robe before they started for the camp: 'When we enter their lodge, pull down the buffalo robe fastened over the door, and take it in with you. We will both sit on it' (to secure power from the buffalo).

"They found the Grizzly Bears gathered together in one big lodge. The men were painted and armed with spears and bows and arrows. Before the game started, the mother of the Bears made a talk, warning them not to gamble with Owl and his friend, but they did not heed her. Red Bear, the chief, asked: 'Who will hide the bones first?' Owl replied: 'My little brother here.'

---

[1] Songs were sung in gambling to distract the attention of the opponents.

[2] Shooting an arrow at his opponent represented a guess, both in this test game and in the real game to follow. If a failure it was counted a wrong guess.

The youngest of the Bears said he would do the guessing. Owl started a gambling song, beating time with arrows on his bow. Little Robe took two bones, one marked and the other plain. He swayed his body and arms in time with the song, while quickly moving his hands and hiding the marked bone from the youngest of the bear warriors. The song grew louder, and the movements of Little Robe quickened. The Bear tribe

CLOUDS LIFTING FROM MOUNTAINS AFTER BLIZZARD.

grasped their weapons with excitement, and fiercely watched the two players. While they gazed at Little Robe, he seemed to them to resemble a bear. Suddenly the youngest Bear shot an arrow at Little Robe. The shaft struck him between the shoulders, but fell harmlessly to the ground. Little Robe said: ' you guessed wrong.' The second Bear then tried, spearing Little Robe in the side, but the spear broke in two.

" Red Bear, the chief, said : ' I will take the last two

guesses.' The song was again started, and as Little Robe waved his hands, the chief struck at him with a tomahawk, which did him no harm and then stabbed him under the arm, but the dagger left no wound. Owl said : 'None of you have guessed right. It is now our turn. My little brother will do the guessing, while you hide the bones.' He arose, and stood beside the door. Red Bear the chief, threw the bones, singing 'Try your best to guess right.' Little Robe shot an arrow into the chief's head and he fell to the ground dead. Owl, standing by the door, allowed no one to go out. He felt glad when he saw the chief of the Grizzly Bears fall dead. He and Little Robe then killed everyone in the lodge. When the Blackfeet knew that their terrible enemies were overpowered, they destroyed all the Grizzly Bears in the other lodges. They feared to let one of them live. Owl became head chief of the Blackfeet and Little Robe a great medicine man. They lived for many years, until they fled from an enemy when both were killed."

Siksikakoan continued his story telling far into the night. After midnight the wind began to subside, and, by morning, had entirely ceased. The light of sunrise in the eastern sky indicated that the clouds were breaking. The horses had left the sheltering willows and were contentedly feeding in the meadow, uncovering the snow from the grass, by pawing with their forefeet. This trait, which is called "rustling," has been so long inbred in the cattle and horses of the great plains of the north-west, that it has become a universal instinct. In mid-winter, while the snows are deep, and the grass is beyond their reach, they are compelled to resort to other shifts for food, and, if none are available, they perish. One food substitute in winter is the bark of the cottonwood tree, which is very nourishing and palatable. If an Indian camp is near a growth of these trees, and they have no summer-cured hay, the squaws will fell large trees for their Indian ponies, from which they will strip the bark completely. Although their horses are very hardy, their winter lot is at the best a hard one, and they are apt to come out of it in the

"HORSE UNCOVERING SNOW FROM GRASS BY PAWING."

spring in a reduced and weak condition. But, they fatten very rapidly, when the prairies grow green with the early-spring grasses. A broncho becomes accustomed to hardship and a precarious living, while a city-bred horse would starve to death under similar conditions.

The clouds lifted slowly from the mountains, unveiling in the clear air the canyons and forests and finally the high peaks. In spite of Siksikakoan's friendly remonstrances, I started off on foot with my camera, over the old Indian war-trail and towards the head of the canyon. He said " it is unwise to go alone and unarmed in the Rockies, especially after a heavy snowfall, when the

THE OLD TRAIL AFTER SNOWSTORM.

wild animals come forth to hunt and are apt to follow any fresh tracks in the snow, seeking for prey." Cut-bank Canyon was filled with winter scenes of wonderful beauty. The outlines of every stone and log were

Copyright in United States by Walter McClintock.]

CUTBANK CANYON AFTER SNOWSTORM.

beautifully rounded with a white mantle of snow and the branches of firs and pines bent under the heavy burdens they had received during the night.

In the early morning, after a snowstorm, one can read by their tracks in the snow, as if recorded in an open book, all the night movements of wild animals. I saw many coyote and wolf tracks crossing and recrossing the trail, and the peculiar footprints of the Lepus americanus, or snow-shoe rabbit, so called because the fur grows long on their feet, making the footprint to resemble a snow-shoe. A pair of mountain lions with large round tracks, resembling those of a large mastiff, were travelling close together towards the head of the canyon, their long tails occasionally leaving their marks behind. The snow told a sad story (whose sequel was probably a tragedy) of two large gray wolves running down a buck-deer. I came to a much trampled place, red with his blood, where he had stood at bay to fight them off, and then they all left the trail together in the direction of Mount Rising Wolf. Because of the ravages by numerous gray wolves, moose, wapiti and deer now show a marked decrease in this part of the Rocky Mountains. The large footprints of a grizzly bear emerged from a rocky ravine and crossed the trail, overturning stones and logs, while on his way down the mountain to drink at the river. While absorbed in taking a picture, with my head under a focussing cloth, I heard behind me several dull thuds, quickly following each other. They sounded so like the heavy footsteps of a large animal, that I quickly withdrew my head, fully expecting to find myself face to face with a grizzly. But, to my great relief, it was only the falling of heavy masses of snow from the fir trees.

When I emerged from the forest on my return to camp, the western sky was aglow with colour. The sun was sinking below the horizon line of the Continental Divide. For a brief moment, the last rays suffused the winter landscape of forest and mountain with a soft and rosy light. The silvery crescent of the new moon and the evening star crowned all with their celestial beauty.

Siksikakoan was waiting, with the lodge fire brightly burning and the horses picketed near for safety, in accordance with an old Blackfoot custom.

CHAPTER V

MAD WOLF GIVES THE BEAVER MEDICINE CEREMONIAL

Mad Wolf's summer camp on the plains.—Preparations for the
ceremonial.—Maka's joke.—Mad Wolf begins the ceremonial with
seven chants —The buffalo song.—Distribution of the rattles to the
priests.—Mad Wolf bids me join in the ceremonial.—Prayers made
by visiting Indians.—Animal songs.—Mad Wolf dances with the
Sacred Pipe.—Pipe Dancing songs.—The Root Digger is brought
forth.—Opening the sacred Beaver Bundle.—Dance of four women
representing beavers.—Two weasel skins are taken from the Bundle.
—The Head Chief gives me the Indian name A-pe-ech eken (White
Weasel Moccasin).—A medicine man decorates me with the sacred
paint.—Mad Wolf continues the ceremonial.—I take part in the
buffalo dance.—Ceremonial closes with a feast.

SIKSIKAKOAN and I returned from the mountains in
good time to keep my appointment with Mad Wolf.
Early in the morning of the first day of the full moon,
when the leaves were falling, I rode across the plains
in search of his summer camp on the South Fork of
Cutbank River. When I reached a high ridge overlooking the river valley, I looked down upon a serene
and beautiful landscape. In a meadow near the river
was a cluster of white lodges. To the west of the
encampment, like a massive wall, extending into the
distant north and disappearing in the far south, was
the main range of the Rocky Mountains. Over the
highest summits floated light, fleecy clouds, the beautiful
snow-capped peaks of Rising Wolf and Going-to-the
Sun standing sharp and clear against the deep blue sky.

Far away over the plains in the east and enveloped in a bluish haze, were the Kato-yi-six (Sweet Pine Hills),[1] resembling distant islands in the ocean. The smoke of many fires was rising from the lodges, bearing the sweet odour of burning cottonwood. Grazing horses dotted the green hillsides, and I met Indian boys riding bare-back and racing their ponies. Groups of Indians in brightly coloured clothing were variously occupied among the irregular rows of tipis. When I rode nearer I recognised the large painted-tipi of Chief Mad Wolf in the centre of the camp.

Clustered around Mad Wolf's were the lodges of O-mis-tai-po-kah, the head chief, Isso-ko-yi-kinni, White Grass, Ear Rings, Medicine Wolf, Bear Child, Drags-his-robe, Double Runner and Elk Chief. The sound of my approach brought forth Mad Wolf's daughter Strikes-on-both-sides. She looked very picturesque in a buckskin dress heavily beaded and a robe of soft-tanned fawn skin with beaded stripes. She wore small white shells in her ears and necklaces of elk teeth and deer bones. Her leggings and moccasins were beautifully decorated with coloured porcupine quills. She called to those within, that A-poi-a-kinni (Light Hair) had come back and laughingly said to me, " I see that you are still smiling." She took my hand and led me inside the lodge. At the back sat Mad Wolf. To his left were the priests—O-mis-tai-po-kah, the head chief, White Grass, a judge and medicine man, Isso-ko-yi-kinni, Stock-stchi, Medicine Wolf, Elk Chief, Bear Child, Ear Rings, and Double Runner. To the right were Gives-to-the-Sun, wife of Mad Wolf, and Natokema, wife of O-mis-tai-po-kah, and other women.

Turning to the head chief, Mad Wolf said : " Because

---

[1] Called Sweet Grass Hills by the Whites.

you are my friend, I request that you select a suitable name for my white son." O-mis-tai-po-kah bowed his head in silence.

Maka, near whom I sat, was an Indian of unusual appearance. He was thick-set and short in stature, with an enormous head, his heavy growth of hair resembling the mane of a lion. He was, however, full of drollery and good nature. There was something upon his mind, for frequently he looked at me, with eyes dancing with merriment, and he occasionally shook with laughter. He kept his joke to himself with difficulty, for several times he was on the point of telling, but changed his mind, when he looked at stern Mad Wolf. Finally he said to me in a low voice, " I have a name which I will give you later." But this little episode did not escape Mad Wolf's keen ears and he turned upon him quickly, with such a piercing and reproving glance, that nothing further was heard of Maka's joke.

Ceremonial of the Beaver Medicine.

Bear Child arose and with a forked stick, covered with sacred paint, selected a live coal from the fire and placed it in front of Mad Wolf. He took dried sweet grass from a small buckskin bag and, holding it aloft to command attention, and as a signal that he was ready to begin the ceremonial, placed it upon the hot coal. When the rising smoke filled the lodge with a pleasing fragrance, Mad Wolf began with seven songs, which were chanted in unison, each song being repeated four times. The first was to Napi (Sun Power, not referring to Old Man).

Mad Wolf led the chants with strong voice, swaying

his body to and fro and marking time with raised finger, explaining to me that the Beaver Chief made this sign when giving instruction to Akaiyan, the founder of the Beaver Medicine.

> 1. " Behold Napi comes into the lodge.
>   He is a strong Medicine Man.
>   He came in.
>   I see him."

MARKING TIME WITH FOREFINGER.

> 2. " The Heavens provide us with food.
>   The Heavens are glad to behold us."

> 3. " The Earth loves us.
>   The Earth is glad to hear us sing.
>   The Earth provides us with food."

Mad Wolf ended this song with the gesture of sweeping his hands towards the ground.

> 4. Song to the " Prongs." (The prongs are sacred sticks painted red. They are forked, and are

used to take hot coals from the fire in the burning
of incense.)

Mad Wolf, O-mis-tai-po-kah and their wives, as the
principals in the ceremonial, knelt beside the Bundle,
and chanted in unison, while laying their hands upon
the " prongs " held in the sweet smoke. Each in turn
held a prong against his shoulder, in imitation of
beavers carrying sticks, while at work building their

HOLDING THE "PRONGS" IN SWEET SMOKE.

lodge, and then, extending their arms together, with
hands raised and parallel (the sign of the beaver
lodge), they prayed together to the spirit of the
beaver,

"Pity us! Grant us your wisdom and cunning that we may
escape all dangers. May our medicine provide us with food. May
all of us be blessed."

5. Two Beaver Songs.

" The Old Man, (Beaver Chief), is coming in.
The Old Man has come in.

He sits down beside his medicine.
It is a very strong medicine."

" The Old Woman (Female Beaver) is coming in.
The Old Woman has come in.
She sits down and takes the medicine.
It is a very strong medicine."

6. Buffalo Song.

During this chant Mad Wolf and O-mis-tai-po-kah
with their wives knelt by the side of the sacred

MAKING THE SIGN OF THE BEAVER LODGE.

Bundle and with deep reverence slowly lifted it, singing
the following in unison :

" I take hold of the sacred Buffalo.
While I am walking, I walk slowly.
I stop with my medicine.
The ground where my medicine rests is sacred."

7. The seventh and last chant was a Buffalo song.

"When summer comes, He will come down from the Mountains."

Mad Wolf directed his wife to bring forth the Kotoki-a-nukko (buffalo raw hides), and turning to me explained that, during the ceremony which would follow, the priests would beat time on these hides with the rattles, in imitation of the way the beavers drummed by striking the water with their tails. Mad Wolf first chanted and then prayed over the buffalo

BRINGING OUT BUFFALO RAW HIDE.

hides with closed eyes, holding his right hand raised impressively with fingers closed and thumb pointing upwards, a sign used by the Beaver Chief. After the hides had been unrolled all chanted in unison,

"The Buffalo likes to live in the mountains during the autumn. He comes down from the mountains to the plains. The mountains are his medicine."

During this chant, Mad Wolf, O-mis-tai-po-kah and

their wives held up their hands with the two index fingers curved towards each other (the others closed) in imitation of buffalo horns, the sign of the buffalo. The hides were spread on the ground in front of the priests during the chant :

> "The Buffalo came down from the mountains.
> He lies down upon the ground."

Gives-to-the-Sun handed Mad Wolf an old medicine

MAKING BUFFALO SIGN.
(Index fingers curved in imitation of buffalo horns.)

sack containing rattles. They were made by stretching raw hide over wicker frames, in shape like gourds, enclosing pebbles and having short handles. While the two women, Gives-to-the-Sun and Natokema, knelt beside the sacred Bundle and raised it reverently, Mad Wolf took the rattles from the medicine sack. He distributed them among the Awa-wa-nukki (singers or priests) and, handing two to me, said : "You are now my son and it is proper for you to join with us in this ceremonial." He then chanted the two Crow songs :

1. "I fly high in the air.
   My medicine (power) is very strong.
   The wind is my medicine."

2. "The Buffalo is my medicine.
   He is a very strong medicine.
       The trees are my medicine.
   When I am among them I walk around my own
       medicine."

TAKING RATTLES FROM MEDICINE SACK.

The Rattle songs came next, all uniting in the song, "The rattles I hold are good." This was repeated four times. The priests then grasped the rattles and beat rhythmically upon the buffalo raw hide, singing in unison "I now take the rattles." I watched every movement Mad Wolf made and when he grasped the rattles and began beating, I did likewise and also joined vigorously in the chant. He had been watching my movements for, at the end of the song, he said, " I like the way you swing your rattles, I feel proud of my white son."

At this moment, a visiting chief from the Bloods raised his voice in prayer, saying,

"Great Spirit in the Sun ! I am praying for my people that they may be able to have food and survive the coming winter. May all

MAKING THE ANTELOPE SIGN.
(Imitating with their hands the movement of antelope running.)

of our children grow and have strong bodies. May they live long and be happy."

During this prayer, Mad Wolf and the entire assembly reverently bowed their heads, joining in an ejaculatory assent (Amen) when he had finished.

Mad Wolf started the Elk song, while the two women, Gives-to-the-Sun and Natokema, imitated the actions of elk rubbing their horns against trees.

In the Moose song four men came forth imitating, with their heads, the movements of moose rubbing their horns.

For the Antelope song Mad Wolf, O-mis-tai-po-kah and their wives chanted while making the antelope sign. Holding their hands closed, one above the other, they changed positions alternately with a quick graceful movement, in imitation of antelope running.

The songs were, at this point, interrupted by the wife of the Blood chief making a long prayer for her own tribe and for the people among whom she was visiting.

Mad Wolf now brought forth the sacred Pipe wrapped in red flannel. Before starting, he explained to me that the ceremonial of the Pipe included two Pipe songs and three Pipe Dancing songs. They chanted the first two, while unrolling the Pipe, one while untying the strings, and one while removing the cover. Mad Wolf, while seated, led the first Pipe song, chanting the words,

"Our father, the Sun! It is now time you were rising.
I want to dance with you."

Mad Wolf then arose and, drawing his blanket around him, held the Pipe in its red cover, while the entire assembly united in chanting the first Pipe Dancing song. Mad Wolf danced, blowing his medicine whistle and circling the fire in the same direction the sun moves through the heavens. O-mis-tai-po-kah took the Pipe for the second Dancing song, and White Grass, the medicine-man, for the third, turning from right to left as he danced around the fire. While Mad Wolf unrolled the Pipe he gave the cry of the beaver and imitated the actions of a swimming beaver. O-mis-tai-po-kah arose and, blowing his medicine whistle, danced around the fire with a slow, graceful step. Taking the Pipe from Mad Wolf, he held it before him, while the priests sang and beat vigorously with their rattles.

O-mis-tai-po-kah then danced, holding the Pipe beneath his blanket and finished by returning it to Mad Wolf, who held it up towards the north, south, east and west. Finally, placing it in the sweet smoke of the incense, he bowed his head and prayed to the Great Spirit in

"HOLDING THE PIPE IN THE SWEET SMOKE, MAD WOLF BOWED HIS HEAD AND PRAYED TO THE SUN."

the Sun for the recovery of the sick. The Root Digger was then taken from the Bundle with the chant,

"I am digging the sacred Turnip."

The two women Gives-to-the-Sun and Natokema placed their hands upon it and prayed, holding it in position for digging.

The ordinary root-digger is a wooden stick, about two feet long, with a sharpened point, in common use by Indian women for digging roots. The sacred Root Digger is similar, but is painted with red paint and figures prominently in the sacred Bundles of the Sun-

dance and Beaver Medicine. The Blackfeet believe
that, according to their tradition, it was originally
brought to them by the Indian maiden, who was loved
by Morning Star, and was taken by him to live in
the home of the Sun. She was compelled by the
Sun God to return to earth and her tribe, because of
her disobedience to his commands, in digging up the
sacred Turnip, and in gazing down at her people on
the earth through the hole she had made in the sky.

The sacred women, Gives-to-the-Sun and Natokema,
seated beside the Beaver Bundle, were distinguished
from the other women by the colour of their blankets,
which were decorated with red paint. They had both
made the vow for the Sun-dance, and were held in
high honour by the Indians. To be eligible as sacred
women they were required to have led perfectly
pure lives before the entire tribe, and they must also
be known for their kindness of heart towards everyone.

The time had now come for the opening of the
Beaver Bundle. The priests sang a lively chant called
the " Song of the Buffalo Bull " :

" The head chief is looking for something to hook that may help
him."

The two sacred women knelt beside the Bundle,
imitating the actions of the buffalo and representing
the buffalo bull, or chief, slowly approaching the
Beaver Bundle. He stopped three times before reaching
it. At the fourth time, the women imitated the Buffalo
Chief, hooking at the Bundle with his horns. Mad
Wolf chanted the Hurrying song and then the String
song, as the women untied the strings and removed
the outside cover, revealing a beautiful beaver skin
called in their ceremonial " His Robe." The song was
changed to a solemn chant led by Mad Wolf, while

the sacred women slowly unrolled the beaver skin, uncovering the many skins of the birds and animals from the plains and mountains.

It is difficult for one of the white race to realise the deep solemnity with which the Indians opened the sacred Bundle. To them it was a moment of deepest reverence and religious feeling.

OPENING THE BEAVER BUNDLE.

Mad Wolf, taking the beaver skin reverently held it up while chanting :

"My medicine (Beaver) says, 'when I go out from the lodge and see an enemy, I dive down into the water where no one can harm me.'"

He then moved the beaver skin in imitation of the animal's movements while swimming, and suddenly blew shrilly upon the medicine whistle, to represent the Beaver's alarm when seeing an enemy and diving out of sight. Mad Wolf and the priests joined in a Beaver song accompanied by the beating of rattles. The sacred women knelt by the side of the Bundle, making mysterious motions with their hands, in imitation of the Beaver swimming and working and building his lodge, gracefully swaying their bodies in time with the rhythmical beating. Each in turn took the Beaver

WOMEN PRAYING WHILE HOLDING ROOT DIGGER.

Skin and with bowed head reverently held it to her breast, praying to the spirit of the Beaver:

"I take you, my child, in order that my children and relatives may be free from sickness."

Two women arose and knelt with Gives-to-the-Sun and Natokema in front of the Medicine Bundle. The four women together imitated a beaver's movements. They covered their heads with blankets to represent the beaver hidden in his lodge, all the time moving their bodies in time with the chanting of the

priests and the rhythmical beating. Then they came
forth to work on their beaver-dams, the women representing beavers rising to the surface by uncovering
their heads, and holding sticks in their mouths like
beavers carrying branches, imitating also the swimming
motions with their hands. Suddenly the beavers dived
under the water, and at this point Mad Wolf slowly
lifted the sacred Beaver Skin, while the four dancers

WOMEN PRAYING WHILE HOLDING BEAVER SKIN.

continued their mysterious and symbolic movements.
Then the dancers imitated the beavers coming to the
surface and swimming across the river. They went out
for a dance upon the shore, sitting upright, wiping their
faces with their hands, and looking carefully in all
directions after the manner of beavers guarding against
danger. The four women arose and stood in single file,
with Gives-to-the-Sun at the head of the line as the
wife of the Beaver Chief. They danced around the fire
with their hands crossed upon their breasts, turning to

and fro and swaying their bodies in time with the chanting of the priests. Mad Wolf handed the Beaver Skin to Gives-to-the-Sun. The singing and drumming became louder as the women circled the fire, imitating the call of the beaver. Gives-to-the-Sun held the Beaver Skin beneath her robe making it appear to swim around her waist and then around her neck. After dancing once around the fire, she handed the Beaver Skin to the woman next in line, saying:

" I do not give you away, my child (the beaver), because I am tired of you, but because the son of this woman is sick and she prays that he might be restored to health."

The woman, receiving the sacred skin, was careful not to let it fall, lest it bring misfortune, and prayed,

" I take you, my child (the beaver) that my husband and children might be free from sickness and that they may live to be old."

She danced once around the fire with the skin across her shoulders. This part was continued, until each one of the four women had taken the Beaver Skin in turn.

Gives-to-the-Sun and Natokema held up two snow-white winter skins of the weasel. They prayed to the spirit of this animal for its skill in hunting, and providing food. The priests chanted the Weasel song, while Mad Wolf, taking one of the skins, held it to his breast, praying for a blessing and then, rising, danced around the fire, blowing at intervals upon his medicine whistle to represent the weasel's cry and imitating its movements when hunting for food. O-mis-tai-po-kah, the head chief, with a gesture of authority, held the snow white skin aloft, so that all within the lodge could see. There was a deep silence as he looked fixedly at me, saying impressively,

" This is the skin of the A-pe-ech-eken (White Weasel Moccasin); one of the animals belonging to the Beaver Bundle. After this sacred animal we now name you. We think you resemble this animal because your hair is light and your eyes are blue. We pray that this name may bring to you long life and good fortune."

Mad Wolf, having expressed his approval of the name, moved to the left, White Grass, the medicine man, taking the leader's seat. The face of White Grass was painted a dark red. Upon the centre of his fore-

WOMEN PRAYING WHILE HOLDING TWO WHITE-
WEASEL SKINS.

head a black spot represented a thunderbolt, from which extended on both sides yellow zig-zags of lightning. He prayed :—

" Great Spirit, bless us all, men, women, and children.
Sacred Medicine Bundle, help us to live a straight life.
Sacred Medicine Pipe, bless us, also the rivers, mountains, prairies, animals, and birds.
Mother Earth, provide for us until we die."

After the prayer, White Grass brought forth the sacred red paint, which he kneaded with his hands, his

body meanwhile swaying to and fro.   First he painted
Mad Wolf and then O-mis-tai-po-kah ; in like manner
the priests, Isso-ko-yi-kinni, Stock-stchi, Bear Child and
Ear Rings.   I was seated next to Ear Rings and when
my turn came, Mad Wolf said, " Here comes my white
son."   White Grass then signed to me to approach.
Going before him, I knelt while he placed the sacred

PREPARING THE SACRED RED PAINT.

paint upon my forehead, chin and hands, the places
where the beaver rubs himself with his paws.   A beaver
song was started by Mad Wolf and O-mis-tai-po-kah, in
which all joined, accompanied by the beating of rattles.

After the song, White Grass, addressing me, said
impressively,

"This lodge is a sacred place, and the ceremonial, in which we have painted you, is also sacred. We pray that you may never be sick."

White Grass then pointed along the ground towards my seat, a sign that he had finished. Bear Child arose and taking the prongs, picked out a live coal from the embers and laid it in front of O-mis-tai-po-kah, the head chief. Placing dried sweet grass upon the coal and holding both hands in the rising smoke, he prayed :—

"My father, Great Sun Chief, who gives us light, look down in favour upon this young man whom we have taken into our tribe. Grant that his relatives and all his friends may have a good life. Protect him day and night from all harm, that he may live long, and return many summers to visit his Indian brothers."

The formal act of naming his white son and making him a member of the tribe having been completed, Mad Wolf returned to his seat beside the sacred Bundle to continue the ceremonial.

It required a wonderful feat of memory to conduct accurately the Beaver ceremonial, with its great number of songs, prayers, and dances, continuing from early morning until after sunset. Every song, prayer and dance must be performed correctly. If any mistakes are made, it is believed that misfortune will surely follow. One instance of the care taken to perform accurately every detail of the ceremonial occurred in the "Dance of the Lynx." Mad Wolf brought from the Bundle the decorated tail of a lynx. It was handed to O-mis-tai-po-kah, who held it aloft while all sang, accompanied by the beating of rattles. Gives-to-the Sun stood a stick, painted red, upon the ground to represent a tree. Natokema took the tail and imitated the movements of a lynx hunting squirrels. First, it walked around and then sat down, looking up at the tree. Several times it ran towards the tree, as if in pursuit of a squirrel, but each time it returned and sat down. Finally, it made a quick dash for the tree, when Natokema carried the tail rapidly up one side and down the other. At this point, O-mis-tai-po-kah raised his hand and stopped the service. The medicine women were astonished. Everyone in the lodge was silent. The chief announced that the ceremonial had not been conducted correctly. The rhythmic drumming and singing began again, as the old chief took the tail. He represented the lynx as making several feints, and then ran suddenly to the tree, just as the women had done. But O-mis-tai-po-kah made it climb more slowly and held it for some time on top, where it had a dance, keeping time with the singing. He then brought it slowly down the other side, clambering little by little as a lynx would do, pausing frequently to look around and listen, making sure that all was well. It finally reached the ground, and, scampering away, was returned to the medicine bundle.

Mad Wolf brought forth two badger skins, taking them out backwards like badgers emerging from their holes. He then imitated the timid actions of the badger, which is naturally a great coward. He moved the skins this way and that, like a badger trying to get away. Suddenly he turned the skins around as if the badger was about to attack but instead it became frightened and ran back into its hole.

During the song of the Wild Goose, Mad Wolf stopped for an instant and, bowing his head, closed his eyes. The entire assembly waited in complete silence. Suddenly Mad Wolf looked directly at me, saying, "There is my son, A-pe-ech-eken. I must ask him to continue the ceremony in my place." This was intended as a humorous diversion. The Indians enjoyed the unusual

occurrence.   The silence was thus relieved, and Mad
Wolf soon continued the service.

The head of a mallard duck was next taken out.
Mad Wolf started a chant, in which both men and
women joined, accompanied by the rattles.   Elk Chief
arose and drawing his blanket around him, circled
around the lodge, imitating the movements of a duck.
From across the lodge Soft Woman arose.   Both danced
towards each other until they met and together circled
the fire, their movements representing the swimming and
flying of a duck.   Soft Woman held up her right hand,
swaying her body from one side to the other, while Elk
Chief spread out both his arms with hands extended in
imitation of a duck flying.   This dance was very
interesting because of the graceful movements and steps
of the two performers.

A woman entered the lodge.   Her dishevelled hair hid
her face and her blanket was closely drawn around her.
She looked pale and emaciated, from fasting and her
arms were bleeding, having been slashed with a knife.
One of her children had died and she was in mourning.
She was indeed a sad and forlorn-looking creature.
She remained standing before the assembled company
until Mad Wolf took a handful of sage and purified
her, praying, that she might begin a new and happier
life.   She then withdrew as silently as she had come.

Four Otter songs were sung and then the Mink
song.   After these were the following Women songs,
Prairie Dog, Lizard, Sitting and Tobacco.   It was now
time to fill the sacred Pipe.   Mad Wolf held the pipe
bowl close to the tobacco.   He slowly picked up the
stone used as a stopper and placed it in the bowl, leading a chant in which all joined :

"The Sun beholds the smoke grow larger and larger."

Picking up the pipe and tobacco he said,

> "The heavens provide us with seeds of the tobacco."

Holding the tobacco up, he chanted,

> "I drop the seeds as I go along."

He filled the pipe and prayed,

> "The place where I sit is sacred."

Then, holding up the pipe with the bowl pointed towards himself, he chanted:

> "Sacred Person! behold I am still alive.
> I ask the spirit of the wild geese to smoke with me,
> The first that came into this country."

> "I know of no medicine so strong as my smoke."

While going through this ceremonial with the pipe, the bowl became loose and fearing that it might fall, which would be an ill omen, Mad Wolf removed it. He held up the stem and placing his right hand upon his breast gazed intently at the sun and chanted:

> "Sacred Spirit in the Sun, it has been a long time since you have smoked with me."

He arose and danced, holding up the sacred Pipe and blowing upon his medicine whistle. Stock-stchi followed and the women also joined, all dancing in single file around the fire, following the direction of the sun's course through the heavens. After the dance was finished Mad Wolf remarked that his Pipe was very old, having been handed down through many generations.

When he came to the skin of the red headed woodpecker, Mad Wolf said it had three songs. In the beginning, when the birds gave their songs to the Beaver Medicine, the woodpecker offered three. Mad Wolf chanted the songs, holding the skin of the woodpecker in his right hand and beating time with the rattles with his left. In closing, he held both the skin and rattles over his head and gave the call of the woodpecker.

For the Buffalo dance, Gives-to-the-Sun and Natokema arose, wearing head dresses having horns, in imitation of buffalo cows. Mad Wolf handed to Gives-to-the-Sun a string of buffalo horns which had been added to the Beaver Bundle as the symbol of the buffalo by the chief, who secured the Buffalo Tipi from the Sacred Buffalo Bull. The Indians found both interest and amusement in this dance, because it represented the mating of buffalo by women choosing their men. Gives-to-the-Sun and Natokema knelt before the Beaver Bundle with heads lowered, making motions of hooking the ground in imitation of buffalo cows digging wallows in the autumn. They pawed the ground and bellowed, simulating buffalo throwing dirt and catching it upon their backs, then shaking themselves and making the dust rise into the air.

Gives-to-the-Sun and Natokema then danced, imitating the capers of mating buffaloes. They stood before their mates pawing the ground and hooking at them with their horns. Mad Wolf and O-mis-tai-po-kah then joined in the dance. The men followed the women around the fire like buffalo bulls following cows. They danced in pairs until Gives-to-the-Sun threw the hoofs to Snake Woman. All then sat down and, amid laughter, Snake Woman danced in front of Medicine Wolf, her relative. When Medicine Wolf arose and joined her, she threw the hoofs to Strikes-on-both-sides, who came gracefully across the lodge and danced before me. While my Indian sister stood there, dancing with quick, short steps and swaying her body in time with the singing and the beating of rattles, I heard them calling, " Get up ! A-pe-ech-eken you are a chief now and should enter the dance." Grasping the string of buffalo hoofs lying before me I danced, following Strikes-on-both-sides around the fire, swaying my body, turning, holding my feet together and bending at the knees. I heard many shrill war cries from both men and women and exclamations of " Good boy, A-pe-ech-eken ! " I stopped at intervals to mimic the call of the buffalo and to imitate its movements, digging wallows, kicking, hooking, pawing the ground and throwing dust. When Strikes-on-both-sides brought our dance to a close I completed the circle and throwing the hoofs to Bear Child's wife, sat down.

Last of all came the Dog dance. Its lively air and fast time made it the most popular of the Beaver Medicine dances. It is a woman's dance, in which all the women within the lodge are expected to join, the men urging them on, singing their loudest and beating time with the rattles. The women entered into the Dog dance with spirit and dash, laughing merrily and joking with each other.

The wife of Stock-stchi, who was not dancing, sat with her little daughter of about twelve years, both intently watching. The dance was just at its height and the little girl's eyes were sparkling with excitement, when her mother, snatching off her own blanket, threw it over the shoulders of the little girl and pushed her into the circle. She looked very pretty with her shining black hair falling over her shoulders, in striking contrast with the brilliant scarlet of her squaw dress, which was beautifully fringed and decorated with beads. Her leggings were also beaded, and around her waist was a miniature squaw belt, closely studded with shining brass-headed tacks. At first she was abashed and

cast her eyes demurely downward, but soon forgot
herself and entered into the dance with animation,
her lithe body swaying to and fro, and her small
moccasined feet keeping perfect time to the beating
of the rattles. As the singers gradually quickened the
time, the steps of the dancers grew faster and faster,
until they were tired out and ceased, saying they could

"AFTER THE CEREMONIAL ALL PARTOOK OF A FEAST."

dance no longer. When the dance was at its height, I
noticed two old white-haired women having a dance of
their own outside the lodge. They were in mourning
and so could not enter the main dance, but they could
not resist the call of the lively Dog dance. They were
surrounded by a circle of young people, who were urging
them on and seemed more interested in their performance than in the main dance.

The sun had already set and the Indians began

preparations for returning to their lodges, bringing in the horses, changing their beautifully decorated clothes and beaded dance moccasins for those of everyday use. But, before they separated, all partook of a feast of sarvis berry stew. It had a delicate, sweet flavour and was a very popular dish. The men were always served first. I noticed, however, that but few of them ate their share. Many children were brought to the ceremonials and the food generally ran short. There was a custom that any man, feeling generously inclined, would call out the name of a woman. His plate with the remaining food was passed to her. If she had children she always shared it with them. Amid a general calling of names by the men and changing of plates, I requested that mine be passed to Morning Plume's wife, who had many mouths to feed. It was eagerly seized, divided into several portions and rapidly disappeared.

While the rest were feasting, I saw Awunna, a kind-hearted old priest and doctor, gathering together a supply of food. Before tasting anything himself, he carried it to his wife, E-kit-o-waki, one of the old women who had been dancing outside the lodge. They were an interesting couple. He always seemed thoughtful of others and in a good humour, while E-kit-o-waki, his wife, was still full of fun and life. Before the ceremonial began I saw Awunna draw her to one side and gently placing his hands upon her, uttered a prayer giving her his blessing. This was because she was about to enter Bear Child's lodge to doctor a sick child.

With the end of the service and the closing day, the Indians separated and the entire camp subsided into quietness, broken occasionally by a crying child in one of the lodges, or the dismal howling of distant prairie wolves and the answering yelps of the Indian dogs.

CHAPTER VI

Legend of the Beaver Medicine

Evening in Mad Wolf's lodge.—His fatherly talk.—He tells the origin of the Beaver Medicine.—In the legend, Nopatsis, jealous of Akaiyan his younger brother, leaves him to die on a lonely island.—The chief of the Beavers rescues him and keeps him all winter in the lodge of the Beavers.—Teaches him the ceremonial of the Beaver Medicine and the make-up of the Beaver Bundle, and bestows upon him supernatural power.—His youngest child, Little Beaver, returns with Akaiyan to the Blackfoot camp to help in teaching the people.—He creates the Beaver Medicine, to which many birds and animals contribute their power.

RETURNING to Mad Wolf's lodge I found him reclining upon his blankets, resting after the strain of the services. There was a long silence, which I did not venture to break, nor to disturb him, while smoking with half-closed eyes. Meanwhile the deepening twilight, which in a northern latitude comes quickly after sunset, but lingers, had settled over prairie and camp. As I looked upon the sacred Beaver Bundle, lying by his side in the flickering light of the small fire, I thought of their mysterious power over the Indian mind and life, and of the strange superstitions centred about them, which had been handed down through many generations. I was aroused from my reverie by Mad Wolf knocking the ashes from his pipe. He looked at me intently for a few moments. His manner was earnest and dignified, and as he sat erect, his long black hair fell loosely over his shoulders. He

answered my inquiring look towards the Medicine
Bundle by signing to me that I should grasp one end of
the rope. We together removed the cover that hid it
from view. He allowed me to gaze upon the sacred
Bundle for a moment, when the robe was solemnly
replaced. He then began to speak in a low voice, with
eyes half closed, as if gazing into the far distance,
saying :

"When I was a young man, I too became interested in the
mysteries of the medicines, which have been taught to me by old
Indians, and what they have told me I know to be true. I have
never before explained those mysteries to white men, because I
have always been afraid to trust them. I am now willing to have
you repeat these to the white race, because I know that you will
speak the truth and because I feel toward you as a father to his
son. When I bought the Beaver Medicine from O-mis tai-po-kah,
there came with it a very old pipe, which now lies by its side.
I will not smoke this pipe for it brings bad luck. When
O-mis-tai-po-kah smoked it his children began to die, so I preserve
it only as a relic. There was a time when I had many relics. If
I had them now I would give them to you, but they are gone."

He handed me the two rattles I had used in the
ceremonial and a small buckskin sack, saying,

"In it are some of the original seeds of the tobacco given to us
by the beavers. They were secured many years ago by Akaiyan,
the man who lived all winter in the lodge with the chief Beaver
and brought back with him the Beaver Medicine. I will relate to
you the story as it has been handed down from our ancestors.
What I will tell you happened long ago, when our people made all
of their tools and weapons from stone, and when they used dogs
instead of horses for beasts of burden."

The Origin of the Beaver Medicine

"In those days there were two orphan brothers.
The younger, named Akaiyan (Old Robe), lived with
his brother Nopatsis, who was married to a woman with
an evil heart. This woman disliked Akaiyan and continually urged her husband to cast him off. One day

when Nopatsis came home, he found his wife with her clothes torn and her body lacerated. She explained that, during his absence, Akaiyan had treated her brutally. Nopatsis said nothing to his younger brother, but planned how he might be rid of him for ever. It was midsummer, the time when the ducks and geese dropped their feathers. He proposed to Akaiyan that they should go together to an island in a large lake and said, ' At this time there will be many ducks and geese there, and we can gather the feathers they have dropped to be used for arrows.' When the brothers came to the lake they built a ' skatstan ' (raft), binding together logs with buffalo raw-hide and then floated on it to an island, far out in the lake. As they walked along the shores of this island looking for feathers, Akaiyan wandered off alone. He was returning with his arms full, when he beheld his brother out on the lake, going towards the shore of the mainland. He implored Nopatsis not to abandon him to perish on the lonely island. But his brother only called back, that he deserved no pity because of his brutal treatment of his sister-in-law. Akaiyan besought him to return, solemnly declaring before the Sun that he had not injured her. But Nopatsis replied heartlessly, ' You can live alone on the island all winter. In the spring, when the ice melts in the lake, I will return to gather your bones.' Akaiyan sat down and wept. He thought his time had come to die. Then he called upon the animals and the under-water spirits for assistance. He also prayed to the Sun, Moon and Stars, saying,

' Haiyu ! Mistapixit Mekape Natotsichpi ! '
' Behold, O Sun ! I cast away whatever of bad I have done,'
' Kokumekis ! Kokatosix Kummokit Spummokit ! '
' O Moon ! O Stars ! pity me ! Give me strength ! '

" After this prayer Akaiyan felt relieved and strengthened. He walked around the island and found a few branches, with which he made a shelter. He also

BEAVER DAM.
(Home of a Beaver Family.)

gathered many loose feathers, piling them up and making a bed that fitted his body so well that he slept warmly on the coldest nights. He killed many ducks and geese before their time for leaving the island to fly south, shooting the wild ones with his arrows and striking the tame ones upon the head with long sticks. He kept some for his winter food, but he skinned others and made a warm robe for himself by binding the skins together with alder bark.

"One day, when he discovered a beaver lodge, he lay

BEAVER BUNDLE OF MAD WOLF.
(It lies at the foot of tripod.)

for a long time watching it and weeping to himself, because he had been abandoned. Finally, a little beaver came from the lodge, and said to him, 'My father wants you to come into his lodge.' Akaiyan followed the little beaver into the lodge, where he saw a big beaver with his wife and family seated around him. This beaver was white from the snows of many winters, and so large that Akaiyan knew he must be the chief of all the beavers. The Beaver Chief bade him be seated, and asked him why he was living alone on the island. Akaiyan told him how cruelly and unjustly he had been treated and left alone to die. The Beaver Chief pitied Akaiyan and coun- selled with him, saying, 'My son, the time will soon come when we will close up our lodge for the winter. The lake will freeze over and we cannot come out again for seven moons, until the warm winds of spring will break up the ice. Remain in our lodge while the snows are deep. We will teach you many wonderful things and, when you return again, you can take knowledge with you, that will be of great value to your people.' The beavers were so hospitable, Akaiyan decided to remain with them. He took with him into the beaver lodge many ducks and geese for food and his bird-skin robe to keep him warm. They closed their lodge before it became cold, leaving a hole for air at the top. During the coldest days the beavers kept Akaiyan warm by lying close to him and placing their tails across his body. He made friends with all of them, but he liked the youngest and smallest beaver best of all. He was the cleverest as well as the favourite child of the Beaver Chief. Akaiyan learned their habits and manner of living. They taught him the names of the herbs and roots, which we still use for the curing of the people. They showed him also the different paints, and explained their use, saying, 'If you should use these, they will bring to your people good luck and will ward off sickness and death.' They gave him the seeds of the tobacco (origin of tobacco), and taught him how they should be planted with songs and prayers. They made scratches with their claws on the smooth walls of the lodge to mark the days, and when the days completed a moon they marked the moons with sticks. He witnessed many dances belonging to their medicines, and listened carefully to the songs and prayers. The Beaver Chief and his wife (Wise Old Woman) taught him the prayers and songs of their medicine and the dances that belonged to them, and said, 'Whenever any of your people are sick, or dying, if you will give this ceremonial, they will be restored to health.' He noticed that the beavers never ate during the ceremonial, and that they beat time for the dances with their tails, always stopping when they heard any suspicious noise, just as they do when they are at work. They told him that they counted seven moons from the time when the leaves fall before they prepared to open their lodge in the spring. When they heard the booming of the ice breaking in the lake, they knew it would soon be time to leave their winter home.

"Little Beaver told Akaiyan that, before he parted with them, his father, the Beaver Chief, would offer him a present and would allow him to choose anything within the lodge. Little Beaver also advised him, saying, 'When my father asks you for your choice, say that you will take your little brother. He will not be willing to part with me, for he prizes me above everything he owns. He will ask you four times to choose something else, but take me with you, for I will have more power to help you than any of the others.'

"The ducks and geese were flying north, when the beavers finally opened their lodge for the summer, and the Beaver Chief said to Akaiyan, 'You will soon leave us now, because it is time for your older brother to return. But, before you start, I will allow you to

choose anything in my lodge to take away with you.'
Then Akaiyan, remembering the advice of Little Beaver,
asked for his youngest child. The Beaver Chief made
many excuses and endeavoured to persuade him to
take something else, but Akaiyan would have no other
gift. After the fourth trial, the Beaver Chief said,
'My son, you show your wisdom in selecting your little
brother to go with you. I am sorry to part with him,
because he is the best worker and the wisest of my
children, but, because of my promise, I now give him to
you.'

"The Beaver Chief also told Akaiyan that, when he
returned to his people, he should make a sacred Bundle
similar to the one he saw them using in their ceremonial.
He also taught him the songs and prayers and dances
that belonged to the Bundle and informed him that,
if any of the people were sick, or dying and a relative
would make a vow to the Beaver Medicine, the sick
would be restored to health.

"One evening, when the Beaver Chief returned from
his cutting, he said to Akaiyan, 'My son, remain in
hiding and do not show yourself. To-day, when I was
among the trees on the main shore, I saw your brother's
camp.' The next day Akaiyan, watching from the
beaver lodge, saw Nopatsis coming to the island on the
raft. He saw him land and walk along the shore hunting for his bones. Then Akaiyan ran, with Little
Beaver under his arm and took possession of the raft.
He was far out in the big lake before Nopatsis saw him,
He at once realised that his younger brother had
secured power superior to his own and had become a
great medicine man.

"Akaiyan now returned with Little Beaver to the

tribal camp.   He went at once to the head chief's lodge
and told his story.   All the people received him with
the greatest honour, when they heard of the wisdom
and power that had been given him by the Beavers.
Akaiyan gathered together a Beaver Bundle as the
Beaver Chief had directed.   He and Little Beaver
had remained all winter in the camp, teaching the
people the songs, prayers and dances given him by the
beavers.   When Spring came, Akaiyan invited all of
the animals to add their power to the Beaver Medicine.
Many birds and animals of the prairies and mountains
came, offering their skins and taught him their songs,
prayers and dances to accompany their skins, just as
the beavers had done.   The Elk and his wife each
contributed a song and dance, also the Moose and his
wife.   The Woodpecker gave three songs with his
dance.   The Frog alone of all the animals could neither
dance nor sing, and it is for this reason he is not
represented in the Beaver Bundle.   The Turtle could
not dance and had no song, but is represented in
the Bundle, because he was wise and borrowed one from
the Lizard, who owned two songs.

" In the following spring Akaiyan returned to the
island with Little Beaver to visit the beaver lodge.   He
saw his brother's bones on the shore and knew the
beavers had not helped him.   The Beaver Chief welcomed
Akaiyan warmly and when he gave back Little Beaver
to his father, the old chief was so grateful that he
presented him with a sacred pipe, teaching him also the
songs, prayers and dances that belonged to it.   When
Akaiyan returned again to the Indian camp he added
this pipe to the Beaver Bundle.   Every spring Akaiyan
went to visit his friends, the beavers, and each time the

Beaver Chief gave him something to add to the Beaver Bundle, until it reached the size it has to-day. Akaiyan continued to lead the Beaver ceremonial as long as he lived and was known as a great medicine man. When he died, the ceremonial was continued by his son, and has been handed down ever since."

CHAPTER VII

MY ROCKY MOUNTAIN GOAT HUNT

The St. Mary's Lakes.—Magnificent mountain scenery.—My mountain camp.—Home of the mountain sheep and goat.—Stalking a herd of five goats.—An exciting climb.—One goat killed.—Pursuit of a wounded goat.—Laborious task of skinning a goat on a dangerous ledge.—A mountain storm.—The back trail.—Ideal camp on the prairie.—Return to Mad Wolf's winter home on Cutbank River.

EARLY on a clear October morning, when the air was peculiarly exhilarating, I threw the "diamond hitch" upon my pack, taking care that the ropes were taut throughout, and headed north-west for the St. Mary's Lakes. The ride across the plains seemed short, for my saddle horse was in fine condition, after his long rest, and Baldy, my pack horse, followed readily.

From the crest of St. Mary's Ridge (the divide running east and west), I saw a beautiful lake country spread out before me, and, towards the west, the magnificent snowy peaks "Almost-a-Dog," "Citadel," "Four Bears," "Little Chief," "Red Eagle," and "Going-to-the-Sun"; while a host of other peaks continued the imposing procession, until they lost themselves in the blue sky of both northern and southern horizons.

Amid such magnificent surroundings, mounted upon my own saddle horse, and followed by Baldy carrying all my possessions, I experienced a delightful feeling of independence and exhilaration, which only those who have had a similar experience can fully appreciate.

Having crossed the ridge, I rode through rich

My Rocky Mountain Outfit.

meadows of long bunch grass along the shore of upper St. Mary's Lake. After climbing well up on the side of " Goat Mountain," where the trail became rough and dangerous, I approached the towering and inaccessible peak of Going-to-the-Sun. It is so called because of the large glacier that lies just under its summit. In winter, it is an unbroken expanse of ice and snow, but, under the melting of the midsummer sun, it takes the outline of a turbaned head, facing the south-west. It is more correctly named by the Indians, " Looking-towards-the-setting-Sun." After sunset I came to Baring's Creek in the dense forest, a large swift stream roaring and plunging down towards the lake. Following the stream, I climbed rapidly upwards, passing many beautiful falls. Near nightfall, I passed from the forest into a large basin. It was surrounded by lofty and jagged peaks, which looked dark and gloomy in the fading twilight. My lodge was pitched at the edge of the forest, on the grassy shore of a beautiful lake, whose waters, fed by the surrounding glaciers, were clear as crystal and cold as ice. The falls of Baring's Creek, not far distant, sent forth a constant roar. Soon the moon rose over the summit of Red Eagle, transforming the scene into one of enchanting and fairy-like beauty. In the clear atmosphere of the high altitude the moonlight was intensely bright, flooding the basin with its silvery light, illuminating the glaciers and snowfields, the peaks and pinnacles, towering above the camp, and making visible the contrasting darkness of the gorge beneath.

Upon waking the next morning, and while still under my blankets, I looked across the gorge and up at the high ledges of Going-to-the-Sun, fully expecting to see a goat, or a mountain sheep gazing down at my camp. The clouds were lifting along the mountains, and the morning mists were fast dissolving before the warm rays of the sun. After breakfast, I saddled Baldy, my sure-footed pack horse, and, with my rifle, started up the basin, watching carefully through my glasses for goats and sheep on the rock shelves, high on the side of Going-to-the-Sun.

At the head of the basin the climbing became so rough and difficult, that I picketed my horse in a convenient place and continued afoot. Many beautiful flowers were blooming by the side of snow-drifts, and I passed through patches of huckleberries of very large size and delicious flavour. At noon I stopped for lunch beside a noisy little stream flowing from beneath a large snow-drift. The day was warm and bright, and the view from my lofty position magnificent. To the north rose the twin peaks of Mt. Siyeh (Mad Wolf), also Mt. Allen and Mt. Grinnell. After the long and fatiguing climb it was a luxury to lie in the warm sun. Several times I was startled by large masses of ice, crashing over precipices with a thundering roar, having been detached by the sun's rays from the glacier high above me.

From behind a clump of gnarled and twisted pines, I looked carefully through my glasses for fresh tracks of sheep and goats in the snow, and examined their well-worn trails on the mountain opposite. The width and depth of many of these trails indicate the large numbers of game formerly inhabiting these mountains. The constant tread of their hoofs through many ages has worn deep paths in the solid granite. As long as the buffalo and antelope were in vast numbers upon the plains and easy of capture, supplying almost all the wants of the Indians, mountain sheep and goats were hunted but little, and their numbers were limited only by the food supply.

In the Northern Rockies, the mountain goat is to be found only among the most inaccessible peaks.

Ordinarily he must be approached from beneath. He is generally found either standing on the edge of a high precipice, or lying upon one of the narrow shelves, or ledges, so numerous among the higher summits. From his lofty perch, he commands a view of the mountain side beneath him, and, if he detects the hunter's pursuit, quickly disappears from sight, or reach. While the "big horn," or mountain sheep, is more keen of scent and sight, the almost inaccessible haunts of the goat make his hunting more difficult and dangerous, and account for the value of his head as a hunter's trophy.

It was now growing so late in the afternoon, that I was fast losing hope of seeing any game that day. After a final examination through my glasses of the side of Goat Mountain, I turned them upon the mountain at the end of the basin. Far up on its slope there was a herd of five goats with fur as white as snow. Had it not been for their jet black horns it would have been impossible to distinguish them from the snow-bank across which they were rapidly moving. Having crossed the summit at the head of the basin, they were headed for a grassy knoll high up on the side of Going-to-the-Sun, and there was a chance that they might delay to feed. My only hope of getting within rifle-shot was to reach the knoll first and to lie in ambush. I waited until they were hidden from view by an intervening shoulder of the mountain. Crawling from my ambush, I climbed with all my strength. The goats were travelling rapidly, and, if I had correctly estimated their course, it would take them but a short time to reach the knoll. Although speed was necessary, I had to take into account that, if I lost my wind, and had to shoot in an exhausted condition, there would be small chance of hitting them. When I reached the knoll, I hid behind a thick patch of grass. Before I had time to get my rifle in position, the head of a goat appeared above the edge of the slope. He took a bite of grass and then stepped into full view. I carefully raised my rifle and cocked it, but the click attracted his attention. He stopped and gazed suspiciously towards me. I lay perfectly still, which apparently satisfied him, for he lowered his head and continued feeding. Then I fired, hitting him directly behind the shoulder, and gave another shot to a large billy which was following, seriously wounding him.

By this time, the first goat had struggled to a snow-drift, where I killed him. In the meantime the wounded billy and a nanny, with her two kids, had disappeared. It did not seem possible that the billy could go far. I started in pursuit, climbing with difficulty through the deep snow. I came upon the nanny with her two kids standing within short range at the edge of a precipice. The kids were beautiful little animals, and though large enough to care for themselves, I had not the heart to shoot them or their mother. I left them to hunt for the tracks of the large billy. While I was following his trail, he started for a precipitous part of the mountain, where I feared I might lose him, for wounded goats frequently go off to die in such inaccessible places, that it is impossible to reach them. He ran along a series of shelves made by the out-croppings of the horizontal rock strata. As he jumped from one to another of these I got another shot. This last bullet slackened his pace, but, with vitality equal to that of a grizzly bear, he still crawled on. The climbing became difficult and dangerous. The goat jumped to a lower shelf, and seeing that if he went farther, he would escape, I leaned over and fired. Fortunately he sank in his tracks, although I fully expected to see him roll from the narrow ledge. Returning to the snow-drift where the first goat had fallen, I quickly skinned him and un-jointed his head. Turning next to the task of passing along the ledges to reach the second goat, I found that, what had been done before with comparative ease, and without any feeling of danger, because of the excite-ment of the chase, now tested to the utmost my strength and self-control. Carefully refraining from looking at the heights above, or the rocks far below, I dropped safely to the lower shelf, which was scarcely wide enough to hold the body of the goat. The natural smell of a goat is offensive, but with the hide partly off it was extremely so. However, there was no escape. Behind was a wall of rock sloping outward, so that I could not stand erect; in front yawned the precipice, over which I dared not look. While skinning in such narrow quarters, it was a difficult problem to turn the carcass of the goat over, for it was very heavy, weighing as much as a large sheep. When I had unjointed the head and finished my work, I crawled to the end of the shelf farthest from the carcass, and sat down to recuperate. While absorbed in the excitement of the hunt, I had not noticed the signs of an approaching snowstorm, which would make my descent difficult and even hazardous. The clouds were lowering upon the mountains, and on some of the peaks the storm had already begun.

There still remained the dangerous and laborious task of removing the head and hide away from the ledge. Fortunately I carried my lariat. Wrapping the head inside the hide, I lashed them with the rope, and throw-ing the end of it to the shelf above, climbed up, pulling the bundle after me. A projecting rock blockaded the way at a point, where the ledge was narrow and the slope steep. While endeavouring to shove the pack across, it began to slide. Fearing that, in such a dangerous place, I might be drawn over the precipice, I let the rope go. The pack rolled from the ledge and fell upon the rocks far below. It seemed as if all my labour had been in vain for, even if I were able to reach the pack, I feared that the head had been ruined by the fall. But, after discovering a way of approach from below, I was delighted to find the head had been saved from serious injury by the thick fur of the pelt. Returning to my first goat I made a new pack of both heads and pelts which, with my rifle, was a heavy load for the return trip. When I reached Baldy, picketed far down the mountain-side, I was very tired. Gathering together sufficient material for making a small fire, I toasted some dry bread and bacon. With an appetite sharpened by hard climbing at a high altitude, they seemed the most delicious morsels I had ever eaten. When I reached camp at dusk the timbered mountain slopes were white with snow and the surrounding peaks hidden from view.

In the morning when I opened my lodge door, I looked out upon a dazzling scene. Over the peak of Red Eagle the sun was shining in a clear sky. Meadow, forest and mountains were covered with a white mantle of snow. It hung heavily upon the balsams and pines and many icicles flashed like diamonds in the sunlight. The deep blue sky and clear images of the high peaks were mirrored in the quiet lake beneath. As if this lovely lake-picture had not enough of beauty, the snow-storm of the night had added a framing of white the brown trunks and dark foliage of the firs and pines serving to soften its dazzling whiteness.

I was delayed in breaking camp by the pranks of my mischievous pack horse Baldy. In roping him, he put his front feet through the noose of the lariat, which then became fastened around his belly instead of his neck. He ran around the camp bucking and kicking until, becoming thoroughly frightened, he galloped away and I had great difficulty in catching him.

MY MOUNTAIN CAMP AFTER THE SNOWSTORM.

The sun was high when the horses were at last saddled and all my belongings were finally packed upon their backs. As I descended, the snow rapidly disappeared and in the lower canyons it had vanished entirely. I travelled rapidly, for the horses were headed towards home and were eager for a better grazing range. While leading Baldy, my pack horse, across a dangerous piece of trail, where the way was narrow, and its side sloped downward towards the edge of a precipice, overhanging the stream, his pack over-balanced and he staggered. For an instant, it seemed as if he must tumble into the river far below. Throwing my whole weight upon the neck rope, I held him fast, until he recovered himself, and in a few moments we were again upon safe ground. My camp for the night was made on the prairie beyond the eastern shore of Lower St. Mary's Lake.

In the evening I stood on the summit of a high ridge to take a last view of the wonderful mountain scenery, unsurpassed by any along the entire Rocky Mountain chain. As the sinking sun slowly disappeared behind the summit of Red Eagle, the forests of pine on the mountain slopes changed from dark green to black, and the heavy cloud masses projected their long shadows upon the prairies and foothills still bathed in sunlight. Far to the east over the plains were the hazy and rounded outlines of the Sweet Pine Hills. The broad prairie surrounding me, with its flowers and long waving grass, bright in the evening sunlight, had never seemed more beautiful, for its openness and brightness were in strong contrast with the deep canyons and gloomy forests from which I had just returned. The all-pervading stillness was occasionally broken by the distant roar of the rapids of St. Mary's River, borne upwards on the light south wind, and by the howling of a pack of prairie wolves. The heavy clouds behind the mountains were lighted up with a glorious colouring that slowly deepened into red until even the clouds overhead glowed like a sea of fire. In the darkening twilight Venus appeared high in the golden after-glow of the western sky. She seemed like a radiant spirit of the heavenly world, gazing down upon the snowy

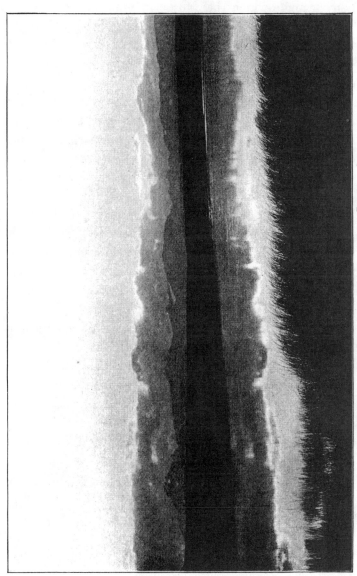

SUNSET ON THE PRAIRIES (ROCKIES IN THE DISTANCE).

"The broad prairie, with its flowers and long waving grass, had never seemed more beautiful."

mountains, an unfailing source of inspiration for the many legends which the Indian imagination has woven about the personality of the " Evening Star."

The following day I crossed the brown plains and rode down into the Cutbank Valley, in search of Mad Wolf's camp. Fording the swift river, I followed a beaten trail, leading up the valley towards his winter home. Ice was beginning to form along the edges of the running stream, and the air was fragrant with the odour of fallen leaves. Towards the west the perennial green of the forests of pine and fir on the foothills stood out clearly in the strong sunlight, while towards the north the table-like summit of the Milk River Ridge formed an unbroken and level line against the horizon. The way led through meadows of long bunch grass and groves of stately cottonwoods. Their foliage, now fast turning to yellow, was in striking contrast with the brilliant scarlet of the sarvis berry and wild rose. Many leaves had already fallen, exposing the silver-grey of the cottonwood trunks, and revealing the delicate purple of the alder bushes and the bright red branches of the thickets of willows. Beneath the large cottonwood tree, marking from afar the home of Mad Wolf, I recognised his large lodge covered with picture paintings. It was after sunset and Mad Wolf was about to close a ceremonial, which he had been conducting on behalf of a mother, who had made a vow to the Beaver Medicine for the recovery of her sick child.

CHAPTER VIII

WINTER ON THE PLAINS

A trip to the mountains for winter wood.—Nature's signs of an early winter.—Narrow escape from death in the forest.—My struggle with a blizzard.—Snow bound.—Legend of the Snow Tipi.—Na-toia-mon's vision.—Power over a blizzard granted him by the Cold Maker.—Supernatural power of the Snow Tipi.

WHEN Mad Wolf said the time had come to secure our winter firewood, Ah-see-tuck (his son-in-law) and I went together to the mountains. We left the camp at sunrise with four powerful bronchos, harnessed to a timber wagon without a bed. Ah-see-tuck was a skilled but reckless driver. He drove standing on the axle between the front wheels, while I sat back upon the reach. It required both strength and agility to hold my uncertain seat, while the bronchos were running at a mad gallop over the plains, the wagon swinging and tilting at times upon two wheels. The bronchos, frightened by the rattling wheels, ran away, but there was no need to hold them, for our course lay across the broad plains, without fences, or obstacles of any kind, and with a constant upgrade towards the mountains. When we reached the foothills and Ah-see-tuck wished to slacken the speed, he put the brakes on hard and skillfully headed them up the steep slope of a butte and brought them to a standstill. He then guided them into a canyon and finally to the edge of a thick forest of pine, spruce and fir. We felled only dead trees. thoroughly seasoned and, having trimmed them free from branches, we had the horses snake them out from the standing timber to be loaded upon the wagon. At midday we rested from our exhausting work, on the bank of a small mountain brook, and were refreshed by the fragrance of the firs and balsams. While reclining upon a thick carpet of moss and pine-needles, we watched

DRAWING OUT TIMBER WITH HORSES.

a golden eagle flying high over the mountains and a flock of white swans passing near the summit of Mount Rising Wolf. Many flocks of ducks skimmed the tree-tops overhead, in their swift and level flight, while far away was heard the faint honking of migrating geese.

Ah-see-tuck then imparted some of his weather wisdom by remarking, " Geese are endowed with great wisdom and foreknowledge of the weather. When they

fly high, it is the sign of an early winter. The movements of other birds and the thickened skins of fur
bearing animals, have already given us warning. The
curlew stopped it's singing in the early summer. The
song birds have gathered into flocks and the yellow
breasts (prairie larks) have disappeared before the
sarvis berries were ripe. The skins of the otter, mink
and beaver are heavier than usual, and the jack rabbits
have turned white earlier than is their custom."

Our work in the forest was brought to an abrupt
close by my narrow escape from death. We were
working together on a large spruce tree, Ah-see-tuck
chopping on one side, while I was standing on the
other. When the tree began to topple, and I saw it
coming in my direction, I jumped for a position of
safety. The top unexpectedly struck a leaning tree,
which caused the butt to be thrown into the air and
then to come rolling towards us. It narrowly missed
Ah-see-tuck, but, notwithstanding his mighty yell,
there was no escape for me. At the same instant I was
struck and hurled to one side. When I came back to
consciousness, I thought my end had come, for I was
unable to breathe, or move. My breath slowly returned
and I sat up. A glancing blow from the jagged butt
of the tree had torn a ragged wound in my side six
inches long, whose scar I shall always carry. If I had
been one foot nearer, I would have been crushed to
death. I carefully bound up the wound, using anti-
septics and other remedies from my small medicine case.
It healed with remarkable rapidity, because of the
bracing atmosphere and my excellent physical condition.

In early November, after returning from the mountains, I rode alone from the camp many miles to the north,
in search of missing horses. The sky was clear and the

air as mild as a day in early summer. At midday, while stopping for rest in a thicket of willows and quaking asps, I was alarmed to see, in the north, a heavy bank of clouds, which spread rapidly, until the high ridge of the Hudson's Bay Divide was completely obscured. Quickly saddling my horse, I started for the camp at a gallop. The thermometer dropped seventy degrees in a few moments and a driving snow storm, with a cold wind from the north, set in. The surrounding plains were shrouded in a white mist and the ground was soon covered with a fine drifting snow. I took a southerly course with the storm at my back. My horse having been purchased from the Kutenai Indians, on the western side of the Rockies, and therefore a stranger to the range, was constantly inclined to turn westward towards the mountains. Finding that he lacked endurance, I changed from a gallop to a slow trot, in order to save his strength in the deepening snow. I followed a small stream, until I recognised the land marks of my former crossing, and then pushed on towards the Milk River Ridge, the most dangerous part of my ride. Having climbed to its summit, I was upon a broad table-land many miles in width. To hunt for a distant camp on the plains, in such a storm, was taking desperate chances, but there was no alternative. The air was bitterly cold, while a fierce gale was driving the snow in blinding clouds. My horse presented a droll appearance with a heavy coat of frost covering him from head to foot, leaving only holes for his eyes. The dripping water from fording the streams formed icicles along his sides and matted his long tail, which rattled like a bunch of bones at every step. Darkness fell, while I was crossing the plateau. The snow grew deeper and deeper, and my horse moved more and more

slowly, losing both spirit and strength. When my
spurs failed of effect, I dismounted and tried leading.
Then he wanted to lie down, so I remounted and by
freely using both whip and spurs, again moved slowly
forward. The storm increased in violence. Everything
was enveloped in a dense white pall and I lost all sense
of direction. I felt as if I were becoming blind and
losing my senses, so I gripped myself and shouted, that
I might hear the sound of my own voice. I knew
when we descended into a coulee by the feeling that we
were going down, down, down, I could not tell how far.
But, when we reached the bottom, my horse was stuck
fast in a deep drift, helplessly groaning without even trying to move. It was now a desperate question of life or
death, with the latter staring me hard in the face. Nerved
with the energy of despair, I seized him by the bridle,
struck him with my whip, and by pulling with all my
strength upon his tail, slowly worked him loose. Just
then the moon broke through the low driving clouds for a
moment, enabling me to correct my course. I struggled on,
until I came at last to the edge of the plateau and then
descended to the lower level of the plain. I was still
far from the camp, having struck the river valley, too
high up through the tendency of my horse to veer
westward towards the mountains. But, it was not
difficult to follow the trail down the valley, sheltered
from the full force of the storm by the big cottonwoods
and dense thickets of willows. At last, the cheerful
lights of the lodge fires appeared, and my hard struggle
with the blizzard was ended. Mad Wolf was rejoiced
at my safe return, having believed that I had been
claimed by the "Cold Maker." Completely exhausted
and chilled to the bone, the warmth and shelter of my
own lodge, on that stormy night, was to me the most

delightful haven of rest and comfort I had ever enjoyed. After finishing my supper, I lay on my blanket-bed listening to the wind whistling through the ropes and poles overhead. Above the roar of the storm, I heard faintly the bawling of frightened cattle, as they drifted helplesly before the driving wind and snow and bitter cold.

When I first wakened on the following morning the

MY LODGE DURING THE BLIZZARD.

terrible blizzard was still raging. Drawing the warm blankets more closely around me I slept soundly until I was aroused at midday by Strikes-on-both-sides calling me to Mad Wolf's lodge to eat. When I looked outside it seemed as if a white sheet had been let down before me. Huge drifts were piled up on the north and south sides of the lodge. Bull Plume, a visiting chief from the North Piegans, appeared on

horseback, struggling through the drifts. He held
Nokoa (a young child) in his arms, completely
wrapped in blankets. Mesamax (Takes-a-long-time-
to-fly—a name derived from the habit of the swans
which are slow in starting to fly)—a boy of eight years,
rode behind holding tightly to his father, while his little
daughter, six years old, Natoya-niskim (Sacred Buffalo
Stone), sat in front. Three women were following on

BULL PLUME AND FAMILY COMING THROUGH THE BLIZZARD.

foot, Ika-sta-pina (Bull Plume's wife), a very pretty
young woman, carrying a baby on her back, Mistina,
her mother, and Itomina, her old and deaf aunt. Bull
Plume explained that his fire-wood was gone and his
travelling lodge was a poor shelter for women and
children during the blizzard.

The storm of wind and snow from the north continued
for ten days. In the meantime the close companionship
round the lodge fire dissolved all reserve and facilitated,

what I most desired, the unbosoming of their experiences, legends and religious beliefs. I heard many thrilling stories of war and adventure, also of strange and unearthly experiences with disembodied spirits. The story-telling generally began in the evening, continuing far into the night, for the Blackfeet, when they feel in the mood, are great talkers, going into minute details

SETTING THE EAR POLES FOR A CHANGE OF WIND.

and giving vivid descriptions of their experiences for which their language is well adapted. They are superstitiously opposed to relating legends in daylight and insist that they should be told after dark and in the winter time.

We were all gathered one night around the lodge fire. There had been a long silence, which Mad Wolf broke by telling

The Legend of the Snow Tipi.

"The Blackfeet have a Winter or Snow Tipi. It was given to us by Es-to-nea-pesta, Maker of Storms and Blizzards. Whenever it is pitched, cold weather and winds are sure to come because of its great power. For this reason the Bad Weather Tipi is rarely seen in our midsummer camps, when the people are most anxious for warm and pleasant weather. That, which

SUNSET AFTER THE CHINOOK (WARM WIND).

I will now tell, happened many years ago during this same autumn moon.

"The ducks and geese had flown south, the last of their flocks having disappeared many days before. It was past the time for the beginning of winter, but the air was warm and the sky cloudless. One morning a band of hunters were running buffalo on a broad plain. Na-toia-mon (Sacred Otter—father of Morning Plume) and his young son had been very successful.

When the hunt was over they began at once to skin their buffalo. While busy on the carcass of a large bull, they did not notice the coming storm. When they had finished, Na-toia-mon saw a heavy black cloud hanging low in the northern horizon and extending high up in the sky. As he watched the cloud it began spreading out and rolling over and over. Soon he saw

SNOW TIPI.

a low, seething, flying mass of clouds advancing rapidly over the plain. He then realised that a terrible Ma-kai-peye (charge-storm or blizzard) was coming, and there would be no chance for escape. They lay behind the dead buffalo bull for shelter, but the cold became so intense he knew they would soon be frozen. With the fresh buffalo hide he made a low shelter behind the bull's carcass and both crawled inside. The snow soon covered the frozen hide with a deep drift, making them warm and comfortable.

" Na-toia-mon then fell asleep and dreamed that he was travelling alone on the plains. He discovered a large tipi in the distance and, as he drew nearer, saw that it was decorated. Its top was yellow like the sunlight, with clusters of the seven stars painted on both sides, representing the North, from whence the blizzards come. At the back was a red disc for the sun, to the centre of which was attached the tail of the sacred buffalo. At the bottom were the rolling ridges of the prairies, with their rounded tops, and a broad yellow band, with green discs to represent the colour of holes in ice, or frozen drifts. Beneath the yellow top and on four sides, where stood the four main lodge poles, were painted four green claws with yellow legs representing the Thunder Bird. Above the door, which was made of spotted buffalo calf-skin, was a buffalo head in red, with black horns and eyes in green,—the ice colour. Horse tails were tied at either side over the door, and bunches of crow feathers, with small bells attached, that tinkled whenever the wind blew, were fastened to the ends of both ear poles.

" While Na-toia-mon was contemplating these picture paintings, he heard a voice saying, ' Who is it that walks around my tipi? Why do you not enter?' So, lifting the door flap and entering, he beheld at the back a large and handsome man smoking alone in the lodge. His hair was white and he was clothed in a long white robe. Taking a seat near the door, Na-toia-mon gazed anxiously around, the stranger continuing to smoke in silence. He was seated behind an altar of fresh earth with juniper laid on the top, similar to the one used in the Sun ceremonial. Smoke was rising like incense

from a hot coal close to the altar. His face was painted
yellow with a red line across his mouth and another
across the eyes to his ears. His medicine stick was
also yellow. In his back hair he wore a black feather
and around his waist strips of otter skin with small
bells attached. Across his breast was a beaded mink
skin, with small bells fastened to its paws and one also
to its mouth. Beside him lay a tobacco sack made also
of mink skin. He smoked a black stone pipe, the stem of
which had been blackened in the fire. The stranger still
smoked in silence for a long time and then finally spoke :

" ' I am Es-tonea-pesta, the maker of cold weather and this is the
Snow Tipi or Yellow Paint Lodge. It is I who bring the cold
storms, the whirling snow, and the biting winds from the north,
and I control them at my will. I have called you to my lodge
because I have taken pity on you. I am going to help you for the
sake of your son who was caught in the blizzard with you. I now
give you the Snow Tipi with its decorations and medicines. With
it I also give you the mink-skin tobacco pouch, the black stone
pipe, and my supernatural power. You and your son will not
perish in this storm. Your lives will be spared. When you return
to camp make a tipi just as you see this one is made.'

" The Cold Maker explained to Na-toia-mon the
decorations to be used in painting, advising him to
remember them very carefully, also the songs and the
ceremonial to be used in transferring the tipi to anyone
who might make the vow. He told him that the mink
skin should be worn as a charm, whenever he went to
war and that the horse tails, hanging over the door,
would bring him good luck, both in keeping his own
horses and in securing others from the enemy.

" Na-toia-mon then awoke from his sleep. He saw
that the storm was abating and knew that the North
Man would keep his promise. As soon as he returned
to camp, he made a model of the Snow Tipi, painting it
just as the Cold Maker directed. He gathered together

the medicines necessary for the ceremonial and in the spring, the time when the Blackfeet make their new lodges, Na-toia-mon made and painted the Bad Weather, or Snow Tipi.

" During the following winter, the Blackfeet found out that the power, given to Na-toia-mon by the Cold Maker, was very great. When the snows lay deep (February), they were camped near the mouth of the Cutbank Canyon. Meat was very scarce, so a party crossed the high plateau to hunt on the North Fork of Milk River. They killed some buffalo but, while skinning them, were caught in a blizzard. They were upon an exposed plain, where there was no shelter. Finding a few small willows they built a fire to thaw out the frozen hides. Part of the expedition started for camp, but lost their way. After wandering around in a circle they came back to the place they started from. When the wood gave out they held a council. It seemed useless to attempt to cross the high plateau in such a storm, but, if they remained, all would be frozen to death. Then, Morning Plume turning to Na-toia-mon said : ' Brother ! will you not try the power given you by the Cold Maker ? If his medicine is strong, now is the time to use it. For the sake of your wife and children, drive back this storm.' Na-toia-mon replied, ' I came not from the Sun ! How can I drive back the Ma-kai-peye ?' ' Try it !' said Morning Plume. ' For the sake of our wives and children I now call upon you for help.' Na-toia-mon had with him the mink-skin tobacco pouch and the black pipe given him by the North Man. When he was ready to open the pipe, he gave directions to wrap up the women and children as warmly as possible, and to place them upon the travois,[1] and told the men to go in advance, and break a trail through the

[1] See Appendix.

deep snow for the horses. When they were ready to start he called out, 'As soon as I begin to pray for power to break this storm, start at once. Travel as fast as you can for camp, for I can only hold back the storm for a short time. When it sets in again, it will come more fiercely than before.' Na-toia-mon filled the black pipe and when he began smoking he gave the signal to start. He blew the smoke first towards the north-east,— the direction the storm came from. Then he held up the sacred pipe and prayed :

" ' Maker of Storms ! listen and have pity ! Maker of Storms ! hear us and take pity on our women and children as you once took pity upon my youngest son ! Pity us now and hold back this storm ! May we survive ! Listen, Oh Maker of Storms ! '

" When he blew the smoke towards the south-east, the sun shone through a rift in the clouds. Na-toia-mon called after the people, 'Hurry now as fast as you can across the high ridge, for the storm will soon come upon you again.' He smoked towards the south-west and the clouds began to break up. When he made his final smoke and prayed towards the north-west, the clouds drew back and the blue sky was seen in all directions. Then Na-toia-mon himself hurried towards camp. He knew the Cold Maker was only holding the blizzard back. They crossed the plateau in safety and were descending towards the river, when the blizzard again enveloped them, and they could not see their way. But, the camp was not far distant, and they finally reached their lodges in safety.

" From that time the Blackfeet have always believed in Na-toia-mon's dream. But he could never again be prevailed upon to try his supernatural power. He always replied, that he knew the power to control the storms would not be given to him a second time."

CHAPTER IX

GHOST STORIES

Superstitious fears of my companions during the blizzard.—Story of
Running Rabbit's ghost.—Old Person ghost story.—Strange story of
Kattana's death.—Methods used by different medicine men during
his last illness.—His visions and death-dream.—Startling apparitions
after Kattana's death.—Story of Crow Eagle and the ghost.—
Blackfeet beliefs as to the future life.—Disposition of the dead.—
Burial customs.—Mourning customs.

When Mad Wolf had finished the legend of the Winter
Tipi, the beating of snow and sleet against the lodge
signified the presence of the mysterious Cold Maker
and filled everyone with awe and dread of His power.
Mysterious sounds were in the air. The singing of the
wood on the fire seemed like voices from the spirit
world. The distant bellowing of the cattle and the
barking of the · dogs sounded weird and ghostly.
Suddenly a furious gust of wind roared through the
poles overhead, shaking the lodge violently, throwing
the door-flap wide open and swirling the smoke.
Mistina said, in awe-struck tones, that a spirit had
entered because she had just heard the dogs giving the
ghost-bark, a peculiar snuffling bark, which the Blackfeet say they use when spirits are about. Mistina
was in a state of mind favourable for both hearing and
seeing ghosts. She, like many others, had been deeply
impressed by the fact that many well-known Indians had
died during the summer and their spirits had been

appearing to the living, bringing fear and sometimes even death. Itomina, the old deaf woman, however, was not disturbed by any of these fears. She sat near the door holding the baby in her arms, swaying slowly

ITOMINA AND LITTLE NATOYA IN A SNOWDRIFT.

backwards and forwards and singing to it softly an old slumber song.

Ika-sta-pina then told of Running Rabbit's spirit which had been harassing the Indians who crossed Two Medicine River at night, by frightening their horses.

Mistina interrupted to say, " It is strange Running Rabbit should have become so mean after death, he was such a kind, and good old man while alive. Not long ago we saw his ghost, when we were crossing the Two Medicine River. He was lying on the ground, but, as we drew near, he raised himself and stood in front of our horses. He came so near, we were frightened lest he might touch us (sure death). Not long ago while Two Strikes and her daughter, Soft Woman, were going to visit Bull Calf, they heard a voice from behind. Soft Woman told me that her mother turned to see who it might be. She fell instantly upon the ground and lay as if dead. When she came to herself, she explained to her daughter that, when she turned, she beheld the spirit of her father, Running Rabbit, who had touched her. Not long afterwards Two Strikes died very suddenly and her family believe that Running Rabbit took her with him to the spirit world."

Strikes-on-both-sides said : " There have been many ghosts this summer bothering people, who travel near the Two Medicine River at night. Old Person was recently riding down the river to Little Plume's. When he was passing the cottonwood trees, where the dead bodies lie in the branches, his horse suddenly reared and plunged, as if frightened by an apparition. Then Old Person heard a voice speaking from the trees, saying, ' Old Person ! what has delayed your coming to the spirit world so long ? I have been waiting for you a very long time.' He was so badly frightened he rode away at a gallop. Next day he was taken sick and in a few days he died. I also heard of another case. When Big Wolf Medicine and Buffalo Hide were recently camped on the Two Medicine with their wives, a ghost harassed them all night, so that they could not sleep.

They first heard something approaching their lodge from the north-west where there was a grove of cottonwoods. It awakened the dogs that were sleeping outside. They gave the ghost-bark and were badly frightened, snuffing the air and growling fiercely. The ghost moved around the lodge to the door, which it threw open. Then it went to the north-east side and hooted like an owl." The Blackfeet have a superstitious fear of owls, believing that the spirits of the dead often appear in that form. " Next morning, they discovered a death lodge in the cottonwood grove and recognised the body of a young man that had been murdered by his jealous brother. It is probably because he was murdered that he annoys the living."

Mistina then told some incidents of the last sickness and death of Kattana. " Many medicine men were present during his last illness. Ketopio, Ominamo, Imo-yis-ocasim, and Paks-ak-ikin. The women doctors were Nits-tos-ape, First Strike, and Snake Woman. The medicine men chanted and prayed night and day. When one was exhausted another took his place. Ketopio's power in doctoring came from the otter; Paks-ak-ikin's from the grizzly bear; Imo-yis-ocasim's from the mink and Nits-tos-ape's from the buffalo. Each drummed and danced in turn, imitating the movements of the animal he represented. Ominamo prayed to the Thunder. He wore a necklace of many coloured beads representing the rainbow which endowed him with supernatural power and wisdom. He blew water from his mouth in imitation of rain falling during a thunder storm. The drumming worried Kattana exceedingly, because he feared its effect on his Wing Medicine—a sacred bundle containing the feathers of many kinds of birds. Unfortunately, he had not taken the precaution to perform the ceremonial required by the Wings before any drumming would be permitted in their presence and he knew, if it were continued, his death would be the penalty. He begged the medicine men to cease, but they explained that their power was secured through the drums and disaster would surely come if they were stopped.

" Akoan, his wife, brought him back to life three times by rubbing his body with the sacred paint and holding the Medicine Pipe before his face. A Black Robe (Catholic Priest) came to the lodge and anointed his body with oil. He also baptised him and made prayers over him. The medicine men were very angry, declaring that the Black Robe was interfering with their supernatural power. But Kattana liked the priest's treatment. He fell asleep and dreamed that his dead grandmother came to him and, taking his hand, as she used to do, when he was a little child, led him away, but, suddenly realising that she was drawing him to the spirit world, he left her and turned back. At dawn a messenger from the Sun appeared to him in a dream, promising that his health would be restored, if one of his female relatives, who was pure, would make the vow to give the Sun-dance. Kattana besought his brothers to bear the message to Natoke, or Mist-chin-awake, either of whom could make the vow. But the brothers said it would be useless, because white men had told them that such a belief was foolish. Kattana replied, ' If my good old grandmother were only alive, she would be willing to make a vow which would save my life.' He then gave up all hope of living. He requested that after death his body might be placed on the summit of the high butte, where he had been accustomed to go to have his dreams. He again fell asleep and dreamed that the Black Robe was leading him to the white man's heaven in the sky. Looking back he beheld the watchers seated around his dead body. When he awoke and told his wife she exclaimed, 'It is your death dream!' and hastening to the doctors besought them to save her man. They again began their drumming, but before the sun had set Kattana was dead.

" One of the last requests Kattana made was that his old saddle horse and a mule which had ranged together for many years should not be separated. The day after he died they came into the camp. It seemed as if they must have known that Kattana was dead for they could not be driven away. They remained standing day and night close to his lodge. One night they disappeared and could not be found, but a rider discovered their dead bodies at the foot of a cliff. Some people believe Kattana's ghost drove them over the cliff that he might take them with him to the Sand Hills, but Akoan thinks they killed themselves in order to follow their master to the spirit world."

The Blackfeet believe that, when people die, their spirits do not start at once for the other world. They feel lonely and are unwilling to leave home and friends. They wander near their old haunts for about two months, when they seem to grow accustomed to the new conditions, and then start for the spirit world. Some spirits are never contented there, but keep returning to their old haunts and are often seen. The night Kattana died, Mistina declared that spirits were hovering near. " When A-koch-pisso, one of the women watchers, was seated near the body, she was alarmed by a cold blast of air. A spirit had entered the door and stood close to her. Later Nits-tos-ape, also a woman watcher, looked into the death lodge and beheld a person standing beside the body. She spoke and it quickly vanished. She knew it was her dead husband, and that he had remained near to protect and give her power, because she wore a lock of his hair in a buckskin sack attached to a necklace. When Akoan (wife of Kattana) came from the death lodge before daybreak, she beheld a ball of fire moving away from Ketopio's lodge. Ketopio declared that it belonged to the spirit world, denying that it could have been caused by his supernatural power, because his power was given to him by the animals. Kattana's body was placed on the high ridge as he had requested. The people who lived near objected because it was so close to their homes that Kattana's ghost would harass them at night."

Bull Plume, the visiting chief from the North Piegans, said that he had heard Crow Eagle, their head chief, relate the following story of his experience with a ghost.

Crow Eagle and the Ghost.

" I was once leader of a war expedition that went south into the Yellowstone country. We were successful in securing many horses from the enemy and were on our way home when I was taken sick, and realising that I must die, I summoned my followers, and when they stood beside me said to them :

" ' My children ! I am very ill and know that my spirit will soon leave my body. It is now evening, but before the sun rises my body will be dead. I know that it is not yet time for my spirit to leave this world for ever. It will be gone for only a short time and I will come back again. I request, my children, that you will not leave my body here alone, but picket my horse near by and place my knife, bow and arrows, and some meat by my side. When I return again to this body, I will need all of these things, because my body is now thin and weak.' It was nearly daylight when I died and they left my body there, just as I had requested. They thought my prediction might come true. The sun was again setting when my spirit returned to my body. I was very weak, but I raised my head to look around, for I heard the sound of strange voices singing. I saw a flock of ravens standing in a circle, and also another circle of magpies. They carried small sticks in their bills, and seemed to be trying to raise me from the ground. They helped me to sit up, and when I was able to look about me I saw that my horse and weapons were missing. Having lighted a fire, I cooked and ate some meat. Then I lay down before the fire and, while I slept, the ravens appeared to me in a dream and gave me a dance (ceremonial), showing me the movements and the manner of dressing, and teaching me the songs to be used. They told me that if any sick person would make a vow to join the Raven society he would recover. Before the ravens left, they endowed me with their supernatural power. I then started north to look for the camp of my people. I travelled in the forest along the edge of the mountains that I might not be seen by an enemy.

"One evening, when a storm was gathering, I came to a fallen tree. The trunk, however, had not separated from the stump, which stood high from the ground. I built a shelter from the storm by placing poles against the tree and covering them with green branches. I made a bed of boughs and built a fire at the end of my shelter towards the top of the tree. Soon after lying down to sleep, I heard something moving through the branches and coming toward my bed. I thought it might be an enemy left behind, just as I had been, so I lay motionless. I did not move, nor turn my head. I thought if I were going to be killed, it would be better not to see my enemy. But this 'Thing' did not act like an enemy. It was making too much noise and sounded as if it had something dragging behind. I heard it creep slowly over to my fire, where it stopped, but when I did not move, it became restless, getting up, moving around, and then seating itself. I finally decided that I might as well take a look at this 'Thing,' whatever it might be. Turning my head, without moving my body, I saw what looked to be a ghost seated on the far side of the fire. It was clothed entirely in white, with white blanket—coat and leggings. There was a hood over its head, which completely hid its face. It was very tall, with long bony legs, which it kept stretching towards the fire, as if it were cold. It was very restless and kept pushing out its long legs, as if trying to touch me. I did not like this and besought it to go away and let me rest. When it paid no attention to my request, I said, 'Pity me for I am weak and sick. If you are still a living person, tell me your name, and we can travel together and be a help to each other.' It acted, as if it had not heard, so I said, 'If you are not a living person, but a ghost, I pray you go away and let me rest in peace, for I am sick.' It paid no heed whatever to my requests, but kept poking out its long bony legs, as if trying to touch me with its toes. They finally came so near, and it was acting so meanly, that I became angry. There was a long heavy stick lying by my side, which I used for a fire poker. Grasping it, I brought it down with all my strength across his shin bones. There was no sound following, for it was a ghost. He vanished so quickly, I could not see him go. I lay down and tried to sleep, but the ghost kept me awake the rest of the night, by sitting in a tree near my bed, complaining, crying like a screech-owl, and saying over and over again, ' You hurt me so badly, You hurt me so badly, You hurt me so badly.' He did not go away until day dawned. In the morning, when I was walking around, gathering sticks to make a fire, I discovered the skeleton of a man lying on the ground near the fallen tree. I understood, then, why the ghost was so restless and acted so strangely. His body had been buried in the branches, and when the tree fell, it had been thrown to the ground and his spirit could no longer rest in peace. I at once hurried away and started North to return to my people."

Crow Eagle died while I was among the Blackfeet, in the summer of 1903. They told me that his spirit left his body, just before daybreak, following the course of the Crow Lodge River eastward toward the Sand Hills. They heard his familiar voice from above, saying, " My children, do not quarrel among yourselves. Live at peace with all people."

The Blackfeet do not have a cheerful or hopeful conception of the future life. They believe that, after death, the spirit goes eastward to the Sand Hills, a very dreary alkali country on the plains. It is inhabited by the ghosts of people and of animals, which exist together, very much the same as in life. It is surrounded by quicksands, so that the living cannot enter. Departed spirits sometimes visit the Sand Hills and return again to remain among the living. Flat Tail once described to me his strange experience, after a severe illness. He felt his spirit starting for the Sand Hills. While departing, he turned and saw his friends and relatives mourning over his dead body. He did not remain long in the spirit world, but returned again to his body. Old Person also said that his spirit had once left his body for the Sand Hills, but had returned to

"THE DEAD WERE PLACED UPON SCAFFOLDS IN TREES."

it, having been turned back because his arrival was premature.

The dead were placed upon scaffolds built in trees, upon the summit of a high hill, or laid in a lodge pitched in a thicket. They were dressed according to their station when in this life, because they were believed to go to the Sand Hills in the clothes with which they were buried. All articles needed for the journey were placed beside the grave. A man would need his pipe, saddle, weapons and blankets and the personal articles

he valued most.   Often a number of his best horses
would be sacrificed beside the grave of a prominent
chief, so that they might serve him in the spirit land.
Mad Wolf's wife told me that in accordance with his
request, my letters and presents were buried with him.
Strangely enough, this intention was announced to me
by Mad Wolf several years before his death, while he
was leading a ceremonial.

When No Chief's brother was killed in battle by the
Crows, he ascertained from the war-party the location
of the body.   After making a journey of several hundred
miles, he found it and brought it home.   He carried
the skeleton about with him in a raw hide case for
many years and had it buried beside him when he died.   No
Chief's touching devotion to his brother was in keeping
with the Blackfeets' high regard and care for the
remains of dead relatives and friends, but such extreme
manifestations of it were only shown by men towards
men and not towards women.

When the Blackfeet went into mourning, they denied
and tortured themselves to excite the pity of the Great
Spirit, to display to the tribe their indifference to pain
and to show their high regard for the departed.   During
this period which often lasted for several months, they
withdrew daily at sunrise and sunset to the summit of
a hill, where they wept and gashed themselves with
arrow points and knives, until a relative, a man, or a
woman, according to the sex of the mourner, went to
urge their return to camp.   They sometimes cut off a
finger, generally the first joint of the small finger.   As a
special act of deep mourning, the men cut off a few inches
of their hair, but the women made a much greater sacrifice by cutting theirs on a level with the eyes.   Another
act of mourning was to make their lodges smaller by

"The Dead were also placed upon the Summit of a High Hill."
(Useful articles were left beside them.)

cutting off a strip around the bottom, which would cause much inconvenience and discomfort to all of the occupants. When a prominent chief died, his family placed their lodge at a distance from the tribal camp for the sake of seclusion. If parents lost an adolescent son, they led his saddle-horse through the camp, loudly lamenting as they went. Those in mourning refrained from all personal adornment. They wore old clothes, gave up painting themselves, braiding their hair and all ornaments. They withdrew from social dances, and ceremonials. They went barefooted, wearing neither moccasins nor leggings. They also cut off the manes and tails of their saddle horses as a mourning sign, although they had a superstition against cutting off horses' tails.

When Wakes-up-last[1] murdered all his children in October, 1903, their grandmother, who had made a vow in their behalf at the Sun-dance, sacrificed her ornaments to the Sun. She hung them in the trees close to our camp on Badger Creek.

New Breast mourned so deeply over the death of his daughter, that he decided to burn his Medicine Pipe, but was restrained by one of his friends, who warned him that such an act would be sure to cause the death of other members of his family. I once saw an elderly chief enter the sweat lodge at the Sun-dance to pray for his son, who was in mourning for one of his children.

Mad Wolf told me that, when his grandchild died, he found relief from his sorrow by withdrawing into the mountains, where he lay in the forest and fasted for several days.

When a man and his wife went into mourning it was customary to give their medicine bundles into the care

[1] See Appendix.

of another couple, with the request, " We ask you to cleanse us." These friends must then make new clothes for the mourners, paint them, give certain ceremonials, and provide a sweat lodge for the man and a medicine smoke for the woman. They were suitably remunerated for all these services. The friends of the mourners kept coming to see them until they finally forgot their trouble and returned to their ordinary life.

It was customary for a woman, who had lost a child, to come before the leader of a ceremonial to be purified with sage, or in the sacred smoke, as a sign that her sorrow was ended and she had begun life anew.

Ceremonials were sometimes postponed, on the death of a distant relative of the owner. On various occasions my work was hindered and I had many disappointments because of the interference of mourning customs. Wolf Plume, one of the Blackfeet judges, with whom I have had a strong friendship for many years, deliberated a long while before deciding that it was proper to allow me to take photographs of his Beaver Medicine ceremonial. After he gave his consent, the ceremonial had to be postponed so many times, that I waited two years before I finally secured the pictures. The deaths of relatives interfered on several occasions, or the weather was not favourable on others, and, at another time, there happened to be ill feeling among his relatives, who were to take part in the ceremonial, and it was not desirable to have them come together.

CHAPTER X

REMINISCENCES OF FATHER DE SMET

Clearing skies.—Big game driven close to the ranch.—Tragedy of Red
Rover, an Indian dog.—Bitter cold.—Starving cattle.—A Chinook.—
Mad Wolf talks about former days.—Tells how the Blackfeet first
met Long Teeth (Father De Smet).—He taught the people to rest
every seventh day.—Fate of Motokis who scoffed at his ceremonial.
—Its salutary effect upon the Blackfeet.—Two Black Robes took the
place of Father De Smet.—One of them went to the Gros Ventres.—
Was badly treated and returned to the Blackfeet.—Gros Ventres
routed by the Blackfeet.—Legend of "The Yellow Buffalo Tipi."
—Buffalo Bull bestows supernatural power upon Chief Mastopeta.
—His death and farewell words.—His body disappears from the
Death lodge.—Final message from his disembodied spirit.—Father
De Smet's tactful use of occurrences for converting the Blackfeet.

A SUCCESSION of storms and blizzards followed each
other during the entire moon. Old Indians could not
recall another early winter of such severity. At the
close of one of these gloomy days an unusual light
appeared along the northern horizon and low hanging
white clouds were rising from the plains. The Indians
watched them at first apprehensively, thinking it might
forebode another blizzard. But, when the strange light
extended towards the zenith they said it indicated a
change of weather.

On the following morning the clouds had rolled
away and the sky was of deepest blue. The plains
were an unbroken expanse of white, so dazzling in the
brilliant sunlight, that I did not dare to remain outside
for fear of snow blindness. Ah-see-tuck reported the

tracks of two mountain lions that had passed during the night close to the ranch. Their tracks were like those of a large mastiff and there were signs of their long tails dragging in the snow. Antelope appeared in large numbers. They had been driven before the storm from the great plains of the North. Many were killed by the Indians for the sake of their meat and for their skins, to be soft tanned by the women for clothing. The big grey wolves and coyotes held nightly carnivals over the carcases of strayed cattle which had perished on the surrounding ridges. When their howling seemed close to the ranch I went after them with my rifle, but never succeeded in getting a successful night-shot.

Two Indian dogs, Isakami and Eko-ats-kene (Red Rover), disappeared—I finally discovered their warm kennel beneath the haystack and visited them daily with food. Isakami, who was accustomed to frequent the lodges, was friendly, but Red Rover was very wild. His father was a coyote, and he had been known to run with coyote packs. At first he slunk away, growling and showing his fangs. But, after several feedings, his distrust disappeared and his friendship was completely won. Whenever I wandered off with my rifle, he came along to join in the hunt. One day Ah-see-tuck and I went upon the hills with a supply of poisoned wolf-baits. Red Rover followed at a distance and, when I drove him back, kept slyly out of sight, behind the ridges. He found and ate one of the wolf baits, probably believing that I had left it for him. It was not very long before he came to me with a pitiful, appealing look in his eyes, staggering and running side-ways. He followed me back to the lodge, where he had never dared to come before, and, struggling to a drift beside the door, lay down and died.

The snow lay so deep on the plains, it became necessary to feed the famishing cattle. With the temperature at forty degrees below zero, Ah-see-tuck and I rode along the river, hunting for cattle among the willows, where they had sought shelter from the blizzard. We galloped swiftly along their deeply worn trails, heading off, rounding up and finally driving the bellowing herd, with clouds of steam rising from their nostrils, safely back to the ranch.

When heavy clouds piled up behind the Rocky Mountains, Mad Wolf predicted that a Chinook (warm wind) was coming. There was a sudden rise of eighty degrees in temperature, and, within a few hours, a strong warm wind blew from the west, carrying the snow before it in dense clouds. During the three days of violent wind that followed, when the snow melted so rapidly that it disappeared in streams of water from the ridges, we remained indoors, while Mad Wolf talked about former days, and told some interesting stories about the life of the Jesuit missionary, Father De Smet, among the Blackfeet.

"My mind reaches far back to the days before the white man came into our country. Then the buffalo were plentiful, and the rest of the game also. It is for this reason that we old Indians can neither read nor write, for we did not then need the talk of the white man. We were taught about the habits of wild animals, and how to cure their skins. We knew about the plains and mountains, and could read the voices of animals and birds. In those days the Indian tribes fought each other, and, in accordance with our custom, I was continually on the warpath. Then we killed white men, but, when the Great Father asked us to cease going to war, I advised the laying aside of our weapons. The old custom of killing our enemies is now under and the white man's way is on top. The only way white men now get killed in our country is by killing themselves. When my father died I looked up to the Sun and vowed I would give the festival sacred to him, not realising that I would one day become a leader of the Sun-dance. From that time I became interested in the mysteries of the medicines, and thoughtful concerning the future of my tribe, praying to the Sun and to the Morning Star, that we might have food to eat and that we might live to be old.

"When Big Lake was our head chief, an expedition, made up from the clan of Small Robes, crossed the Rocky Mountains to visit the Flathead Indians. They met there a Black Robe [1] (Father De Smet). He was a good man, so they persuaded him to return with them. We named him Innu-e-kinni (Long Teeth), because of the appearance of his teeth. He lived with us for a long time, occupying a large tipi near the centre of our camp, in which he kept his religious outfit and held his ceremonials. He had a large bell which he always rang before beginning. Whenever our hunters or warriors returned to camp, he visited their lodges and taking them, with their wives and children, to his big tent, bade them all kneel down and give thanks to the Great Spirit for their safe return. He taught the people to rest every seventh day, and, on that day, to remain in camp, and not to go off on war and hunting expeditions. On the seventh day he always held an important ceremonial, which began in the morning and lasted until midday.

"One spring, just after the big rains, when we were camped close to the Rocky Mountains hunting grizzly

[1] See Appendix.

bears, Long Teeth rang his bell and rode through the camp announcing that it was the seventh day, and he would hold a ceremony in the lodge of O-mis-tai-poye. It happened that a man named Motokis, when he heard the bell, began preparing for a hunt. His wife made objections, and said they should go together to the ceremonial. But Motokis derided her and scoffed at the ceremonial, declaring defiantly that he intended to go on a hunt to kill a bear. He ordered his son to bring in the horses and to go with him on the hunt. When O-mis-tai-poye saw these preparations he went to Motokis and requested him to wait until after the ceremony, saying, ' Even if you do not want to pray yourself, come over to my lodge and listen to what the Black Robe has to say. You can then go off on your hunt.' Long Teeth himself warned Motokis not to go. But it was in vain. Motokis laughed at them all and started with his son towards the mountains. Soon after the ceremonial, when the sun was high, the boy rode into the camp at a gallop, shouting that a grizzly bear was killing his father. He said that soon after he and his father had entered the mountains, they discovered a grizzly bear turning over stones and hunting for grubs. The bear did not see them, so Motokis directed his son to hold the horses while he crawled up to kill him. Motokis circled around for an approach through some trees. But the bear turned and made a sudden charge. The boy saw the grizzly bear rise on its hind legs and seize his father, who fell with the bear standing over him. He did not wait longer, but rode as fast as he could to camp. The men caught their horses and followed the boy to the place, where they found Motokis dead. The bear had killed him and then covering the body with dirt had gone away. They followed the bear's tracks to the heavy timber, where they hesitated to go further, fearing that the grizzly might have supernatural power. They firmly believed that death came upon Motokis because he had disobeyed the Black Robe. Afterwards Long Teeth made a speech, warning the people against disobedience, and declaring that Motokis had been punished by the Great Spirit for scoffing at the sacred ceremony.

" From that time, the Blackfeet believed Long Teeth was endowed with supernatural power. When some of the women saw that their lives were made easier by his good influence over their men, they said the Black Robe's power was very great and advised everyone to obey him. The three clans, Worm People, Buffalo Chips, and Small Robes became his followers and were obedient to his teachings. Little Plume, the great war chief and leader of the Worm People, was the first man to be baptised by him and many people then followed his example.

" When Long Teeth left us and returned to the Flatheads, he sent two Black Robes (priests) to take his place. We named one of them Short Man and the other Scar Cheek because of a mark on his face. Short Man remained with the Blackfeet, but Scar Cheek went eastward to visit the Gros Ventres.

" When Scar Cheek appeared in the Gros Ventre camp he was set upon and roughly treated. They stripped him of his robe, making him wear a buffalo skin coat and leggings like themselves. Scar Cheek remonstrated with the Gros Ventres, saying he would rather be killed than stripped of his robe and have his ceremony ridiculed. The young men scoffed at him and treated him with so much indignity that Scar Cheek finally returned to the Blackfeet, after warning the Gros

Ventres that the Great Spirit would surely punish them for their wickedness.

"The things I will now tell you happened in spring, at the time we were beginning to gather buffalo tongues for the Sun-dance. Scar Cheek accompanied us to the Cypress Hills, where we went, because the buffalo were plentiful. Early in the moon when berries are ripe, according to our custom, the most prominent of our young men were sent on a buffalo hunt, to secure raw hide for binding together the poles of the Sun lodge. Among those selected for this honour were Seven Head, Lazy Boy and Prairie Chicken. They killed a buffalo bull and were taking off the hide when they were surprised and killed by a war party of Gros Ventres. When it became known that seven of our leading young men were killed, there was mourning throughout the entire camp. Our warriors held a council and decided that they would at once follow and punish the Gros Ventres. But Scar Cheek, the Black Robe, walked through camp admonishing the people :

"'My children, my heart is heavy because these brave young men were killed, and it makes me sad to hear the women mourning and to see them cutting themselves. But I warn you not to go to war against the wicked Gros Ventres. The Great Spirit is watching. He will punish them and help you if you remain here and pray.'

"The Blackfeet were afraid to disregard the warning of the Black Robe. They did not go to war, but continued their mourning for the dead warriors six days and six nights.

"Soon after this, a heavy fog settled down upon the plains. The war party of the Gros Ventres, surprised that we did not pursue them, returned. Four of their warriors, hidden in the thick fog, stole unobserved into camp. We saw them, when the fog suddenly lifted. They were in the very centre of the camp, and were preparing to drive away a herd of horses. We killed all four, but when we made no further sign of revenge, the Gros Ventres thought we were afraid, and became very insolent. One of their warriors rode to a butte overlooking our camp and called out :

" 'You Blackfeet are cowards. You have short horns like buffalo calves, and are helpless and unable to fight. We intend to kill all of your warriors, and will take your women and your children prisoners.'

" The following day, when the sun was high, we saw objects moving on a distant ridge. At first we thought it was a herd of buffalo, but, when they came nearer, we saw that a large party of Gros Ventres were approaching. They flashed mirrors into our camp, making signs and daring us to come out and fight. Our people hurriedly prepared for battle. The warriors marched out fully armed, while our women followed, carrying additional powder and bullets. Scar Cheek, the Black Robe, also came upon the battle field to encourage the warriors, and to help our wounded. It was midday when we began the fight, but before the sun was setting the Gros Ventres were in flight. We followed them until dark, shooting them down like buffalos, and taking their scalps. Sitting Woman, who was their war chief, saved himself by hiding in the underbrush. We have always taunted him with this fight; even his own people ridiculed him. After this battle Scar Cheek had great influence over both Gros Ventres and Blackfeet."

The following story of the origin of Chief Ma-sto-peta's Yellow Buffalo Tipi indicates the tact with which

Father De Smet utilised events and circumstances for converting the Blackfeet to Christianity.

LEGEND OF THE YELLOW BUFFALO TIPI.

"A large band of our people were once camped on the Okoan River hunting buffalo in the moon when the

YELLOW BUFFALO TIPI.

leaves were falling. Ma-sto-peta, a prominent chief, brought down a large bull with his spear. While he was removing the hide, the bull rose unexpectedly to its feet and, catching him upon its horns, tossed him many times into the air. The other hunters, hearing it bellow, and seeing it run with hide hanging loose, hastened to his aid. They found him lying as if dead, and carried him back to his lodge. While they were doctoring, Ma-sto-peta opened his eyes and said, ' My children, it is useless for you to try to cure these wounds. While I was lying on the ground the Buffalo Bull stood over me saying, ' My son, I have done this because you showed me no pity, and to prove to you my supernatural power. You must die from the injuries I have inflicted, but I will bestow upon you my power, through which your spirit will return to your body, if you follow my directions. You must be painted all over with yellow paint, which is sacred to me (the yellow paint was secured from the buffalo's gall). Your body must be wrapped with your pipe in a buffalo robe, coloured with yellow paint, and thrown into the river, where the current is swift and the water deep. In this way you will recover from these injuries, and you will come forth unharmed from the river.' When the sun was setting Ma-sto-peta's spirit left his body. The instructions of the Buffalo Bull were carefully followed by the Blackfeet. After painting Ma-sto-peta's body they wrapped him with his pipe in a buffalo robe painted yellow. Four noted warriors bore him to a place where the banks of the river were steep. They swung the bundle three times, and after the fourth swing tossed it far out into the stream where the current was swift and the water deep. The shores of the river were thronged with people. When they saw the bundle sink beneath the water many thought they would never again see Ma-sto-peta, but some ran to the summit of a ridge to look down the stream and see if he might appear. To their astonishment, they beheld him walk unharmed from the river. After this the Buffalo Bull continued to appear in dreams to Ma-sto-peta, giving him the Yellow Buffalo Tipi and instructing him in the ceremonial. The Yellow Buffalo Tipi can be

seen in our big camps.   It now belongs to Mu-koi-sapo.
You will recognise it by two buffaloes painted yellow
around the middle.   A yellow buffalo calf skin is used
for a door flap.   The top is painted black to represent
a night sky, with many small discs for stars, and around
the bottom is a black band with a single row of dusty
stars.

"Many years later, in the moon, when the grass is
green (spring), Ma-sto-peta was taken very sick.
Realising that he must die, he summoned his friends
and relatives and bade them farewell, saying, 'My
children, you may well feel anxious about me now, for
I will not recover.   My spirit has left my body three
times during my life, but has always returned,.   This
time I must go away for ever.'   Ma-sto-peta died soon
after daybreak.   His wives made a Death-lodge to
receive his body, pitching it in a dense thicket where it
would not be disturbed by heavy winds.   They used
new poles, pinning the bottom of the lodge securely to
the ground and tightly lacing the front with raw-hide
so that no wild animals could enter.   They dressed him
in war clothes, decorated with porcupine quills, placing
his spear and bow and arrows beside him, and tying his
Pipe to the lodge poles over his head.   All of Ma-sto-peta's
possessions were distributed among his relatives.   As a
proof of their sorrow his wives gave away everything
they had.   They kept only the clothing they wore, also
a robe and a travois.   The youngest wife, because she
had a young baby, retained also a parfleche of buffalo
meat for food.   Not long after Ma-sto-peta's death, when
the tribe were preparing to move camp, Sa-koi-niski, his
favourite wife, with her daughter, Akaniki, went to visit
the death lodge.   They found the door securely
fastened, just as they had left it, but when they looked

inside Ma-sto-peta was gone. The Pipe still hung from the lodge poles over the spot where the body had lain, and everything, including his spear, bow and quiver full of arrows, were undisturbed. The women aroused the camp and everbody joined in the search. They thought perhaps he had come back to life and wandered away. They examined carefully the thicket around the lodge, but could find no signs. Some rode far out on the plains and watched from the high buttes. After the tribe had moved camp, the relatives remained behind to continue the search, but it was in vain. No trace of Ma-sto-peta was ever found. Sa-koi-niski and Akaniki continued their mourning for Ma-sto-peta. By day, they walked through the camp, scourging themselves and cutting their bodies with sharp arrow heads and, at night, they went to the summit of a lonely ridge to cry and mourn.

"During the time of heavy rains (early spring) Sa-koi-niski and Akaniki were camped with the clan of Small Robes. They were alone in the Yellow Buffalo lodge and were startled to hear a long deep sigh as from someone with a heavy heart. They sat in silence and to their surprise heard the voice of Ma-sto-peta. It seemed to come from overhead down through the top of the lodge and said :

"'Tamasa ! no-kok-siks ki-taki-ma-po-ans,' etc. 'Alas ! my poor children, I pity you still living where you are. I do not desire to come back again to your life, for I would soon long to return again to the spirit world. There always will be trouble upon your earth, because the people who live there must suffer from famine and pain. Here is a beautiful country. It is neither too hot nor too cold. There is plenty of game here, and the people never suffer from pain. Your unhappiness alone troubles me. My heart is heavy when I see you cutting your bodies and when I hear you crying and mourning upon the ridges. I have now come to tell you that I am happy in the spirit world, and to ask that you mourn for me no more. If you lead straight lives and keep your heart good towards all people, when you die you too will come to this country where I now live.   My Children ! This is the last time I will come near you, and you will never again hear my voice.   Farewell ! '

" Sa-koi-niski and Akaniki told these things throughout the camp of the Small Robes, so that none of them mourned again for Ma-sto-peta. It happened that, at this very time, Long Teeth (Father de Smet) was living among our people. When Sa-koi-niski and Akaniki told these things to him, the Black Robe said, ' What the spirit of your father has told you is true.   There is a beautiful country, where those who have lived good lives will go when they die and will be happy.   Your father is there now and you too will go there, if you lead good lives just as he did.'   Akaniki, with her children, and many of the clan of Small Robes were baptised by Long Teeth, the Black Robe.   They and their children have ever since attended his church and believed in the white man's heaven after death."

CHAPTER XI

Religious beliefs.—Origin and meaning of "medicine" and "medicine-man."—The reasonableness of Sun Worship in the light of nature.—Religious significance of the Sun-dance.—Mad Wolf's letter inviting his white son to the Sun-dance.—Reason for the vow to give the Sun-dance by Mad Wolf's wife.—My return to attend Sun-dance.—First-night impressions in Mad Wolf's camp.

THE Blackfeet are firm believers in the Supernatural and in the control of human affairs by both Good and Evil Powers in the invisible world. The Great Spirit, or Great Mystery, or Good Power, is everywhere and in everything—mountains, plains, winds, waters, trees, birds, and animals. Whether animals have mind and the reasoning faculty admits of no doubt with the Blackfeet, for they believe that all animals receive their endowment of power from the Sun, differing in degree, but the same in kind as that received by man and all things animate and inanimate. Some birds and animals, such as the grizzly bear, buffalo, beaver, wolf, eagle, and raven, are worshipped, because they possess a larger amount of the Good Power than the others and so, when a Blackfoot is in trouble or peril, he naturally prays to them for assistance.

His ideas of the Evil Power are vague and undefined. That problem of all time, the origin of evil, its continuance, and the suffering in the world because of it, are mysteries to the Indian, as well as to the greatest minds of the Christian races. Without knowing why, he believes that bad luck or misfortune, such as accident and loss of property, sickness or death, is inflicted upon him as a punishment by the Evil Power because of his violations of the laws of the "medicines." A Blackfoot has no fear of the Good Power, because it is his friend ; but he is an abject slave to his constant dread of the Evil Power, or Evil Spirits, who are ever ready to pursue and punish him. Death, like the fabled "sword of Damocles," is always suspended over his head, ready to drop in punishment for any one of the multitude of offences against the sacred medicines, which he is liable to commit.

It is impossible for the Christian races to understand, or estimate the powerful influence, which the "medicine" beliefs have for ages exerted upon the Indian character and tribal life. It being their universal belief that illness of the body signified possession by an evil spirit, their methods of healing, in common with those of all savage tribes, naturally took the form of incantation and occult ceremonies for exorcising it. No doubt the title of "medicine," by which their doctors were known in our early chronicles of the Indians, had its origin in this manner with the early French colonists. By a natural transition it passed into that of "medicine men," with English speaking people. A "medicine man" is believed to control the weather, to heal the sick and exorcise evil spirits by means of incantations and magic arts. He is really more of a magician than a medical doctor, although he constantly assumes the functions of the latter. His vocation is to instruct and guide in the avoidance of acts that are "bad medicine" and therefore unlucky, and in the use of the best means for propitiating the

Evil Power, because of unlucky acts already committed. When an Indian is " making medicine," he is performing mysterious ceremonies, or using other approved means for controlling the supernatural powers and averting the malevolence of the evil spirits. Some authorities have understood the word as meaning " mystery," and the medicine man as " mystery man." But this is not an adequate expression. While there is no corresponding word in the English language to express the equivalent of the Indian idea, the phrase " supernatural power " is probably the nearest equivalent to the word " medicine," in its common Indian use.

Without the medium of a divine revelation, through which the Christian races received knowledge of the true God, and with only their senses and reason, and the light of nature to guide them, the Blackfeet evolved a very reasonable form of pagan religion in their Sun-worship. Unaided, so far as we know, and circumscribed by the horizon of their own experiences, they determined the phenomena of nature, and connected causes and effects into a system of natural religion, which did credit to their reasoning powers, their piety and their imagination. Whether they derived any of it from the South, through the Aztecs, or from Asia via the Behring Straits, or otherwise, is, as yet, one of the unsolved problems of ethnology.

The Sun, as the great centre of power and the upholder of all things, was the Blackfeet's supreme object of worship. He saw that every bud and leaf and blossom turned its face towards the Sun as the source of its life and growth ; that the berries he ate reddened and ripened under its warmth ; that men and animals thrived under its sustaining light, but all perished when it was withdrawn. He saw that in the darkness and cold of winter, nature retired into silence and sleep; that when the sunlight and warmth of spring returned, all nature awakened and put on its robe of green; the bears left their hibernating dens and the beavers their winter lodges. The Sun made the grass to grow and the trees to be covered with foliage for the subsistence of birds and animals, upon which he himself in turn depended for food. The devout Blackfoot therefore called upon men, women and children and everything that had breath to worship the all-glorious, all-powerful, Sun-God who fills the heavens with brightness and the earth with life and beauty. To them, he is the supreme source of light, of life, and of power.

The Sun-dance was not, as has been commonly believed, " merely an occasion for the self torture of youths, who are candidates for admission to the full standing of warriors." It was, on the contrary, their great annual religious festival, their holy sacrament, the supreme expression of their religion. It must always have its beginning in a woman's vow, made to the Sun-God for the recovery of the sick. The entire tribe were accustomed to come together every summer for the Sun lodge, some to fulfil vows made for the recovery of the sick, some to fast and pray, others seeking diversion, while warriors came to inflict self torture in fulfilment of vows made to the Sun for deliverance from peril.

It was my good fortune to witness several Sun-dances and to have had exceptional facilities for their study and observation, especially in the one given by Mad Wolf and his wife, my Indian parents by adoption. I have been surprised that so little has been known as to the remarkable symbolism of the ritual and the elevated religious ideas and teachings contained in the ceremonial

of the Sun-dance. Much stress has been mistakenly
laid upon its demoralising tendencies, chiefly because of
the self torture, which was formerly practised under
an intense religious fanaticism, but now entirely
suppressed and overlooking entirely the high morality
it inculcated. The silence of literature as to its true
religious significance and its highly developed symbolism, is doubtless owing to the barriers with which
all explorers have found it surrounded. These have
been a difficult and unwritten language ; the Indian's
natural reserve, especially concerning religion, and
the impenetrable secretiveness of the medicine men,
who were the custodians of the religious rites and
mysteries. Their very livelihood depended upon a
strict and jealous maintenance of that secrecy.

Early in the spring, I received the following letter
from Mad Wolf, written through an interpreter :—

" MY DEAR SON : —
    " I am now feeling good in my heart because I
received a letter from my white son and read in it so much
that I wanted to know. We are glad to hear that
Ka-ach-sino (great grandfather, President) is a good
man, that he cares for his red children and will protect
them. We all feel good in our hearts, when you write
telling us so many things from the outside that we do
not know. After you left us, at the time of the first
snowfall, some white men tried to take away our lands,
but my people refused to allow it. We want to move
away from civilisation, but there is no longer a place to
which we can go. We have been continually driven
westward, until the Rocky Mountains now face us like
a wall and we can go no farther. We have made many
mistakes, but I consider the greatest was when we
allowed white men to live with us upon our lands. We
were not satisfied with one trading store. There are
now two stores, but the prices are even higher.

Why is it that the Great Father does not send us a good man for agent? He is wise and should know what his red children need. We have never had one whole-agent, they have all been half-agents. I have come to feel now, as if there was no one to trust except you, my son. I ask that you continue writing to me, even if you should not hear in reply. I am experiencing great difficulty in getting my letters written because there are so few white men, upon whom I can depend. Last winter, my youngest son was taken sick with a fever. When the Indian doctors said Little Crane must die, my heart was heavy. I went alone to the mountains and entering the forest, I fell asleep and had a dream. I saw you coming through the trees and walking towards me carrying two large birds. You came to my side, and said 'My father, you are in distress, but I have come to help you. These two birds I have killed are your troubles and they will no longer grieve you.' I awoke feeling relieved. You are far away towards the rising sun, but I know you have influence among the white men and can help us. When I returned from the mountain, my wife met me, saying, 'Little Crane will now recover because I have made a vow to give the festival sacred to the Sun God. I know it will cost us many horses and I must fast and suffer, but it was necessary to make the vow to save the life of our son.' Little Crane is well again, and in the coming summer, when the grass is green, we will give the Sun ceremonial. I ask that you come again soon to visit your brothers and sisters and Indian parents. Tell your white father that no harm will come to you in the Blackfeet camp, because you will be safe and at home with your Indian parents. I now feel good in my heart towards you, my son, and shake hands with you and with all your friends.

Your Indian Father,
Siyeh (Mad Wolf)."

Early in the moon of flowers (June), I rode across the plains towards Mad Wolf's home on Cutbank River.

The prairies were brilliant with wild roses in various shades of colour, and on all sides larks and Savanna sparrows were singing. I crossed a long and irregular procession of hills, sweeping northward to join their mighty leader the Hudson Bay Divide. Far to the north, as if rising from the plains, and separated from the main range of the Rockies, stood the sharp peak of Chief Mountain, a perpetual landmark of the Indians. I recognised the familiar scenes, the streams, the lakes, and the cut-banks, the piles of stones used for guidance and safety during storm and blizzard, and the lonely graves upon the ridges. I found Mad Wolf camped on the South Fork of Cutbank River. When I entered the lodge, he was seated at the back with Gives-to-the-Sun, his wife, their heads bowed in prayer. It was Gives-to-the-Sun who had made the vow, and around her, as the sacred woman, all the ceremonies would centre. Mad Wolf exclaimed, " It is my white son ! " He gave me a warm hand-shake, and bidding me be seated looked me over searchingly. I was deeply touched by the evidence of his warm friendship for me, when he took a package from an old medicine bag, and unrolling the outside cover, which was decorated with sacred red paint, produced a number of my letters, the envelopes soiled and worn. He first passed them around the circle for examination, and then, after gazing at them for a moment in silence, returned them to the bundle, saying he would always preserve them carefully and they would be buried with him when he died. Sweet grass was burning on a hot coal, and as Mad Wolf saw me watching the smoke, he explained that it was incense rising to the sky, and said : " Ever since you went away, I have been praying to the Sun that you might return in safety, and now you are here. We are

glad to have you present, and I will reveal many things
in order that you may know there is nothing harmful
in our worship. You can then explain our religion to
the white people, for we know you are straight and
will speak the truth.

"Last winter when Little Crane was sick and about to

A WOMAN'S VOW TO THE SUN.

die, it was very cold. For many days the sun did not
shine and the snow lay deep over the plains. The
medicine men, White Grass, and Bull Child danced and
beat upon their drums, but the evil spirits could not be
driven out. In vain Ear Rings sang his strongest songs
and administered root medicine by means of hot stones.
Our son only became weaker. One evening at sunset

the clouds broke, and my wife seeing the bright rays coming into the lodge went outside, and prayed to the Sun :

" ' Pity me, Great Sun God ! for you know that I am a pure woman. Give back health and strength to my boy, and I promise to build a sacred Sun lodge for you before all the people.'

" She then stood beside Little Crane and said, ' Rise up, my son, for I am a pure woman and have vowed to give the Sun-dance that your health may be restored.' She then went to Bull Child, the medicine man and was painted by him. Next morning at daybreak they stood together facing the east. As the sun rose from the plains, Bull Child prayed,

" ' Great Spirit in the Sun ! I know that this is a pure woman. If her sick boy recovers, I promise you that she will give a Sun-dance and will eat of the sacred food with you and with the Underground Spirits.'

" Before the snow melted Little Crane was restored to health, and when the warm winds of spring began to blow and the grass was green, we began preparations for the Sun-dance in fulfilment of our vow. We are now waiting for Flat Tail to bring tongues from the south. When he arrives, we will hold a ceremonial, and will consecrate them as the sacred food."

There is always so much uncertainty in the movements of Indians, that, in order to be present without fail and miss nothing, I determined to stay night and day beside Mad Wolf's lodge. He gave me every facility for accomplishing my purpose. He even stopped the ceremonies that I might photograph the dances, write down the words of the chants and prayers and secure graphophone records of their sacred songs. He also made a speech into the graphophone, asking that it be sent as his message to the Great Father at

Washington.   My lodge was pitched by Strikes-on-both sides, my Indian sister.   She was the Chief's favourite child, and with good reason, for she was skilled in the Indian arts and always thoughtful and considerate of others.   It was she who gathered my firewood, called me whenever my horses strayed from camp, and showed where a cool spring lay just over the ridge.

When night fell, and a cold breeze blew from the

WHEN NIGHT FELL.

snow-covered Rockies, it was delightful to lie once more upon my comfortable bed of robes and blankets, watching the flickering light of my small inside fire, and to hear again all the well known sounds of lodge life.   The gentle flapping of the lodge ears, when the wind changed, causing the smoke to swirl and even the mournful singing of wet wood on the hot embers were familiar sounds.   It was interesting to distinguish the different odours of burning firewood, the sweet fragrance of birch and cottonwood, the resinous scent of pine, and the disagreeable odour of alder, called mic-cisa-misoi (stink-wood) by the Blackfeet, because of the offensive smell of its smoke. I went to sleep listening to the musical flow of the river upon its rocky bed, and it was the first sound to greet my ears when I wakened in the morning.

CHAPTER XII

BEGINNING OF THE SUN-DANCE

Preparations of Mad Wolf and Gives-to-the-Sun.—Rules and customs observed within the sacred lodge.—Ceremonial of consecrating the tongues.—Methods of Medicine Men for impressing their supernatural power upon the tribe.—Sudden death of Good Hunter, sacred woman at a former Sun-dance.

IN former days, when the Blackfeet were constantly hunting the buffalo, the man and his wife giving the Sun-dance would begin to collect tongues for the sacred food in the early spring, and continued gathering them until the sarvis berries were ripe (midsummer). They went on the buffalo hunts, but took no part in the killing. They sat upon a robe, watching from a distance the hunters run the buffalo, praying that there might be no accident.

When Mad Wolf and his wife began their preparations for the Sun-dance, she became the " sacred woman." In her tipi the ceremonials would take place. The fire burned day and night. It must not be allowed to die out, nor the door to remain open. A sarvis berry stick or buffalo chip [1] must be used to light the pipes. No other fire was allowed within. Gives-to-the-Sun and Mad Wolf remained in fixed places, with heads bowed and blankets drawn closely around them, praying to the Sun by day and the Moon by night:

---

[1] Dried buffalo dung.

"Great Spirit! have pity on me and my people. Help me to be pure and to lead a straight life. Grant that I may be kind-hearted to all my people, and may our children and relatives live to be old."

They seldom spoke to each other, and did not go outside, while the sun was above the horizon. Before sunrise and after sunset, a relative came in to assist them to rise. Before they left the tipi, they chanted a sacred song. Mad Wolf filled a pipe, and with Gives-to-the-Sun carrying many presents, they went together to the home of O-mis-tai-po-kah, the lodge maker of the year before, and presented the pipe to him. It was a custom of the Black-feet that the lodge maker and his wife be instructed by those who had given the cere-monial the year before. The sacred bonnet, to be worn by the woman, was purchased from them and they were paid for their assistance. O-mis-tai-po-kah, Mad Wolf and their

THE SACRED WOMAN.

wives smoked together and prayed to the Sun. Hence-forth, during the Sun-dance, Mad Wolf and Gives-to-the-Sun addressed O-mis-tai-po-kah and Natokema as father and mother, for, by smoking the pipe, they agreed to lead and instruct them. When the tongues were dried and ready for cutting, Mad Wolf invited to his tipi the Sun-dance priests, White Grass, Ear Rings, Curly Bear, Stock-stchi, Double Runner, Morning Plume and Blessed Weasel, with their wives; the men to help in chanting and praying, the women to assist Gives-to-the-Sun in curing tongues and other necessary preparations. When they were assembled, O-mis-tai-po-kah (as father or instructor) produced two buffalo chips, a bag of red paint and dried sweet grass. Placing the sweet grass upon a hot coal he started a chant. As the smoke arose, Natokema (the mother) took Gives-to-the-Sun s hand and held it in the sacred smoke for purification. She then gave her the red paint, which Gives-to-the-Sun rubbed over the buffalo chips. Natokema took a

"THEY PRAYED CONTINUALLY WITH HEADS BOWED AND BLANKETS DRAWN CLOSELY AROUND THEM."

tongue, which, during the ceremony that followed, was called "chief of tongues." Holding the end towards her, she painted the north side red and the south black, and handed it with a knife to Gives-to-the-Sun, who arose and prayed, holding the tongue before her. After placing the knife in the smoke of the sweet grass, she cut the tongue into thin strips for boiling. Tongues were then distributed to the other women, who arose in turn, and, after making confession, also cut them into thin strips.   If a woman made a mistake, or cut herself, while preparing the tongues, the rest suspected that she was not pure.   Two women were selected to go to the river for water.   They carried a bucket painted with red and black bands, forming a cross on either side. While dipping the water with small shells they avoided careless splashes, which might bring on a sudden storm, and on the way back to the tipi stopped four times to pray.   If a storm came, the people believed it was caused by an error in some part of the ceremonial.   The women sang in unison while they placed the tongues in the bucket and hung it over the fire.   When it boiled, Gives-to-the-Sun chanted

"I want to go to a sacred place,"

and threw in sweet grass that the meat might have a pleasant fragrance.   The ceremonial of preparing the tongues was finished, when Natokema held the bucket in the fragrant smoke.   The priests and their wives again assembled to place the sacred meat in parfleches. At this ceremony a feast was given, but before eating, a blessing was asked upon the food, not so simple in form as our Christian custom of giving thanks, but very devout and expressive as a symbolic act.   Each broke from his portion a small piece, holding it up as an offering to the sun, all praying in unison to the Spirit for long life; then, after planting it in the ground, they supplicated Mother Earth for an abundance to eat.   The sacred meat was then placed in parfleches in readiness for the Sun-dance, all the men and women chanting in unison

"The buffalo will wait for us."

The same ceremony was repeated for every lot of tongues secured, until a sufficient quantity had been prepared. Formerly about three hundred buffalo tongues were gathered for a Sun-dance. They now seldom secure more than thirty beef tongues. An occurrence at another Sun-dance, during the ceremony of preparing the tongues, illustrates the methods employed by medicine men to impress upon the people their supernatural powers and the importance of implicit compliance with their directions. An Indian from Canada named Big Swan, with his wife, Good Hunter, were giving the Sun-dance. Big Swan selected as his adviser for the ceremonies, Spotted Eagle, and invited, to assist him, Red Wing, Wolf Eagle and Big Moon, with their wives Strikes-on-top, Feather Woman and Calls Back. They camped together on Two Medicine River, and were preparing the tongues. Big Swan interrupted the services by going to Willow Creek. There he met Spotted Eagle, telling him that additional tongues had been secured and the ceremonial would be continued that evening. For a moment Spotted Eagle made no reply, but gazed intently at the distant Rocky Mountains where his trained powers of observation detected signs of a storm. He said to Big Swan : " When you return to your tipi, do nothing further with the tongues to-night, put them away." No more was said. Big Swan returned to Two Medicine River and told the waiting men and women of Spotted Eagle's warning. Thinking they had insufficient reason for delay, they continued the service. In the midst of the ceremonial, a violent storm from the Rockies moved eastwardly over their camp. A bolt of lightning struck the lodge, prostrating the three women, Good Hunter, Strikes-on-top and Feather Woman. The last two recovered, but Good Hunter, the sacred woman, was killed. Big Swan discontinued the service, and, after placing the body of his wife upon a high cliff, overlooking the river, returned to Canada. In telling me of the event Spotted Eagle said : "It cast a deep gloom over the entire Sun-dance. If Big Swan had followed my directions it would not have happened. I saw signs of a storm over the mountains at the head of Two Medicine Canyon. They were bad medicine, so I warned him." Some of the Indians, however, believed the Sun God had stricken down Good Hunter because she had falsely declared in her prayer that she was a pure woman.

CHAPTER XIII

MARRIAGE CUSTOMS

IN former times immorality was rare among Blackfeet women. Chastity was held of supreme importance in their family life. It is remarkable how constantly the greatness of this sin was impressed upon women, both by the teaching of their religion and the severity of the punishment involved. Women's prayers uniformly began with the declaration of their purity. They believed that, without it, their prayers were in vain, and brought only a curse, if the declaration was false. Their most important ceremonial, the Sun-dance, began with the vow of a virtuous woman, made for the recovery of the sick. If the patient died, or if disaster came during the ceremonial, as in the case of Good Hunter, the sacred woman killed by lightning, the woman who made the vow was suspected of unchastity. Consequently an unchaste woman would have a superstitious dread of making a vow, or of assuming the part of a sacred woman in·a ceremonial. Sickness and death were believed to be the penalties for false vows, visited either upon the woman herself, or upon her relatives. If a married woman was unfaithful, her husband had the right to kill her, or cut off her nose himself, or he could call a council of the head men to pass judgment. Immediately following a verdict of guilty, a powerful law-and-order society inflicted the punishment, by cutting off her nose. The woman generally chose death in preference to carrying such a hideous life-brand of disgrace. As in civilised society, so among the Blackfeet, the woman suffered, but the man went free. There are, to-day, some women without noses among the Blackfeet. They, however, live secluded lives and are seldom seen by strangers.

Besides the fear of punishment, there were other considerations for a Blackfoot mother's chastity. If her children were sick, she could then make the vow to give the Sun-dance and thus secure their recovery. She could become the sacred woman in that great ceremonial and be entitled to the respect and veneration of the tribe. Parents pointed to the sacred woman as a notable example for their daughters to imitate, that, like her, they might be esteemed as above reproach.

The sacredness of marriage and the purity of family life among the Blackfeet, before contact with the white race, doubtless contributed largely to the high average of mental, moral, and physical development, which characterised so many of their former leaders.

Marriage generally took place when a girl became about fourteen years of age, and sometimes as young as eight. When she attained a marriageable age, her

parents selected a husband for her. If it happened
that a young man fell in love with her, the proposal
came from his parents. This, however, was unusual.
It was not customary for unmarried girls to associate
with men.

When a girl's parents decided upon a son-in-law, the
father made the proposal by saying that his daughter
would carry food to the young man's lodge. If he was
favourable she carried food to him daily for a moon.
Everyone would know of the girl's actions and the
engagement would be talked of throughout the camp.
During this period it was customary for the father,
realising that his daughter would soon leave his
control, to admonish her as to how she should conduct
herself after marriage. When she became engaged,
her parents were expected to give a pair of moccasins,
ornamented with porcupine quills, to each member
of her intended husband's family. They also arranged
for a feast to be given at the lodge of their future son-
in-law, to which his relatives only were invited. When
everything was in readiness, the mother and daughter
carried the food and moccasins to his lodge. The girl
then entered alone. Without a word being spoken she
took her seat on his right and distributed the moccasins
and food. During the feast her mother remained
outside. It was not proper for her to enter the lodge
of her prospective son-in-law. After the feast
the man gave to his prospective wife many presents,
bidding her to distribute them among her relatives, who
had given presents to his family. The girl's mother
made a new lodge for the young people, preparing the
poles and furnishing it with blankets, buffalo robes,
lodge backs, parfleches, mountain lion skins, a buckskin
dress for the girl and a buckskin suit, trimmed with

ermine, for the young man. The mother waited until the tribe moved to a new camping ground, when she pitched the new lodge for the first time, and, with her daughter's assistance, completed the necessary preparations. When the first lodge was worn out, it was customary for the mother-in-law to make a new one for the young couple. If by this time they did not own a lodge decoration, the father-in-law, if able, might purchase one for them. When a girl married, she left the clan of her parents and lived among her husband's relatives, with whom she and her children became identified. It was not customary to marry within the same clan because of blood relationship. After their marriage, as long as their lodge remained beside her father's, he was expected to build their fire in the morning, and the mother-in-law to carry food to them. But, under no circumstances, could she enter the lodge of her son-in-law, or have any dealings with him. Even if he appeared unintentionally in her presence, it was a breach of etiquette and placed her in such an embarrassing position, that he must make amends by presenting her with a horse. It was proper for a mother to visit her married daughter, only during her son-in-law's absence. A man never spoke to his mother-in-law nor to her sisters. He must be careful of his conversation before his own sisters, not to offend their modesty, but he might talk as unreservedly before his cousins, or his sister-in-law as before his own wife.

It was the custom for a man and his father-in-law to have many dealings with each other and to be on the best of terms. At the marriage of his daughter, a father gave from thirty to forty horses as a present, but they were promptly repaid by a like number from the son-in-law, together with his best buffalo-horse, saddle and war bonnet. Whenever a son-in-law went on a hunt, he was expected to share the proceeds with his father-in-law. If he brought in three horses laden with meat and hides it was proper for him to direct his wife to take one of them to her father.

During the period of childbirth, when the young couple were usually camped beside her parents, the father-in-law recognised the event by inviting to a feast at his daughter's lodge his friends and relatives, whom he desired to make acquainted with his son-in-law. He furnished the food, also the pipe and tobacco. If the company remained long enough to smoke twice round, they were said to have enjoyed themselves. If, however, they were inclined to continue talking and joking, or became so interested in story-telling, that the pipe circulated three times, they were said to have had an exceptionally good time. When the host decided it was time for the feast to end, he rapped with the pipe saying, "It is burned out." The guests were then expected to depart.

The first wife sat on her husbands' right—the position of honour—and was called his "sits-beside-him-wife." She stood higher in his affection than his other wives and she was expected to direct them in their work.

The practice of polygamy by the Blackfeet may seem to the reader inconsistent with the spirit, which maintained their strict regulations upholding the integrity of the family. But it should be remembered that polygamy was a natural and necessary expedient, growing out of their tribal organisation.

The Indian division of occupations, between men and women, always made the men the providers and defenders against the enemy, and imposed upon the women a wide range of drudgery and manual labour, which included the rearing of children, the care and cooking of food, the tanning of skins, and the making of clothes and lodges.

All were joint owners of the resources of the tribal domain. All stood on an equality as to personal rights and the acquisition of wealth by hunting and warfare. There was no such thing as hired servants, their free and independent life making them too proud to serve.

Although a chief or successful warrior might secure orphan boys to look after their horses in return for their keeping, and could engage young men to hunt for them by furnishing their mounts, these were incidental and not a part of their system.

Of necessity women took the place of servants in the capacity of wives. Their number in each family would naturally be regulated by the husband's means and the requirements of his station. All his wives were under the direction of his first, or " sits-beside-him " wife.

A chief must be kind-hearted and open-handed, ever ready to share his food supply with the poorest of his tribe. His tipi must always welcome the stranger, and it devolved upon him to entertain generously the visiting chiefs and delegations from other tribes. One can readily see that such responsibilities required a family organisation that was not possible to the Black-feet, excepting through polygamy.

Another condition, that operated strongly in favour of polygamy, was the preponderance of women over men, caused chiefly by the death losses sustained in the constant wars waged with surrounding tribes.

It was considered desirable for a girl to marry a chief with several wives, because the work would be divided among them. If a girl married a poor man, who could afford but one wife, her life would probably be filled with drudgery and hard labour. Frequently an Indian would marry several sisters. In such an alliance, there was not likely to be much friction, because sisters were already accustomed to living together. Parents naturally preferred such an arrangement, if they were satisfied with a son-in-law, because they would thus avoid the many complications involved in having several sons-in-law.

The Blackfeet had a Love medicine, which they called Ito-wa-mami-wa-natsi (Cree medicine), because it was generally obtained from the Crees, who were specialists in its manufacture. In talking with E-kum-makon about the Cree medicine, he said that he had used it to regain the affection of his young wife. When she left him and returned to her father's lodge, he made a long journey north, to visit a Cree medicine man, from whom he purchased some of the Love medicine. It consisted of a small beaded buckskin bag containing a sweet-smelling powder. As the Cree magician had directed, he secured one of his wife's hairs and, winding it with one of his own, placed them together in the medicine bag. He carried it with him everywhere, fastened around his neck by a buckskin string and wore it beneath his shirt. He firmly believed in its power, because his wife had returned and became so much attached to him, that she was unwilling to leave his side and they went everywhere together. Soon after this E-kum-makon had a severe illness, lasting so long he thought he must be bewitched by Little Plume, who owned a Porcupine-Quill medicine. It consisted of a small stone, or wooden image of a person, a porcupine quill and some red paint, by which the owner was able to cast an evil spell over people.

If he placed the red paint between the eyes of the image, the one whom he desired to injure became ill; if over the lungs, he had a hemorrhage; if on the top of the head, he became crazy; if over the heart, it caused death. E-kum-makon became so worried over his health, that he again sought the advice of the Cree medicine man, who informed him that his sickness was caused by the improper use of the Love medicine. It should not have been carried around with him, but left inside his tipi, tied to one of the lodge poles, where it properly belonged. The medicine man also explained, that it was wrong to put the hairs into the bag without the burning of incense, which was necessary to ward off the Evil Power.

There was also a medicine for counteracting the Love Power. This was employed, whenever it was discovered that the Love medicine was used by anyone who was unacceptable and therefore to be resisted.

The Blackfeet have always been ready purchasers of Love medicine, for which they paid the Crees a horse, or even more. They have also secured it from the Flatheads and Pend d'Oreilles. The Blackfeet say that the Sioux and Assiniboines also made a love medicine, but that the Crows and Cheyennes bought theirs from other tribes.

CHAPTER XIV

FORMING THE SUN-DANCE CAMP

Mad Wolf announces time for moving to the Sun-dance camp.—Care of the sacred woman and the loading of her travois.—My journey with Mad Wolf and his clan.—An interesting and impressive procession. —Mad Wolf selects a site for the Sun-dance camp.—Formation of the camp according to clans.—Origin of clan names.—Pitching the Sacred Tipi.—Guests in my tipi.—Arrival of Running Crane with prominent chiefs from the south.—Visitors from many Indian tribes.—Mad Dog society as police.

In response to the summons to prepare for the Sun-dance, the Indians north of Willow Creek continued to gather around the lodge of Mad Wolf, until the camp was widely spread upon the plain. For many days the sun had been hot, and the people waited impatiently for the signal to move to the fourth and last camp. Finally, when the evening sun was approaching the summits of the Rockies, Mad Wolf stepped from the sacred tipi. His strong voice rang far out over the quiet plain with the announcement :

"Hear, my children ! The grass is now green and long upon the prairies, and the time has come, when we should move together to the big flat near Willow Creek for the Sun-dance. Be prepared to start at the rising of the sun ! Let everyone go !

He sent a messenger to Badger Creek, where the southern division of the tribe had assembled, and were waiting under Seco-mo-muckon (Running Crane), to instruct them also to move at the appointed time to Willow Creek. On the following morning, the occu-

pants of the sacred tipi were astir before daybreak.
All the labour of moving was performed by the chosen
assistants of Gives-to-the-Sun. She sat apart, behind
the sacred travois,[1] on a buffalo robe and a pillow stuffed
with antelope hair. With head bowed in prayer, she
faced towards the south, the direction in which they
would move for the last camp. I heard Natokoma

"GIVES-TO-THE-SUN SAT APART, BEHIND THE SACRED TRAVOIS, HER HEAD
BOWED IN PRAYER."

uttering a prayer, while placing the sacred travois
before her, and then again while loading it with the
ceremonial clothes of Gives-to-the-Sun. These were a
buckskin dress, decorated with elk tusks, beaded
leggings and moccasins, the medicine bonnet and robe
of soft-tanned elk skin ; together with parfleches of
sacred tongues, juniper branches and the medicine

[1] See Appendix.

bundles to be used in the Sun-dance ceremonial. Gives-to-the-Sun's own saddle horse was hitched to the sacred travois, which, as well as the harness, was painted red. She had become so weak and exhausted by fasting and close confinement that it was necessary for O-mis-tai-pokah and his wife to lift her into the saddle. The fasting of those who took a prominent part in the

GIVES-TO-THE-SUN MOUNTED ON THE TRAVOIS HORSE.

ceremonial was believed to excite the pity of the Great Spirit and to be of the greatest importance for securing a favourable answer to prayer.

All eyes were now fixed upon Mad Wolf's lodge, waiting for the signal to move. When it was taken down, the entire camp became a scene of confusion. Mad Wolf mounted his horse, singing a chant. He rode with O-mis-tai-pokah to a ridge near by and was closely followed by Natokoma and Gives-to-the-Sun with the

sacred travois. There they waited till the rest were
ready to start. Then Mad Wolf slowly led the way,

NATOKEMA AND GIVES-TO-THE-SUN WAITING WITH THE SACRED TRAVOIS.

following no trail, but directing his course southward
across the open plains. He was followed by many well-
known chiefs, among whom I recognised White Grass,
Isso-koyi-kinni (Heavy Breast),
Ear Rings, Bull Child, Double
Runner, Three Bears, Morning
Plume, Bear Child, Maka, Stock-
stchi, Blessed Weasel, Cream Antelope and Medicine Weasel. I
rode with the clan of Hard Top
Knots, the relatives and friends
of Mad Wolf. Near by were
Kionama and Menake ; also Onesta
and Nitana with their families.

"O-MIS-TAI-PO-KAH WITH
LONG GREY HAIR FALLING
OVER HIS SHOULDERS."

Directly in front rode Anatapsa, my pretty Indian
niece (Mad Wolf's granddaughter), with Dives-under-

water, a granddaughter of the head chief. They were both astride the same horse and greatly interested me, because of their vigorous conversation in the sign language. Anatapsa, gaily dressed, sat in front, her long black hair flying in the wind. Her blanket of brilliant scarlet fell loosely from her shoulders,

GIVES-TO-THE-SUN'S OWN HORSE WAS HITCHED TO THE SACRED TRAVOIS.

confined at the waist by a belt heavily beaded. Her small feet, clad in dainty moccasins, were continually kicking the horse's sides to urge him forward. Dives-under-water, clothed in a robe of soft-tanned fawn skin with beaded stripes, was seated behind. She was deaf and dumb but full of life and skilled in the sign language. Her busy hands moved gracefully while talking with Anatapsa.   From their mischievous looks and frequent peals of laughter, I knew their jokes were at the expense of those around them.

I passed a travois bearing three aged squaws.   They were berating their horse, a raw-boned, old cripple,

ANATAPSA AND DIVES-UNDER-WATER RODE ASTRIDE THE SAME HORSE.

trying to urge him from a slow walk, so that they could keep pace with the procession.   One was vigorously beating him with a stick, but it was in vain, for he hobbled placidly along, with eyes closed and head

hanging down, unmindful both of the stick and their
execrations. The way led across rich meadows brilliant
with roses and wild flowers, winding in and out among
the ridges and through deep ravines.

Leaving the line, I rode ahead and climbed a high
ridge, where I could have a better view of the interesting and impressive procession of Mad Wolf and his

"The two Noble Chiefs were in the lead and were followed by
the Medicine Women with the Sacred Travois."

tribe, moving slowly across the plains. When the line
crossed the summit of the ridge, the dark forms outlined
against the sky made a striking picture. The two
noble chiefs were in the lead, Mad Wolf gazing straight
ahead, tall, erect, and with head thrown proudly back,
and O-mis-tai-po-kah at his side, much older, somewhat
stooped, his long grey hair falling over his shoulders.
They were closely followed by the medicine women,
with the sacred travois and its mysterious bundles, the

poles crossing in front, high above the horse's head and
their butt ends dragging behind on the ground.   There
was a long line of warriors, with rifles and war bonnets
of eagles' feathers, and bearing the sacred Spear and
Shield and also the Medicine Pipe.   Bells fastened to
the legs of the riders and around their horses' necks

THE THREE CHIEFS.

jingled at every step.   Then came a number of travois,
laden with lodges and supplies in charge of squaws.   In
the rear were groups of old men, women, children and
young girls.   Each family had its pack of dogs, all as
gaunt and hungry-looking as prairie wolves.   To the
south lay Willow Creek and the broad plain selected
by Mad Wolf for the camp, resembling an enormous

arena with hills rising on all sides. It was covered
with long prairie grass, still green from the many rains
of spring. At one end was a small lake, and beyond, as
far as the eye could reach, were green rounded ridges,
closely following each other like great billows of the
ocean. I overtook the procession while it was stopping

"THERE WAS A LONG LINE OF WARRIORS WITH RIFLES AND WAR-BONNETS
AND BEARING THE SACRED SPEAR AND SHIELD."

at Willow Creek for the fourth and last time, as
required by the Sun ceremonial.

Mad Wolf slowly advanced to the centre of the plain
and all waited while he selected a site for the Sun
lodge. There was no confusion. The site having been
chosen, the camp circle was formed in an orderly
manner, according to the different clans or blood
relatives. Each family knew where they belonged, and
took their accustomed positions. Mad Wolf as leader of
the Nee-ah-kinna clan (Hard Top Knots), with his
followers, occupied the north side of the plain. The

Hard Top Knots were so named because of the peculiar arrangement of the hair of the chief, who founded the clan. There were also the Small Robes, Worm People, and Grease Melters, the last so called because they covered their roasted meats with melted grease. The Lone Eaters were so named, because one of their chiefs had been accustomed to rise early with his family and finish breakfast, before the rest of the tribe were astir, to avoid inviting guests.

MOUNTAIN CHIEF.
(A noted warrior.)

When his peculiarity was noticed, his clan became known as the Lone Eaters. The Don't Laughs name had its origin in the eccentricity of one of their women who shunned men and was never known to smile. But to the astonishment of the tribe she suddenly fell in love with a young man and eloped with him. After this incident, the clan took the name, Don't Laughs. The name of the Skunks had its rise in an occurrence which caused much

BIG MOON.

amusement in the tribe. A young man wanted to marry an Indian maiden, but his suit was refused, because of his slovenly habits. She made a song and sang it publicly with the words, "Young men appear well at a distance, but when you are close to them, they smell like skunks." From that time his band

PITCHING THE SACRED TIPI.

was named Ah-pi-ki-yix = Bad Smelling Animals (or Skunks).

Mad Wolf sat apart smoking, until everything was finished, but speaking to no one. Gives-to-the-Sun, too weak from fasting and the exertion of the journey to sit upright, leaned with bowed head and covered face against Natokema. The women assistants pitched her sacred tipi, before they attended to the wants of their own families. They scattered green branches

around the outside as a sign that Gives-to-the-Sun, the
sacred woman, must not be disturbed. The medicine

ARRIVAL OF RUNNING CRANE LEADING THE SOUTHERN DIVISION OF THE TRIBE.

bundles were placed inside and the sacred travois, with
cottonwood branches, against the back of the lodge.

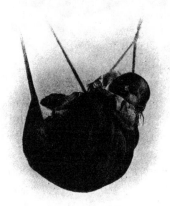

TEARS-IN-HER-EYES IN HER BLACKFOOT CRADLE.

My tipi was shared by Kionama and Menake, Indian
friends, who later went with me on my expedition into

the north, with their daughter Sinopa (Kit-fox), two sons, Emonissi (Otter) and Seeyea, and Isto-kopena (Tears-in-her-eyes), a baby six months old. Tears-in-her-eyes was a niece of Mad Wolf's.

When her mother died, soon after her birth, she was nursed by sympathetic squaws, but continued to waste

CHIEF OF THE MAD DOGS.

away, and would have died, had it not been for the motherly Menake. Under her watchful care she changed into a happy, healthy child, so pretty and lovable, that everyone was delighted to show her attention. Her cradle was a little hammock made of blankets, ingeniously folded over buckskin thongs and swung from the lodge poles. In the evening Menake rocked her to sleep, singing a Blackfoot cradle song.

When buffaloes were numerous, the udders from dead buffalo cows have been taken for suckling babies, which had lost their mothers. There is a Blackfoot woman, now living, who was thus kept alive on buffalo milk.

Seco-mo-muckon (Running Crane) appeared later in the morning, leading the Indians from the south. He

MAD DOG LODGES (BLACKFEET POLICE).

took his position on the south side of the plain, opposite to Mad Wolf. With him were Neno-kyio (Bear Chief), Morning Eagle, Little Plume, Nena-estoke (Mountain Chief), Little Dog, Spotted Eagle, O-muck-ah-tose (Big Moon), Shoots-in-the-air, Brocky, Big Beaver, Flat Tail, Curly Bear, Stomick-onesta (Bull Calf), Elk Horn, Black Bear, Strangling Wolf, Kattana (No Chief), and

White Man.   During the day, the Indians continued to come from all directions, until they numbered about two thousand.   There were representatives from many leading tribes of the north-west, the Nez Perce, Sarcees, North Blackfeet, Bloods, Crees, Assinniboines, Gros Ventres, Flatheads, Bannocks, Kutenai, Pend d'Oreilles, Mandans and Sioux.   The camp was formed in an enormous circle, with the site for the sacred Sun-lodge in the centre.   Many tipis of the leading chiefs were strikingly decorated.   They were pitched, for the most part, in the inner circle, the most conspicuous part of the encampment, while the small and inferior tipis were relegated to the outskirts of the great circle.   The three lodges of the Mad Dog Society (Blackfeet police) were grouped near the centre of the great circle.   To them the chiefs looked for the enforcement of their orders and the policing of the encampment.   In moving camp, they saw that none lagged behind, and in making camp, that every lodge was in its proper place, and that the great circle was symmetrically formed.   I have never seen an equally large gathering of white men where there was as little disturbance.   Although I was continually present, I saw no fighting in the great encampment, and it was a rare occurrence to hear even angry words.   In their largest lodge, the Mad Dogs kept their weapons and society clothes, and assembled to feast and to dress for their dances, which took place both day and night.

Copyright in United States

INNER CIRCLE OF PAINTED TIPIS

By Walter McClintock

CHAPTER XV

PAINTED TIPIS

OF all types of primitive dwellings, the tipi of the plains-tribes, with its conical shape, tapering poles and ingeniously devised "ears" for facilitating the upward draught for the inside fire, is one of the most picturesque and beautiful. It has been evolved in the distant past to meet the requirements of a nomadic people for shelter. Like the snow igloo of the far distant Esquimaux, it displays much skill in the adaptation of available materials to the necessities of their environment. It is a perfect habitation for comfort, convenience and good ventilation in both summer and winter. Its design and interior arrangements are so complete, they never change. In recent years canvas has been substituted as a covering in place of buffalo skins, because of the practical extinction of the buffalo.

No one who has seen the "White City" of the

Blackfeet, during their annual Festival of the Sun, can ever forget the strange and fascinating beauty of the scene. With the snow-capped Rocky Mountains for a background, hundreds of white tipis, uniform in shape,

CROW TIPI IN 1896 (MADE OF SKINS). REAR VIEW.

and pitched in perfect order by clans, are spread upon the plain in a great circular encampment.

The rapidity with which such a great camp can be either "pitched" or "struck" is almost incredible. Catlin, in describing the sudden striking of a similar camp by the Sioux, says: "At the time announced, the lodge of the chief is seen flapping in the wind, a part of the poles having been taken out from under it. This is the signal, and in one minute 600 lodges (on a level and beautiful prairie), which before had been strained tight and fixed, were seen waving and flapping in the wind, and in one minute more all were flat upon the ground. Their horses and dogs, of which they had a vast number, had all been secured upon the spot in

by Walter McClintock.
CROW TIPI IN 1906 (MADE OF COTTON DUCK). FRONT VIEW.

readiness, and each one was speedily loaded with the burden allotted to it, and made ready to fall into the grand procession."

The tipi has received an added element of individuality and picturesqueness, originating, no one knows when, by the use of painted decorations in colours, representing prominent events in the history of the tribe, or of the owner, or symbolical designs of religious significance. The symbolical designs, medicine bundles and ceremonials attached to them, which are believed to secure for their owners and their families protective power from sickness and misfortune, suggest a large and interesting field for investigation and study. These designs and the make-up of the medicine bundles were always

BIG ROCK TIPI.

secured through dreams, after long fasting and solitary communion with nature. They thus became, by right of discovery, the exclusive property of their owners, who might transfer them to others, but there could be no duplicates. When a painted tipi became worn out, a new one, with the same decorations, could take its place, but the owner must destroy the original, sacrificing it to the Sun by spreading it upon a lake, and sinking it beneath the water. The Yellow Buffalo Tipi, also the Crow, Otter, Serpent, Cross Stripe, Black Buffalo, Big Rock and others, with their bundles and the legends of their origin have been handed down

SERPENT TIPI.

through many generations, and are considered preeminent in their strong protective power. Their ownership is still jealously guarded by the head men of the Blackfeet, who, because of their sacred character and power, and consequent value to the tribe, will not sanction their disposal to white men. Through several years of repeated failures, in trying to purchase a painted tipi, I was made to realise the force of the rigid customs governing their ownership, the religious barriers of ceremonial requirements and the strict secrecy of the owners. I finally secured an Otter Tipi from an Indian, out only because of the unusual circumstance, that he

CROSS STRIPE OR BEAVER TIPI.

believed it had lost its protective power, his wife and all his children having died.

Painted Tipis may change ownership, in the fulfilment of vows, made by either men, or women in time of peril, or in behalf of the sick. Anyone, who is willing to observe the rules of the medicine and to keep the secrets of the ceremonial, can make the vow. There are, however, certain penalties, in the form of sickness, or loss of property, which are believed will fall upon their owner, if the ceremonial is not carefully followed. Each painted tipi has its medicine bundle composed of the skins of birds and animals, or other articles, that

THUNDER TIPI (ON LEFT), RED STRIPE TIPI (IN CENTRE).
(Thunder Tipi was painted blue, with Thunder-bird at the back.)

are used in the ceremonial of transfer, and at other times. The man, receiving the tipi, makes payment to the owner with horses and other gifts. His relatives generally contribute, to show that they take a deep interest in the transaction, and to demonstrate to the tribe that they are willing to sacrifice their property to help their clansman.

The ceremonial and feast are also given at a certain time of the year. The time for the Thunder Tipi is when the first thunder is heard in the Spring, and for the Beaver Tipi when the first grass is seen,—the time when the beavers are opening their winter lodges.

During a Sun-dance camp, Wolf Tail, in fulfilment of a vow to buy the Cross Stripe or Beaver Tipi, called upon Wipes his-eyes, the owner, and gave him a horse and a pipe as a retainer. According to the rules of the medicine, Wipes-his-eyes could not refuse to part with the sacred tipi. The ceremonial, with full payment, took place at a later time. On the day following, when I was told of the occurrence, I visited the Cross Stripe Tipi and saw Wolf Tail's horse tied outside, while the wife and children of Wipes-his-eyes were mourning because they must give up their home, to which they had become deeply attached, having lived in it for many years. Later in the day I saw the tipi taken down, to be pitched by Wolf Tail among the clan of the Skunks.

Although the use of paints as a preservative was unknown among the Blackfeet, the decorative painting of tipis and the symbolic marking of sacred objects, were in such general use, as to make the procuring and preparing of paints a business in itself. Onesta and his wife Nitana, my companions while visiting the Bloods and North Piegans in Alberta, were known as " paint gatherers." They traded in them with their own people and also with other Indian tribes. Onesta told me of the best places for securing the different coloured paints and their methods of preparing them.

There were formerly men who made a speciality of painting tipis. Their names were Marrow Bones, Calf Looking and Eagle Flag. Whenever anyone had a tipi to be painted, he gave a feast and invited his friends. After songs and prayers, all present would assist the leader chosen to do the painting. The pencils used for painting were made from buffalo bones, which were porous and readily absorbed and held the paint. A different pencil was used for each colour. Willow sticks were used for ruling the lines, which were first traced out with a white liquid scraped from a hide.

BLACK BUFFALO TIPI.

The paints were dug from the ground. The yellow and black colours were found at certain places along the Marias River. The yellow clay was first worked into a dough-like mass, and then roasted on a hot fire of coals, when it became a red powder. This is called the sacred red paint and is used in the ceremonials. Black was made from charred wood. The green paint was formerly secured from a large lake north-east of the Katoysix, (Sweet Pine Hills). It was made from the scum taken from the surface of the water and dried. Most of the yellow came from a place on the Yellowstone River near some warm springs, but was also made out of the buffalo's gall.

"There was once a large camp of Blackfeet at these springs. Some of them had made a tunnel into a high cut-bank and were hard at work getting out yellow paint. One old woman, who made a speciality of paints, was digging, while about eighty women, with their paint bags, were waiting outside. Suddenly, the old woman called from the cave that her arms were caught. She was frightened and said that she wanted to come out. An Indian, seated on a butte not far away, shouted to them that the bank was caving in. At first it came slowly, and then with such a rush, that the women could not escape. They were buried beneath great masses of earth. Almost all of the women were caught. The Indians worked night and day to uncover them, but many were taken out dead."

Nitana then said, "just before we started on our northern expedition, I was digging paint on Birch Creek. When I had finished, I prayed for the old chief, Many-white-horses, and then examined my paint, only to find it had turned to worthless dirt. I was so frightened that I hurried back to the lodge. Soon after this, we heard that Many-white-horses had died." Onesta replied to his wife, " If you had prayed for Heavy Breast, as you should have done, because he was then giving the Sun-dance, your paint would not have been changed to dirt." It was the custom, when a woman was digging paint, to offer prayers in behalf of some prominent medicine man."

No Blackfoot would venture to copy the design of a painted tipi, unless it had been regularly transferred to

him, or been received in a dream, believing that such
an infringement would incur the penalty of sickness, or
death.   I first realised the strength of this superstition
when I attempted to have a tipi of my own painted.   I
went to Medicine Weasel—an old friend of Mad Wolf's—
asking his assistance and promising to reward him for
his trouble.   He willingly agreed, not realising fully the
character of my proposition.   Next day, when I handed
him the paints and suggested his making it into an
Otter Tipi, he begged to be released, explaining that he
had no right to copy the Otter design, and to do so
might bring on a severe illness, or even cause his death.
After several futile efforts I abandoned my purpose,
because of the alarm it caused among my Blackfeet
friends.

In the Sun-dance camp, consisting of three hundred
and fifty lodges, I counted thirty-five painted tipis—
one-tenth of the entire number.   They included a great
variety of designs, but lack of space forbids my taking
more than a few descriptions from my notes.   There
were five Otter Tipis, each differing from the others,
but all having a separate and distinct origin.

In nearly all of these painted tipis, there is an
appropriate and logical arrangement of the decorations.
There is generally, at the bottom, an encircling band of
dark colour representing the earth.   Within this band
is a row of discs called "dusty stars."   The Blackfeet
have given the name "dusty stars" to the puff-balls
which grow in circular clusters upon the prairies,
because they are supposed to be meteors, which have
fallen from the night-sky and spring up into puff-balls
in a single night.   They call them "dusty stars"
because they emit a puff of dust when pressed.
Resting on this lowest band, we often find a row of

rounded, or of pointed projections, representing rounded ridges or pointed mountain peaks. Upon the broad central space above these is portrayed the protective design of animal, bird, sacred rock, thunder-trails, or other emblems, which imparts to the lodge its protective

OTTER TIPI.

power and from which it receives its distinctive title.

Surmounting all, and including the "ears," a broad encircling band of black represents the night sky, on which are portrayed the sun and crescent moon, the constellations of the Seven Brothers and Lost Children (Great Bear and Pleiades), and a Maltese cross, the emblem of the Morning Star. This cross is also said to represent the Butterfly (or Sleep Bringer), which is believed to have great power in bringing dreams to the owner.

I was once a guest for a week in an Otter Tipi, and had the opportunity of learning the symbolic meaning of its decorations, the ceremonial belonging to it and

WAR TIPI OF RUNNING RABBIT.

the pictures and signs which had been painted on the owner's body for the ceremonial of its transfer. A section of the top was painted black to represent the night-sky. On it the Morning Star was represented by a yellow cross, to the centre of which was attached a sacred buffalo tail. On opposite sides of the black band the two constellations were painted in yellow clusters. A procession of otters, painted on the middle space beneath, made it an Otter Tipi and gave it the protective power promised in the dream, which originally revealed the design. At the bottom of the canvas a broad band in dark colour represented the earth, and on it two parallel rows of discs were painted in yellow, to represent the "dusty stars" of the prairie.

For the ceremonial of transferring the Otter Tipi, all the painting on the face and body of the purchaser was made symbolical of the Otter. Parallel lines on both sides of his face represented otter trails. Upon his arms were painted otter paws. Over his body were otter tracks and upon his breast a circle representing an otter lodge on the river bank.

The painted War Tipi of Running Rabbit was of an entirely different character, being covered with picture records of tribal victories. It is an interesting fact that Indians never make records of their defeats. The War Tipi had a broad red band encircling the bottom. The top was painted black, with a red star at the back. The picture records in the central space, which were all in red, represented battles with the Crows, Sioux, Snakes, Cheyennes and Flatheads. There was depicted a daring horse-stealing expedition of a Blackfoot chief, who was in the act of cutting loose a horse, tied close to a lodge, in full view of the owner. A warrior was engaged in a fierce hand-to-hand conflict, while seizing his enemy's rifle. A number of successful scouting expeditions of a brave chief were marked, each expedition being portrayed by three sides of a square. A circle around a number of arrows pointing in all directions represented a small entrenchment where a Blackfoot warrior repelled the enemy after a desperate fight. On a long crooked line, representing the course

of a river, was marked the bend, where a famous fight
with the Crows took place.   The brave act of a warrior
was recorded, who saved the lives of two wounded
comrades, by carrying one with him on his own horse

WAR TIPI (REAR VIEW).
(The crooked lines represent rivers where famous fights took place.)

and leading a second horse carrying the other.   The
making of the first treaty with the whites, by a
Blackfoot chief, was recorded as an event of great
importance.   A warrior stealing the first mule from
the white soldiers was also regarded as an act of

special renown, because mules had never been seen before by the Blackfeet.

My own tipi, which was made by Ips-e-nikki (Kills-close-to-the-lake), wife of Big Eyes, was decorated with symbols of the Blackfeet religion, and pictographs of

My own Decorated Tipi.

interesting events, both of war and hunting, in her husband's life. The top was painted yellow and had the usual stellar constellations on both "ears." The Sun and Morning Star were at the back with sun dogs at the sides and a rainbow beneath. In two perpendicular rows, one on each side of the door, were representations of Rocky Mountain peaks. At the

bottom was a yellow band, with a single row of discs for
" dusty stars." Figures of men, animals and Indian camps
were painted in yellow, black and red on the central
space of the canvas.   There was an attack by a band of
Sioux upon Big Eyes, while travelling with his family,
and also his hand-to-hand fight with the Sioux Chief.
He was represented as stealing by night a horse picketed
close to a Crow lodge, also a mule from a white man ;
also as suddenly descending at daybreak upon a white
man milking a cow; and also in a desperate fight on
horse-back with a band of Cree Indians.

On the north-side was depicted Big Eyes' thrilling
fight in the Rocky Mountains with five grizzly bears (a
mother bear with two large cubs and two other bears)
in a berry patch,—his wounding the she-bear,—her
charge and the desperate struggle, when he plunged his
knife into her breast and she tore him with her teeth
and claws, then, leaving him for dead, to attack and
lacerate his horse.

A white man looking upon the inside circle of
Painted Tipis, in the great encampment of the Sun-
dance festival, would be impressed with their imposing
array and with the spectacular effect of their novel
colourings and fantastic decorations.   But, it probably
would never occur to him that he was looking upon
pictorial representations of the tipi-owner's religion.
As the wearing of the crucifix is the outward sign to the
world of the inward faith of many Christians, so these
tipi representations of the Buffalo, Beaver, Elk, Otter,
Eagle and Antelope proclaim the belief of the Blackfeet,
that these sacred animals and birds have been endowed
with power from the Sun, and, therefore, that the owner
and his family may secure from them aid in danger and
protection from sickness and misfortune.   Just as patron

saints are worshipped to-day, and the Lares and Penates of pagan Rome were worshipped two thousand years ago for household protection, in like manner the spirit of the otter, or buffalo, or beaver, is worshipped and its visible representation on the tipi is held sacred by the Blackfoot family as their powerful protector.

These symbolic decorations, having a religious significance are an ever present reminder to the family of their obligations to their tutelary medicine, and of the protection they may expect as a reward for their strict observance of its rules. Wherever the ascending smoke of their fires denotes their abode, there they piously display the symbols of their religious faith.

CHAPTER XVI

THE SUN-DANCE CAMP

THE first day in the Sun-dance camp was warm and
pleasant. The Indians remained outside their tipis
greeting their friends and watching for late arrivals.
All were light-hearted and glad to be assembled in the
great tribal camp. On all sides were scenes of activity,
boys galloping bareback over the hills while rounding
up the horses, men picketing their horses and driving
large herds of them to the lake for water. Women
were arranging the lodges, caring for the medicine
bundles and bringing in wood and water in preparation
for the evening meal.

An inseparable feature of an Indian camp is the
large numbers of dogs of all kinds. They mostly run
in packs, continually brawling, or, for the sake of
excitement, racing after horsemen and riderless horses
on the hills, or even worrying a single dog that had
incautiously ventured out alone.

Little Owl's large family were seated about an outside

fire in front of his lodge, while Poi-o-pa-ta-mach-ka (Coming Running) prepared their supper. She was young and very pretty, although the mother of a numerous flock of children. As my lodge was close by, I had an opportunity of observing her overburdened life. She was entertaining visitors from the Flathead tribe in her single-roomed home. A crowd of small

COMING RUNNING.

children were hanging about her, demanding attention, one of them a young baby, and another, a little daughter, suffering from a dangerous abscess. But, in spite of her cares and labours, she was always smiling and in a good humour. I did not once hear her complain, or speak an angry, or impatient word. Her bright and cheerful disposition radiated sunshine to all around her.

Wolf Chief came from his lodge to announce that he was giving a feast. He invited his guests by shouting each of their names several times in succession. The simplicity of this Blackfoot custom of issuing social invitations contrasts with the complicated forms observed in civilised society.

Morning Eagle, a noted old warrior and the hero of many battles, led through the camp his old white war-horse, decorated with medicine emblems and picture writings, representing his achievements in early days, while, in a loud voice he called the people's attention to his "advertising horse," and proclaimed his deeds of valour. Although a very old man, he was still alive during the Sun-dance camp of 1909, when his lodge was close to mine. He was then nearly blind and had completely lost the use of his legs, but he still

LITTLE OWL'S FAMILY AROUND AN OUTSIDE FIRE.
(Coming Running is surrounded by children.)

retained his old-time enthusiasm and love of excitement. He had the young men lift him upon his war horse, that he might ride through camp as of old and take part in the sham battles. He awakened me every morning at sunrise (4.30), when he began to chant his medicine songs, repeating the performance at precisely the same time each day. The songs seemed very similar, the principal variations consisting in changes of rhythm and in the different bird, or animal calls at the end of each. During a heavy storm, and in spite of his age

MORNING EAGLE AND HIS OLD WHITE WAR HORSE.

and feebleness, he crawled from the lodge on his hands and knees and seated himself in the pouring rain, with only a blanket thrown over his head, to pray and to chant medicine songs, for the purpose of driving away the storm.

Standing before his small tipi among the North Blackfeet, was an elderly chief named Natosin (Sun Chief). His two travois, one with a wicker frame constructed over the seat as a protection from the weather, were ingeniously raised together for a sun shade over the door. He was over six feet in height and of dignified bearing. His long hair was tinged with grey and his

NATOSIN'S TIPI AND TWO TRAVOIS.

face manly and earnest. He seemed pleased, when I stopped to tell him that I had once visited his people. At that moment his wife came from the lodge and joined in welcoming me. Natosin said, " We have come here in fulfilment of a vow. During the past winter, when very sick, I vowed that if my health was restored, I would attend the next Sun-dance. When we heard the ceremonial was to be given here, we came from the far north, that I might fulfil my vow and that we might partake of the sacred food."

In another tipi I heard a woman singing softly. Looking within I saw a little hammock, ingeniously made by folding a blanket over two buckskin thongs, swinging from the poles. The baby slept, while its old grandmother gently rocked the hammock, singing a lullaby, just as our affectionate grandmothers do.

Two Women Tanning a Green Hide.

Two women were tanning a green hide, which was pegged to the ground, hair-side down. They first fleshed it with large sharpened elk-bones, and then scraped it with an adze-shaped tool to make it of uniform thickness. An old woman was patiently softening a hide, which is the last step in tanning. She pulled and worked it against a raw-hide rope, fastened at both ends to an upright pole. When the hide became sufficiently soft and pliable, she whitened it by rubbing with a piece of fungus.

Running Fisher's wife was making parfleches (raw-hide cases) near the Otter Tipi. They were used by the Blackfeet as receptacles, and for packs on horses while travelling.

I found greater difficulty in photographing women than men. I was at a loss to understand the cause of my trouble, until I discovered that they were unwilling

OLD WOMAN SOFT TANNING.

to have their pictures taken dressed in their ordinary clothes, as I usually found them while pursuing their daily avocations. But they took an entirely different view of the matter when dressed in their finery. I was told, however, that some women believed that the machine had magical power, and were afraid of it. This belief was started by a medicine man who was jealous of his wife's frequent visits to a photographer's place. But he effectually stopped them when he explained to her that, by means of the camera, the white man was able to see through her clothes.

A group of women were seated on the ground, sewing a large tipi covering which was spread out before them. They seemed to be thoroughly enjoying themselves,

WOMEN SEWING A TIPI COVERING.

gossiping, smoking, and eating while at their work, much after the fashion of the neighbourly quilting bees of our grandmothers. The tipi coverings were so large and heavy that it would have been impossible for one woman to do the work alone. Joint labour was a necessity, at the same time furnishing a means of social enjoyment. When the group had finished one tipi they moved on to help another woman, who was waiting for their assistance on her tipi covering.

Not only the manufacture, but also the keep—the "pitching" and "striking" of the tipi, was the office of women. They became so expert in both, that either was the work of only a few minutes. In former days, when buffaloes were numerous, the Blackfeet made

WOMEN PITCHING A TIPI.
(Lifting the covering into place.)

their tipis of buffalo skins. They now use canvas, or duck. The skins were tanned white but, in use, became smoke-coloured in the upper part of the tipi. When a lodge covering was discarded, it was cut up for moccasins, because they would not harden or shrink.

It required eight buffalo skins to make a small lodge, and from twenty to thirty to make a very large one. The average size was about sixteen feet in diameter at the base, while large ones measured twenty-five feet. From fourteen to twenty-six poles were used for the supporting framework, and two others as " ear-poles " for facilitating the escape of smoke. The best poles are made of the slim and straight mountain pines, which the women cut and peel and season slowly, to keep them straight. Their length varies from fifteen to thirty feet according to the size of the tipi. A good set of poles having been secured, it is carried everywhere in their wanderings.

The following method of pitching a tipi was taught me by the Blackfeet. Four poles of equal length were selected. Lashing them together near their tops with a strong cord, we stood them up like a tripod and spread out their butts on the ground, very much on the same principle as the stacking of arms, with fixed bayonets, by infantry. This made a firm basis or skeleton for the completed framework. The other poles were then placed around, equi-distant from each other, their tops falling into the forked seat, made by the crossed tops of the four poles first put into place. Then, spreading the canvas covering upon the ground, we tied a pole to its middle and raised it to its proper position against the standing poles. The covering was then drawn around the framework of poles and the two ends were pinned together above the door opening in front, with seven slender sticks, or keys. By spreading out the poles uniformly at the base, the tipi was made symmetrical and by pegging the canvas down tightly all around, it was made to fit snugly. Last of all the two " ear-poles " were put in position, suited to the direction of the wind, and regulating the draught of the smoke-hole at the top. Inside, the fire-place occupied the centre, being made of stones, to confine the fire in a small circle. Around it were placed the beds, provisions and cooking utensils. There was keen rivalry among the women in the matter of pitching the first new tipi in the spring, also as to who would excel in having the neatest tipi and the best tanned robes and skins.

Although it was customary for Indian women to

MAKING PARFLECHES.

perform the menial work, while men filled the more exalted vocation of providing and defending, yet it is a mistake to conclude that Blackfeet women rebelled against their lot. A Blackfoot mother conscientiously trained her daughter from childhood in the tanning of hides and converting them into clothes and shelter, the making of lodges and travois, and in the knowledge of herbs and wild vegetables used for eating and healing.

Women considered that this work was their rightful vocation and allowed no interference from the men of the family. In fact as the men lacked the necessary training they naturally were unfitted for these tasks.

The superiority of women in all household arts, which was developed by careful training from childhood, was

WOMAN CARVING A POLE.
(Used inside as part of a lodge-back.)

a marked feature of their social life. The same idea is suggested in a very primitive and curious Blackfeet legend, which tells of a period before the institution of the family, when men and women lived in separate camps. It describes the clothes and lodges of the men as poor compared with those used by the women, and alludes to the great benefits resulting to the men, after the women chose them as mates.

In front of the war-tipi several women were engaged in drying and smoking meat upon poles erected for the purpose. From the time, when the men killed the game, the cutting of the meat, packing it on horses into camp, curing it, and finally cooking it, all was the work

WOMEN DRYING AND SMOKING MEAT UPON POLES.

of women. The preparing of pemmican, the Blackfeet's "staff of life," a palatable form of condensed food, which was used for long journeys and for winter supplies, was also their duty. Their method of preparing it consisted, first, of cutting the meat into strips and drying it in the sun. It was then well pounded in a mixture together with wild cherries. To this was added shredded meat, forming a kind of mince-meat, which was again dried and stored in parfleches for future use.

The Blackfeet subsisted mainly upon buffalo meat, when it could be secured. They also used sarvis berries, wild cherries, buffalo berries and vegetables such as camass, wild turnips, wild onions, wild potatoes, bitter root and wild rhubarb. They secured wild ducks and geese by striking them over the head with long sticks. Beaver tails were considered a great delicacy. They

My Puppy Neighbours Asleep in Their Small Tipi.

snared rabbits with willow sticks and fish with horse-hairs, but did not often eat them, because they preferred meat, which was abundant. They ridiculed the custom of eating dogs practised by the Crees, Gros Ventres and Assinniboines. The Cree Indians were not particular as to their diet for they are said to have eaten skunks, badgers, prairie dogs and even wolves and coyotes.

I once had an opportunity to witness the preparation of a dog feast by a band of Assinniboines, who were visiting in a Blackfeet camp. It happened that my

lodge was next to Eagle Child's, who was the owner of
a litter of fat puppies. He had erected close by, a
small tipi where they slept, and they played daily before
my door. One night the puppies suddenly disappeared,
Eagle Child himself could not explain what had become
of them. The mystery, however, was solved when I
went to call upon the Assinniboines. I saw that some of

ASSINNIBOINE WOMAN MAKING SOUP OUT OF MY
PUPPY FRIENDS.

my puppy neighbours had already been cut up and were
boiling in a large pot, while others lay in the hot ashes
to have the hair singed off. Nothing was wasted.
Near by was a collection of small legs and feet which
were to be used for soup and was afterwards described
in jest by my Blackfeet friends as " the puppy paw soup
of the Assinniboines."

CHAPTER XVII

EVENING SCENES IN THE CAMP

A wonderful prairie sunset.—Distant view of the big camp at night.—
Young men and women singing Riding songs.—A Love song and the
rendezvous of the lovers at the river.—Ceremonial chants and Dance
songs.—Wolf song and an ancient war custom.—The Kissing dance.
—Visit to the lodge of a sick friend.—Scenes by the lodge fire.—A
pet coyote.—Gossip of the women.—I assist a medicine man and his
wife in doctoring their patient and have permission to photograph
the performance.—Indian methods of doctoring.

WHEN the sun was setting, I walked through the camps
of the Lone Eaters and Don't Laugh bands along the
shore of the lake. The picturesque lodges, with their
painted decorations and blue smoke rising from their
tops, were perfectly reflected on the surface of the quiet
lake. I crossed a rich meadow, very beautiful in the soft
evening light, with its long waving grass and brilliant
wild flowers, and climbed to the summit of a neighbouring butte, where I had an excellent view of the entire
encampment. On all sides larks, thrushes, and Savannah
sparrows were singing. In the surrounding meadows,
large herds of horses were quietly feeding, while upon
the summit of a ridge was a solitary horseman, who
had left the noisy camp for quiet and meditation. He
stood gazing out over the vast expanse of country
towards the mountains. The sun, sinking behind the
Rockies, lighted up the sombre cloud masses with a
splendid colouring, while its pencilled rays, streaming to

Copyright in United States

by Walter McClintock.

IN THE SURROUNDING MEADOWS LARGE HERDS OF HORSES WERE QUIETLY FEEDING.

either side and extending to the zenith, formed a magnificent " sun-burst," with Mount Rising Wolf for its centre. Later in the deepening twilight the great cluster of Indian lodges showed a ghostly white against the darkening blue of the eastern sky. When the tipis were lighted by bright inside fires, the circular encampment looked like an enormous group of coloured

by Walter McClintock.
UPON THE SUMMIT OF A RIDGE WAS A SOLITARY HORSEMAN.

Japanese lanterns, and the flickering lights of the many outside fires resembled fireflies in the summer's dusk.

Young men, with their wives, or sweethearts, were making the rounds of camp on horseback singing Riding songs in unison. I heard the plaintive voice of a young brave singing a Love [1] song near the lodge of his sweetheart, begging her to come forth and meet him.

[1] Song 1.   See page 283.

WAR PARTY SINGING "WOLFSONG"

By Walter McClintock

It was probable the girl alone knew for whom the song was intended. He stood waiting in the meadow and she soon joined him, both going together to the river for water, the common rendezvous of Indian lovers. The sound of beating drums came simultaneously from six different lodges, where dances and ceremonials were taking place. In Mad Wolf's sacred tipi a solemn chant, accompanied by heavy and regular beating of rattles on the ground, was being given as a preparatory ceremonial of the Sun-dance. In the clan of the Grease Melters a group of young men and women were singing and dancing round an outside fire. The Brave Dogs were assembled in their big lodge drumming and singing a society song. A group of Crazy Dogs were dancing in front of the lodge of a chief, who was under obligations to their society and from whom they expected a feast.

Beside O-mis-tai-po-kah's tipi, a band of young men were singing a Wolf [1] song together, reviving the custom of former days, when an expedition was starting upon the war path. They stood in a circle, holding a raw hide between them, upon which they beat time with sticks. They sang no words, but gave the wolf howl at regular intervals, the young women, who stood near, joining in the wolf howl. They said this song was very ancient, having been handed down through many generations. It was sung in time of danger when hunting, or upon the war path, in the belief that the wolf would inspire the singer with his cunning.

In another part of the camp a large throng was gathered about Sepenama's tipi to see the Sina-paskan (Sioux dance).[2] The men and women dancers stood in opposite lines, the women advancing towards the men.

[1] Song 2. See page 513.   [2] Song 3. See page 514.

Each woman singled out the man of her choice and, dancing towards him, kissed him on the face. For this favour he was expected to give her a handsome present. The people always attended the Sioux dance in great numbers, because of their curiosity to see who would be chosen. The story was told of a woman who became so infatuated with the Sina-paskan that she danced every afternoon and evening. Her husband becoming tired of her neglect of their tipi, and jealous of her favours to an old rival, appeared unexpectedly one night at the door of the dance-lodge and killed her before the assembled people. After this tragedy, the Sina-paskan was discontinued for several years.

When I descended from the butte, and again entered the camp circle, twilight had faded into darkness. The bright inside fires revealed upon the canvas of the tipis their weird decorations and the moving shadows of those within. But I soon became confused in my wanderings and lost my way. In the darkness, the tipis all looked alike. There were no streets nor paths, nor any landmarks on the plains, by which I could identify my lodge. Fortunately I met Awunna, the medicine man, with Ekitowaki, his wife. He was carrying his drum, while she bore her medicine sacks of herbs and paints. I joined them, for they were on their way to doctor Stuyimi, whose tipi was close to mine. He was the father of Menake, who, with her family and Kionama, her husband, shared my lodge. Stuyimi had been sick for many months. He had grown steadily worse, and his robes and horses were rapidly dwindling to pay the Indian doctors. We found him looking very weak and sick, with sunken eyes and emaciated body. He was an old friend and, when I entered, looked up with a smile of welcome. Awunna the medicine man seated himself at the back. He was a large man with a pleasing personality, and yet with an air of self-confidence and importance. He held his head erect, and his long thick hair fell loosely upon his shoulders, like the mane of a lion. Fresh wood was thrown upon the fire, the brightening flame showing many women present—Stuyimi's mother, his wife,

AT TWILIGHT THE TIPIS WERE LIGHTED UP BY BRIGHT INSIDE FIRES.

Akoan, and their two daughters ; also Menake and her daughter Sinopa.

A beautiful little coyote puppy, with long sharp nose and bright sparkling eyes, suddenly emerged from the blankets, where I had taken my seat. I put out my hand to feel its soft, fluffy coat, but drew back quickly, when it turned and snapped at me, opening and closing its jaws like a steel trap. It resented my intrusion, snarling and threatening me with its shining fangs, until one of the little girls called to it by name (Apis), when it hopped across to her on three legs, dragging its tail, after the manner of coyotes, and went to sleep in her arms.   They also had a dog named Sa-sak-si (Freckle Face), which seemed to understand the Blackfeet tongue, for, when Stuyimi, his master, called "ha-im-mit" (laugh), he lifted his upper lip, as if smiling, and, at the same time, wagged his tail.   When he said "iks-skat-sit" (watch the door), the dog took his seat by the entrance, to defend it against any comer.   The Blackfeet make pets of all kinds of birds and wild animals.   In former days they tamed and kept in their tipis cranes, hawks, eagles, beavers, wolves, antelopes, and even grizzly bears.

The women were earnestly discussing the runaway match of young Mountain Chief and the sixteen-year-old daughter of a visiting chief from the north.   She had been last seen with a party of children gathering berries.   Her mother and father opposed the match, because they did not consider the young man able to provide for their daughter.   But, as is often the case in civilised society the world over, the young people decided the question for themselves by a runaway match, and went to live in a remote spot in the mountains.   Awunna sat in silence, taking no interest in the gossip about the elopement.   The pose of his head and the expression of his countenance indicated unmistakably his impatience for the women to finish, yet he was too dignified to interrupt their conversation.   Meanwhile Ekitowaki had placed four round stones in the fire to be used in the doctoring.   While waiting for them to become heated, Akoan passed around a small parfleche containing sarvis berries for refreshment.   When Ekitowaki pronounced the stones sufficiently hot,

Awunna removed the cover from his medicine drum and warmed it over the fire.   Its head was painted yellow to represent a clear sky, with a red ball in the centre for the sun.   Beating the drum was believed to bring him power in doctoring the sick.

The Blackfeet have a superstition that a doctor should not relate his dreams (sources of inspiration),

DOCTORING THE SICK.
Ekitowaki taking herbs from medicine sack.

nor reveal his methods, nor hand them down to others. On the other hand, leaders of religious ceremonials were expected to teach their rituals to anyone who made a vow to purchase them.   Sometimes a doctor was a specialist, his power being confined, by the command received in his dream, to a certain form of sickness.

Because the presence of spectators is believed to weaken the doctor's power, even the patient's family are ordinarily excluded from the ceremony. As I had never been permitted to witness a medicine man's methods of doctoring, I fully expected to be asked to withdraw. To my surprise, Awunna called upon me to assist in the incantations, saying that if I would join in the chants it would give him greater power in his doctoring. I consented, but asked for permission to photograph the ceremonial during his visit on the following morning. Awunna hesitated and Ekitowaki, his wife, at once raised objections, but it was decided in my favour by the patient himself, who requested that the pictures be taken, so that I could explain to the white people the Blackfeet methods of doctoring.

Stuyimi's shirt and blanket being removed, he lay upon the bed stripped to the waist. Awunna then signed to his wife to begin. She took some herbs from her medicine sack and threw them into a pot, which she placed on the fire to brew into a hot drink. Removing a coal from the fire, she placed dried sweet pine upon it, and holding her hands in the smoke, prayed to the Spirit of the buffalo that she might be endowed with power to discover the place where the disease lay. Kneeling by his side, she placed her hands upon his body, feeling gently with the tips of her fingers until she announced that the trouble lay in the breast and was worse on the left side. She took a hot stone from the fire and placed it in a kettle of water. As the steam arose, she dropped roots into it, one by one, and prayed :

"Hear us, Great Spirit in the Sun! Pity us and help us! Listen and grant us life! Look down in pity on this sick man! Grant us power to drive out the Evil Spirit and give him health!"

At this point, Awunna raised his drum and signed to me that we should begin the chant. With eyes closed and head thrown back, he started the chant (in which I joined), accompanying it with his drum. Ekitowaki brought from her sack a small disc of buffalo raw hide. She held it towards Stuyimi, with many mysterious motions in imitation of the buffalo, breathing upon it, swaying her body, keeping time with the drum and also joining in the chant. She laid the disc upon the hot

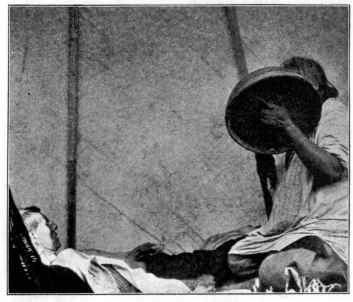

Doctoring the Sick.
Awunna drumming.

stone and placed it quickly upon his breast on the left side. She wet both hands in the root medicine and laying the tips of her fingers upon a stone, so hot that I heard them sizzle, she then placed them, with a quick movement, upon the body of the patient. In this way, she used three hot stones, one after the other, and then, turning Stuyimi over, proceeded to make hot applications to his back in the same manner. When Ekitowaki retired, Awunna knelt beside the patient, beating rhythmically upon his medicine drum, while I united with him in his chant, praying for power from the eagle. Taking yellow paint from a small sack, he sprayed it through his medicine whistle over Stuyimi's breast, arms and back. Grasping a large eagle wing, he imitated the motions of an eagle flying, and beat the

DOCTORING THE SICK.
Awunna spraying patient with yellow paint.

wing against the patient's body. When the doctoring was finished, and I was taking leave of Stuyimi, he suggested that I should accompany his clan on the third day of the Sun-dance, when they went to the river valley to secure their share of the branches and poles for the building of the Sun lodge, explaining that, as he was sick, he desired me to go as his substitute.

CHAPTER XVIII

AN INITIATION INTO THE MEDICINE PIPE SOCIETY

Mysterious methods used in securing a new member.—Medicine Pipe given to the Blackfeet ages ago by the Thunder Chief.—Disturbing sounds in the big camp at night.—Excitement at daybreak caused by herald announcing an election to the Medicine Pipe Society.—Initiation of the new member.—Initiation ceremonial in Tearing Lodge's tipi because of a superstition.—Large fee for membership.

As I walked through the camp of the Grease Melters, bright inside fires lighted up the Otter, Elk and Antelope Tipis, revealing the characteristic animal paintings in soft Indian colours on the canvas. A fresh breeze blew from the mountains, gently moving the lodge ears, and tinkling the small bells attached to their decorations of buffalo tails. Hearing strange noises from a tipi, I went near to listen. The fire had burned so low that I could see nothing, but from the grunting and blowing sounds I knew that a medicine man was doctoring within, by invoking the power of the grizzly bear.

While standing in the dark shadow I noticed two men, with blankets drawn closely over their heads, moving stealthily towards Big Spring's lodge. A bright fire was burning inside. When they drew near, they stopped, as if listening. One of them approached cautiously to peer inside, and then both hurried away. When I told Mad Wolf, he explained that they were two members of the Medicine Pipe society, choosing a new member in place of Lone Chief, who had kept his Pipe for four years and was ready to give it up. He

MEDICINE PIPE BUNDLE OVER LODGE DOOR.
(Position when in a permanent camp.)

said, " It is a difficult matter to secure an acceptable member, because the society can only take in prominent men, who can afford to pay well for the Pipe, and to give the customary feasts and ceremonials. It is always known when a member is to be taken in, so that those who are unwilling to be chosen can sleep away from their lodges. Big Spring is sleeping to-night on a ridge to the west of camp, because he is unwilling to stand the expense and trouble of keeping a Medicine Pipe. The society is now assembled in Lone Chief's lodge, singing Owl songs and drumming. They will keep representatives out all night, with Lone Chief as leader, carrying the Pipe hidden beneath his blanket and endeavouring to find a prominent chief inside his lodge. If they catch a man unawares and offer the Pipe to him, he dare not refuse, lest sickness or even death come to him, or to some member of his family. The Medicine Pipe was given to the Blackfeet long ago, when the Thunder struck down a man. While he lay on the ground, the Thunder Chief appeared in a vision, showing him a pipe, and saying, ' I have chosen you that I might give you this Pipe. Make another just like it. Gather together also a medicine bundle, containing the skins of the many animals and birds, which go with it. Whenever any of your people are sick, or dying, a vow must be made and a ceremonial given with a feast. The sick will then be restored to health.' The Grizzly Bear afterwards appeared to this same man, and said to him, ' I give you my skin to wrap around the sacred bundle, because it is larger than the skins of other animals. Whenever you transfer the Pipe to anyone, steal quietly upon him just before daybreak, the time I am on the move, and take him by surprise, just as I do, chanting my song, and making the sound of a bear charging. When you catch a man and offer him the Pipe, he will not dare to refuse, but must accept it and smoke. It is sure death to refuse, because no one may dare to turn away from a grizzly bear.'

"The Owl is also a prominent figure in the Pipe ceremonial, because he is a bird of the night. When the society are after a new member, they chant Owl songs and pray to the Owl for power to enable them to catch him in a deep sleep. In this way a spell is cast over him and he cannot escape. In order to propitiate the Owl they also, in the ceremonial, make use of the Siksocasim-root, which is his favourite food. The Indian made the Medicine Pipe, just as the Thunder and the Bear had instructed him. It is wrapped with raw hide and decorated with feathers and the winter skins of weasels. He also gathered together many animal and bird skins for the sacred bundle, wrapping them in a large grizzly bear skin. In the spring, when the first Thunder was heard, the Pipe was brought forth and held up. The Blackfeet had never before seen a Medicine Pipe, but they have ever since continued the ceremony."

When I finally lay down upon my blanket-bed, it was not to sleep. All in our lodge were disturbed by the many different sounds and even little Tears-in-her-eyes was restless in her hammock cradle. There were numberless dogs throughout the camp, fighting and barking. Some were on foraging expeditions, sneaking silently into the lodges in search of food. Menake saw a thieving dog in the act of making away with a side of bacon from our lodge. She made such an outcry, that he fled through the doorway with frightened yelps.

Although it was late at night, two small boys, the sons of Running Fisher and Long-time-sleeping, came to our lodge and sang a Night song as a serenade.

According to the Blackfeet custom, it was expected from me to go outside and give them food.

In Morning Plume's lodge near by, a small boy was very restless. The night air was cold and, when the fire burned low, he kept begging his old grandmother to cover him more warmly. She finally went to him, but had no sooner returned to her own bed than he began to whimper that the robes were not tucked underneath.

THE DAY HERDER.

As he was the old woman's pet, she went to him again, but said very sharply, that the night was not cold and she would do nothing more for him. Then his baby brother cried violently and I heard his mother softly crooning as she rocked him to sleep.

Beyond Morning Plume's was the small tipi of a poor young Indian named Okio. His only child, a young baby, was very sick. During the night a medicine man was sent for. The monotonous drumming, so different in sound from the dance drum, began after midnight. It was not loud but rapid and regular, like the beating of a human heart. With the first grey signs of dawn the drum suddenly ceased, and I knew the little life was gone. For a brief moment there was a deep stillness. The mother sobbed violently, as she took the lifeless body to her breast; then, suddenly realising that it was dead, she broke into a mournful

Copyright in United States *by Walter McClintock.*

THE NIGHT HERDER.

wail, the universal utterance, the world over, for a mother's grief over a dead child.

Such incidents in the daily life of an Indian camp are like the human experiences we constantly find in the compact cities of civilisation. Though the striking extremes of wealth and poverty are absent, the lights and shadows of domestic joy and sorrow, of health and sickness, of pathos and humour, of the grave and the gay, of love and hate, of the old man's wisdom and thoughtfulness and the young man's folly and recklessness—all of these are present in an Indian camp, with even sharper and more impressive contrasts, because of the close association of the people.

With the dawn, a light breeze came from the Rockies, making a low humming sound in the tightly stretched canvas and causing the lodge ears to flap gently like a loose sail. The quick movement of horses' hoofs, passing in the direction of the meadow, where the herd of horses was feeding, meant that the day-man was going to the relief of the night-herder. A sudden beating of many drums, accompanied by shouting and singing, came from the clan of Grease Melters. When I opened my door, the morning star had risen above the plains. In the uncertain light, I could distinguish a crowd marching through the camp. People in the surrounding lodges were talking excitedly and I knew something unusual had happened. Then the powerful voice of Elk Horn, the herald and a leader of the Grease Melters was heard, as he rode around the camp circle beating upon a drum. He called upon all members of the clan to build their fires and prepare the morning meal, announcing :

" The Medicine Pipe men have caught Mu-koi-sa-po, one of the leaders of our band. He has smoked the Pipe and will now become a member of their society. I call upon all of you to do your share towards the expense, for it is a great honour and will cost many horses and blankets. Do not delay for day is breaking, and the sun will soon rise. Let each one of you carry what you can give to Mu-koi-sa-po's lodge, whether it is a horse, robe, blanket, or provisions. Let everyone come."

The drums began again and Mad Wolf called to me that the society had clothed Mu-koi-sa-po in his ceremonial dress. It was the signal for them to appear and, if I did not hasten, I would be too late to see them march through the camp bearing the Medicine Pipe. I hurried forth with my camera and was just in time to see them emerging from Lone Chief's lodge. I was fortunate in securing several photographs of this unusual and interesting ceremony. The light, however, was very weak. It was between three and four in the morning and the sun had not

ELK HORN, THE HERALD, AROUSING THE CAMP.

yet risen. Lone Chief and Mu-koi-sa-po were in the lead, the latter bearing the sacred Pipe covered with weasel tails and feathers. Etomo-waki, his wife, accompanied the wife of Lone Chief, bearing together the medicine bundles and the tripod. Then came the drummers with the rest of the society and their wives.

Before entering the lodge, prepared for their reception, they paused to perform certain rites. I noticed

Mu-koi-sa-po's old mother standing near the door, waiting to receive them. She was bent with age and leaned heavily upon her staff. As they marched up with Mu-koi-sa-po bearing the sacred Pipe, singing in unison and with the beating of drums, the old woman was so overwhelmed with delight that she waved her staff in the air, calling loudly to her son, and joining in the chant. Then the society slowly entered and took

WOMEN CARRYING MEDICINE PIPE BUNDLES.

their accustomed seats. The ceremony was performed in the tipi of Tearing Lodge, Mu-koi-sa-po's father-in-law, because Mu-koi-sa-po owned a Beaver Bundle, which did not permit of drums. The beating of rattles on a buffalo hide was required in the Beaver ceremonial, because it was supposed to resemble the striking of the water by the beaver's tail. The Medicine Pipe, on the other hand, required drums, because they imitated the drumming of the grouse, which had given its power to the Pipe. The drums were decorated with symbols representing the sun, moon, and stars. The figures also of birds and animals were used as decorations, in accordance with the requirements of the dream, which originated the ceremonial.

The women deposited the sacred bundles against the back of the lodge. Mu-koi-sa-po and his wife, with the wife of Lone Chief and other women, sat on the right, while Lone Chief, who was giving up the Pipe, and the members ·of the society, were on the left of the medicines. Mu-koi-sa-po was dressed in the ceremonial clothes by Lone Chief, and Etomo-waki (his wife) by the women. Mu-koi-sa-po wore around his head a decorated band of buffalo hide and a feather in his hair, a beaded buckskin shirt, fringed with scalps and ermine; also beaded leggings with ermine tails and moccasins to correspond. His blanket was decorated with red marks to represent the stars. In addition to the clothes, Lone Chief gave him the horse, saddle, bridle, whip and lariat which belong to the sacred Pipe. Etomo-waki, his wife, received from Lone Chief's wife the buckskin dress, beaded moccasins and leggings, and the soft tanned elk-skin robe decorated with red paint, which were to be worn by her, only during the Pipe ceremonials. Spectators from all sections of the camp thronged about the lodge. The clan of the Grease Melters came, leaving their presents with Tearing Lodge, who announced them and the names of the givers in a loud voice. Menake brought my gift of a blanket in bright colours, which was announced with the rest. Because of the high honour conferred on one of their clansmen, the Grease Melters gave to Mu-koi-sa-po forty horses and an enormous pile of clothing, blankets, and provisions. These, with many additional presents were all turned over by Mu-koi-sa-po to

Lone Chief as his fee for transferring the Medicine Pipe.

The Blackfoot *esprit de corps* and large-hearted generosity were strikingly displayed on this occasion. But, it was not unusual, for they were characteristic of the tribe. The support of their Sun-worship by offerings, always of their best; their generous gifts to their chiefs, medicine men, and leaders of their societies, and their open-handed hospitality to visiting tribes, were always conspicuous when the opportunity offered. The aged, the fatherless and widow, the sick and helpless, and those who had no one to hunt for them, were not allowed to suffer for want of clothing, or meat, or a place by a lodge-fire. The strong and successful hunters were always ready to give of their abundance to those who lacked.

CHAPTER XIX

CEREMONIAL TRANSFERRING THE MEDICINE PIPE

Bird and Animal dances.—The Grizzly Bear dance.—Many varieties of songs.—The Woman's Pipe.—Four chants towards the cardinal points.—Rules governing ownership of the Pipe.—Care of the Pipe a heavy burden.—The Indian firmly held in mental slavery by his medicine superstitions.

THE ceremonial transferring the Medicine Pipe from Lone Chief to Mu-koi-sa-po began just as the sun rose from the plains. Its bright rays streaming into the open lodge, fell upon the priests chanting the seven Thunder songs, beating on their medicine drums, and burning sweet pine as incense. After the Thunder songs, Lone Chief, as the giver up of the Pipe held it in his arms singing :

"I am now moving around."

The Pipe was laid down during the tenth song, all chanting in unison :

"I will sit down."

In the eleventh, or buffalo song, all chanted :

"I will take away the Chief's (Pipe's) robe,"

and made the sign of the buffalo with their curved forefingers, while Mu-koi-sa-po and his wife opened the outside cover of the medicine bundle. They chanted the Antelope song and imitated with their hands the motions of an antelope walking, while the strings of antelope raw-hide were being loosened. It was explained that the antelope is supposed to be opening the bundle with his hoofs. While loosening an inner wrapper, bound by strings of elk-hide, they chanted an Elk song and made the Elk sign, holding their hands open on either side of the head with fingers extended to represent antlers. They imitated the actions of an elk as if loosening the wrapper with his hoofs. The time had now come for the dances to be held over the

MEDICINE PIPE PRIESTS WITH DRUMS.

skins representing the spirits of the birds and animals included in the medicine bundle. Only members of the society danced with the Pipe, although it was customary for anyone, who made a vow, to fulfil that vow by dancing with a skin provided for that purpose. Whenever a prominent chief arose to take part, or an Indian who had performed some unusual feat, he was applauded by the spectators. Mu-koi-sa-po, as the recipient of the Pipe, did not rise to dance, but remained seated beside the medicine bundle, receiving the skins as they were turned over to him by those taking part in the ceremonial. For the Grizzly Bear dance, the drummers chanted

"I begin to grow restless in the spring,"

representing a bear making ready to come from his winter den. Lone Chief drew his robe around him and arose to dance, imitating the bear going from his den and chanting,

"I take my robe.
My robe is sacred.
I wander in the summer."

Placing both hands upon the Pipe, he chanted,

"Sacred Chief, (Pipe)! Every one, men, women, and children will now behold you."

Slowly raising the Pipe, he sang,

"The Great Mystery beholds our Chief arise.
The Chief is sacred."

He shook the Pipe in imitation of a bear, but was careful not to handle it roughly, lest a storm should come, nor to make a miss-step in his dance, nor allow a skin, or feather to fall, lest some misfortune would befall him. He again laid the Pipe down, with the chant,

"This lodge is sacred; the ground, also, where the Chief lies is sacred."

While Lone Chief danced with the Pipe, the drummers beat time and chanted Bear songs. He imitated with his hands a bear holding up its paws, and, placing his feet together, moved backward and forward, with short jumps, making the lumbering movements of a bear running, breathing heavily and imitating his digging and turning over stones for insects. Then he blew shrilly upon his medicine whistle, representing the sounds made by the wings of the Thunder Bird, which comes forth in the spring at the same time that the bear leaves his winter den. He held the Pipe in his right hand, spreading out the fingers of his left in imitation of the wings of the flying Thunder Bird.

During the Swan song, Bear Child danced alone, representing the chief Swan, the leader of the flock. He made the Swan sign, with both hands held before him, palms out and fingers spread in imitation of a swan sailing through the air with extended wings.

In the Antelope dance, Red Fox made motions with his hands, in imitation of an antelope walking, moving the Pipe in the same manner and looking keenly alert, as if watching for an enemy.

During the singing of the Crane song, the dancers imitated the motions of flying Cranes and gave the crane call. There were no dances for water birds, but the people remained seated, while songs were sung for the ducks and geese. Mu-koi-sa-po and his wife were painted, during the four Horse songs, sometimes called Resting songs. It was necessary to sing all the words and notes of these four songs accurately, because, if anyone made a mistake, misfortune would surely come to his horses. After a short rest, during which a pipe was passed around for a smoke, seven Owl songs were sung. They were followed by seven Buffalo songs, in honour of the power that went with the band of sacred white buffalo skin, which was to be worn around the head of the Pipe owner. Seven songs were also sung to a water bird called Good Rusher, because it runs so fast along the surface of the water and is believed to possess great power. It is said to drown people by dragging them beneath the water. The muskrat skin was used by its owner to wipe the paint from his face accompanied with the song,

"All the water birds and little water animals are my friends."

The Bee songs are sung by the owner of the Pipe as a warning, when he is angered, because anyone that angers a bee will be stung. The Bee songs are also believed to possess, not only power for making the owner proof against any spell, or evil charm, but also to cause the evil power to react upon the enemy that is trying to injure him. The woman's pipe, which goes with the Medicine Pipe, has a plain flat stem and is not decorated. During the ceremonial, it was unrolled by Etomo-waki and was smoked only by the women. The Medicine Pipe is decorated with feathers and weasel tails. The owner begins smoking it by blowing a whiff first towards the sky and another towards the ground. The closing song of the ceremonial was the Good Luck song, which should bring good fortune to Mu-koi-sa-po. Whenever he might wish for anything, as owner of the Medicine Pipe, it would only be necessary for him to sing this song to have his desire fulfilled.

At sunset, Lone Chief led Mu-koi-sa-po and his wife, Etomo-waki, from the lodge and, facing in turn the four directions, chanted first towards the West,

"Over there are the mountains. May you see them as long as you live, for from them you must receive your sweet pine as incense";

then towards the North,

"Strength will come from the North. May you look for many years upon 'the star that never moves'" (North Star);

then towards the East,

"Old age will come from below (East) where lies the light of the sun";

then towards the South,

"May the warm winds of the South bring you success in securing food."

There were many rules in which Lone Chief and his wife—the former owners, must instruct Mu-koi-sa-po and his wife, when transferring the Pipe. The long category of *musts* and *must nots* taxed both their memories and consciences to carry the burden of their observance. If not obeyed to the smallest detail, misfortune would come upon them and their family. They were as follows :

"You must not lie down until we chant the Bear song and place you in certain positions, to be retained until morning, when we will assist you to rise. You must not paint your clothes with the sacred red paint, until we first perform certain rites and chant the Buffalo song. You must not smoke a pipe, or remove your moccasins before we have given you proper instructions. You may not enter the river to wash, without having sprinkled yourself and chanted the Water Bird song. You and all your family should wear necklaces of small shells because they will bring you long life. When you enter a lodge, always take seats at the back, no matter how crowded it may be, and under no circumstances take seats near the door. No one should be allowed to sleep in your bed Firewood and burning embers must not be taken away from your lodge, because they belong to the Pipe. The firewood must lie in the same direction that the Pipe hangs. Ashes must not be removed, until the Pipe is first taken outside of the tipi. You must not be present while the ashes are being taken out, lest you become blind. When you return do not fail to burn sweet pine as incense. Permit no one to curse, or talk loud, or aim a gun inside the tipi, where the sacred pipe is kept. Allow no one to strike the tipi, or throw anything towards the owner. The word ' bear ' must never be named before the Pipe, lest it cause bad dreams and bring sickness upon your family—the word ' badger ' should always be used instead. The Evil Power in such a violation may be averted by burning sweet pine as incense. You must not reply to anyone, who stands on the outside of your lodge. Insist that everyone, who wishes to speak to you, must enter. Every morning, when you arise, burn sweet pine as incense before starting the fire. When you are in a permanent camp, the Pipe may be tied over the door, but, if you are soon to move, from the tripod behind the tipi, one leg of the tripod must point in the direction you intend to go. Never allow the Pipe to hang outside in bad weather. Carry it out every morning after sunrise and hang it from the tripod behind the tipi. Always take it out on the right hand side and bring it back on the left side. Allow no one to ride, or place meat upon your Medicine Horse, or borrow its bridle and saddle. It once happened that our people captured a herd of horses from the Crows and loaded them with meat. Some of the herd suddenly sickened and died. We could not understand it, until the Crows told us, a long time afterward, that they were Medicine Horses. People should not dare to pass in front of a sacred horse. An accident is sure to befall anyone who follows its trail. Never strike a dog or horse. I once whipped my favourite horse and as a result he was afterward fatally injured. Do not cut a horse's tail. This act once caused a Pipe owner to lose five horses. You must not drink from a blackened bucket. Dangerous storms will arise if you do not drink properly, or if you throw water upon children. Never allow a dog to leap against you, for it will cause your body to ache. You must not scratch yourself with your fingers, lest it bring on a skin disease—use the sharpened stick provided in the medicine bundle. Never curse, nor swear, nor say anything injurious against the character of anyone. Never touch a dead person. Never point toward anyone with your fingers, always use the thumb. Never move anything burning with a knife, lest it start your teeth to ache. Never pick up a lost article, without first taking care to chant,

"The earth where I walk is sacred: this article lying on the ground is sacred: I therefore take it.

" If you neglect to do this you will be sure to lose something. If you invite anyone to smoke, you must always furnish tobacco for four pipes. If you are not satisfied then, you must smoke four more. If you have not time for four, explain this to your guest and let him smoke alone. Never light your pipe with willow—always use cottonwood, or sarvis berry. As a member of the Society, the Pipe must be handed to you bowl first. You must always take hold of it with both hands, just as the bear does. Never smoke with a woman, nor with anyone who presses the tobacco into the pipe bowl with his fingers. A special stick must always be used for this purpose. If anyone seeks to borrow tobacco, or asks you four times for a pipe, he runs the risk of your turning the Medicine Pipe over to him. It must then be transferred with the ceremonial and paid for by him, just as if it had been taken because of a vow. The Medicine Pipe must not be opened in winter, while the snows are deep. But, in the spring, at the time of the first thunder, the Pipe should be opened and held before the people, and the tobacco changed in the Bundle."

The ceremonial and instruction by Lone Chief continued through four days. During this period Mu-koi-sa-po and Etomo-waki learned the ceremonial prayers, chants and dances. They also fasted, that they might have dreams by night.

The Pipe ceremonial is generally given in fulfil-ment of a vow. If a child is sick and the father makes a vow to the Pipe, he makes his vow known and fulfils it, after the child is restored to health, by giving a feast with the ceremonials. Payment must also be made to the owner of the Medicine Pipe. If the vow maker is not a member of the Society, he cannot dance with the Pipe itself, but he may dance with the Eagle Feathers, which are provided in the Bundle for such a case. Much of the knowledge of the Pipe is unknown to members of the Society, because they are unwilling to pay for the instruction. This knowledge is of great advantage to him who cares for his Pipe, for he, who carefully follows its laws, will have abundance, while he may lose everything, if he is negligent of its rules. In the case of Lone Chief, the knowledge he had gained about the Pipe proved to be a good investment, because his property meanwhile increased and Mu-koi-sa-po also paid him well for his instruction.

Mu-koi-sa-po was not gratified, but rather depressed, with the honour conferred upon him by the Medicine Pipe Society. Of all the Blackfeet medicines, the Pipe is believed to have the greatest power, but it also brings the greatest burden. Mu-koi-sa-po was already the owner of the Yellow Buffalo Tipi and a Beaver Bundle. It depressed him to think of the additional burden his wife would have, in caring for the Medicine Pipe, and observing its rules, during the four years it must be retained. The heavy burden, involved in Mu-koi-sa-po's acceptance of the Medicine Pipe, illustrates the mental slavery with which the Indian is bound, hand and foot, to the superstitions, exactions and penalties of his medicines. A proper consideration of these conditions should not only mitigate our race prejudice, but also convince us of the injustice of judging the Indian by our own standards of right and wrong, without allowing for the influence of his mental environment.

CHAPTER XX

DANCE OF THE KISAPA SOCIETY

ON the morning of the second day of the Sun-dance, Elk Horn, the herald, rode through camp, announcing with his powerful voice that the Kisapa (Hair Parters, a social organisation composed of young men) were preparing for a dance and invited everyone to be present. In his left hand he carried a long spear. At regular intervals along its staff, eagle feathers were attached, falling free and fluttering in the wind. Coyote tails, representing his medicine animal, were fastened to his stirrups. He wore a buckskin shirt and a blue beaded necklace of many strands. About his waist was draped a red blanket decorated with a band of white beads. His leggings and moccasins were ornamented with porcupine quills, and large pieces of cottonwood punk were fastened to his blanket for their sweet perfume. When the young men, coming from different

Copyright in United States

By Walter McClintock

RETURN OF A VICTORIOUS WAR PARTY

parts of the camp, assembled for the dance, they were dressed in their gayest and finest clothes. They wore war-bonnets of eagle feathers tipped with coloured horse-hair, and ornamented with beads and porcupine quills, and caps made by winding otter and mink skins around their heads, the tails hanging down behind. Some were stripped and their faces and bodies were painted; others had war-shirts and leggings of soft-tanned deer skin heavily beaded, or decorated with coloured porcupine quills and trimmed with ermine along the shoulders and leggings. They wore necklaces variously made of beads, small bones, elk-teeth, shells and grizzly bear claws. They also had dog-skin ankle-bands with bells attached and arm-bands of deer skin and brass, with pendants of grouse and woodpecker

Two Bears with War Bonnet of Eagle Feathers tipped with Horse Hair.

feathers. They carried shields, spears, bows and arrows, tomahawks and rattles made of deer and elk-hoofs tied together in bunches.

All sat down in a semi-circle, and when forty or fifty had arrived, the singers began, accompanied by the drums.

First came the dance of the warriors, in which every-one who took part had been in battle. A prominent chief had eight parallel black lines on his leggings, representing the number of chiefs, or medicine men he had killed ; another had a war-shirt covered with marks representing picket pins with short lariats attached. These signified the number of horses, picketed close to the lodge of the enemy, he had cut loose, with great risk of being captured. This was followed by the dance of those who had been wounded. Wolf Eagle, a fine looking fellow, whose arm had been shot off by the enemy, entered into the dance with great energy, carrying in his single hand the feather-decorated bone of his missing arm. One dancer, named " Behind-the-ear," continually aimed his rifle, as if in the act of shooting. He had received his name from shooting an enemy behind the ear, and was now going through the motions which recalled the deed. Another warrior, who had been a

MAKA WITH BUFFALO HIDE SHIELD DECORATED WITH EAGLE FEATHERS

noted stealer of horses from the enemy, carried a horse carved out of wood. Others had tomahawks, spears, arrows, feathered shields and war-bonnets. Every movement of the dance and the distinguishing marks of the dancers had a significance, which it is impossible for an outsider to understand.

When an eagle feather fell from Sepe-nama's war-bonnet, he selected Bear Chief, a noted warrior, to pick it up, because it would bring him bad luck to do it himself. With Bear Chief as their leader, they danced in single file three times around the feather. When passing it the fourth time, Bear Chief picked it up and they returned to their seats.

The leader was Black Weasel, a tall and handsome

WOLF EAGLE DANCING.

Indian, whose seat in the surrounding circle was marked by a feathered wand driven into the ground. He wore a large war - bonnet of selected eagles' feathers, and a soft-tanned buckskin suit trimmed with ermine tails. It was decorated across the shoulders and along the arms and legs with coloured porcupine quills, beautifully laid. When it was time to commence a figure, he moved about the circle, wand in hand, hustling the dancers out and giving sharp raps to those who lagged behind. He was as considerate, however, as he was energetic, in enforcing discipline, for he devoted part of his efforts to seeing that visiting Indians were comfortably seated, and that the women and children were supplied with drinking water.

The most interested of the large circle of spectators seemed to be Nokoa, the small son of Wolverine. He was seated beside his mother, watching with filial admiration every movement of his father, who was taking part in the dance. Nokoa wore a beaded necklace of many strands and a fringed buckskin suit. His

LEADER OF KISAPA DANCE.

bright eyes fairly danced with excitement, when his father led him out before the company. He stepped forward fearlessly, swaying his small body to and fro, aiming his stick as if it were a gun, while his little moccasined feet kept perfect time with the beating of the drums.

While they were feasting, Running Crane addressed the people :

"I am now glad in my heart to see you gathered together. The young men are dressed in their beautiful clothes, and they dance well. It is not often that we have such a good time,—only once a year. Lawless shooting has all been stopped, and we have ceased to count coups, yet we are all happy. I hope that the Great Father (the President) will not stop our coming together, for it

RUNNING CRANE ADDRESSING THE PEOPLE.

does not last long. Let the old people restrain the young men, so that we may break camp and return to our homes without having any disturbance. I have now finished. My name is Seco-mo-muckon (Running Crane)."

Nena-es-toko (Mountain Chief) then arose to tell of the old days and how he used to dance. He urged the people to be generous and give many horses to the Sioux, because they were visitors, and had come on a long journey from the far east. He held a small stick, which represented a horse, and, when he had finished speaking, stepped across the circle and handed the stick to a Sioux Indian.   From the crowd of spectators there came the voice of another old chief singing, "Good man, giving away your horse so generously."

A band of Indians, under Chief Little Plume, appeared on a high ridge to the north, representing a victorious war party returning to the tribal camp with spoils.   Their faces and horses were decorated with paint, and they were dressed in beaded buckskin clothes

by Walter McClintock.
SHAM BATTLE BY HORSEMEN.

and war-bonnets.   They rode rapidly across the plain in single file, and entered camp at a gallop with war whoops and piercing yells.   Then, forming into line, with Little Plume in the lead, they marched slowly around the camp circle, with rifles in the position of firing, holding aloft the sacred Spear and singing their song of victory.[1]   The warriors then gathered together in the large open space in the centre of the camp, where they gave exhibitions, before the tribe, of sham battles,

[1] Song 4.   See page 514.

both on horseback and on foot, re-enacting their victories of former days.

I also witnessed some exciting horse races. The course lay over a level stretch and along a low ridge, where crowds of Indian spectators were seated. On one side was the tribal camp of picturesque lodges. The surrounding prairies were dressed in the living green of spring, embroidered with wild flowers. The distant snow-covered peaks of the Rocky Mountains furnished a magnificent background, at the head of the course. The young riders were completely stripped. They were excellent horsemen, riding fearlessly the wildest bronchos, using no saddle, and, for a bridle, only a rope passed through the horse's mouth. I secured an excellent view of the most exciting race of the day, by standing near the finish, where a large crowd of Indians had gathered, wagering, instead of money, horses, cattle, robes, blankets, and even provisions upon the result. At the start, the horses could be seen rearing and plunging, until a loud shout was heard, and we realised that they were off. As they passed us in a cloud of dust, the riders, excited by the shrill war whoops of the spectators, shouted in turn to their horses for greater speed, lying low upon their backs and beating them with raw-hide quirts. They finished amid intense excitement and rejoicing by the Indians, who bet on Bull Shoe, their horse, which won by a narrow margin.

While eating our evening meal, Strikes-on-both-sides suddenly opened the door, exclaiming, " Come quickly A-pe-ech-eken, and see the Pena-pes-ena Warriors (Below People or Sioux)." I was just in time to photograph them passing in a long line. They were led by Lone Dog as chief, and riding beside him were Red Boy, Bear Paw, and White Eagle. They were dressed in beaded

by Walter McClintock.

THE HORSE RACE.

Copyright in United States

clothes of bright colours, with horned head-dresses and
feathered shields on their backs.   Many tinkling bells
were attached to their horses, which were also painted
and otherwise decorated.   They marched slowly through
camp, holding their spears and feathered ensigns aloft

PARADE OF SIOUX WARRIORS.

and singing in unison a striking Celebration song [1] with
the words :

" Oh, Blackfeet ! we have heard you boast in the past that you
were becoming like white men.   We now behold you taking part
in these ceremonials, poorly dressed, and with few of your Indian
clothes left."

In accordance with a time-honoured Indian custom,
it was expected that those before whose lodges they
stopped and sang would give them presents.   If the
Blackfeet were not generous, they could not expect
many gifts, when the return visit to the Sioux would be

[1] Song 5.   See page 514.

made. After completing the circle they dismounted
at the lodge of Ahkiona, where they gave a ceremonial.
When Ahkiona had visited the Sioux they presented
him with a Medicine Pipe. On this occasion the Pipe
was to be returned to its former owners.

Exhausted by the excitement and heat of the day,
I returned to my lodge and was soon asleep in spite
of the singing and drumming of the dancing Sioux.
But it was not long before I was rudely awakened by the
fierce snarling and yelping of a vicious dog-fight near
by. The fight of this single pair quickly roused other
dogs and they rushed together to engage in a mass fight.
Soon hundreds of dogs in all parts of the camp, excited
by the uproar, united in a great deep-throated mournful
howl, such as is only heard in a large Indian village,
and resembles the howling of an enormous pack of
wolves.

When their dismal chorus had finally died away, I
stepped outside the lodge. The full moon was rising
from the plains, flooding the camp with its light. The
lodges with their crowns of tapering poles stood out in
sharp relief against the burnished eastern sky. To the
west were the dim outlines of the rugged Rockies,
behind which a large planet was slowly sinking. The
constellation of the Northern Crown (called " The
Camp," by the Blackfeet, because of the suggestiveness
of its outlines) had passed over into the west, while, in
the east, the sparkling Pleiades (Lost Children) were
rising above the plains. Although it was late, the
camp was still so throbbing with life that sleep was
made impossible. Many young men were on horseback, singing Riding songs[1] as they rode around the
circle of the encampment. The dance at Ahkiona's

[1] Song 6. See page 514.

lodge was finished, and the Sioux were returning to their quarters, singing a Travelling song in their own tongue. When they had finished, the answering notes of a Night song [1] were heard from a small band of Blackfeet, sitting on the shore of the lake. A large company of men and women on horseback, having learned a Celebration song [2] from the visiting Sioux, rode slowly through the camp singing it at intervals. Red Fox and his young wife, riding the same horse, made circuits of the camp, singing a Night song of remarkable beauty. I saw them very distinctly, when they passed, their strongly coloured Indian clothes showing in the bright moonlight. The woman rode in front, wearing a magnificent bonnet of eagle feathers, belonging to her husband, and a buckskin dress heavily beaded across the shoulders. Red Fox wore a band of weasel skin around his head, with an eagle feather erect in his back hair. A beautifully tanned elk-skin robe, decorated with red stripes of porcupine quills, extended in graceful folds from his shoulders backward over the horse's tail. He carried a string of bells, which he used in marking time for their singing. Their song had a very pronounced rhythm, which was in perfect time with the slow trot of their horse. They continued their striking duet at intervals through the night, not stopping until day began to dawn.

When I first heard the Blackfeet singing together in unison, with untrained voices, the women's an octave higher than the men's, my impressions were not pleasing. But, having learned several of their airs, and mastered the peculiar intervals and difficult voice vibrations, so that I could join in their singing, the wild beauty of their music dawned upon me. Their music seemed so

[1] Song 7. See page 515.   [2] See page 514, footnote.

thoroughly original in its conception, and so unique in the method of expression, that I became filled with the desire to do something for its preservation. It strongly appealed to me, that its development through past ages had been independent of all sources of inspiration or colouring, other than those of their natural environment of mountains, forests and plains, their wild life of hunting and warfare, their Sun-worship, and those emotions and passions which are common to the human heart the world over.

I also felt that the beautiful motives of their sacred hymns, war-songs, love and night songs, springing from these aboriginal sources, like pure water from a mountain spring, were so entirely original and thoroughly American, that they ought to be rescued from oblivion and permanently preserved.[1]

[1] See Appendix, pp. 513–15.

LOVE SONG

CHAPTER XXI

CEREMONIAL OF THE SUN-DANCE

The Mad Dogs build the sweat lodge.—Ceremonial of the sweat lodge.—
Tribal parade of men and women on horseback.—Elaborate and
interesting costumes.—Impressive evening ceremonial in Mad Wolf's
tipi.—Prayer of the head chief.—Indian humour.—Practical jokes.—
Dance of the Brave Dogs.—Bringing in the poles and branches for
constructing the Sun lodge.—Ceremonial of felling a tree for the
Centre Pole.

TEN of the Mad Dogs rode to the river to cut one
hundred long willow branches for the large sweat
lodge. On their return, they entered from the side that
faced the setting sun. Forming in line, they marched
slowly round the camp circle, holding the green branches
high in the air, and singing their society song in unison.
When they returned to the place where they had
entered, they built the framework of the lodge there,
by firmly setting the willow branches in the ground,
and bending them into the form of an ellipse, about
four feet high, facing the entrance toward the rising
sun. The north side was painted red and the south
black. When the sweat lodge was finished, other Mad
Dogs were called upon to gather one hundred stones of
the size of a man's hand. If a stone were to fall, it
foreboded misfortune, and if, during the day the men
building the lodge either drank, or washed, it was
believed to bring rain, which would interfere with the
ceremonies. A fire was built for heating the stones.

Blankets and robes were thrown over the framework of
the sweat lodge and, when all was in readiness, the
occupants of the sacred tipi came forth. Mad Wolf
led, followed by O-mis-tai-po-kah, Bull Child, Spotted
Eagle and Natosin. Then came Natokema and Gives-

FRAMEWORK OF THE SWEAT LODGE.

to-the-Sun. They walked once around the sweat lodge
and Gives-to-the-Sun took her seat on the west side.
She sat smoking and praying, while the priests, with
their helpers the Mad Dogs, stood on the south side.
A hole was dug inside the sweat lodge to receive the
heated stones. The earth was carefully placed on one
side, because it symbolised the earth thrown up by the

underground animals (beaver, otter, badger, and coyote). Mad Wolf then arose and, taking off his blanket and moccasins, placed them beside Gives-to-the-Sun. He entered the sweat lodge followed by O-mis-tai-po-kah, Bull Child and Spotted Eagle, for inward purification and to pray to the Sun, Moon and Morning Star in behalf of their people. The paint was blessed

MAD DOGS RIDING WITH WILLOWS.

by Gives-to-the-Sun and along with a buffalo skull was handed to Mad Wolf. He placed the skull beside the hole, the nose pointing toward the west. It was laid upon the Soyotoiyis, a luxuriant meadow grass gathered from beside springs. Spotted Eagle worked the paint in his hands and, using the tips of his fingers, marked black spots on the north side of the skull to represent stars, and red for the sun on the south side. While all were chanting in unison,

"I now put you into the sacred place,"

Spotted Eagle stuffed the grass into the nose and ears of the buffalo skull and tied it around the horns, symbolising the feeding of the buffalo. The Soyotoiyis (Carex Nebraskensis praevia) was the favourite food of the buffalo. Those inside the sweat lodge waited until they saw smoke rising from the sweet grass burning

PRIESTS WALKING AROUND SWEAT LODGE.

outside, a sign that the stones were fully heated. They then sang four songs, the fourth being,

" This spot is a holy place,"

and handed out the buffalo skull to the Brave Dogs, who reversed the head, pointing the nose towards the east, and laid it upon the pile of earth, which represented the underground animals. One by one the heated stones were passed into the sweat-lodge and dried sweet grass laid upon the stones. Mad Wolf placed his hands in the rising smoke and, rubbing them over his body, chanted and prayed to the Sun :

"May our lives become as strong as the stones we have placed here."

Water was thrown upon the hot stones, and, as the vapour arose, he prayed again :

"May our lives be as pure as the water, that we may live to be old and always have water to drink."

SPOTTED EAGLE PREPARING BUFFALO SKULL FOR SWEAT LODGE CEREMONIAL.

The Mad Dogs uncovered the sweat lodge four times, that those inside, dripping with perspiration, might cool off. Each time it was closed, water was thrown upon the hot stones. While the priests inhaled the vapour, they chanted and prayed to the Sun, Moon and Morning Star, that their children might live to be old, and always have plenty of food. When the Mad Dogs uncovered the sweat lodge the fourth time, the priests came out. They were given meat, but before eating, a blessing was asked upon the food, each breaking off a small piece and, with a prayer, planting it in the ground. The ceremonial was finished, when the Mad

LITTLE PLUME.

Dogs tied the buffalo skull, with strips of bark, to the framework of the sweat lodge, the nose pointing towards the rising sun. Mad Wolf then arose, and, followed by the priests and medicine women, led the way back to his tipi. They walked slowly and in single file, with heads reverently bowed, carefully avoiding the crossing of the trail, by which they had left the tipi.

A sweat lodge had been built in each of the four camps, made previous to the large encampment, in which the Sun-lodge was constructed. In the first camp, it was built on the east side; in the second, south; in the third, west and in the fourth, on the north side, following the course of the sun through the sky in summer.

Preceding the "Raising of the Pole," it was

BLACKFEET ASSEMBLING FOR TRIBAL PARADE.

customary for the tribe, both men and women, to dress in their finest clothes and to paint and decorate their horses with feathers for a parade through the camp. On this occasion the women, who were to take part in the Scalp-dance that followed the parade, were permitted to wear their husbands' eagle feathers in their hair. There were many elaborate and handsome costumes. Little Plume, a leading chief, wore a

hat made of a beautiful red fox-skin wound round his
head, the tail of the fox hanging down behind.   The
crown of the hat was decorated with pieces of white
weasel-skin, and two large eagle feathers stood erect
at the back.   His shirt and leggings were of soft-
tanned buck-skin, heavily beaded and ornamented with
many black-tipped ermine tails.   The wife of Mikosta

THE WAR CHIEFS, LITTLE PLUME AND LITTLE DOG, LEADERS OF THE
PARADE.

wore an otter-skin hat, with many shells as ornaments ;
a buck-skin dress with two hundred and fifty elk tusks
attached and an otter-skin across her shoulders.   Her
saddle had deer-antler pommels with beaded pendants
and a beaded buck-skin crupper.   Brightly coloured
feathers were fastened to her horse's tail and a large
cluster of eagle feathers hung from his neck.   One
young man was dressed as a clown, or jester.   He

TRIBAL PARADE.

rode a black horse, his face and hands painted black, and he wore a long black robe, which extended from his shoulders over his horse's tail and flowed out behind when he galloped. All marched slowly around the great circle of the encampment, singing in unison, some holding aloft scalps tied to long willow sticks,

SACRED TIPI WITH GREEN BRANCHES OUTSIDE.

others long streamers of eagle feathers and feathered shields fastened to poles. On the evening of the third day, the Sun-dance priests came, one by one, to Mad Wolf's tipi. In this service O-mis-tai-po-kah and his wife gave final instructions to Mad Wolf and Gives-to-the-Sun, concerning the important ceremonial of "Raising the Centre Pole," which would take place on the following day. Green branches had been

placed around the lodge on the outside, as the sign
that only those bidden should enter. I stood near
the door listening to a weird chant led by Mad Wolf.
At intervals the low monotone of the priests was
joined by the shriller voices of the women. Gradually
the chant died away and there was silence, finally
broken by Mad Wolf's voice directing that the fire
be replenished. When a brighter flame lighted up
the lodge, I decided that this was the opportune
moment for entering, and so opened the door. In
the uncertain firelight I was not recognised and two
priests motioned me away. When I gave my Indian
name, they bade me enter. On Mad Wolf's left were
O-mis-tai-po-kah, Natosin, the chief from the north,
and the Sun-dance priests ; on his right, Gives-to-the-
Sun, the sacred woman, Natokema and their assistants.
All the women wore gray blankets coloured with dull
red paint. Apisaki, daughter of Natosin, alone wore a
blanket of brilliant colours. She was unmarried and
had accompanied her father, that she might witness the
medicine-lodge and become familiar with its ceremonials.
Over the head of Mad Wolf hung the Medicine Pipe,
and near by were the sacred bundles of the Beaver
Medicine and Medicine Bonnet, the latter to be worn
by Gives-to-the-Sun, during the ceremonial of " Raising
the Pole," on the following day. In front of Mad
Wolf was an altar, or holy place, made by cutting out
the grass and smoothing the soft earth. It was lined
with juniper (red cedar). At the foot, and bending
towards the west, was a single stalk of wild rhubarb
(cow parsnip), with an eagle plume fastened to the
top. The wild rhubarb and plume were used by the
Indians in the Sun-dance ceremonial as symbols of
lightness, and were believed to favour the safe raising

of the Centre Pole. A young warrior was chosen to secure a rhubarb plant in bloom. Carrying it to the sacred tipi, he stood outside and announced,

"Here is the wild rhubarb."

When Mad Wolf bade him enter, he passed on the south side of the fire, laying the plant across the altar.

Copyright in United States   by Walter McClintock.

INTERIOR OF SACRED TIPI WITH SUN-DANCE PRIESTS AND MEDICINE WOMEN
(Altar is in foreground.)

Mad Wolf rubbed it with black paint, and, tying an eagle plume to one of the stalks, placed it upon the altar. Soft tanned buffalo and elk-skins were spread out, and rattles for beating time were distributed, Mad Wolf directing that two be given to his white son. Two redstone pipes were passed around, one for the men and the other for the women. It was Morning Plume's duty to see that the pipes were filled, and by his side lay a large beaded tobacco bag, extra stems, and a tobacco board for cutting. O-mis-tai-po-kah, as the father or instructor, gave directions for conducting the ceremonies, the way the medicine bonnet should be worn, and the songs that should be sung, while placing it upon the head of Gives-to-the-Sun. He warned Mad

SACRED WOMAN AND HUSBAND WITH RHUBARB STALK.

Wolf that if the ceremonials were not accurately performed, misfortune would follow. He advised him to refrain from the use of sweet pine (balsam fir), as incense during the Sun-dance. He made this injunction because in the tradition the Sun instructed Scarface to use sweet grass as incense. He also cautioned all to use great care in " Raising the Centre

Pole," and in building the Sun-lodge, reminding them of the well-known chief, who had died soon after the Pole had been carelessly allowed to lean towards him, and warning them that, if any part of the sacred lodge should fall, sickness and death would result. O-mis-tai-po-kah then prayed:

"Great Sun Power! I am praying for my people that they may be happy in the summer and that they may live through the cold of winter. Many are sick and in want. Pity them and let them survive. Grant that they may live long and have abundance. May we go through these ceremonies correctly, as you taught our forefathers to do in the days that are past. If we make mistakes pity us. Help us, Mother Earth! for we depend upon your goodness. Let there be rain to water the prairies, that the grass may grow long and the berries be abundant. O Morning Star! when you look down upon us, give us peace and refreshing sleep. Great Spirit! bless our children, friends, and visitors through a happy life. May our trails lie straight and level before us. Let us live to be old. We are all your children and ask these things with good hearts."

During the prayer of the head chief, all heads were reverently bowed, and at the close they joined earnestly in an Amen. While inside the sacred tipi, I took part in the ceremony, beating time with my rattles and joining with the priests in the solemn chants.

Sounds from the outside attracted my attention and led me to leave Mad Wolf and his company. They were so deeply engrossed in their solemn service that they did not seem to notice my withdrawal.

Going out from the dimly lighted sacred tipi, I met a group of young men dressed in their gay trappings on their way to a dance. They were singing a Society song in unison, the bells fastened about their legs jingling at every step. A horse passed, ridden by two young fellows, singing together the "Black Tail Deer" song, while making the rounds of the camp. Suddenly a band of Indians rushed out from behind a lodge.

With piercing war whoops they closed around the two singers and beat their horse, causing it to buck and plunge, but the riders pluckily held their seats. Finally, amid laughter and shouting, they distanced their pursuers, galloping off over the prairie.

Gaiety and humour are unexpected qualities to find concealed behind the habitually stoical and solemn exterior of the Indians. But, when one has been intimately associated with them in their camp life, he will find many indications of their playfulness and keen sense of humour, and that, when free from care and enjoying plenty, they are as light-hearted and as happy as children.

While passing a lodge, I heard a man's voice calling loudly, " What has become of the fellow that went after my horse ? " When he repeated it, those in the near lodges took up the cry, as a joke. One clan after another quickly joined in the clamour, until the entire encampment was in an uproar, to the great amusement of everyone.

Awunna told me of one of his pranks when a youth. With some companions they captured a wild yearling colt, and pushed it into the lodge of one of the older chiefs, who was unpopular, tying down the door flap. The thoroughly frightened colt bucked and squealed, scattering the inside fire, upsetting everything and kicking at the occupants, who almost overturned the lodge in their mad scramble to escape.

It was considered a practical joke for young men to lasso and overturn the tipis of old women at night, especially those of elderly single women, who lived alone near their relatives. One of them passing on horseback, would skilfully throw his lariat over the tops of the poles and, with the other end securely fastened to the horn of his saddle, would start off at a gallop. The tipi would be jerked from its fastenings, the old woman would be startled from her slumber by the disappearance of her home, as if struck by a hurricane, and she would be left sitting up among her

OLD WOMAN'S SMALL TIPI.

belongings, frightened and embarrassed by her sudden exposure to the public view.

The sounds of drums came from the large lodge of the Mutsaix (Brave Dog Society), where a crowd was gathered to watch their dance around an inside fire. Crawling beneath the side of the tipi, I found myself among the squaw spectators, who were so completely absorbed in the dance, that they took no notice of my sudden appearance in their midst. The dancers laid aside their blankets and their naked painted bodies looked as savage and frightful in the firelight, as they could make them. All had eagle-bone whistles in their mouths, which they blew while dancing. They wore belts, made of grizzly bear skins, with the tails hanging behind. Mikasto, as the chief of the band, had other distinctive marks. He alone carried a rattle. On his head was the scalp of a large gray wolf, the skin of which was split and hung down his back with the tail almost touching the ground. Four of the dancers were painted black. Four others, as gray wolves, were covered with white clay, and had black streaks painted under their eyes, also a black circle on the back. They carried long spears painted white, with four eagle feathers attached to them at regular intervals. They circled around the other dancers imitating wolves driving together a herd of buffalo. Two other dancers sat in a hole, near the door, representing grizzly bears in their den. Their bodies were painted red and they had black streaks downward across the eyes. Whenever the wolves herded their band together, the grizzly bears jumped from their den, and pushing to the centre of the throng, drove the dancers out and scattered them. The bears returned to their den, while the wolves again began herding. After the dance was finished, the Mutsaix marched through the camp, singing their society song and calling out, " Let everyone be quiet to-night, because the sacred woman is going through her ceremonial and should not be disturbed. Let all rest well, for to-morrow we will build the Sun lodge." After completing the circle of the camp they separated.

The labour of securing poles and branches for the Sun-lodge had been evenly distributed among the tribe. Each clan was required to furnish and put its share in place. Women mounted on horseback carried the poles to camp, riding on either side of them and holding them up from the ground with lariats fastened to their saddles. The men also walked beside the poles, as an extra precaution to prevent their touching the ground, which was considered unlucky. Followed by a large crowd, singing war songs and with the Mad Dogs shooting their rifles, they entered camp from the north, south, east and west, carrying the poles to the place chosen for the Sun-lodge. Mad Wolf selected the tree to be cut for the Centre Pole. He struck the tree four times, and then handed the axe, which was painted red, to Gives-to-the-Sun. While she chopped, she prayed,

"Oh tree! I ask that you will fall easily. I promise to plant you in a new place and to give you many presents. May you stand firmly in your new home."

A large crowd watched the cutting of the tree, praying to the Sun that it might fall with its prongs flatwise, and not be broken. The crowd cheered, when it swayed, and, while it was falling, many of the warriors fired guns into the branches. When it struck the ground, they jumped from their horses, and with shrill war-whoops broke the branches, "counting coups," as if it were an enemy. After they had trimmed the tree, its forked top was lifted upon a double travois. It was then borne to camp and laid beside the open hole made to receive it.

CHAPTER XXII

RAISING THE CENTRE POLE

Ceremonial of painting Mad Wolf and clothing the sacred woman.—The priests and sacred women appear before the tribe.—The Feast of Tongues.—Making vows in behalf of the sick.—Awasaki's prayer for her grandchildren.—Ceremonial of "Cutting the hide."—Warriors assemble according to clans.—They march holding long poles aloft. —The tribe sing the Hymn to the Pole in unison.—An impressive scene.—The priests and sacred women bless the Centre Pole.—The warriors raise the pole and complete the Sun-lodge.—Points of resemblance in the Feast of Tongues to feasts of the Jewish and Christian Churches.

On the morning of the fourth day many assembled to witness the ceremonial of decorating Mad Wolf with the black paint and clothing the sacred woman. As Gives-to-the-Sun put on the ceremonial dress, made from the skins of antelope and black-tail deer, the women assistants sang and made signs in imitation of deer and antelope. While putting on her medicine bonnet they sang :

"I want the weasel tails."

When the elk-skin medicine robe was thrown about her they sang the Elk song, making signs with their hands, imitating the movements of elk, swaying their bodies like trotting elk and giving the elk call.

Food was carried to the side of the Sun lodge, where the entire tribe assembled for a feast, seating themselves in long rows upon the ground. When the waiting people heard the Elk song, they knew the ceremonial in

Mad Wolf's tipi was nearly finished, and some eagerly exclaimed, " It is now time for the sacred woman to come forth." Gives-to-the-Sun, her face completely hidden by the medicine bonnet, was lifted to her feet by Natokema. She waited, leaning upon her cane for support. A line was formed, led by O-mis-tai-po-kah. Then came White Grass, Natosin, and Mad Wolf,

PROCESSION OF PRIESTS AND SACRED WOMEN.

carrying the wild rhubarb stalk with eagle feathers attached. He was followed by Natokema, Gives-to-the-Sun and their assistants. The procession moved slowly to a temporary shelter, or " lean-to " of canvas, near the site selected for the Sun-lodge, where they seated themselves. The parfleches of sacred tongues were opened. At this time, if there were any sick among the people their female relatives or friends came forward to pray to the Sun for their recovery. They took pieces of the consecrated meat and came before the tribe, the priests, and the givers of the Sun-dance. On all sides women were standing and facing the setting sun, each with right hand upraised, holding aloft portions of the sacred food, making vows,

PRIESTS AND SACRED WOMEN BENEATH THE SUN SHELTER.

confessing aloud and praying for their relatives standing beside them.

Awasaki, an old woman, the wife of Painted Wing, came forward with the children of Wakes-up-last,[1] her son. When the small line was properly formed, Awasaki, raising her voice, called upon all to hear. The silence and respectful attention of the spectators, the grandmother, and the children by her side, standing before the venerable chiefs and medicine women, made

[1] See Appendix.

an impressive scene.   Awasaki said, " I now give Spotted Eagle a good horse, and ask him to pray for my sick grandchild."   Spotted Eagle arose and prayed,

" O, Sun! I am praying for this woman because she is pure. She will take some of the holy food and will eat with you and with the Underground Spirits that her sick one may recover.   Listen, Sun, and hear us!   Grant us all life and health!"

Awasaki having taken a piece of tongue, broke off and

AWASAKI PRAYING FOR HER GRANDCHILDREN.

ate a morsel of it, facing the sun.   Holding up another piece, she prayed,

" Great Sun Power! I give you my life to-day, because I have always been a pure and honest woman.   I promise now to eat with you and with the Underground Spirits, that my grandchild may recover.   I am praying also for these children standing before you, that they may grow and be strong, that they may have long life and may never suffer from hunger.   Hear us and pity us!"

She planted another piece of tongue in the ground, and divided the remainder among her friends, to help them lead good lives.

A green hide was stretched and pegged upon the ground, to be cut into strips for binding the framing poles together. For this ceremony, Three Bears, a noted warrior, was chosen, because he had once killed an enemy with his knife. He was selected by Eagle Head, the cutter of the hide of the year before. It

WOMEN MAKING VOWS HOLDING UP PIECES OF SACRED TONGUE.

sometimes happened that men cut the hide because of a vow. Three Bears sat beside a fire, in which sweet grass burned as incense, and was painted by Eagle Head—red over his body, and a black circle around his face. Eagle Head also prayed to the Sun that he might cut the hide properly. Three Bears stood before the assembled people with a painted knife, half red for the Sun and half black for the Moon. He first prayed to the Sun for power, and then, holding the knife high in the air, he called out, "Hear! men and women, for what I speak is true. Once I made an expedition against our enemy, the Snakes; I captured a band of horses and killed two men." He then cut several strips from the hide. Again he said, "I was on the war-path in the north, and fought with a chief of the Crees. I killed him and brought his scalp back with me." In this manner Three Bears cut as many strips as were need-ed, "counting a coup" [1] before each cutting. Each time his wife was heard singing, and after he had finished, his relatives arose and danced, because their brother had

THREE BEARS "COUNTING COUPS" WHILE CUTTING HIDE.

gone through many dangers and had returned safely to his people. For conferring upon him the honour of cutting the hide, Three Bears gave to Eagle Head the customary gift of several horses. Many presents of moccasins, blankets, and old clothing were fastened to the Centre Pole, as sacrifices to the Sun and Moon. It was explained that articles, which

[1] See Appendix.

had been worn, were used as gifts, because the Sun and Moon expected offerings, but never made use of them.

When the Sun was setting, O-mis-tai-po-kah, the head chief, arose and in a loud voice directed the people to prepare for the ceremony of " Raising the Centre Pole." The men dispersed to their lodges, but soon reappeared, dressed in paint and war clothes. They

WARRIORS WITH POLES SINGING TRIBAL HYMN.

formed in four lines towards the north, south, east and west according to the clan, or camp to which they belonged. They held aloft long poles lashed together near the top, for lifting into place the heavy timbers of the Sun-lodge. The camp of Chiefs-all-over was first in line. They led off in singing the grand old hymn, " Raising the Pole," [1] given to the Blackfeet by the Sun through Scarface, and sung by them, in order that

[1] Song 8. See p. 311.

the Centre Pole might rest firmly in the ground.   The singing was taken up by the different camps as they formed in line, the Bloods, Big Top Knots, Buffalo Chips, Don't Laughs, Skunks, Lone Eaters, Grease Melters and Small Robes.   The lines moved forward from the four points of the compass towards the centre. Mad Wolf, with the priests and medicine women, passed slowly and in single file into the Sun-lodge.   Gives-to-

THRONG OF WOMEN AND CHILDREN SURROUNDING WARRIORS WHILE RAISING "CENTRE POLE."

the-Sun took her position with Natokema beside the forks of the Centre Pole.   Four times the lines of warriors advanced and stopped.   On the fourth advance, they stood in a large circle around the unfinished Sun-lodge, singing in unison.   The solemn and inspiring notes of their great "Hymn to the Pole" floating out over the quiet plain, the light of the evening sun, now sinking behind the Rocky Mountains, falling upon the strong and earnest faces of the chiefs and medicine women and the religious dignity of the occasion, combined to make the scene most impressive, one never to be forgotten. When all was ready, O-mis-tai-po-kah called in a loud voice, "Hurry! raise the Centre Pole quickly, that the sacred woman may eat and drink, for she is famished."

A bundle of willow branches was tied in the forks of the Centre Pole, representing the nest of an eagle. Mad Wolf stood upon the branches waving his robe in imitation of an eagle about to fly. When the priests shook the branches as if driving the eagle from its nest, Mad Wolf blew shrilly upon his medicine whistle, in imitation of an eagle screaming, and jumped from the Pole. The eager throng of women surrounding the lines of warriors closed in, shouting, "Hurry!" and praying,

"Great Sun Power! May our part of the sacred lodge go up safely, for we do not want to lose any of our relatives."

The lines broke and the warriors rushed towards the Sun-lodge, with shrill war-whoops. The Centre Pole was quickly raised by means of lariats. The young men with poles lifted the girders into place and branches with foliage were placed against the sides.

A small opening towards the west was left free from branches. These were secured and put in place by Mad Wolf and Gives-to-the-Sun, at dawn on the following day, that they might do their share in the labour of building the sacred lodge. The Sun-lodge was thus completed and ready for occupancy. In it the entire tribe assembled, during the remaining days of the festival, to witness the ceremonies and dances under the leadership of Spotted Eagle, Bull Child, and other medicine men.

Gives-to-the-Sun's fast was now ended. She returned

to her tipi and was given a small quantity of nourishing soup, while Mad Wolf again entered the sweat-lodge to remove the black paint, and to pray for his people.

The preparatory services, the consecration and setting apart of the food before its distribution, the religious assembling of the people, the symbolic act of eating a small portion of the consecrated food by each, the giving of thanks and prayer before partaking and the purification beforehand of those conducting the ceremonies,—all these impressed me by their religious significance, and the many respects in which this Blackfoot Feast of Tongues resembled the Jewish feast of the Passover and the Lord's Supper of the Christian Church.

TRIBAL HYMN, "RAISING THE POLE"

CHAPTER XXIII

INSIDE THE SUN-LODGE.

Three medicine men have charge of ceremonies.—Bull Child's famous medicine robe.—Sacred booth of the medicine men.—Great crowd of people at Sun-lodge.—People are painted by medicine men.—Society dances and "counting of coups."—Big Beaver tells of his vow.—Kit-sta-ka's song to her dead lover and suicide from a high cliff.—Self-torture by warriors at the Sun-dance in former days.—Story of the fulfilment of a vow by Two Bears.—An approaching storm.—Interesting contest between two medicine men as weather-makers.—Mad Wolf's farewell speech.—The tribe breaks camp.—Death of Mad Wolf.

SPOTTED EAGLE, Mas-te-pe-ne and Bull Child, prominent medicine men, were chosen by the chiefs to take charge of the ceremonies to be given inside the Sun-lodge. On the morning of the fifth day they walked slowly through camp, dancing and blowing their medicine whistles as a signal to the tribe that they were proceeding to the Sun-lodge.

Bull Child wore a robe,[1] famous among the Blackfeet, and purchased by him from "Brings-down-the-Sun," a celebrated medicine man of the north. Many bird and animal tails were attached, including those of the eagle, owl, weasel, mink and gopher. It had also a small bell, two shields and several pieces of fragrant punk from the cottonwood tree. There were paint marks on the back of the robe to represent stars. One group of seven, across the shoulders, to represent the

[1] See Appendix.

312

BLACKFEET CAMP BY MOONLIGHT

By Walter McClintock

Great Bear, and, under the right shoulder, a cluster of six to represent the Pleiades. In the centre of the back, the Sun was represented by a double circle in black and red, and there was also a small Maltese cross for the Morning Star. Before entering the Sun-lodge, Bull Child gave a long dance outside. In one hand he held owl and crow tails, which belonged to the medicine of his robe; and, in the other, an eagle wing that went with his medicine bag.

The symbolic designs painted upon his face and body had been revealed to him by the Sun in a dream, while sleeping in the medicine booth of a former Sun-dance. The marks upon his arms represented the rainbow, those upon his cheeks stars. Across his mouth was a red cross, the sign of fasting. Upon the

BULL CHILD WITH HIS CELEBRATED MEDICINE ROBE.

centre of his forehead was a red disc for the Sun and upon either temple two yellow streaks for sun dogs. Upon the front of his otter-medicine-hat was fastened a white shell representing the sun, and above it was painted a crescent for the Moon. At the back of the hat were two spotted eagle feathers, and in his hair a single red eagle plume.

When he danced, he faced first towards the rising sun, blowing his medicine whistle and making mysterious motions with both arms extended towards the sky. Then he danced facing the west and waving the eagle wing in the direction of the setting sun.

The door of the Sun-lodge faced towards the east. Opposite the entrance upon the inside, was a small booth for the exclusive use of the medicine men. It was closely interwoven at the sides and back with ground-pine to bar inquisitive eyes from the outside. The

THE SUN-LODGE.

floor was made of earth taken from the foot of the Centre Pole. It was hardened by wetting and then covered with white clay. Pine boughs were spread within upon which they slept. When the medicine men entered the booth they announced that they would fast four days, which meant to the tribe that the Sun-dance would continue four days longer. During this time the medicine men ate but four bites of dried meat before sunrise and four more after sunset, with an allowance of but one small shell of water. They might eat gooseberries and sweet cottonwood pulp, provided they were brought to them. They could not gather them, nor leave the booth during their fast.

The Indians surrounded and crowded into the Sun-lodge in such numbers that it was almost impossible for more to enter, or for those that were within to withdraw. Seats were reserved for the lodge-giver with

THE THREE MEDICINE MEN IN THEIR BOOTH.

his wife and their assistants. Gives-to-the-Sun was indeed highly exalted among Indian women, when she entered the Sun-lodge with Mad Wolf, O-mis-tai-po-kah and Natokema, for she was the object of honour and veneration from the entire tribe. Robes were spread, and they took their seats near the Centre Pole, on the north side of the medicine booth. The people brought offerings, which they presented with a filled pipe to one of the medicine men. After smoking he painted the faces of the givers and blessed them with " long life and

good luck." Many women carried young children
to Bull Child to receive his blessing. He took them
in his arms, and, holding a bunch of eagle feathers
in one hand and a buffalo tail in the other, gazed
intently at the bright sun and prayed, that " they might
be endowed with power, and have an abundance to eat
throughout their lives."

The space in the centre was kept open for the
different societies. They were recognised, as they entered,
by their characteristic dress and the painting of their
bodies. Hanging their shields and weapons upon the
Centre Pole, they sat down in rows to the north and
south of the fire and later gave their different dances.
Warriors also " counted coups," narrating their deeds of
bravery and illustrating them by their sham battles.

The Blackfeet believe that men, who have been brave
in battle, have acquired extra merit and, by recounting
their deeds publicly in the Sun-lodge will thereby help
their sick relatives and friends. One of these was
Mukoi-sa-po who arose and prayed,

"O Sun take pity on my sick mother and restore her to health."

He built a miniature lodge of branches to make more
realistic his description of his attacking alone a Sioux
lodge, and securing two scalps.

Big Beaver, dressed in a buckskin suit, decorated with
weasel skins and holding a piece of the sacred food,
stood before the people saying :

"Hear me ! my brothers and sisters. During the moon, when
snows are deep (February), I went with Esto-ko-atto to visit the
Crows. On our way home, at the time of the big Chinook (Warm
Wind), we were crossing the Yellowstone River. The water was
high and carried us against an ice-jam. Esto-ko-atto went under
and was drowned, but I crawled out upon the ice, which floated
down the river. I then vowed to the Sun that, if I escaped alive,
my sister would partake of a tongue for me at the time of the

next Sun-dance. I jumped from one ice-cake to another and escaped to shore, reaching my home in safety."

He handed the tongue to his sister, who held it up, praying to the Sun Power for all of the people. Breaking a small piece from the tongue, she buried it in the

MEDICINE MAN PRAYING FOR BIG BEAVER AND HIS FAMILY.

earth, praying to the Underground Spirits that all might have plenty to eat. Big Beaver then said to his sister, "Here is my horse and the clothing I wear. Give them to the medicine man, Spotted Eagle, and ask him to pray for us."

The entire assembly became hushed, when Kit-sta-ka

arose from a group of squaws and, with trembling voice, sang to her dead lover,

"This is the sacred place where I was last with my lover. Now I am left alone, for he has gone to the Spirit World where I hope to join him soon."

After the Sun-dance, Kit-sta-ka was camped with the clan of Lone Eaters on Two Medicine River. One evening she was seen standing on the edge of a high cliff in full view of the camp. The Indians heard her singing this same song to her dead lover, and then saw her jump to her death.

Many years ago, when the Indian tribes were at war, it was customary for warriors, who had made vows, to fulfil them at the time of the Sun-dance. These acts were not performed, as is sometimes asserted, for the making of warriors, nor were they regarded as deeds of bravado, but as religious expiations to the Sun, in return for favours granted. The vows were made under various conditions. For instance, a man, starting upon an important war expedition, would pray to the Sun, promising self-torture, if he could be successful and return home safely. Sometimes a warrior, hard pressed in battle, or a hunter in a desperate conflict with a wild animal, vowed that, if his life were saved, he would cut himself at the next Sun-dance. The devotee, in fulfilling such a vow, would choose a friend to do the cutting and have charge of him during the ordeal. Having made the incisions and thrust wooden skewers under the muscles, on both sides of his breast, he made them fast to the loose ends of one of the half dozen raw-hide ropes suspended from the top of the Centre Pole. He then danced around the pole until the skewers were torn loose. The spectators spurred him on by loud and continual singing, shouts of encouragement and admiration, and violent beating of the tom-toms. Weakened by previous fasting, he would often fall senseless to the ground, to be revived and started again, until his flesh was torn loose, when he would withdraw within the tipi of a relative for healing treatment and a feast. In their frenzy greater tortures were often voluntarily undertaken. Extra incisions would be made in their shoulders and back, from which buffalo skulls, guns, saddles and other heavy articles were suspended. The dancers would run about, dragging these heavy objects after them, until torn off by the violent strain.

Once, Two Bears, a young chief in a desperate battle with the Sioux, was surrounded and cut off from his comrades. When death seemed certain, he made a vow to the Sun and escaped. The next summer, he rode through the Sun-dance camp, telling the story of his deliverance and announcing that he was ready to fulfil his vow. He presented himself before a medicine man, who covered his body with white clay, painted black streaks on his cheeks, representing tears, and a black shield on his back,—the emblem of war. A wreath of juniper was placed upon his head and sage leaves tied around his wrists and ankles. He chose a noted warrior, who had done great deeds in battle, to cut the incisions in his back and breast. In these slits skewers were inserted, to which lariats were attached. During the ordeal Two Bears displayed no sign of pain. He directed that a herd of his own horses be sent for ; that the lariats be fastened to them, and that they be stampeded by the waving of blankets. He announced also, that he gave these horses as an offering to the Sun. The young chief was dragged a long distance before the last skewer was pulled through his flesh and he lay as if dead upon the plain. He was carried on a litter to his tipi, and root medicine was applied to his wounds. Next day he returned to the Sun-lodge, bringing a present and a filled pipe for the medicine man, who smoked and prayed for him. It is said that those who underwent self-torture generally seemed to recover, but not many of them lived long afterwards, because of the severe nervous shock sustained.

The medicine men were believed to have power over the weather, and at the time of the Sun-dance were expected to drive away all storms. The following incident illustrates the extraordinary skill with which they acquire and maintain a reputation with the tribe for supernatural power.

A dark cloud, with its eastern side extending far out over the plains, was seen slowly advancing along the main range of the Rockies towards the encampment. The people anxiously watched the medicine men, who were quick to realise that the occasion had great possibilities of success, or failure for their office. Spotted Eagle and Mastepene standing in front of their people, entered into a sort of competition as weather-makers, but with much better success than the competing prophets of Baal. Mastepene, blowing his whistle and facing the black cloud, called in a loud voice,

"Behold! A storm comes from the mountains, and you people would get wet, but I am powerful and my medicine is strong. I will now dance to keep the weather clear."

He left the booth, and stepping forth into the circle danced alone. He was short, but sinewy, and as he danced, circling around with agile step, he held an otter skin towards the north, south, east and west which, with a final gesture, as if driving back the clouds, he waved over his head. A sudden change in the wind averted its course and it divided, as Mastepene predicted.   Spotted Eagle, jealous of the success of his rival, then left the booth.   He wore the powerful medicine handed down to him by Four Bears.   On his head was an otter-skin cap to make him strong and active ; in his hair an eagle feather to preserve him in battle ; while around his waist was a medicine belt to keep his body free from sickness.   In one hand he

A MEDICINE MAN MAKING INCANTATIONS TO DRIVE AWAY A STORM.

carried a magpie and in the other a mink skin.   Standing before the waiting people, he said,

"Mastepene, you are wrong, for my supernatural power over the weather comes from the Sun, and is therefore stronger than yours.   The storm has indeed separated, but it will again unite and return to wet the people."

Again the eyes of the Indians eagerly watched the divided clouds, which actually came together and continued to spread until they passed over the encampment with a heavy rain.

The Sun had set on the last day of his Sun-dance, when Mad Wolf, the greatest orator of the Blackfeet, arose to make a farewell talk. A deep stillness fell over the assembled people as the venerable chief, with hand upraised to command attention, stood before them. He spoke with a strong full voice, saying:

"Hear! my children, for I speak to you with a good heart. It does us all good to assemble every summer around the Sun-lodge. We have smoked the Medicine Pipe, and the rising smoke has carried away all of our bad feelings. Many have given presents to the Sun, and some have fulfilled their vows. The old people have fasted and prayed, and now feel better in their hearts. The young men have listened to the wise counsels of the chiefs, and the young girls have seen the medicine women, chosen to fast and pray, because their lives are pure and their hearts are kindly disposed towards everyone. The Great Sun God is our father. He is kind, for he makes the trees to bud and the grass to become green in the spring-time. He gave the people good hearts, that they also might be kind and help each other. The grass is now long, and the sun is bright and warm upon the prairies, but the cold and frost of winter, with its deep snows and biting winds, will soon come, and I know not where our women and children will get their food. We are not moving; we are just standing still. The buffalo are all gone, the antelope and the rest of the game also. The white men have continued driving us westward, until now the Rocky Mountains face us like a wall and we can go no farther. I care not for myself, for I will soon go to the Great Spirit. I am anxious for the little children, for I know not what will become of them.

"You have all heard of our Ka-ach-sino (Great Grandfather, President), who calls us his red children. He is the only one upon whom we can depend, and we must now look to him, as in the past we have prayed to the Sun God. All of you my children should obey his laws and give heed to his advice. He lives far away towards the rising sun, but I shake hands with him now, for our hearts feel good toward him. Prepare to return to your ranches and look well after your cattle, for, with diligence and perseverance, you can make a good living. Let everyone keep away from fire water, and send your children to school. If they can learn the talk of the white men, they will be a great help to us, for the white man's way is now on top. I shake hands with all of you, my children.   I wish that you may feel the sunshine of joy in your hearts and that you may have no trouble.   What I speak with my mouth I feel in my heart.   Farewell ! "

Early on the following morning, Running Crane, followed by his band, departed for the south, and on the next day Mad Wolf also departed, followed by the rest of the tribe.   I remained alone in the midst of the recent encampment, watching them as they slowly

MAD WOLF WITH HIS BAND DEPARTING FOR THE NORTH.

made their way northward.   When they disappeared over a distant ridge, I turned for a last look at the Sun-lodge, which was now the one conspicuous and solitary object in the midst of a broad and desolate plain, surrounded on all sides by the smoking embers of the deserted lodge fires.

Mad Wolf died, May 28, 1902, during the moon, when the grass is green.   Just before his death, four large crosses of light appeared about the moon, the sign a great chief is about to die.   He was ill but three days.   Ear Rings and White Grass, skilled doctors of the Blackfeet, were called without avail. Mad Wolf grew steadily worse. It was the second night of his illness, when Ear Rings said, "Mad Wolf, you should make your farewell talk, for your sickness is hard to cure and it is doubtful if you will recover." The chief would not think of death. He directed that Snake Woman, a celebrated herb doctor and medicine woman, be consulted, but her remedies brought no relief. At early dawn of the fourth day, Mad Wolf suddenly raised himself. He said, "I want to go alone into the open, that I may see the blue sky and breathe again the fresh air."

He walked slowly to the door, and when outside, the watchers heard him speaking. Gives-to-the-Sun, hastening to him, found him kneeling, his face towards the rising sun, with arms outstretched and praying to the Morning Star, which had already risen and was shining upon the face of the dying chief. She heard him exclaim, "Wait!" and when she hurried to his side, he said, "Do you not see, standing there, the ghost of my old friend Double Runner? He says he is waiting for me, and it is now time for me to go with him."

Morning Plume ran out and caught the dying chief in his arms. Mad Wolf sank back as if tired. Reaching out, he took the hands of his wife in his own, and looking up tried to speak. She leaned close to his face and heard him whisper, "I love you and I love Morning Plume also." With these last words, Mad Wolf passed to the Spirit World over the "Wolf Trail" (Milky Way), the path worn across the heavens by the travelling spirits of many generations of the Blackfeet dead.

CHAPTER XXIV

ALONG THE OLD NORTH TRAIL

Our camp on Two Medicine River.—Sudden plans to start for Canada.—
Members composing our expedition and its object.—First camp at
foot of Hudson's Bay Divide.—Evening visit to tipi of the widow of
Screaming Owl, a former head chief.—She talks about former days
and of her dead son.—His ghost makes a night visit to our camp.—
Crossing the Hudson's Bay Divide.—Descent of its northern slope
into the beautiful valley of the North Fork.—Arrival at Spotted
Eagle's camp on St. Mary's River.

IN the early summer of 1905, I was in camp with
Kionama and Onesta on Two Medicine Lake in northern
Montana. The sun had set behind Mount Rising Wolf.
The rugged summits of the Rockies were silhouetted in
sharp outlines against the golden light, which still
lingered in the western sky. The distant snow-capped
peaks, the intervening forest-covered ridges and the
silver crescent of the new moon hanging over all, were
reflected in the quiet lake. Menake and Nitana, their
wives, were busily engaged preparing our evening meal,
over an outside fire. They were, at the same time,
taking a prominent part in discussing with their
husbands a proposed trip across the border into Canada,
to visit relatives and friends among the northern
divisions of the Blackfeet.

Menake was in favour of starting at once, urging that
the weather was undoubtedly settled, and that it was
the best time of year for travel. But Kionama doubted

Two Medicine Lake.   (Mount Rising Wolf in the distance.)

if permission to leave the reservation could be secured from the Kino (father or agent), and besides, we would not be able to get through the " Red Coats " (the Canadian North-western Mounted Police). He knew permits to go north had been refused to Ne-sots-kena, Ketamoken and many others. I reassured them by saying that I was a friend of their agent, and as I had

LODGES OF KATOYA AND HER SON.

come into their country with the permission of Ka-ach-sino (the Great Grandfather, or President), I could secure the permit, and we would go together. All were greatly pleased, and Onesta said, " We will not only visit our relatives and friends among the Blood Indians, but we will also see my uncle, Natosin Nepeë (Brings-down-the-Sun). He is a noted authority upon our ancient customs and religion. He lives in a camp with his children and grand-children near the Porcupine Mountains, on the Crow Lodge River. If you will go with us on the north trip, we will make you chief of our expedition. We will take you to Brings-down-the-Sun as our friend, and will persuade him to tell you about the old days." When I agreed to their plan, all doubts as to our ability of making the expedition were removed, and they decided, in characteristic Indian fashion, to start at once.

Next morning the horses were driven in at daybreak, and soon after sunrise we were on our way towards the north, over the Old North Trail, which has been trodden by unnumbered generations of Indians, and used long before the white race came to divide the country and to fix a border line. We had two teams, Kionama driving the first wagon with Menake, his wife, Onesta following with Nitana, their little daughter, O-tak-kai, (Yellow Mink), and Moiyami (Woolly One), the dog. I rode on horse-back in company with Sinopa (Kit Fox), daughter of Kionama, and her two brothers, Emonissi (Otter) and Seeyea.

We camped, for the first night, in a meadow of tall bunch grass, at the foot of the Hudson's Bay Divide, and near a stream of cold and sparkling water, fresh from the snow peaks of the Rockies. Not far distant, were the black timbered slopes of the mountains from which came a gentle breeze laden with the fragrance of the pine forest.

The Indians were delighted to be upon the trail again. They were as light-hearted and happy as children. When we gathered around the fire, Menake and Nitana busied themselves preparing the meat for our long journey, cutting it into broad strips and hanging it to dry upon poles near the fire. Thin strips

were roasted on the hot embers for supper, and the
"boss ribs" boiled in a large kettle for the morning
meal. Not far distant, up the river, were two lodges,
where lived Katoya, widow of See-pis-tok-komi
(Screaming Owl), former head chief of the Blackfeet,
and her married son Ekum-makon.

In the evening Kionama and I went to pay our

OUR CAMP NEAR THE HUDSON'S BAY DIVIDE.

respects to the old woman. There was no apparent
sign of life about her tipi, save the blue smoke, slowly
curling from the top, and carrying the sweet scent of
burning cottonwood. Katoya was at home and bade
us be seated. I leaned against the comfortable lodge
backs, made of small pine branches skilfully woven
together, and sat gazing at the medicines and the other
objects of interest in the lodge, revealed by the cheerful

firelight. I broke the long silence, by asking her to relate the circumstances that brought her husband into prominence before the tribe. She lapsed into a reverie, but finally, after filling her pipe, began :

" Many years ago, when we were at war with the whites, and in great dread of them, our tribe was camped near the Cypress Mountains. It was then that my husband, Screaming Owl, made a treaty with the white men. Early one morning he awoke me, saying, ' Catch our best horses and dress in your finest clothes, for I intend to start to-day for the camp of the Long Knives' (United States Cavalry). When this news had spread throughout the camp, there was great excitement. The people thought we were going to certain death and, crowding round our lodge, urged us not to go. But Screaming Owl said to them, ' Are you all women, that you should so fear the Long Knives ? I know the whites will do me no harm, for I go to make friends with them. Many times in the past I have advised you not to fight. It does no good to kill them, for they are as many as the grass on the prairies. Whenever we have taken their scalps they have brought bad luck and caused us much trouble.' We started off on our long journey and travelled towards the south for many days. When we drew near the white settlement, my husband rode to the summit of a high butte. He made signals with a mirror, flashing it into the fort, and then walked four times along the butte, backwards and forwards. The white chief rode towards us with some other men, making signs of peace. My husband also made signs to them that his heart was good, and we rode together down the hill. They shook hands with us, and, having entered their camp, we smoked a pipe with them. We remained there ten days, and then returned again to our people. We found the Blackfeet camped on Milk River. They were anxious for our safety and had followed our trail, but turned back, when it approached the white settlement. Screaming Owl told them of our journey, and how kindly the white men had received us. He finally persuaded the whole tribe to return with him to Fort Benton, where they camped many days. The great treaty was then made. My husband was given a medal by the Great Father, and he was also made head chief of the Blackfeet."

It was late when we returned to camp. The night air was cold, and we sat closely around the fire, built at the edge of the willows. Menake was relating the story of a ghost, which took the form of a large owl, and harassed a camp of Blackfeet. In the midst of her story, she abruptly stopped, and, turning, gazed intently towards the meadow. For a moment there was a deep stillness. Then a rustling was distinctly heard in the long grass, just beyond the circle of firelight. We all rose to our feet, while Kionama reached for his rifle. The strange object continued to move stealthily through the grass of the meadow and glided into the thick willows. Onesta said, " It must be a cougar, or a lynx." But Menake thought it was an Indian watching our camp. Before retiring to my blanket-bed, I stood, for a moment, looking up at the bright moon, and again closely scrutinised the dark line of the willows where the mysterious visitor had entered. As the sequel proved, it was my first meeting, face to face, with a real ghost, which has always remained a mysterious and inexplicable experience.

The following morning, when we went back to Katoya's tipi, she unconsciously furnished us with a startling explanation of the apparition. She said :

"Our talk yesterday brought back to me many things, and, since you left, I have been going over in my mind the happy days of the past. Last night I did not sleep, but lay thinking until the darkness became pale, and I watched the dawn as it came into the tipi. The spirit of my dead son, Pakapse, came here. He is my protector, and often visits me. Whenever he comes he is hungry; and last night, while eating, he said : 'My mother, there are strangers near you, but you need not be afraid, for they are good people and will do you no harm. I have been watching their camp and recognised Kionama, A-pe-ech-eken (referring to myself), and Menake. They were seated by the fire, talking together. I went too close, for they heard me, and Kionama picked up his rifle. I feared lest he might shoot and alarm you, so I went away. I then met the ghost of my dead father, Screaming Owl, coming down from the ridge, where his body lies. He said he was coming to watch over you, my mother. I advised him to go back and rest quietly, because I would see that no harm came to you.'"

Katoya continued in a reminiscent mood, "I was seven years old when I became the wife of Screaming Owl. I lived with him until death separated us. During our married life I gave the Sun ceremonial three times; the first, when I was fourteen years of age. The vow for our last Sun-dance was made by my son, Pakapse, when he was living on Badger Creek. I had been very sick, and some one brought to him word that I was dying. It was night when he received the message, and the moon was in the sky. He had always before prayed to the Sun, but, that night, he stood before his lodge, and looking up to the sky, prayed,

"'Great Spirit in the Moon and in the Stars! Have mercy on my mother that she may live. Pity her, for she is a pure woman, and I vow that if she recovers from the sickness of this night she will give the festival sacred to the Sun.'

" When Pakapse came in the morning he kissed me, saying, 'Rise up now and get well, because I have made the vow and have prayed for you.' I became strong again, and in midsummer, we gave the Sundance, as our son had promised. Since my husband died, I have been very poor. The agent has taken away my ration ticket, and I know not where I will get food. I would not have clothes, if my son Ekummakon, did not provide for me. He is also poor and has a wife and family to care for. The agent now says he must take me from my home and send me, with other old Indians, to the 'Country of the Dead' (referring to the 'Old Agency,' which was so named by the Blackfeet because of its dreary surroundings, the many graves on the hills and the quantity of bones lying around, bleaching in the sun). If this is done there will soon be no old people, for we shall all die of loneliness. We need our children around us. They provide for us, when we are in want, and care for us, when we are sick. I wish to live always on the banks of this river, where I lived with my husband, where his body now lies, and my children and sister are buried. When I die, I want my body to be placed beside theirs, on the summit of yonder ridge." When Katoya ended her talk, she bowed her head in silence, allowing her long hair to cover her face in order to hide her tears. We quietly left her to the companionship of her ghostly dead and returned to our camp, for we had a long drive ahead of us.

Heavy clouds settled down so low over the divide, that our camp was enveloped in a thick fog. Fearing that a heavy storm was gathering, we hurriedly finished breakfast, packed our outfit, and started in the face of a cold north wind. I lagged behind to get out my thick gloves and heavily lined leather coat. Closely muffled in their blankets the Indians made an interesting procession, moving forward through the heavy mists, and slowly climbing towards the summit of the divide. While we were descending its northern slope, a magnificent view was spread before us. The clouds were lifting from the Rocky Mountains, and the higher peaks stood out sharply in the clear sunlight. When we at last rode down into the broad valley of the North Fork of Milk River it was a lovely summer day, with balmy air and sky of deepest blue. At the head of the grassy valley, the sharp peak of Chief Mountain rose like a great pyramid. On either side of the stream the luxuriant meadows were radiant with masses of sweetbriar roses, and its course was marked by green groves of balsam poplars and willow thickets.

Arriving at the Green Banks (St. Mary's River), we camped beside the lodges of Spotted Eagle and Big Smoke at the edge of a grassy plateau overlooking the river. Spotted Eagle, a medicine man of the South Piegans, was recrossing the border with his wife and family bound south, having made a long stay among the northern divisions of the Blackfeet in Alberta. Big Smoke was a Blood Indian. He and his wife were on their way to visit their daughter who had married among the South Piegans.

CHAPTER XXV

SPOTTED EAGLE'S MYTHICAL STORIES OF OLD MAN

The camp of Spotted Eagle, a noted medicine man.—His jovial disposition and reputation for wit and humour.—He relates mythical
adventures of Old Man.—Old Man plays with the ground squirrels.—
Punishes the lynx and the birch tree.—Takes part in an elk dance.
—Joins in the mouse dance and gets into trouble.—Travels with a
fox and punishes a rock.—His adventures with coyotes.—He flies
with the cranes and falls to the earth.—He is tricked by a small
bird.—He dives after berries reflected in the water.—Starts the
custom of scalping dead enemies.—Induces men and women to mate.
—Steals the magical fire leggings.—Spotted Eagle's morning bath.—
His remarkable weather prediction followed by a violent electrical
storm.

WE found Spotted Eagle reclining on his bed of robes
and blankets, fanning himself with a large eagle wing.
He was a noted medicine man, who made a speciality of
the Sun-dance ceremonial. He was generally chosen to
sit in the sacred booth of the Sun-lodge, to pray for
those who came before him. If the man and his wife,
who gave the Sun-dance, were not competent to lead in
the ceremonial, Spotted Eagle was their paid adviser, to
guide them through the long and intricate rites.
Commanding in person, and with a face indicating much
force and strength of character, he had an imposing
presence—a most valuable qualification for a medicine
man. His hair, now streaked with grey over his
temples, was separated into braids by bands of otter
skin.

Because of its supernatural power, the use of otter-skin for all sorts of ornamentation of their tipis, war dresses and articles used in the ceremonials was very general among the plains-tribes. It was also prized as a handsome article of personal adornment, especially in wrapping their hair braids, and twisting it into their hair and scalp locks. "Otter-skin twists" were fashionable among the young men and were generally admired.

Spotted Eagle was accustomed to give special attention to making his toilet. We found him pulling out straggling hairs from his face with a small pair of tweezers (the Blackfoot substitute for shaving), and dressing his hair with a comb made of a porcupine's tail, ornamented with bead work, and a hair brush made of the skin of a buffalo tongue. Its pointed papillæ, when carefully dried, made a good substitute for bristles. These toilet articles were not modern, but they served the purpose equally as well. The making use, or wearing as an ornament, of any part of an animal, was often the Indian's way of honouring that animal. Spotted Eagle's comb and brush (especially the latter) had a superior value for a medicine man's toilet over the best comb and hair brush to be had from the Indian trader's stock.

SPOTTED EAGLE.

He complained to Big Smoke of the extortion of white traders, when he tried to barter some of his horses for provisions. But he had such a jovial disposition that he soon forgot the white traders and began telling stories. Spotted Eagle had quite a reputation as a wit, and was widely known as a joker. When startled by a sudden noise, such as the barking of a dog, or the whinney of a horse, he had a comical way of giving an odd cry, made more ridiculous by the peculiar intonation of his voice and the expression of his face. After each of his jokes, he would turn towards me, winking vigorously, and was greatly pleased if I laughed at them, which I did at every opportunity.

He was specially fond of telling stories about the marvellous adventures of Old Man (Napi), a mythical character of the Blackfeet, whose contradictory qualities are difficult to understand, or reconcile. Old Man was also known to other plains-tribes and by different names.

Some of these myths are fragmentary and incomplete, but all bear an unmistakable stamp of the primitive and childhood period of Blackfeet history.

Others are samples of Indian humour, told as we tell fairy tales and using Old Man for their central figure.

Many of them were vulgar and even obscene, which have an ethnological value, but cannot appear in a book for general circulation. Spotted Eagle had a fondness for them because they had been handed down from the ancients, and he also had that common trait, which finds enjoyment in hearing and telling such stories, because of a keen sense of the humour in them.

The character of Old Man as revealed, even in the more serious of these myths, is a strange composite of opposing attributes, of power and weakness, of wisdom and passion, of benevolence and malevolence. He associated intimately with the birds and animals. He conversed with them and understood their thoughts and language, and they understood him. Although believed to be the creator of all things, and as having omnipotent power, he was often helpless and in trouble, and compelled to seek the aid of his animal friends. He was, in fact, like an animal in his instincts and desires, which, strange to say, were exercised in conjunction with his supernatural power.

Old Man, like Hercules of Greek and Roman legend, and Thor of the ancient Scandinavians, was the personification, in human form, of strength and super-natural power. But it was a power uncontrolled by reason, and wanton in its exercise. He was a deceiver and a trickster and his name was a synonym among the Blackfeet, at least in later years, for mischievous and immoral adventure.

Spotted Eagle said of him : " Old Man first came to the Blackfeet from the south. The last we heard of him, he was among the Crees, and disappeared towards the east, whence he is not likely to ever return."

In the following myths about Old Man, related by Spotted Eagle, the reader will observe the striking contrast between their crude character, and the beauty of conception, dignity of imagery and vividness of description, characterising the star-legends as told by Brings-down-the-Sun.[1]

Old Man Plays with the Ground Squirrels and Punishes the Lynx and the Birch Tree.

" Old Man came to a place, where many ground squirrels were seated around a fire, playing a game.

---

[1] The ancient Indian traditions of Old Man have left their impress in many geographical names of this region, as Old Man's River, Old Man Mountains, Old Man's Slide, and Old-Man-on-His-Back Plateau.

They would bury one of their number in the ashes, until he squealed, when they pulled him out. Old Man said that he would like to learn the game. The squirrels explained that it was very easy, and invited him to take part. He asked them to bury him first, but, as soon as he was covered over, he yelled, and they quickly pulled him out. Old Man then said that it was the squirrels' turn, but since there were so many of them, it would save time to bury them all at once. They agreed, so he covered them all over with hot ashes, excepting one mother squirrel, who was afraid. He warned her to run away, so that there might be other squirrels, but left the others in the ashes, until they were well roasted. He ate so many of the roasted squirrels that he fell asleep, when a lynx came along and ate up the others. Old Man followed the lynx, until he came upon him fast asleep. He was so angry, that he seized him by the ears and shortened his head by hammering it against a stone. He pulled out his long tail and, breaking it in two, stuck the brush part on his rump, making a bob-tail. He stretched his legs and body, making them long and slender, and then cast him upon the ground saying, ' You bob-cats will always look like this, and you will always be so short-winded, that you will never be able to run far.'

" Old Man having been burned by the fire called upon the wind to blow. The cool air made him feel better, so he continued calling upon it to blow harder and harder, until there came such a fierce wind that he was blown away. Every tree that he caught hold of was torn up by the roots, and he could not stop himself, until he lay hold of a birch tree. When the wind went down and he was rested, he denounced the birch saying, ' Why have you such strong roots, that you cannot be pulled up like other trees ? I was having a good time being blown around by the wind, until you spoiled my fun.' He was so angry that he drew his stone knife and gashed the birch all over.

"This is the reason why the bark of a birch tree always has such a nicked appearance."

Old Man Takes Part in an Elk Dance.

" Old Man come to a herd of elk having a dance. They were following their leader in single file. Old Man persuaded the chief elk to allow him to be the leader. When they became tired, and it was so dark that they could not see where they were going, Old Man led them to a precipice, and throwing his rattle over, to make it sound as if he himself had jumped, he hastened to the bottom. The elk were at first suspicious but when Old Man called to them to follow him, they jumped over one after the other and were all killed, excepting one, which was a cow. Old Man told her to go away, in order that there might be more elk. Old Man then ate his fill of elk meat, keeping the tongues to the last by placing them upon poles to be safe from the animals. When a lame coyote came along and whined for some meat, Old Man refused, but finally promised to give him some, if he would beat him in a long foot race. The coyote, at first, said he was too lame. When Old Man insisted he agreed, but first went to the top of a neighbouring butte, and barked to the north, south, east and west, summoning all of the animals to come together to witness the race. At the start the coyote pretended to be so lame, that he could scarcely walk, but when they were far out on the

plains, he let down his lame leg and quickly passed Old
Man. Old Man seeing that he was beaten, called after
the coyote to leave some of the meat for him. When
the coyote arrived at the finish, he found the animals
waiting. They had a great feast together and finished
eating all the elk meat, excepting the tongues, which
they could not reach. But the mice crawled up the
poles, and ate the insides out of the tongues.

"When Old Man arrived there was nothing left."

Old Man joins in the Mouse Dance and gets into Trouble.

"Old Man found large a elk-skull lying upon the
ground. He looked inside and saw some mice having
a dance. The Chief Mouse always started the dance
by singing Ka-wa-skiau ap-a-nok-se = 'Mice-winking-
their-eyes.' Then all stood up and joined in the singing, taking hold of each other's paws and dancing in a
circle. Old Man asked if he could join them. The
Chief Mouse replied, that his body was too large
to get inside the skull, but he might stick his head in
and keep shaking it up and down, which would be
almost the same thing as dancing. He told him
however, that the dance would last all night, and
advised him not to fall asleep. In spite of the warning
Old Man soon fell asleep, and the mice ate off all his
hair. When he awoke in the morning, the mice had
gone, and he was unable to pull his head from the
skull. He could not see, because the skull covered his
eyes. Losing his way, he walked over a steep bank
into a river. He swam down stream with the elk-
antlers sticking out of the water, until he drew near an
Indian camp, where his appearance caused great excite-

ment. When Old Man heard the people shouting, 'Here comes an elk,' he made a noise like an elk, and kept on swimming. The Indians roped him with lariats, and pulled him ashore, but they did not discover that it was Old Man, until an old woman broke open the skull with a stone-hammer."

Old Man Travels with a Fox and Punishes a Rock.

" While Old Man was travelling with a Fox, they came to a large rock, where they stopped to rest. It was a very hot day and Old Man was very tired of carrying his robe. As they were leaving, he said, ' Poor Rock ! You have been living here uncovered so many years, that you are turning black. I am so sorry for you that I will give you my robe for a cover.' He and the Fox then continued their journey. A big black cloud soon came up, and he decided to send the Fox back for the robe. But the Rock refused to give it up saying, 'Whenever anything is given to me, I never part with it.' Old Man asked the Fox to try to borrow the robe, but it was in vain. Old Man then ran back himself and said, 'Rock you have stood here many years without a cover and now you have become too particular.' He angrily pulled the robe from the Rock, and continued his journey with the Fox. They had not gone far, when they heard a mighty roar, and saw the Rock coming after them. Although they ran their fastest, the Rock gained on them so rapidly that Old Man called upon the night hawks for help To rescue him they kept swooping down upon the Rock and each time a piece fell, until finally it broke into pieces.

" The remains of the Rock can be seen to-day scattered over the plains."

Old Man's Adventures with the Coyotes.

" After leaving the camp, he saw a coyote on the shore of a lake, eating a piece of fat. When Old Man inquired where he got it, the coyote explained that he made it from the lake foam. He said that Old Man could easily make it, if he would first cover his hands with mud and, after skimming the foam from the lake, put it in his mouth, when it would turn into delicious fat. Old Man did as the coyote said, but, when he put the mixture in his mouth, it made him very sick.

" Farther on, he saw two coyotes on a frozen lake jumping up and down on the ice, and at the same time, singing, ' Pokoto kima ho ! hoi ! ' Whenever the ice crackled, they barked and yelped with excitement. Old Man came near, and asked what they were doing. They explained that, where the ice broke, juicy meat and rich fat came through. Old Man said he would like to try, but, when he jumped on the thin ice, he broke through into the cold water and had a hard time getting out."

Old Man Flies with the Cranes.

" During Old Man's travels, he came to a lake, where he saw many ducks, geese and cranes gathered into flocks and ready to fly south. He begged them to allow him to go along. The Chief Crane said, that he might join them, if he would wear feathers just as they did. When Old Man agreed, the Chief Crane directed each one of his flock to give him a feather until he was covered with a complete outfit of feathers. Before starting, the Chief Crane warned Old Man saying,

'When we fly over the Indian camps, you must not look down, no matter how much you may want to see what is going on.' The cranes then mounted high into the air and started towards the south, Old Man flying along with them. When they passed over an Indian camp, Old Man remembered the advice of the Chief Crane and looked straight ahead. When they came to a camp, where there was much noise and shouting, he could not help looking down to see what was happening. He quickly lost his balance and fell headlong into the Blackfeet camp, striking the ground so hard that he was stunned.

" When he came to himself there was a large crowd of people gathered around and they recognised him."

Old Man Tricked by a Small Bird.

" While travelling through the forest, Old Man saw a small yellow bird sitting on a long elk horn. When he stopped to ask what the horn was used for, the bird said that it was his bow. There was a long log lying near by and Old Man asked if it also belonged to him. The bird replied that it was his arrow. Old Man said, ' You cannot shoot me with it.' The bird answered, ' Yes, I can shoot you with it." Old Man then tried to lift the log, but it was too heavy, so he sat down on one end and laughed loudly, because the bird was so very small. The bird asked Old Man to move to the other end of the log saying, ' I will then shoot you with it.' The bird kept urging him to move over and he obeyed until the bird suddenly cried, ' Look out brother, I am going to shoot !'

" The other end, being overbalanced, flew into the air. Old Man was thrown off, but was not badly hurt."

Old Man dives after Berries reflected in the Water.

" Old Man came to a river, where he saw in the water, the reflection of a bush covered with ripe berries. He jumped into the river but could not get them. He tried again several times, but in vain. He then tied stones around his neck, arms and waist with willow bark, to make him sink deeper. This time he reached the bottom, but was unable to rise again to the surface. While tearing the stones loose, he became so filled with water, that he was almost drowned. He crawled out upon the shore and lay upon his back, feeling very weak. He then looked up and saw the berries hanging from a bush above him, and, for the first time, realised that he had been diving after the reflection. He was so angry, that he seized a stick and beat the bush, knocking off all the berries, and said to it, ' Old bush, from this time forward, the people will gather berries from you in this way.'

" This accounts for the custom, which Indian women have of knocking the berries from bushes with sticks."

Old Man starts the Custom of Taking Scalps.

" The Old Man, who made us, and all things, gambled with another Old Man, who created the people on the other side of the mountains. We have seen the great stones, which they used in their games. The Old Man from over the mountains won all the mountain sheep and elk, leaving the antelope and buffalo. After all the game had been lost, our Old Man wagered his head against the head of the other Old Man, and won, but, in consideration of a return of part of the game, he only took his scalp. In doing this, he said : ' When any of your young men kill mine, they shall take their scalps, and when any of mine kill yours, they will do the same and will thus become chiefs.' "

The Blackfeet believe, in common with all Indians, that one, killed and scalped in battle, goes to the happy hunting grounds, with all the glory and honour given to a successful war party returning with the scalps of their enemies, while one, who dies from old age, or sickness, departs in a much less honourable manner.

Old Man induces Men and Women to Mate.

" Men and women formerly did not live together as they do now, they were in separate bands like animals. Old Man was the means of bringing them together. The women were then camped on Crow Lodge River, beside a piskun,[1] and secured their game by driving them over a high cliff. They were skilled in the art of tanning, and knew how to make good clothes and lodges from skins. The men, on the other hand, killed their game with bows and arrows. They did not know how to tan skins, or sew. Their lodges were made of green hides and their clothes of rough skins, roughly fastened together. When Old Man came to the women's camp, he met the Chief Woman and told her about the condition of the men. She asked him to bring the men to their camp, that they might each choose a mate. Old Man led the men to a hill outside of the women's camp, where they all stood in line. The Chief Woman, who had first choice, came out very shabbily dressed. She walked along the line of men and selected Old Man for her mate. But he did not recognise her in her poor clothes and refused to go with her. The Chief Woman

[1] See Appendix.

was very angry. She returned to camp and instructed the other women to pass by Old Man in their choosing. She dressed in her best clothes and returned again to the men. This time Old Man liked her appearance so much, that he kept getting in her way, seeking to be chosen. But she selected another mate. When the other women selected their mates, Old Man was left out. The Chief Woman then changed him into a pine tree.

" There were formerly three pine trees beside the Women's Piskun. There is now a fourth, which we call Old Man."

Old Man Steals the Magical Fire-leggings.

" Old Man came to the lodge of a man who owned a wonderful pair of leggings. Wherever he went they set fire to the grass. If he wished to kill buffalo, he had only to walk around them when they would be caught in a circle of fire. Old Man wanted these leggings very much. He said that he had come a long journey to get them, but the owner refused to give them up. Old Man then decided to remain all night in the lodge. When the owner and his wife were sound asleep, Old Man stole the leggings. After running a long distance he became tired and lay down to sleep in a thicket with the leggings under his head. But, when he awoke in the morning he found, to his surprise, that he was back again in the lodge. When the owner asked him how it happened that he had his leggings under his head, Old Man told him a lie, saying, ' I had nothing else, so I used them for a pillow.'

" On the following night, Old Man made another attempt to carry off the leggings, but morning found him back again in the lodge where the leggings belonged. The owner then told Old Man that, if he wanted the leggings so badly he would give them to him. He warned him, however, not to make use of them more than three times. Old Man was so proud of the fire-leggings, that he put them on to show off in every camp he entered and paid no heed to the warning of the owner. He used them three times successfully, but the fourth time he put them on he set fire to the grass, wherever he stepped. The grass burned so fiercely that Old Man became frightened and started to run. The fire followed him, wherever he went, burning his clothes and his hair, until he was compelled to jump into a river. But the magical leggings were burned up."

An incident happened in Spotted Eagle's Camp that illustrates the remarkable control, which the mind has over the pain and ailments of civilised and savage alike, when the will is directed by an implicit faith in the means prescribed. Kionama had been complaining of severe pains in his side, resulting from an old injury of a horse. I suspected from the frequency of his complaints, that his pains were more or less imaginary. I accordingly doctored him with harmless pills of a pronounced taste, which I took impressively from my medicine case in his presence. During the night I was aroused by groans from Kionama who was sleeping beside me. Suspecting that they were intended to waken me, I asked him if he was ill. He replied that he had those terrible pains again. When I suggested more pills, he said that he regretted giving me so much trouble, but he was confident that, if I could give him more, he would quickly recover. I soon found and administered the magic pills, with the wonderful result that, in a few moments, he was fast asleep.

Next morning while we were packing for an early start, Spotted Eagle came to bid us farewell. He was on his way from a bath in the river and was clothed only in a blanket and moccasins. In one hand he held a red stone pipe, and in the other his eagle-wing fan. Remembering, that it was required of the Blackfeet, to perform certain in-cantations before entering a river, in order to prevent sudden storms, I inquired if he had taken the precaution to make medicine, before going into the water. Spotted Eagle, giving me a keen and inquiring look, replied that he had not. It was a beautiful clear morning, without a cloud in the sky, and with no indication of a storm. So I said,

SPOTTED EAGLE'S SON RIDING A DOG.

with a laugh, "I suppose then it will rain?" He saw that I was sceptical as to his power over the weather. Gazing intently at the sky and the distant mountains, and then looking solemnly at me, he replied, "Yes, it will surely blow up a storm."

When we rode away, Spotted Eagle was superintending the packing of his outfit. Turning in my saddle for a last look, I saw him seated very grandly, watching his wife and daughter taking down the tipi, while his youngest son was trying to ride one of the dogs.

While climbing the long ridge beyond the St. Mary's River, I was mindful of Spotted Eagle's prediction, and my curiosity kept me on the look-out for any sign of a storm. The sky was cloudless, but the sun was very hot and a warm breeze blew from the east. When we gained the summit of the ridge, and had a distant view of the mountains and plains, I saw clouds forming over the high peaks of the Rockies. To my surprise, they spread with astonishing rapidity, and, dividing, a heavy rain passed to the south, while dense black clouds moved rapidly northward along the main range. I suggested that Spotted Eagle would probably be grati- fied with the apparent results of his prediction. But Kionama was non-committal, while Onesta only shook his head ominously. The clouds continued to spread rapidly, throwing a black pall over plains and moun- tains. Sheets of brilliant lightning darted from the clouds in the north and heavy rains were falling in many directions. An angry looking cloud, from which extended curving black lines, advanced rapidly towards us—the infallible sign of a dangerous hail storm. When we felt a sudden drop in the temperature, we halted. The horses were quickly loosened and secured with ropes, so that they could not stampede, while we all crawled beneath the wagons to escape the pelting of the hail, which soon covered the ground. When we were again on our way, another storm burst over us with vivid flashes of lightning and a rain so heavy that my slicker afforded but little protection, the water running down my neck and into my shoes. We had just passed through a herd of cattle, all huddled together, when there came a vivid flash, and, almost simultaneously, a deafening crash of thunder. The bolt entered the plain in the midst of the herd, killing four steers. I was riding in advance, and did not feel the electrical shock, but the others were stunned. Kionama complained of Spotted Eagle's use of his supernatural power, as if he had directed the storm in pursuit of us, and said : " I do not see why he could not have sent the storm in some other direction." The day's events brought forcibly to mind the reason of the Blackfeet's frequent prayers for protection from " sudden storms." My own experience and observation have convinced me that the remarkable success of medicine men in predicting weather is the natural result of long training and their habit of constant and expert observation of weather signs.

CHAPTER XXVI

ONESTA AND THE BEAR SPEAR

Gift of supernatural power from the Sun, conveyed to men through certain animals.—Onesta's watchful care of the Bear Spear.—He gives the ceremonial for an auspicious entrance into a new country.—Relates legend of the origin of the Bear Spear.—The Mink Ceremonial.—Curiosity of white emigrants visiting our camp.—Extreme heat.—Changed outlook after crossing the International Line.—Indian theories for "Fairy Rings" on the plains.—My botanical collection of herbs and plants used by the Blackfeet.—Perfumes used by women.—Arrival in the Blood Country.

MANY of the Blackfeet legends relate to the origin of their medicines, and the manner in which supernatural power was transmitted to men by the Sun. When an Indian desired to know the future course of his life, or to receive knowledge, that would be of value to his tribe, he went off alone upon the plains, or to a remote region among the Rocky Mountains, to fast and pray, sometimes for many days, that he might receive a dream or vision. If he was worthy, a message would be transmitted to him from the Sun, through some animal, or supernatural being, whose compassion had been excited by his fasting and exhausted condition. The revelation, and with it the gift of power, generally came in a dream through the medium of one of the more powerful animals, such as the buffalo, beaver, wolf or grizzly bear, which were believed to have supernatural attributes, or through one of the personified natural forces, such as the Thunder Chief, the Wind Maker, or Es-to-ne-a-pesta,—Maker of Storms and

Blizzards.   The Blackfeet believed that this power was conferred upon the animals by the Sun, and they in turn were able to transmit it to men.   If, for instance, the grizzly bear bestowed his power upon a man, that man would attain the nature of a grizzly.   It would be difficult to kill him in battle, because of his wonderful vitality, or

ONESTA WITH THE BEAR SPEAR.

life force, and like the bear, he would inspire fear among his enemies.   At the death of the owner of this power, or medicine, it was handed down to his son, or someone worthy to possess it, along with the ceremonial and the story of its origin, which became one of the most valuable of his possessions and was made known only upon special occasions.

Onesta was the owner of the sacred Bear Spear. During our travels I found it very interesting to observe his watchful care of it. When we made camp, the Bear Spear was always attended to first. It was never allowed to lie upon the ground, but hung from the tripod behind the lodge. After sunset, it was carried inside and tied to the lodge poles. In the morning, it was again taken outside to hang in the sunlight, but was never exposed to a storm. The evening we camped on the border of the reservation of the Kainau (Blood tribe), Onesta made preparations for the ceremonial necessary before entering a strange country. He and Nitana put on their ceremonial clothes of yellow,—the colour sacred to the Bear Spear. Nitana led Yellow Mink, their small daughter, to a stream, where she was washed, her hair was neatly braided, and she was clothed in her little yellow dress, with beaded leggings and moccasins to match. Onesta and Nitana burned sweet grass as incense and painted their faces. They sang a chant over the Bear Spear, which was laid before them, and made prayers for a prosperous journey. Having become familiar with the chants, I joined with them in the singing, doing my part in giving more power to their prayers. When the ceremonial was finished, and we were gathered around the evening fire, Onesta related the following legend of

The Origin of The Bear Spear

" Many generations have passed since the events I am about to relate took place. They happened at the time, when the Blackfeet used dogs, instead of horses, as beasts of burden. Our people were travelling in the moon, when the leaves fall (late autumn). One evening, when they went into camp for the night, a herald announced that a dog travois owned by the head chief was missing. The herald said further, that the chief's ermine skin-suit, and his wife's buck-skin dress, and her sacred elk-skin robe were all on this travois. No one could recall having seen the dog during the

ONESTA HOLDING UP PIPE WHILE PRAYING TO THE BEAR SPEAR, WHICH HANGS FROM THE TRIPOD.

day. A band of warriors rode back to their former camp, but they could find no sign of the missing travois. Sokumapi, a young boy about twelve years old, was the only son of the head chief. When the warriors returned, after their fruitless search, he went to his father, and said : 'My father, let me return to our old camp. I am now old enough to make this trip alone, and I feel that there is in me the power to find out what has become of our travois dog.' The head chief was, at first, unwilling

that his son should go so far alone, but the boy was so
eager, that he finally consented. Sokumapi travelled
alone to their former camping grounds, which were close
to the Rocky Mountains. He went first to the place
where their tipi had stood, believing that, if the dog had
strayed away, he would return there. Then he walked
slowly around the circle of their old encampment,
carefully examining the ground. When he discovered a
single travois track leading away from the camp, he
followed it, until it ran into a well-worn trail, leading in
turn into a deep and rocky ravine. Near the head of
this ravine, he discovered the entrance to a large cave.
Its mouth was almost covered with large sarvis berry
and choke-cherry bushes. On a fresh mound of earth,
in front of the cave, he found the missing travois.
While he stood gazing at it, and was wondering what
had become of the dog, a huge grizzly bear suddenly
appeared in the entrance. He walked out from the
cave and, rising upon his hind legs, gave a terrible roar,
which so frightened Sokumapi, that he could neither
speak, nor move. The grizzly grasped the boy in his
paws and carried him back into the cave, where it
was very dark. Gradually Sokumapi's eyes became
accustomed to the darkness and when he discovered the
enormous size of the bear that held him, his spirit left
his body. When he came to himself, he was lying
on the floor of the cave. He was so close to the head
of the grizzly, he could feel his hot breath. When he
moved, the bear placed his heavy paw across his body and
stretched out his great claws. After that, the boy lay
still ; for a long time he did not even move, but gazed
straight ahead. Finally, the grizzly spoke to him saying :
' Do not be alarmed, my son, for I will do you no
harm. I am the head chief of all the bears and my

power is very great. I know that you have wandered
to my den because you are trying to help your father.
It was my supernatural power that drew you here,
because I want to help you. Live with me here while
the snows are deep. I have provided plenty of food
and no harm will come to you. Before you leave my
cave in the spring I will bestow upon you some of my
supernatural power, so that you will be of great help to
your people.' The grizzly then stood upon his hind
legs, his head almost touching the roof. He first walked
around and around and then led the boy to a large
pile of branches bearing different kinds of berries and
said : ' You will have plenty of berries for food. The
bear eats them, stems and all, but you can pick the
berries from the stems if you prefer.' Taking
Sokumapi to the other side of the cave, the bear
uncovered a hole filled with buffalo chips. He showed
him how to transform them into food. Lifting one,
he held it between his paws and danced slowly four
times around a circle, making many mysterious
motions. As the boy watched the buffalo chip, he
saw it change into rich pemmican and wild berries.
Sokumapi lived all winter in the cave with the
bear, doing just as he did. His eyes became so
accustomed to the darkness, that he could see just as
well as the bear himself. He observed that, when the
snows lay deep the bear lay on one side. He did not
even move. But when the warm winds of spring began
to blow, he became restless. One day he rolled upon
his back, and, after lying for some time with his legs in
the air, he sat up. Finally, he yawned and rising
walked around the cave, turning now and then to look
out of the entrance. The bear then told the boy that
spring had come and it was time for them to leave the

cave. When Sokumapi looked out, he saw that a Chinook (warm wind) was blowing and that the snow had melted from the hills. But, before they left the cave, the Medicine Grizzly bestowed upon Sokumapi his supernatural power. He brought forth a long stick and, raising himself upon his hind legs, stretched out his arms and extended his claws. Throwing up his head, he snorted and rolled back his lips, showing his long sharp teeth. He said, 'Behold my nose, with its keen scent, and my claws and teeth which are my weapons! Everything fears the grizzly bear. There is nothing living upon the earth that dares to defy my power. When you return again to your people make a Bear Spear. Secure a long stick like this I am holding. To one end of it attach a sharp point, to represent my tusks. Tie bear's teeth to the staff and a bear's nose, which must always go with the teeth. Fasten eagle feathers to the handle and cover the staff with bear skin painted with sacred red paint. Grizzly claws should also be tied to the handle, so that they rattle like the noise a grizzly makes when he runs. When you go into battle, always wear a grizzly claw in your hair, and my power will go with you. Whenever you attack, imitate the noise a grizzly makes when he charges, so that your enemy will be afraid and will run away, just as everything that lives on earth runs from a grizzly.' The bear taught him the chants to be used in healing the sick. He also showed him how to paint his face and body, so that he would not be struck in battle, red over his body, black across the forehead, and two curved black lines at either side of his mouth, to represent bear's tusks. The bear warned him that the Spear must be kept sacred. Its supernatural power must be used, only in battle and for healing the sick. When anyone is near death, a relative can make a vow to purchase the Bear Spear, and the sick will then be restored to health by the supernatural power that goes with it. The Medicine Grizzly accompanied Sokumapi, until they saw an Indian seated on a distant butte. The bear then left him, saying, ' Go now, my son. That person is a sentinel of your people and the camp is not far distant.' The sentinel recognised Sokumapi and inquired where he had spent the winter, and told him that his father and mother had mourned him as dead. But the boy was silent. He would not answer. When the sentinel called out that the lost son of their head chief had returned, the entire camp was thrown into great excitement. Everyone came out to meet him. The head chief was proud of his son. He gave a feast and invited many prominent men to his lodge. When they had finished eating, and all were seated to listen, Sokumapi related the story of his journey, the visit to the den of the Medicine Grizzly, and the gift of the sacred Bear Spear. Sokumapi began at once to make the Spear, as the grizzly had directed, and the tribe did not move camp, until it was finished."

Not long after Sokumapi's return, it happened that the Blackfeet were preparing to meet the Crow Indians in battle. The two battle lines were drawn up, but, before they met, Sokumapi appeared in front of the Blackfeet warriors, bearing the sacred Spear on his back, with the sharp point up, and the feathers hanging down. He was stripped and his body was painted red. There were black curving lines at either side of his mouth for tusks, and in his hair he wore a huge grizzly claw. He walked along the line, singing one of the Bear songs, and back again, singing another, then holding the Spear up towards the sun, so that all could see, he prayed, and started a charge against the enemy, calling upon all the warriors to follow. The Blackfeet followed the sacred Spear and, knowing that the power of the Bear was with them, rushed upon the Crows with such fury, that they turned in flight. It was a great victory. The Blackfeet killed many of their enemy and, when the battle was over, they put Sokumapi on a large horse and he led the warriors back to the tribal camp, chanting the Bear songs. After this victory, Sokumapi was made a war chief, and the people knew that the Bear Spear was endowed with supernatural power. It was often taken to war, and was also used for healing the sick. Its ceremonial lasted an entire day. The man, who made the vow to receive the Spear, pitched his lodge at a distance from the main camp, on the side where the sun rises. He remained there alone for four days and four nights. If during that time, the tribe moved camp, one of his relatives was required to change his camping place four times, before his lodge could be pitched again in the main camp. After the Spear changed hands the owner hunted for a bear-den, and securing some of the dung, he placed it on the ground, where the Spear was uncovered, and also upon the spot where the incense was burned. Sweet grass is used as incense in the spring and in summer, when it is at its best. In the autumn and winter, the root of the big turnip is used instead, because it gives forth such a strong odour at that time of the year. The owner of the Bear Spear must always keep it near him. It cannot be placed on the ground, but must hang from a tripod. No dogs are allowed within the lodge, because they fight bears. All openings must be kept closed and parfleches placed against the door, so that dogs cannot find an entrance. The sacred Spear is unrolled and taken out in the spring, when the first thunder is heard, just as with the Medicine Pipe, because the bear appears in the spring, and remains out all summer, like the thunder. In the late autumn, when the bear disappears for the winter, the sharp point is removed from the staff and the Spear is put away. Wipes-his-eyes owns a Bear Knife given him by the Black Bear. The songs belonging to its ceremonial are different from the Bear Spear songs. Women are not allowed to handle, either the Bear Knife, or the Bear Spear. When Onesta was leaving camp, not expecting to return before dark, he asked me to remove the Bear Spear from its tripod at sunset and hang it from the poles inside the lodge. He explained that his wife could not do this for him, because women were not allowed to touch the sacred Spear.

Next morning, Onesta brought forth a Mink Skin, over which he held a short ceremonial, explaining to me that it had been in his possession for thirty years, and had formerly belonged to the Bear Spear Medicine. The incense he burned for the Mink Skin consisted of small dried seeds which gave forth a pleasing odour. He called it Pono-kan-sinni (Elk Food) (Narrow Leaved Puccoon), and said it was prepared by drying the tops of the plant. While painting his face he said, " A-pe-ech-eken, it would be well for you to paint your face also, in order that the Bloods may know that you are an Indian, and besides, the red paint protects the face from the hot sun." Nitana then decorated my moccasins with paint, thinking that it improved their appearance.

At some distance down the stream, was a camp of

white people. They were evidently emigrants moving into Canada, for they had several prairie schooners and a large herd of horses. They all came in a crowd, men, women and children, to stare, and to gape at the Indians, and to examine everything belonging to us. Many were the surprised and curious glances directed at me, but I escaped by going upon the prairie after my

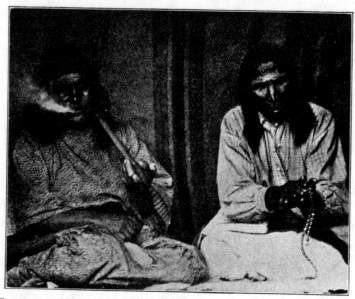

ONESTA AND NITANA HOLDING CEREMONIAL WITH SACRED MOUNTAIN LION CLAW NECKLACE.

(Onesta is chanting while painting necklace. Nitana is praying with the Pipe.)

saddle horse. By the time we were ready to start the sun was intensely hot, with a warm breeze from the south. My thermometer registered 98 degrees in the shade and 125 degrees in the sun. Suddenly the wind changed, and blew furiously from the north, carrying with it clouds of dust and sand, which filled our eyes and mouths. In a few minutes there was a fall of more than 60 degrees in the temperature, compelling me to dismount and walk, to keep warm.

A great change now appeared in the face of the country.   Instead of the high and rocky ridges of Northern Montana, the Alberta country was undulating. The soil was rich and black and the prairie covered with luxuriant grass.   I saw everywhere many " Fairy Rings," both large and small, made by the peculiar growth of a species of fungus, or puff balls. They are identical with the mushroom growths common in our eastern fields, and popularly known as " Fairy Rings," or " Fairy Dances," supposed to be caused by fairies in their dances.   Kionama's idea of them was, that they were buffalo wallows, which had gradually filled up.   But Onesta advanced the Indian belief, that they had been caused in olden times by the dances of buffalo, the large circles by old buffaloes, and the small circles by buffalo calves.   Puff Balls, called Dusty Stars by the Blackfeet, because supposed to be meteors fallen during the night, grow around the circles and emit a puff of dust when pressed.   We may have in this belief the origin of their use of the broad band of dark colour, with its circle of discs or Dusty Stars, as the bottom decoration of the Blackfoot tipi. This band, usually painted in red, with the discs in yellow or other colour, suitably symbolises the Earth as the foundation for all things.

Menake and Nitana were industrious collectors of medicinal herbs and edible plants.   Whether in camp, or on the trail, whether in the forest, or along the streams, or even on the dry and dusty plains, they never lost an opportunity for collecting them.   They dried them before the camp fire, or in the hot sun.   They used some of them in seasoning the meats and stews, others as medicines for the children's sore throats and other complaints, and as a tonic for Kionama's weak stomach. Menake showed me a special collection she was taking as a present to Brings-down-the-Sun, containing plants he used in doctoring, but did not grow in the north country. When I started a botanical collection [1] of my own, the women were constantly on the look-out to aid me, pointing out the different varieties, telling their Indian names, and explaining their different uses and methods of preparation. Our outfit was frequently halted to secure additional specimens.

It surprised me to learn the number of perfumes used by the Blackfeet. Menake said that sweet grass was the most popular among the women. It is dried and made into braids and placed among their clothes, or carried in small bags. They also use beaver musk, red cedar, punk from the cottonwood tree, buds from the balsam poplar and dried blossoms of dog fennel and meadow rue. The leaves of sweet pine are also valued for their delightful odour, when confined in small buckskin bags, and are also used to give a pleasant fragrance to hair grease. In gathering sweet pine, the women distinguished the right species from others by its branches turning upwards.

In the late afternoon I saw, in the far distance, a green line, which Kionama said consisted of trees, marking the course of the river Okoan (Belly), so named, because the outlines of the hills along its course resemble those of a buffalo's paunch.

Riding ahead of our party, I was the first to enter the valley, and soon found myself in the midst of the Kainau camp (Blood Indians). I looked with keen interest at everything about me,—the decorations on

[1] See Appendix.

CAMP OF THE BLOODS.

their lodges, the picturesque travois and the costumes of men, women and children. It was a warm evening, and the fronts and sides of the lodges were lifted for better ventilation. The centre of interest was a large gathering of Indians near a big lodge. It was evidently a ceremonial, for they were seated in a circle, beneath a shelter made of an old lodge lining, and held in place by a cluster of poles tied together near the top. Because of the warm day, the men had discarded their clothing. At the back reclined a distinguished looking Indian, one of their leading chiefs, and, in front of him, was seated an elderly chief, who was evidently a visitor. He held a long red-stone pipe, from which he drew copious whiffs of smoke. A fire burned at one side, over which a large kettle hung from a tripod. A squaw had arrived from the river, with a travois, to which were fastened pails filled with water. On the edge of a high cut-bank nearby, an old Indian was seated, placidly smoking, facing the setting sun.

Meanwhile, a horseman came to meet me. When he saw I was a stranger, he raised his hand, and signed to know who I was. I replied, that I was travelling with a party of Pi-kun-ni (South Piegans), and that my people were behind. He closely inspected everything I had, from my horse's brand to each article of clothing I wore. Kionama, with the rest of the party, soon came in sight, and my new companion rode back to meet them. He proved to be Wolf Robe, an old friend of Onesta's. After conversing a few minutes, Wolf Robe led the way down the river to One Spot's camp, a near relative of Menake's. One Spot, with Snake Woman, his wife, also Cotton Tail, Good-young-man, and others hurried forth to greet us. One Spot insisted upon our sharing his lodge, but Kionama and Onesta replied, that in such warm weather we preferred camping in the open. He directed us to a place, sheltered from the west wind by a large grove of poplars and cottonwoods, and where the Pome-piskun (Greasy Cliff) stream flows into the Okoan River. Before our wagons were unpacked, the Blood women came · with presents of food. This is an old Indian custom, originating in the desire to obviate the inconvenience to visitors of preparing their first meal, when the tipis had to be pitched. Snake Woman, wife of One Spot, was the first to come with her baby on her back, bearing sarvis berries, a pail of tea and dried meat. To the South Piegans these sarvis berries were the first of the season and therefore it was necessary, before eating, to make an offering to the Sun. All waited, while Onesta held a berry up, with the prayer that we all might have abundance of food during the coming year, and then we followed his example, by planting a berry in the ground, with a similar prayer to the Underground Spirits.

When the Blood women returned to their lodges, their presents were promptly repaid by Menake and Nitana with tobacco, rice, flour and meat.

CHAPTER XXVII

CAMP OF THE BLOODS

Reserve and haughtiness of the Bloods.—Pathetic mourning of a mother for her son.—Tragedy of Opiowan, "The Mad Indian."—Journey along the Okoan River.—Onesta and Nitana pray for a prosperous journey and my success.—Onesta teaches me two queer Blackfeet songs.—Beautiful valley of the North Piegans.—The trail along the Crow Lodge River.—Interesting Indian names for local topography. —Lookout Butte and the Indian watchers.—Camp of Brings-down-the-Sun.—His dignified and hospitable welcome.—Our attractive camp under the cottonwoods.—Indian custom of exchanging gifts.— Ideal camp of a happy and contented Indian clan.

WE remained several days in the Blood camp to rest our horses and visit Indian relatives and friends. The Bloods are a fine looking tribe, but reserved and haughty. They seem to be on the best of terms with the North Blackfeet, but are not popular with other tribes, because of their conceit and arrogance. The Piegans have a saying, "He is just like a Blood, he likes to show off." They also speak of the Bloods as "generous givers, but always seeking to get back as large a return as possible."

An incident occurred, while I was present at a Sun-dance of the Piegans, which illustrates the peculiar manners of the Bloods. It was in a large assembly of Indians, including representatives from sixteen different tribes, guests of the Piegans, who were gathered around the Sun-lodge, listening to the war stories of prominent chiefs. Unlike their white brothers, it is the custom of

Indians to always listen with respectful attention to the speeches of their leaders, without regard to their importance.   But not so with a visiting band of young men from the Bloods.   While the old Piegan chiefs were recounting their brave deeds in battle, the Bloods

HEAD CHIEF OF BLOODS.

gave great affront and transgressed all custom and etiquette by publicly ridiculing their stories.

For my own part, I have found that the Bloods are not so approachable, and lack the cordiality and open hearted friendliness so characteristic of the Piegans.

After sunset, on our way to One Spot's lodge, we were startled by the mournful wailing of a woman, standing upon a lonely butte, overlooking the river valley.

Snake Woman told us that she was the mother of Has-many-guns-in-the-camp, mourning over his death. The sad news had just come, that he had died in the camp of the North Blackfeet. While absent on a long journey, he had heard that his wife had left him for another. Has-many-guns mourned so deeply over the loss of

BLOODS DANCING.

his wife, that he refused to eat and finally died from starvation.

The similarity of the cause of this pathetic incident,—the infidelity of a wife,—reminds me of a much more tragical event, which happened in the winter of 1896, during my visit among the Piegans.

Opiowan, a Blood Indian, living just across the border in Alberta, killed his rival, who had stolen his wife's

affections.   For many weeks he kept the Indian families
on both sides of "the line" at the highest pitch of
excitement and alarm because of his sudden attacks
and cold blooded murders.   He proved himself more
than a match for the Canadian Mounted Police in his
Indian cunning and resourcefulness in evading arrest.

This Opiowan tragedy illustrates the capabilities of a
single Indian for cunning, ferocity and physical en-

BLOOD CUSTOM OF PILING WINTER WOOD.

durance, when fired by revenge for wrongs suffered.
When one such was multiplied into a band, or tribe united
for revenge, as in the cases of the Sioux, Apaches and
Nez-Perces, it meant a bloody war against the whites.
War meant extermination for the Indian, for it
developed among the whites that bitter animosity
which was universal along the frontier and still finds
expression in that laconic but barbarous saying, "The
only good Indian is a dead Indian."

Opiowan was reported as frequenting so many localities

and as moving about with such incredible swiftness, while murdering indiscriminately, that all, whether in the mountains, or on the plains, were in dread of a surprise by him. The Piegan women spoke of him in great fear as the "Mad Indian," while the mere mention of his name filled the children with terror. When I asked Snake Woman for the Blood account, she related the following thrilling story of vengeance under the "unwritten law."

Tragedy of Opiowan, "The Mad Indian."

"Opiowan once lived at peace with all our tribe. He was known as an industrious man, living contentedly in a lodge with his two wives, his mother and his only child, a boy of eight. A young man named Natomina, a former lover of Pretty Wolverine, his favourite wife, began coming to the lodge. When he became so deeply enamoured that his attentions were the talk of the tribe, Opiowan warned him to desist. One day Opiowan prepared for a journey, as if he would be absent for several days. He rode off over a ridge, but, instead of going farther, lay in ambush to watch his lodge. When he saw Natomina and Pretty Wolverine cross the meadow together, he quietly returned and with drawn knife came unexpectedly upon the guilty lovers. He mutilated and killed Natomina, but spared his wife. Having ordered her to return quietly to the lodge, he continued his journey. When the Mounted Police discovered Natomina's dead body, some days later, they carried it through the camp, vainly endeavouring to find some trace of the murderer. When Opiowan returned from his journey, he heard the people talking about the mysterious murder. At night the face of Natomina was always before him, so that he was unable to sleep. He dreaded hearing a rider enter the camp, lest it might be one of the Mounted Police coming to arrest him. He became morose and gloomy and shunned his friends, imagining that all had turned against him. He thought he must be going mad and desired to live no longer. Resolved to die the death of a brave, he vowed he would kill as many people as he could, both Indian and white. Passing the store at night, and seeing the trader standing near a window, he raised his rifle and fired. He saw the trader fall forward upon his face and then fled in the darkness. Returning to his lodge, he told his wives that he had shot a white man, and he must hide in the mountains. The lodge was quickly taken down, and their belongings packed upon a travois. Opiowan put on his war charm and, painting his face, chanted a war song. They entered the Rocky Mountains, camping in a small glade, where their lodge was hidden by the trees. When the Mounted Police heard of Opiowan's escape, they knew he must be the murderer and followed his trail. But Opiowan, watching from a neighbouring cliff, saw them coming. Knowing they would enter the glade from below, he left his mother and son in the lodge and with his wives circled through the forest. The police tied their horses at the lower end of the glade and advanced on foot. They shot into the lodge, but the boy and woman lay flat and were not hit. Opiowan then came quickly from the forest and made off with their horses. The police captured the old mother and the boy and withdrew, after destroying the lodge, but Opiowan, with his two wives, escaped by going northward along the Rockies. When they came to the country of the North Piegans, they entered the Porcupine Mountains and hid

themselves in the forest.   Whenever they ran short of
food, or ammunition, Opiowan stole down at night into
an Indian camp, shooting anyone who would oppose his
demands.   One day he rode boldly through the main
street of a small town (Cardston), and shot one of the
police.   They followed him many miles, but were unable
to capture him.   On a big flat beyond the Kootenai
River, Opiowan killed another of his pursuers, whose
horse had outrun the others, and seizing the policeman's
rifle and ammunition, escaped into the forest.   The
autumn passed and winter came on with intense cold
and deep snow, but no one could find his hiding place.
One night, in a heavy snow storm, Opiowan left the
camp of Brings-down-the-Sun, where he had suddenly
appeared to demand food and amunition.   He lost his way
and was followed by the police, but again managed to
elude his pursuers.   At last, fearing that his wives might
desert him while absent on foraging expeditions, he
hobbled them, tying their hands and feet, but leaving
them separated from each other.   Managing to free
themselves, they made their way down the mountains
by night and came into the Blood camp on the plains,
where they were arrested.   Opiowan, deserted by his
wives, without food and suffering from the intense cold,
was finally driven from the mountains by starvation.
He came one night to the lodge of his brother Sixepe,
who kept him in hiding.   The information was carried
to the police, who surrounded the camp, and ordered
them to give up the outlaw.   Our chiefs in their
alarm finally prevailed upon Sixepe to betray his
brother into the hands of the police.   As he lay tied
hand and foot, Opiowan warned his brother that he
would die first.   Within four days Sixepe suddenly
sickened and died. Opiowan also died soon after, killing

himself by piercing the arteries of both wrists with a sharp awl."

We left the Blood camp soon after sunrise, riding along the Okoan River, and through groves of large

SUN-SHELTER AT MIDDAY.

cottonwoods.   After fording the river, we turned towards the mountains and the country of the North Piegans.   Heavy clouds covered the plain, completely hiding the rising sun.   But the snow-clad summits of the Rockies in the west, glowed in the rays that shone above the clouds.   We followed an old Indian trail known to Kionama and Onesta, a short cut, that took us across a broad plain.   When we entered the hill country beyond, the clouds disappeared and the hot sun again shone in a clear sky. My thermometer registered 98 degrees in the shade and 130 degrees in the sun. We rested our horses at midday near a small lake. The women erected a shelter from the sun by throwing canvas over a wagon pole, supported on a tripod. The sides were then raised, allowing the breeze to blow through.

In the early afternoon clouds gathered over the Rocky Mountains. Electrical storms appeared in all directions and the air gradually became cooler. While slowly winding our way among the high hills, I heard Onesta and Nitana chanting a religious song. I quietly rode behind them and, after becoming thoroughly familiar with the air, joined in the chant. They explained that it was an ancient custom, while travelling towards a strange country, to chant and offer prayers to the Sun for a prosperous journey and safe return. Onesta said, " On this occasion, we have been praying also, that you may be successful in securing the information you desire from the North Piegans. I intend giving the Sup-weyo-kinni (Crow Beaver) ceremonial in their camp and I will teach you some of the chants, so that you can help us in the singing." Nitana expressed her uneasiness, lest some misfortune might overtake us, because one of the medicine sticks of the Crow Beaver Bundle had been broken while in the Blood camp.

Onesta taught me the Worm song, which the Blackfeet use to make worms dance. When we came to a wild rose bush covered with cobwebs enclosing small worms (Tent Caterpillars), he directed me to stand near and sing, " Kom-i-os-ché ! Kom-i-os-ché ! (Worms ! Worms !), beating time by clapping my hands. To my surprise, the worms, which had been perfectly still, began to move as if slowly waking up. They soon became more active, until all stood erect and swayed their heads to and fro. Onesta sang another song, with which, he said, he could make a sand-piper dance, by clapping his hands and singing, "Ék-si-sa-que ! Ék-si-sa-que !" (Meat ! Meat !)

He called my attention to the swallows hovering over the horses to secure hairs for their nests, and also to the grasshoppers flying high in the air "to colour their wings." Grasshoppers' wings are said to be without colour, until they fly into the sunlight, which turns them red, yellow and black.

When we finally gained the summit of the ridge, we looked down upon the broad valley of the North Piegans, through which flowed a river, bordered with huge cottonwood trees. Towards the north were the Porcu-pine Mountains covered with dark forests of pine, and westward were the snow-capped summits of the Rockies. While descending towards the valley, we met several young men of the North Piegans, guarding their tribal herds of cattle and horses. They guided us towards the camp of Brings-down-the-Sun. One of them, whom I afterwards discovered was the son of Crow Eagle, the head chief, rode with me. He pointed out an enormous solitary rock upon the prairie, and said : "Many years ago a huge grizzly lived in a cave beneath that rock. Around it grow different varieties of berry bushes from seeds carried there by the bear." The Porcupine Moun-tains are so named, because the ridges bristle so thickly with tall trees that they resemble a porcupine's back. The river in the valley before us was called Old Man's River by the white men, but Crow Lodge by the Indians, the vision for the Crow Lodge having been received in former days near its source. The high mountain, with a broad slide shining like a huge glacier, is called Turtle

Mountain by the whites, but is named Lodge Lining by the Indians, because its slopes are uniform and regular, resembling the inside lining of a lodge.

Having reached the river, Crow Eagle's son invited us to his tipi. But, when Onesta explained that we must go direct to the camp of Brings-down-the-Sun, he

HERDER LASSOING WILD HORSE.

pointed out to us a distant bend in the Crow Lodge River, saying that we would find Natosin Nepe-e (Brings-down-the-Sun) there among the big trees on the north bank.

After the young men had left us, I observed a single horseman appear upon the summit of a distant ridge and remain to watch our course, that we might not go astray. The trail led down a steep hill and into the

valley. A wolf standing motionless, watched us from
the head of a small ravine. The colour of his coat was
so like the grass and willows surrounding him that he
had an excellent colour protection. The deep shade
of the big trees and luxuriant vegetation of the river
valley were most refreshing, after the fierce sunlight and
heat of the plains. The meadows were bright with a

"A Single Horseman Appeared upon a Ridge
to Watch Our Course."

beautiful pink flower called Manekape (young man) by
the Blackfeet, but known by botanists as Horse Mint,
or Monarda scabra. The trail ran sometimes close to
the broad, swift river, now through meadows of grass
and flowers and now among the cottonwoods. Passing
through an opening among the trees, I saw, in the
distance, a group of Indians, wrapped in blankets,
standing on the edge of a high cut-bank overlooking the
valley. They were watching our approach with evident

interest.   Onesta explained to me that it was a " Lookout Butte" for the camp of Brings-down-the-Sun.
From its summit, not only the river valley, but also the
surrounding plains could be viewed for a long distance.
As we drew nearer, I discovered that the watchers were
women.   One with a baby on her back, her long black
hair flying in the wind, and her figure distinctly
outlined against the evening sky, was standing surrounded by children.   Nitana recognised her as Long
Hair, favourite daughter of Brings-down-the-Sun.   As
we approached the edge of the clearing, a group of
white lodges among the trees came into view.   It was
the camp of the noted medicine man, with his children,
grandchildren and great-grandchildren.   In front of a
lodge, beneath a huge cottonwood, and close to where
the trail again entered the trees, a tall figure, with a
blanket wrapped closely around him, stood gazing
intently at us.   When he recognised Onesta, he hailed
us and said : " My children, I will be glad to have you
pitch your lodges close to mine, under the big trees on
the other side of the trail."   I rode nearer to observe
him more closely.   He was an elderly man with clean-
cut Indian features.   His hair was grey and the deep
lines in his face indicated a strong character, burdened
with care and responsibility.   With hand upraised and
head thrown back, he had the air of one accustomed to
command.   Pointing to the meadow, he continued,
" However, if you wish, you can camp in the open at
the edge of the cottonwoods.   Sometimes heavy
wind-storms tear branches from the trees, and if your
lodges were beneath they might injure you.   On the
north side of the clearing you will find a spring, where
the water is cold and good to drink.   It will be better
for you to take your horses upon the hills, where they

can feed upon the abundant bunch grass." With these
words the chief withdrew into his lodge.

The cool shade of the woods proved such an attrac-
tion that we promptly selected the spot beneath the big
trees pointed out by Brings-down-the-Sun. While our
lodges were being pitched, Sis-tse (Bird), wife of the
chief, with her daughters and daughters-in-law, arrived,
bearing many presents. This exchange of gifts among
the women was always an interesting performance.
They often gave many objects, that were highly prized
by themselves, although they might seem of little value
to white people. For instance, Nitana received on this
occasion an old tea-pot, a wash tub and board, a small
bag of beans, two plates, two cups, a copper kettle and a
butcher knife. In return, she gave two blankets, two
pairs of moccasins, paints dug by herself on Birch Creek,
and a few trinkets. Bird brought an invitation from
Brings-down-the-Sun, for Onesta, Kionama and their
friend, the white man, to eat with him at sunset.
When we walked down the wooded trail towards the
tipis of the chief and his son Running Wolf, standing
close together at the end of a grove of huge cottonwoods,
we came upon an ideal camp and the most peaceful and
charming picture of a happy and contented Indian
family it has ever been my good fortune to see. A large
outside fire sent a shower of golden sparks into the air.
It lighted up the white tipis with their clusters of
tapering poles, and tops deeply browned by smoke, and
brought them into sharp contrast with the dark trunks
and green branches of the big cottonwood trees.
Grouped around the fire, and dressed in brightly
coloured Indian clothes, were women and young girls
engaged in animated conversation, while cooking,
making clothes and moccasins and playing Indian games.

To one side a little baby hammock, swung between two saplings, was rocked by a mother singing a Blackfeet slumber song. When we stepped into the circle of bright firelight, this peaceful scene was rudely disturbed by a dog dashing at us, with flattened ears and snarling fiercely. A squaw shouted, " Puksiput ! kokun ! Kops-ksis-e ! " (Come back here ! you pup ! Swell Nose !), but the damage was done. The group of young girls, warned of the approach of the strange white man, fled precipitately into the woods, and the charming circle was quickly broken.

CHAPTER XXVIII

CAMP OF BRINGS-DOWN-THE-SUN

We dine with Brings-down-the-Sun. —Onesta introduces me to the old chief.—He declines to impart his knowledge.—Recites the wrongs which caused his mistrust of the white race.—Allows me to remain in his camp.—I meet his wife and youngest daughter.—He offers us free use of their wild berry supply.—His statesmanlike reasons for preserving their natural resources of trees and berry bushes.—First thunder of the summer is heard marking time for opening Medicine Pipes.—I meet my friend Bull Plume conducting a Pipe ceremonial. —Hospitality of Brings-down-the-Sun.—Indian children's fear of white men.—Interesting scenes along a stream.—A contented family of beavers.—A miniature camp with complete doll outfit.—Games of boys and girls.—"Wheel and arrow," a gambling game of men.—An extended sunset view from Lookout Butte.

WE found Brings-down-the-Sun reclining against his lodge-back, waiting our arrival. He directed Onesta, his nephew, to a place on his right, while Kionama and I took seats on a comfortable blanket-bed on his left. A small fire burned in the centre, and, from a hot coal, arose the fragrant smoke of dried sweet grass. Everything inside the lodge was scrupulously neat and clean. The shining cooking utensils were stored in boxes by the door. The provisions and clothing were hidden away behind the beds in bags and painted parfleches, while articles decorated with beads and coloured porcupine quills hung from the lodge poles. After a preliminary smoke and a simple meal of bread, dried meat and tea, Onesta addressed Brings-down-the-Sun :

"We have brought this white man, A-pe-ech-eken, the adopted son of Mad Wolf, a long journey under a hot sun to see you. On our way we met Spotted Eagle and Big Smoke. We also visited the lodge of One Spot in the Kainau Camp. I have told them all that we were taking A-pe-ech-eken to the North Piegans, to learn from you about our legends and customs and that you might instruct him concerning the worship of the Sun. You are my uncle, A-pe-ech-eken is my friend, and I ask that you do this."

Brings-down-the-Sun gazed keenly into my face and then replied very earnestly: "The white race have always cheated and deceived us. They have deprived

BRINGS-DOWN-THE-SUN.

us of our country. Now they are trying to take away our religion, by putting a stop to the ceremonial sacred to the Sun. Our religion was given to us by the Sun and Moon, and we will never give it up, while the Sun and Moon last. The white people have given us no good reason why they wish to take away our religion. We do not fight, nor drink whisky at our ceremonials, and there is nothing harmful that can come from them. We have been struggling to keep up our religion, in order that our people may be happy, and that they may lead better lives. When I began preparations for a Sun ceremonial this spring, in accordance with the vow, made by one of our women for the healing of her sick son, the agent shut off our rations. He would not allow my family to receive the food, upon which we are dependent. Because of these things my heart has become bitter, and I have made a vow, that I will have nothing more to do with the white race. It does not now seem to me advisable to talk further about these things, and to explain our religion to a white man. However, Onesta is my kinsman and has brought this white man a long distance. He can remain in my camp for a few days to rest, and, during that time, it is possible that we may grow to know each other better."

At this moment Bird, the chief's wife, entered the lodge with her daughter, a very pretty young woman. The mother was small and slender. In her youth she must have been remarkably good looking. She gave me a smile of welcome, and the old chief explained, that the girl was his youngest daughter, and that she was called "Whistling - all-n i ght," because she was born in

"WHISTLING-ALL-NIGHT" AND "CRIES-EARLY-IN-THE-MORNING," DAUGHTER AND GRANDDAUGHTER OF BRINGS-DOWN-THE-SUN.

January, the moon when the jack rabbit whistles at night, in calling his mate, just as the bull elk is accustomed to do. Brings-down-the-Sun said to Kionama, " I am glad in my heart that you have come to stay in my camp. We pitch our tipis in this grove of cottonwoods every summer, to gather sarvis berries for our use, when the snows are deep. You will find many kinds of berries on all sides. You can eat them now, or gather and dry them for your winter supply, just as we do. I ask, however, that you will be careful not to injure the trees, or break the branches of the berry bushes. I make this request. because I am looking ahead for my tribe. I am anxious to preserve these big trees and the berry bushes for our children. I am accustomed to admonish my people, in this manner, warning them not to be short-sighted like the Bloods. They once had many large trees along their river, but they cut them down for firewood. Now their country is bare and they have few berries. I am continually advising my people not to cut down the trees along the river, but to haul their wood from the forests on the mountains. They have followed my advice and we still have our big leaf trees (cottonwoods). The long leaved trees are the spear-leaf trees (Balsam-Poplar). We also have round-leaf trees (Quaking-Asps) and brush-sticks (Willows). We always speak of large trees as ' The Old Time Trees' and the small ones as ' Young People's Trees.'" When leaving, I presented the chief with a large silk handkerchief, his wife with a blanket, while the daughter, Whistling-all-night, showed great delight, when I gave her a set of pearl buttons.

The first night of our arrival in Brings-down-the-Sun's camp, I spread my blankets beneath a large cottonwood tree. Although I was very tired after our long ride in the hot sun, and from assisting in the laborious work of making a permanent camp, caring for the horses, unloading the wagons, cutting the lodge poles and firewood, pitching the tipis and starting the fires, I was too restless to sleep. The night was unusually warm and sultry. Heavy clouds had gathered over the Rockies and extended over the plains, bursting upon us, during the night, with wind, lightning and crashing peals of thunder.

Next morning, Onesta said that it was the first

thunder heard by the Piegans. In Montana it had thundered earlier and the South Piegans had already brought out their Medicine Pipes, but the North Piegans had been waiting, and now they must give the ceremonial of unrolling their Pipes and renewing the tobacco in their sacred bundles. A messenger came into camp, announcing that Running Antelope would

BULL PLUME LEADING THE CEREMONIAL.

open his Medicine Pipe and invited us all to the ceremonial. Onesta, Nitana, Bird and Long Hair were going, so I accompanied them several miles up the river to Running Antelope's camp. When we entered the lodge, the ceremonial had already begun. To my surprise, I saw that the leader was Bull Plume, the chief, whom I had met when visiting Mad Wolf. He was so astonished at my unexpected appearance, that the rattles fell from his hands, and he stopped in the middle of a chant. When he had recovered himself, he shook my hand, telling the assembled people my Indian name, and explaining that I was the adopted son of Mad Wolf. Bull Plume then turned to me and said: " I can tell you how many moons have passed, since I last met you in Mad Wolf's lodge, for I have kept count and have marked the moons in my records." He handed me a pair of rattles, requesting me to join in the chant and take part in the ceremonial. After a number of dances, followed by a feast, the Medicine Pipe was opened and held up. Fresh tobacco was also inserted in the Bundle, in place of the old, which was distributed among the people. When the Medicine Pipe ceremonial was finished, Running Antelope's wife availed herself of the opportunity to open a Medicine Bonnet, in fulfilment of a vow made by her son. During the winter, when he was very sick, he made a vow to the Sun, that, if he recovered, his mother who had given the Sun-dance and owned a Medicine Bonnet, would give a ceremonial. The boy recovered, and the mother was now fulfilling his promise.

On this same day, Brings-down-the-Sun drove thirty miles across the plains, under a burning sun, that he might secure, from the nearest trading store, provisions for his visitors. He took with him Mysterious Woman, his young daughter-in-law, and Sinopa, the daughter of Menake. When they returned, Brings-down-the-Sun carried all of his purchases (five loaves of bread and some fresh meat) to our camp, at the same time offering apologies that he had so little to offer. He said: " Some people may think me foolish for taking two young women with me, but I thought they would be pleased at seeing the strange sights of the town." Sinopa afterwards told her mother that, when they reached town

(Macleod, Canada) the old chief took them to a restaurant
and ordered a fine turkey dinner for them. While
they were eating, he visited the bakers to buy bread,
and hunted for a good store to secure the best meat.
Before they started home he gave Mysterious Woman
five cents with which to buy candy, remarking that " it
was not well to spend more for sweet stuff."

When I walked through the wood to explore the
trails, I noticed groups of children slyly peeping through
the trees to get a look at the " strange white man."
They had been taught from infancy that white men are
dangerous monsters, for whenever I came near, they
quickly disappeared like frightened deer, but I gradually
overcame their instinctive dread ; at first by seeming
to ignore their presence, and finally gaining their
confidence, by small presents and bribes of candy. I
investigated the spring pointed out by Brings-down-the-
Sun for our water supply. It proved to be the stillwater of a very beautiful stream. Along its shady
banks, I found delicious wild strawberries, choke
cherries and sarvis berry bushes, growing high above my
head and laden down with ripe fruit. In the wood,
were great numbers of beautiful song birds. I recognised the yellowthroat, cat bird, whitethroat, goldfinch,
white crowned sparrow and many varieties of warblers.
In a grove of cottonwoods, beside the river, I discovered
the fresh tracks of a family of beavers. There were
tiny footprints of the children in the soft mud and the
large tracks of old beavers. I saw their recent cuttings
and also weather-beaten stumps of trees felled by them,
many years ago. When I spoke to Onesta of my find,
he said ; " Some beavers, like many people, never seem
to be satisfied and are continually travelling, but this
family, you speak of, have lived here undisturbed for

many years. They have a sandy beach and a mud bottom, with plenty of food, and are contented with their home."

Following a trail, leading past Brings-down-the-Sun's tipi, and crossing the stream near the deep pool, where every day the old chief and his entire family took their early morning plunge, I met Long Hair coming from the stream with a bucket of water. Nitana sat nearby upon a grassy bank washing Yellow Mink. It was a beautiful spot. In the mirror-like stillwater were perfect reflections of the arching trees, the tipis close to the shore, and the blue smoke floating from their tops. The children and young people had congregated along the banks, to wade and swim and play their primitive games. I saw a young girl poling a raft. She looked very picturesque in her squaw dress, with hair hanging in long braids over her shoulders. She wore white shell earrings, a braided health-charm fastened in her front hair, and a long necklace of dried sarvis berries. When the craft finally grounded upon a large rock in mid-stream, I felt like going to her assistance but, realising that it would only subject her to the gossip of the camp, I remained at a distance, and contented myself with taking her picture.

In an open glade was a miniature encampment, where a group of little girls were playing. They had men and women-dolls dressed in buck-skin, and cloth costumes, with real human hair and leggings and beaded belts and moccasins. There were gopher skins for robes, little knife-sheaths, tanning-tools and baby-cases. In the centre of the camp circle of miniature tipis, they had the largest tipi with long poles, for the head chief, also small lodge backs, painted parfleches and a diminutive medicine case, hanging from a tripod.

A boisterous game was being played by lively boys and girls. The game was similar to our 'catcher,' in which all endeavoured to avoid the touch of one of their number, at whom they sang derisively, "Ape-koi-ya-soma-tia-kake-kina" (You are a mangey old skunk with no hair along your backbone).[1]

The young girls played a game called, "Throwing

CHILD'S PLAY TIPI.

willow arrows." They used a large arrow with a string of plaited horse-hair attached to one end. The first in turn threw it into a bush. If the second thrower could hit the larger arrow with a smaller one, or even touch the horse hair, she won an arrow from the first player. But, if she missed, and the first player in turn threw a

[1] Song 9. See p. 515.

small arrow touching the second arrow, the latter became the winner. The girls also had a game of "hiding bones," made of antelope bones, beautifully carved and decorated. The boys had another curious and amusing game. They sat in two long rows. One of the players, with his eyes closed, walked back and forth between them, each side trying to confuse him, by calling to him to go this way, or that. If he came too close and touched one of the players with his foot, that boy jumped up, and taking him upon his back, held him by the legs with his head hanging down. All then rose and, taking hold, swung him round and round. If he called out the name of a girl, saying : "She is my sweetheart," they stopped, but, if he was ashamed to do so, they kept swinging him until they were tired out. If the boy lacked nerve to endure the swinging, he acknowledged it by spitting and they dropped him at once.

The boys had a bow-and-arrow game. A stake arrow was driven into the ground and they shot in turn, each trying to hit the stake, or come as near as possible. If the first player shot so close, that the second in turn thought he would have difficulty in beating it, he walked up to the stake arrow and danced beside it, to secure "power" for shooting, beating time with an arrow upon his bow while singing, "I am going to hit it first." If the second player shot well also, the third danced, seeking for even greater skill, singing, "No, I am the one, who will hit the stake arrow first."

There was also the "wheel and arrow," a gambling game played by men with arrows and a small wheel with beaded spokes. The wheel was rolled over a smooth and level course, each player throwing an arrow at it. The points were counted according to the position of the arrows when the wheel stopped. Its origin is very

ancient and it is often mentioned in old stories and
legends.   Its use as a gambling game was very general
among the plains-tribes.

Passing from these interesting scenes of camp life,
I climbed the steep ascent of " Lookout Butte," which
Onesta told me had been used for many generations by
Brings-down-the-Sun and his ancestors, as a place of
meditation and prayer.   A wonderful prospect was
spread out in every direc-
tion.   By the winding
course of green cotton-
wood trees, I could trace
the beautiful valley of
the Crow Lodge River
westward to its very
source among the snow-
crowned summits of the
Rocky Mountains, and
then follow it eastward
like a shining silver
band, far out upon the
prairies.   A rainbow from
a straggling storm ap-

WHEEL AND ARROW GAME.

peared in mid air, hanging over the river.   As the sun
was sinking behind the mountains, the clouds became
suffused with red up to the zenith.   At the foot of
the butte, and among the trees below, lay the picturesque Indian camp, with its white lodges and
brightly blazing outside fires.   The continuous beating
of drums came from our South Piegan camp, where
Onesta was making preparations for his Crow Beaver
ceremonial, to be held on the following day.

Seated in this ancestral place of meditation, and
under the spell of my peaceful and beautiful sur-

roundings, a strong doubt entered my mind as to whether the white races, in the pride of their civilisation, fit their natural environments much better than this patriarchal settlement of Blackfeet.

While we have mastered and harnessed the forces of nature to do our bidding, and have achieved wonderful things in science and industrial combination, have we, with all of our striving and complex life, attained a much higher average of character, contentment and loyalty to the community interests, than was attained under the simple life and few wants of the average Blackfoot family, before the invasion of the white race ? We could look in vain in such camps as that of the North Piegans, nestled among the cottonwoods, to find the depravity, misery and consuming vice, which involve multitudes in the industrial centres of all the large cities of Christendom.

CHAPTER XXIX

Various methods used in obtaining proper names.—Interesting illustrations of naming children.—Manner of changing men's names.—Women's names.—Names for strangers.—Names for animals.—Extended use of sign language among plains-tribes.

It is a wonderful provision of nature, which preserves the identity of the individual by infinite variations and combinations of facial features and other characteristics. All races of men emphasise this individuality still further by giving to such human entity a proper name. The various methods, by which this is done, furnish an interesting field of investigation. I found it so with the Blackfeet, but was not able to make an exhaustive study of the subject. I, however, discovered that the queer and fantastic proper names of the Blackfeet, which seem to most people either curious, or amusing, have often been improperly rendered into English equivalents which fail to express the Indian ideas.

I met with a reluctance among the Blackfeet to tell their names, which was prompted by a superstitious fear of the bad luck, or misfortune that might follow.

In common with other Indian tribes, the Blackfeet have no patronymics to denote ancestry, or surnames to designate family. It was, however, sometimes the case, that a distinguished name would be handed down from father to son. Thus Brings-down-the-Sun, having received in infancy the name of his distinguished father, Running Wolf, and being proud of the name, and the brave deeds it stood for, gave the same name to his son.

The Blackfeet used great care in the selection of appropriate proper names, being guided by certain customs and employing a variety of methods in obtaining them. Parents ordinarily entrusted the task of naming their children to others, usually to an old person, because they believed this would favour their reaching old age. When names were formally given, it was with the prayer that they might live to be old. They had a superstition against the choosing of children's names by young persons.

NITANA.

Names were often given because of some physical mark, or characteristic. The use of horses and the capture of horses from other tribes having been a prominent feature of their life, it was but natural that the word horse was used in a great variety of name combinations.

Dreams were depended upon for suggestions, which were said to come from the "Dream People," and they were also received from the animals. When Onesta's wife, Nitana, was once sleeping on the bank of the Missouri River, she heard, in a dream, a strange voice calling "Go away from there, Green Snake Woman, do not disturb that sleeping person!" and then again, "Go away from there, Green Snake Woman, do not waken that person!" When she awoke, she saw, by a strange coincidence, a rattlesnake near by with head erect, as if calling to her children. The young snakes were crawling beside their mother, and all went off together. When Nitana was afterwards asked to name her sister's

Two Sisters—Green Snake Woman and Blue Snake Woman.

little girls, she gave them the names of the rattlesnake's children.

Spotted Eagle, the medicine man, once dreamed that he was walking under the ground, following a man, whose comrade called him " Walking Underneath." The first male child Spotted Eagle was asked to name he called " Walking Underneath."

When Brings-down-the-Sun lay watching a family of beavers at their work, he heard the mother beaver calling her children by the names, Sa-ko-wai-stai (Last

Diver) and Sa-kowa-et-sosin (Last-one-to-swim-in-with-the-willows, referring to the beavers' food).　When the chief was asked by a relative to name two of his boys, he gave them the names of the beaver children.

Another custom was to name a child in honour of a

LAST-ONE-TO-SWIM-IN-WITH-THE-WILLOWS AND HIS SISTERS.

medicine animal, or bird, thereby invoking their protection, or the gift of their supernatural qualities for the child.　This had its counterpart in the custom of the Pilgrim Fathers of New England of choosing Christian names from Biblical characters and qualities and even sacred phrases.　It resembles, too, the more modern custom, which many observe, of giving the names of the saints to their children.

The name of the wife of Curly Bear, who is still alive, although now an old woman, had a singular origin in a religious act of her father. Many years ago, during a scourge of smallpox, her father prayed to the Sun, offering his girl baby as a propitiatory sacrifice to ward off the "great sickness" with the prayer, "Take her, O Sun! and leave the rest of my family!" But they all died save this baby. She alone was spared. From that day her name has been "Given Away."

Running Fisher and his wife (Lone-Charge-Woman) became discouraged because of the death of all their children, although they had carefully complied with the customary precautions and observances, to insure their living to old age. When another child, a girl, was born, they decided upon a different method. They named her Sis-toi-tsi-ma (Something-that-is-given-away). They allowed her to run wild, hoping by that method to escape the bad luck that had befallen their other children. She is alive to-day and the mother of a family.

Other names of girl babies that I met with were :—

 A-sa-na-ki = Cries-all-the-time.
 Ska-na-sa-ne = Cries-early-in-the-morning.
 A-na-to-ki = Pretty Head.
 So-ya-ksi-wa-wa-kas = Water-spider-woman.
 Sit-so-a-ki = Good-looking-water-bird.
 Sit-a-ka-poki = Stays-in-different-lodges.
 A-ka-no-kim = Everybody-down-on.
 also Blue Wings and Born-with-teeth.

The names of females were not changed after childhood as was the case with males. A boy's name was frequently changed when he became 16 or 18 years old and his character was sufficiently developed to make some trait prominent, or give promise of his after life. But, when he reached manhood, his name might be changed again to commemorate some deed of valour, or notable event.

" Behind-the-ear " was so named, because he shot an enemy behind the ear, and Many-white-horses, because his herd was composed entirely of white horses. Brings-down-the-Sun told me that his present name originated in a dream, in which the Sun God came down and stood beside him and said, " I take you for my friend, and I bestow upon you my supernatural power." When he related his dream to his people, they changed his name from Running Wolf to Natosin Nepe-e or Brings-down-the-Sun.

When a man distinguished himself as a warrior, in the face of the enemy, it was customary for him to name his girls in honour of his exploits. But they had a superstitious belief that if his claims were false, the child would die.

The following names of women will illustrate :

A-kops-iso = Took-many-things-with-a-scalp ; Kills-many ; Strikes-on-a-horse ; Catches-the-enemy ; and Catches-two-horses.

Mad Wolf named his daughter Strikes-on-both-sides, because as he said, "when captured by the enemy, I saved her life by striking them down on both sides of her."

The wife of Big Eyes was named by her father, Its-u-e-nikki = Kills-close-to-the-lake, because he killed an enemy in a fight close to a lake. I found many names of women, the first syllable of which was either " Strikes " or " Kills."

Strangers were given names from some peculiarity of their personal appearance. When Arthur Nevin, the musical composer, went with me among the Blackfeet,

they called him " Don't-lace-his-moccasins," not because
of any carelessness in tying his shoes, but because he
was said to resemble a Blood Indian of that name.
They called the author, A-pe-ech-eken = White Weasel,
because I was a blonde. They called Father De Smet
" Long Teeth " because of a peculiarity of his mouth.
" Long Knives " is their name for United States
cavalrymen equipped with sabres ; " Red Coats " for the
Canadian mounted police ; " Black Robes " for Catholic
priests, and " White Ties " for Protestant missionaries.

Names for animals are in like manner similarly
expressive, although sometimes difficult of rendering
into equivalent English words.

> Beaver ; Ksis-stukki = Cuts-trees-with-his-teeth.
> Buffalo ; Ee-neu-ah = Black Horns.
> Badger ; Me-sin-ski = Striped Face.
> Deer (White-tail) ; Au-a-tu-yi = Wags-his-tail.
> Coyote ; Kis-see-noh-o = Bastard ; or E-muck-o-tis-
> ah-pi-ce-yi = Small Wolf.
> Mule ; O-muck-stow-ki = Big-Ears.
> Horse ; Pono-kom-i-ta = Elk Dog.

Pono-kom-i-ta (horse) is a compound word composed
of Ponoka = Elk, and Emita = dog. Its etymology seems
to have been as follows. The elk was known and named
by the Blackfeet long before the appearance of horses.
When horses were introduced, and because they
resembled the elk in form, they applied to the new
animal their name for elk, but differentiated it, by
affixing their name for dog, expressing its use, the dog
having been their beast of burden before horses were
known.

Further illustrations of the appropriateness of
Blackfeet names for things will be found in Brings-

down-the-Sun's topography of the Old North Trail
(pp. 434–440); in his discourses on the names and
habits of birds (pp. 481–484); and on the names of
the different moons, the constellations and signs in the
heavens (pp. 486–488).

They also had phrases and proverbs tersely expressing
both wisdom and humour.

The phrase, " Ik-is-kaks-ksisi," = " His nose is short
for good nature," describes a man who loses his temper
quickly.

The phrase, " Ah-kit-kats-a-pin-soye," = His eyes are
dry from looking around so much," or, more literally,
" He has been looking around so much, that he winks
his eyes as if they were dry," describes a sight-seer, or
one absorbed and staring at the sights around him.

The art of talking by sign language, *i.e.* by a combination of facial expressions and bodily movements, which
is natural to man, attained a high degree of perfection
among the plains-tribes. Having different vocal
languages, their contact, when coming together in war
or in hunting buffalo, of necessity developed the use of
gesture-speech in the remote past. A tradition of the
Arapahoe tells us that the original Arapahoe,
the creator of all things, " taught them to talk
with their hands." Iron Hawk, a Sioux chief,
said to Captain W. P. Clark, " the sign language was
the gift of the Great Spirit. He gave the whites the
power to read and write and convey information in this
way. He gave us the power to talk with our hands and
arms and to send information to a distance with the
mirror, blanket and pony, and when we meet with
Indians who have a different spoken language from
ours, we can talk to them with signs." Alex. Henry,
a partner of the North Western Company (Montreal),

records in his journal (1806), " It is surprising how dexterous these natives of the plains are, in the art of communicating their ideas by signs. They will hold conference for several hours together upon different subjects and, during the whole time, not a single word will be pronounced on either side, and still they appear to understand each other perfectly."

The Blackfeet, because of their central location on the

VISITING INDIANS CONVERSING IN SIGN LANGUAGE.
(Second from left end is making sign for buffalo by crooking forefingers.)

Buffalo range, and frequent contact with other tribes, had constant use for sign language and were very proficient. I attended one of their large camps where representatives from 16 different tribes were present. Although unable to understand each other's spoken language, they talked freely and rapidly together in gesture speech. Each evening the visiting Indians withdrew to a ridge, overlooking the big camp, where I watched, with great interest, their graceful and expressive gestures, while conversing with the Blackfeet chiefs in the sign language.   I learned the equivalent ideas representing the names of the following tribes present and saw them expressed by signs readily understood by all.

> Arapahoe = Spotted People, because they had many spotted, or pinto horses.
>
> Blackfeet = Black moccasins, because the bottoms of their moccasins were black.
>
> Blood = Streak-across-the-mouth, a peculiar way the Bloods had of painting.
>
> Cheyenne = People - who - part - their - hair - in - the-middle.
>
> Crow = Bird flying.
>
> Flathead = Peculiar shape of the head.
>
> Gros Ventres (of the prairies), = Big Bellies, because they eat so much.
>
> Kutenai = Mountain People, People-who-live-in-the-mountains.
>
> Mandans = People-who-live-in-dirt-lodges.
>
> Nez Perce = Users-of-black-paint.
>
> Pend d'Oreille = Paddling People, or River-people-using-canoes.
>
> Piegan = Users-of-paint-on-the-cheeks.
>
> Sioux = Cut Throats, from the olden-time tradition that they cut off the heads of their victims in battle.
>
> Snake = A crawling serpent.

As an illustration of the Indian's method of conveying ideas by signs, I quote the manual equivalents for some of the above mentioned tribal names, for which I am indebted to "Indian Sign Language," by Captain W. P. Clark, Second Cavalry, United States Army.

Sioux = Concept.—Cutting off heads.

Sign : Hold right hand, back up, in front of left shoulder, height of throat, index finger extended and pointing to left, other fingers and thumb closed, move the hand horizontally to the right, index passing near throat.

Blackfeet.   Concept = Black Moccasins.

Sign : For moccasins, pass spread thumbs and index fingers over feet and toes to ankles, right hand over right foot, left hand over left foot, palms of hands towards and close to feet.   For black, point to something black in colour.

Crow.   Concept = Bird flying.

Sign : Bring extended hands, backs nearly up, in front, a little higher than and slightly to right and left of shoulders ; move the hands simultaneously a little downwards, slightly outwards, and a trifle to right and left, indicating motion of wings.

Flathead.   Concept = Peculiar shape of head.

Sign : Press the upper part of forehead and head with palms of hands, fingers extended and touching, tips of fingers touching above head.

Nez Perce.   Concept = Powder, because of their excessive use of a bluish black paint.

Sign : Hold extended left hand in front of body, back down, and rub tips of fingers and thumb of right hand just over left palm.

Snake.   Concept = Motion of a snake.

Sign : Hold right hand, back to right, in front of right shoulder about height of waist, first and second fingers extended, touching and pointing to front, and, by wrist action, give a wavy sinuous motion to extended fingers.

CHAPTER XXX

ONESTA GIVES THE CROW BEAVER CEREMONIAL

North Piegans gather around our camp fire.—Dances by the children Emonissi and Yellow Mink.—Embarrassing relations between a mother-in-law and son-in-law.—Running Wolf and myself entertain a gathering with Blackfeet songs.—At Onesta's request I sleep in the sacred Thunder Tipi.—Story of my vision has an advantageous result.

ONESTA was drumming and chanting religious songs, inside his tipi, when he requested me to join with him and help in the singing. The women, having finished their evening cooking, opened the front of the lodge and seated themselves to listen. The North Piegans, attracted by the chanting and sound of the drum, also came to our camp and joined the audience. Onesta and I continued our singing, while his little daughter, Yellow Mink, danced for the amusement of the company. When she had finished, Kionama directed his son, Emonissi, a young boy about eight years of age, to go through some of the Medicine Pipe dances he was teaching him. When his father picked up the drum, and began beating time, the little fellow started off with the Grizzly Bear dance, stepping slowly backwards and forwards, imitating the clumsy movements of a bear, holding out his arms, with his hands hanging, and then moving them about, just as a bear does, all the while breathing hard like a grizzly, when running. In the Antelope dance, Emonissi imitated, with his hands,

the graceful movements of an antelope, and turned his
head alertly, like an antelope. For the Swan dance,
he held his arms in front with the palms spread out, in
imitation of the swan sailing through the air. Kionama
explained that the boy was representing the chief swan,
who leads the flock. In the Thunder, or Pipe dance,

THUNDER TIPI.
("Lookout Butte" in distance.)

Emonissi held a pipe in his right hand, while his left
was extended, to represent the Thunder Bird flying.
After the performance, Onesta announced that he and
Nitana would give the Sup-we-yok-kinni (Crow Beaver
ceremonial), and invited all the North Piegans to
attend. He had been so pleased with my singing
during our evening dance, that he asked my help for
his ceremonial, and suggested that I should be the

owner of a medicine drum. Nitana had spent the entire day gathering sarvis berries for the feast, also sage and the different herbs required for the ceremonial.

Early in the morning of the day of the dance, the women pitched the sacred Thunder Tipi. The top was painted black to represent a cloudy sky, with a cross at the back, symbolising the Butterfly, the Bringer of Dreams. A band of Dusty Stars circled the bottom, symbolising the earth and, resting upon it, were representations of mountains. Between the top and bottom decorations were four serpentine bands of red representing the trails of the Thunder Bird (Lightning).

A huge kettle hung from the tripod over our outside fire, in which the sarvis berry stew was cooked. Onesta and Nitana chanted and offered prayers, while placing the berries in the kettle, and when all preparations had been completed, they reverently carried the food and their medicine bundles to the sacred tipi. Onesta beat loudly upon his drum, the signal to the people to assemble. The North Piegans, having never before witnessed the Crow Beaver ceremonial, attended in great numbers. One exception was a fine-looking man, who was holding himself aloof from the rest of the company. Noticing that he remained apart in the South Piegan camp, and wondering what could be the cause of his absence, I made inquiries. Menake explained that Bird was his mother-in-law and, according to the tribal custom, two persons of such relationship could not be present at the same time. If she chanced to meet him face to face, she would be greatly annoyed. If a man came unexpectedly into the presence of his mother-in-law, he would be expected to make her a handsome present for such a breach of etiquette.

Brings-down-the-Sun did not enter the sacred tipi,

neither did his wife, nor any of the family, but sat outside, for only those who took part in the ceremonial were expected to enter. Menake said, that, "It was their custom to refrain from participation in any ceremonial, excepting that of the Sun-dance. He was the high priest of the Sun-dance and his wife one of its sacred women. It was necessary for them to be careful,

ONESTA GIVES THE CROW BEAVER CEREMONIAL.
(Onesta is second from right end.)

not only in respect to their own, but also their children's actions. They were expected by the tribe to lead straight lives and to be above reproach." In this instance, they all attended as onlookers, because Onesta was a relative, but maintained their dignity by not participating.

The Crow Beaver Society ceremonial was introduced in recent years by a Blackfoot Chief, after a visit to the Crow Indians. It is participated in by both men and women. Their ceremonial is generally given for healing the sick. The society is invited to the home of the sick person, where the ceremonial is held. They bring their medicine bundles, and opening them, dance, with feathers and skins of the different birds and animals, and offer prayers for the recovery of the sick.

The priests, assisting Onesta in the ceremonial, were seated by his side. The North Piegans, who were to be instructed sat opposite, or were "against him," as the Indians expressed it.

When the Crow Beaver dance was over, and the people had dispersed, Onesta inquired if I would be willing to sleep in the sacred Thunder Tipi, explaining that it was contrary to the rules of the medicine to leave it unoccupied during the night. He said that, if I slept inside, I might possibly secure a dream, or a vision. He was much gratified, when I agreed to the proposal. Onesta, Nitana, Kionama and Menake came to sit with me during the evening. We were also joined by Running Wolf, Star-that-sets-over-the-hill, and their wives.

When we were all gathered around the lodge fire, Running Wolf asked me to sing some Indian songs. I agreed, if he would sing in turn. In reply to my wolf song, he sang a dance song, used by young warriors during a test for bravery. He gave me the following explanation of the occasion, when it is used.

"The bark of a pitch pine tree was set on fire. A group of men stripped naked, and holding hands, gathered in a circle about the tree. Two of them with long poles stood close to the tree, scraping the burning bark. This caused showers of sparks, which fell upon the bare bodies of the candidates, dancing around the tree, and singing 'Sats-to-o-komo' (Rub under the jaw). When the live sparks struck the faint hearted and cowardly, they could not withstand the pain and ran from the circle, but the men with brave, strong hearts continued dancing and singing, unmindful of their burns."

After my dance song, Running Wolf sang a song used in a man's game. The oldest man present takes two burning brands from the fire. All the others fall in line, each holding tightly to the one in front, and all singing in unison. The leader strikes the burning brands together, throwing off showers of sparks, while he leads them, winding in and out. The sparks falling on their bare bodies make the faint hearted shrink from the ordeal.

Nitana sang the song of a maiden disappointed in love. The words were,

"My lover looked like an eagle from a distance, but alas ! when he came nearer I saw that he was nothing but a buzzard."

My guests, especially the women, were much interested, when I sang the love song I had heard in Mad Wolf's Sun-dance camp, and they insisted upon hearing it over and over again. When Mysterious Woman entered the lodge, a request was made that I would again sing the love song for her.

It was after midnight, when my visitors departed. Before they left, Onesta was careful to inform me of certain things I must avoid, while occupying the sacred Thunder Tipi, to guard against bad luck. Running Wolf also warned me, that a skunk visited the locality every morning, just before daybreak, but assured me that if he were to enter the lodge, he would go out without causing any trouble, if I would lie perfectly still.

The night was very cold, after the Indians had departed. I built a warm fire and, comfortably wrapped in my blankets, lay for a long time, thinking of the varied events of the past day. It was a strange experience to be occupying a sacred tipi, to fulfil the laws of the medicine and to await a vision, like a

medicine man.   The rustling of the cottonwoods overhead, the faint murmur of the river rapids near by, and
the weird shapes of the lodge decorations, in the fitful
glow of the dying fire, made favourable conditions for
a vision.   As I went to sleep I remembered having
seen a large eagle, sailing high above the plains, on the
day we entered the North Piegan country.   He stood
beside me in the night, advising what message I should
bring to the North Piegans.

I was wakened by the bright rays of the morning
sun, shining into the lodge.   Smoke was slowly rising
in the still air from our South Piegan camp fire.
Menake and Nitana were already cooking breakfast.
Kionama called me, while I was at the river endeavouring to wash the red paint from my face and hair.
Before long, as I had expected, Onesta inquired if
anything had disturbed me during the night.   I replied,
" No," and relapsed into silence.   Menake then asked if
I had seen a vision.   When I replied that I had had a
very strong vision, Onesta urged me to tell it.   I said,
with the greatest seriousness,

" Before sunrise, just as day was breaking, an eagle stood beside
me, saying, ' My son, it is the chief of all the eagles that is speaking
to you.   I am going to help you because you are alone among a
strange people.   It is a good thing for you to visit the North
Piegans, to learn about them, and to take their pictures.   It will
bring good luck to you and to those, who take part in the ceremonials.   Good fortune and long life will come to all who may help
you.' "

My companions looked to see if I were joking, but,
when I maintained a solemn countenance, nothing
further was said, and I knew that my vision was taken
seriously, and would soon be heralded and discussed,
in its smallest detail, throughout the North Piegan
camp.

During the day a violent storm passed over the camp. Onesta questioned me closely as to my having disobeyed any rules of the Thunder Tipi. When I told him I had washed off the red paint in the early morning, he said that that was undoubtedly the cause of the storm.

CHAPTER XXXI

THE RIVAL LEADERS

Jealous anger of Bull Plume.—He urges me to visit his camp.—Brings-down-the-Sun is angered by the intrusion.—Onesta explains the cause of the rivalry.—Brings-down-the-Sun makes a friendly visit.—He agrees to impart his knowledge.—Stories of his father Running Wolf.—Origin of the name.—Winter counts kept by him as head chief of the tribe.—His initiation into the Medicine Pipe Society.—Discovers cavern of the Thunder-bird on Chief Mountain, who gives him a sacred Pipe.

On the day of the Crow Beaver ceremonial, while seated by the door of the sacred lodge, I was honoured by Brings-down-the-Sun seating himself beside me. To the Indians his act was a conspicuous recognition of me, and was noticed by everyone. Bull Plume was inside the lodge seated opposite to Onesta. When he observed Brings-down-the-Sun's action, he was much disturbed. Unable to control his jealous anger, he harangued the people seated near him. Even the family of Brings-down-the-Sun heard his words. He said : " My heart is now black because A-pe-ech-eken, who is my friend, has not come to my camp. I know that someone must have turned his heart against me." During the rest of the ceremonial Bull Plume was morose and silent. Next morning he came early to our camp to see me. We seated ourselves on the ground, and while engaged in a friendly smoke he made inquiries as to my journey, and how long I intended remaining in his country. He said he felt offended because I, an old friend, was visiting another man. He suggested that his camp was not far distant, on the other side of the river, and asked me to return with him. Knowing well the jealousy that pervades an Indian tribe, and the rivalry between all medicine men, my replies were careful and guarded. I explained that I had come a stranger to visit in his country, along with relatives of the chief, in whose camp I was now staying. It was necessary that I should remain with the people, with whom I was travelling. Bull Plume then became more urgent. He said, " I have some interesting tribal records to show you. They were handed down by Wolf Child, my grandfather, and are very old. If you come, you may copy them and you can make as many pictures in my camp as you wish." I replied that I was eager to see his records, and to take the pictures, but that our horses were running loose upon the hills, and I had no means of crossing the river. Bull Plume then departed, leaving me much disturbed in mind. It was the last I saw of him.

I learned afterwards, that he was so disappointed at my refusal to visit his camp, and angered, because Brings-down-the-Sun had practically won a victory over him, that he and all his followers struck their lodges and started for the north. Onesta explained this very strange occurrence by the fact, that Bull Plume and Brings-down-the-Sun were rival leaders. Bull Plume was a comparatively young man, ambitious for reputation and influence, while the aged Brings-down-the-Sun was universally revered, because of his honesty and kindness of heart, and his life-long reputation for high character and knowledge of their sacred ceremonials. Onesta said that Bull Plume was also a constant source of irritation to Brings-down-the-Sun, because of his aggressive methods, and that, if I had associated with him, it would have injured me greatly in the estimation of the older chief.

Political human nature is the same the world over. How like the rival ambitions and struggles for pre-eminence between the chiefs of our political parties, and political antagonists anywhere, was this manœuvring for recognition and leadership between these rival chiefs of the Blackfeet !

When Brings-down-the-Sun heard that Bull Plume had been in the South Piegan camp, trying to persuade the white man to go with him, he was very indignant. In the afternoon he entered our camp for the first time. Seating himself upon a big log, near the outside fire, and, filling his every-day pipe, he spoke as follows :

" For several years I have endured many things from this Bull Plume. I will no longer be silent, but will now speak plainly. If you desire to go to the camp of this man, I will not hinder you." When I replied that I intended remaining with him, he seemed relieved and continued : " I would prefer to have you stay with me, inasmuch as you came first to my camp and I have been preparing myself to relate to you many things that have happened to my people in former days. If you should be instructed by another man, there might be confusion. However, I do not wish to interfere, if you want to learn from Bull Plume." I again assured him that I desired to learn from him alone, and said, " When I started north with the South Piegans, they promised they would take me to your camp, because you know more than any of the chiefs. When I met the Blood Indians, I told them also that I was on my way to visit you. I do not care to go to the camp of Bull Plume and I want to learn from you alone." Gazing steadily

Copyright in United States   THE WAR CHIEF   *By Walter McClintock*

into my face for a moment, he said, "I can read a man's character in his eyes and by the look I see in his face. I know this Bull Plume is tricky, because he cannot look a man straight in the eyes. He is like a crooked stick and his words and his schemes are as many as the branches in yonder thicket. He told you that he has in his possession tribal records handed down to him from his grandfather. This is not true. Bull Plume is a young man. We do not even know who his father was. I remember him as a small boy. He was so poor he used to walk barefoot behind the travois. When, as a young man, he was gathering together the records he now boasts about to you, he secured the knowledge from me. This same information was given to me by my father, who was the head chief of the

BRINGS-DOWN-THE-SUN.
(Eagle feathers fastened on both sides of head.)

Blackfeet. Bull Plume has lied to you and, if you had gone with him to his camp, he has no records of value to show. Since you were not deceived, and have remained true to me, I now take you as my son, I will be your father in the north, and the people in my camp henceforth will be your brothers and sisters. As long as you remain in my camp, I will give myself up to you and will tell you all the information you may desire

to know. I also take as my friends your white father and
mother who live towards the rising sun. I ask you to
send them word that my heart feels good towards them."

After expressing, in a few words, my deep appreciation
of his kindness and goodwill, I asked him to tell me
about his father, and also about his own life.

His manner was very impressive as he turned and,

" I will tell you nothing but the truth."

pointing towards the setting sun, addressed me. " The
Sun looks down upon us both, sitting here together,
and hears everything that we say. I declare, before
the Great Mystery in the Sun, that I will tell you
nothing but the truth.

" When my father became a man he was named
A-pe-so-muckka (Running Wolf). My grandfather,
Little Mountain, was once alone in the mountains,
when a wolf came to him in a dream saying, ' My son,
you have often heard my voice, for I am Running Wolf,
the head chief of all the wolves. I run all over the

country. My tracks are to be found everywhere, and I will always continue to wander. If you should ever have sons, name one of them Running Wolf after me. If he should have a son, let the name be handed down. All of your descendants, who bear my name, will be blessed with long life.' I was the only one of my father's sons to be named Running Wolf, and I in turn have given this name to my son whose tipi stands there next to mine. My father was the third son, and I will relate the events, which proved that he was worthy to bear the name of Running Wolf.

" When he was a boy fifteen years old, he was watching a large war party, of which his two older brothers were members, making ready to start on an expedition against the Snake (Shoshone) Indians. They rode to my grandfather's big lodge, in the centre of the camp, dressed in war clothes, and with horses painted, singing a wolf song and beating time on their parfleches. When they finished their song with the wolf-howl, Little Mountain directed his wives to go out and join them in another song, that their expedition might be successful. After smoking a pipe with their head chief, they marched four times around the camp circle, stopping to sing at the four largest tipis, located towards the four main directions (cardinal points). They then dispersed, and after saying farewell to their friends and families, started for the south. All these preparations were very thrilling to my father, and, as they rode away, he longed to accompany them, but he well knew that they would say he was too young. After the war party had gone, young Running Wolf secured his father's rifle, making the excuse that he was going on a hunt. Instead, he circled around, and, by fast riding, finally overtook them. The war-chief was not pleased to see him, and ordered him to turn back, explaining that they were starting upon a long and dangerous expedition, and that he, as their leader, would be held responsible for his safe return. Running Wolf made no reply, but his two brothers spoke: ' If he is so eager to go to war, let him come along. He can make himself useful by leading these two travois dogs.' No further objections were made, so Running Wolf took charge of the dogs and remained with the war party. Nothing of interest happened for many days. One night, after crossing the Yellowstone River, when the boy was sleeping on the outskirts of the camp, he was awakened by the growling of his dogs, and discovered not far away a band of Snake Indians. He gave the alarm, and the Blackfeet hastily made ready, but waited to make their attack just before dawn. When they were starting out, my two uncles directed Running Wolf to hand over his rifle, because it might be needed, and because he was too young to enter the fight. He pleaded with them to allow him to try at least one shot at the enemy. When the Snakes saw the Blackfeet coming, they hastily retreated towards some high cliffs. The Blackfeet warriors followed, but held their fire, thinking the Snakes were out of range. Young Running Wolf was the only one to fire a gun. He took a long shot, and, strange to say, killed a Snake warrior, the bullet entering his head. When he fell, my uncles ran out and took his scalp and clothes. The Snakes reached the cliffs, where they were in such a strong position that our warriors could not dislodge them. The victory had already belonged to the Black-feet, so they left the country to return home. It was in midsummer when they came back. The people were all outside the lodges, the women playing a game of bones, and the young men gambling with the wheel and arrow, when a band of horsemen unexpectedly appeared upon a high butte.   It was the returning war-party.   They had come back so quickly, no one believed it possible they could have gone far enough to en-counter the enemy.   The warriors tied the scalp to some long willow branches.   The chief instructed young

WAR-PARTY RIDING THROUGH CAMP HOLDING UP SCALPS.

Running Wolf to hold them aloft when they entered camp, and to cry out, ' My name is Running Wolf.   I am the youngest of the war-party, but I was the only one to kill a Snake Indian.   Behold ! here is his scalp.' Then they marched around the camp, shooting their rifles in the air, and singing the song of victory, ' We have hair.'   Many years afterwards the Blackfeet were told by the Snakes, that the man my father killed was also the son of their head chief, and that his name was Running Wolf.

" My father was the leader of the clan of Grease Melters. Later, when he was chosen head chief of the Blackfeet, he was known by the name of Iron Shirt, because he wore a buckskin shirt decorated with pieces of shining metal. He was a large, muscular man, with a wonderful memory and a great knowledge of our customs. He could tell a horse's age by its whinny, and a man's by the sound of his voice. He kept ' winter counts ' on buffalo hides, marking the principal events in the history of the tribe. He recorded our tribal camps, the battles, the names of our leaders, when the great chiefs died, the years of sickness (scourge of smallpox), the summers of droughts and the hard winters, when game was scarce and snows lay deep.

" Sixty-nine winters have passed, since we had our first ' Great Sickness ' (smallpox, 1836). Fifty winters, since eight Indian tribes assembled together in a big camp on the Yellowstone River, when Little Dog, Big Snake and Lame Bull were the head chiefs (1855). Thirty-one winters since the coming of the Mounted Police (1874), and twenty-nine since the severe winter, when many of our horses were frozen (1876). One year later, there was a big camp in the north, when Big Crow Foot was head chief (1877).

" Other important events that my father marked in his ' winter counts ' were : the winter, when many of our people died from the ' Cough Sickness.'

" The winter, when the children broke through the ice.

" The winter, when the moose came into camp.

" The winter, when our horses had the mange.

" The winter, when it was necessary to eat dogs to keep from starving.

" The winter, when the antelopes broke through the ice.

" The winter, when buffalo were scarce.

" The winter, when we caught antelope in the deep snow.

" The winter, when a treaty was made with the white men.

" I was born in the year, when white men were seen for the first time in our country, and in the spring, during the moon, when the grass is green. Grass, as you know, is the head chief of everything. The animals depend upon the grass for food, and without the animals our children could not live.

" I was still a young boy when my father was made a member of the Medicine Pipe society. It happened at the time of the Sun-dance camp in midsummer. Wolf Child had owned a Pipe for four years. It was time for him to give it up and to select his successor. He chose my father, and told the society that they must catch him. Now my father was a Bear Man, that is, his power came from the grizzly bear. His medicine, which was a bear skin, always hung from the lodge poles over his bed It was for this reason, that the Medicine Pipe men had never chosen my father before. The word ' bear ' was believed to exert an evil power over the Pipe, and should never be spoken in its presence. They feared to offer the Pipe to my father, with the bear skin so near, lest it bring misfortune upon all of the society. But, Wolf Child, the owner of the Pipe to be transferred, finally prevailed, urging that, ' Iron Shirt is head chief and is so powerful, no harm can come to him. For our part, I believe we can safely take the Pipe into the presence of the bear skin without danger, if all of us are careful to use the word ' Badger,' instead of ' Bear ' and, at the same time, burn sweet pine as incense, which will avert the evil power. We must catch both Iron Shirt and his wife inside their lodge. Don't let either of them escape.' In this way he persuaded them and overcame their fears. It was after midnight, when I heard them come into our lodge. Wolf Child entered first, holding the sacred Pipe hidden beneath his blanket. My mother tried to run out, but Wolf Child held her fast, until the others entered. He offered the Pipe to my father and, when he grasped it with both hands, the society men began to drum and sing. When my father had finished smoking, he said : ' I have many horses, which of them is it you wish to take ?' Wolf Child said : ' Your black buffalo horse.' He knew well that he was the most valuable of the herd and the fastest horse in camp. He was so high spirited that it required three raw hide bridles to hold him. My father answered quickly : ' Take him ! He is yours.' It was an honour, but also a great burden for my father and mother to own a Medicine Pipe. But few men dare to refuse it. I remember the case of a young man, who declined a Medicine Pipe, because the society asked for his racehorse. As a result his father-in-law soon died, then the racehorse, and finally the young man himself.

" I was once camped with my grandfather and father on the Green Banks (St. Mary's River), close to the Rocky Mountains. They were digging out beavers, which were very plentiful. My father went off for a hunt to supply our camp with meat. He followed the trail of some elk up the side of a steep mountain, until he came to timber-line, where he saw a herd of mountain sheep. He followed them towards Nin-ais-tukku (Chief Mountain). When he drew near the summit, he discovered a dense, foul-smelling smoke rising from a deep pit. He pushed a huge boulder into it to hear it fall. There came back no sound, but a cloud of smoke and gas arose so dense and suffocating, that he turned to flee, but it was only to meet a black cloud coming up the mountain side. He was frightened and tried to escape, but suddenly there came a terrible crash, and my father fell to the ground. He beheld a woman standing over him. Her face was painted black and red zig-zag streaks like lightning were below her eyes. Behind the woman, stood a man holding a large weapon. My father heard the man exclaim impatiently, ' I told you to kill him at once, but you stand there pitying him.' He heard the woman chant, ' When it rains the noise of the Thunder is my medicine.' The man also sang and fired his big weapon. The report was like a deafening crash of thunder, and my father beheld lightning coming from the big hole on the mountain top. He knew nothing more, until he found himself lying inside a great cavern. He had no power to speak, neither could he raise his head, but, when he heard a voice saying, ' This is the person who threw the stone down into your fireplace,' he realised that he was in the lodge of the Thunder Maker. He heard the beating of a drum, and, after the fourth beating, was able to sit up and look around. He saw the Thunder Chief, in the form of a huge bird, with his wife and many children around him. All of the children had drums, painted with the green talons of the Thunder-bird and with Thunder-bird beaks, from which issued zig-zag streaks of yellow lightning.

" We call the thunder Isis-a-kummi (Thunder-bird). We believe that it is a supernatural person. When he leaves his lodge to go through the heavens with the storm-clouds, he takes the form of a great bird with many colours, like the rainbow, and with long green claws. The lightning is the trail of the Thunder-bird.

" Whenever the Thunder Maker smoked his pipe, he blew two whiffs upwards toward the sky, and then two whiffs towards the earth. After each whiff the thunder crashed. Finally the Thunder-bird spoke to my father, saying, 'I am the Thunder Maker and my name is Many Drums (expressive of the sound of rolling thunder). You have witnessed my great power and can now go in safety. When you return to your people, make a pipe just like the one you saw me smoking, and add it to your bundle. Whenever you hear the first thunder rolling in the spring-time, you will know that I have come from my cavern, and that it is time to take out my pipe. If you should ever be caught in the midst of a heavy thunder-storm and feel afraid, pray to me, saying, ' Many Drums ! pity me, for the sake of your youngest child,' and no harm will come to you. (This prayer is often used by the Blackfeet during dangerous storms.) As soon as my father returned, he added to his Medicine Bundle a Pipe similar to the one shown to him by the Thunder-bird."

CHAPTER XXXII

EVENTS IN THE LIFE OF BRINGS-DOWN-THE-SUN

Death of his father.—The sacred Pipe and leadership of the tribe were handed down to him.—He chose instead to become a medicine man.—His wise and benevolent manner of dealing with the people. —Eagle-catching his means of livelihood.—His method of trapping eagles.—The Spirit of the Mountain gives him a Medicine Robe.—His reasons for not using the sweat lodge.—He tells the names of his children and of their remarkable deliverance from a dangerous flood.

" My father was not killed in battle, nor did he die of sickness, but of old age. When he knew the end was near, he called me to him, and gave into my care the Pipe of the Thunder Maker, explaining that it was a Long Time Pipe, and should not be buried with him. I still have it in my possession, and smoke it only upon important occasions. He also gave me a large silver medal, which he wore as head chief, saying, ' My son, it is yours now. Take with it also my wisdom and power, and lead our people straight.' After my father's death, I came north to live. I became deeply interested in the mysteries of the medicines, which I have continued to study diligently. I was formerly called A-pe-so-mucca (Running Wolf), and am still known to many by that name. But, afterwards, when I became the leader of their Sun-dance, and their instructor in the worship of the Sun, the North Piegans called me Natosin Nepe-e (Brings-down-the-Sun, literally the Sun Bringer). I have always tried to give my people sound advice, and to lead them in the right trail. Whenever they gather in assemblies, I go among them to guide them straight. At horse races, I endeavour to keep them from fighting, and, if they quarrel, I reason with them, and try to persuade them to hold the matter over until another day. I advise the women to be obedient to their men, and am continually impressing upon the young, to keep their hearts kind and not to be wild or quarrelsome. Some of our leaders become angry with the people, when they go wrong. I believe you have more power with men, if you are patient with them, when they wander from the right trail.

" For many years I have helped to support my family by catching eagles. I dispose of most of the feathers among the South Piegans, who use them for their head-dresses and medicine bonnets. It is very difficult and exhausting work to take eagles alive. When I was a young man my father taught me his methods, for he was a skilled eagle-catcher. I camp in an unfrequented place, near the foot of the mountains. After digging a deep hole, so that I can stand erect inside, I kill a coyote and stretch the tanned hide on sticks, with raw meat laid along the sides, as if it had just been cut open. Long before sunrise, I enter the hole, covering the top over with branches and leaves. The coyote bait lies on top, just over my head. I must stand in the hole all day, not able to eat, nor drink, nor even smoke, lest the eagles scent the smoke. All day long I chant the coyote medicine song,

> " ' I want the eagles to eat my body.'

The power of this song draws the eagles towards the bait. First I see the Mami-as-ich-imi (Long Tails or Magpies) coming. They walk around chattering and talking, saying to each other over and over again, 'Magpies go on ahead, and hang your sack upon a tree.' An eagle sees the Longtails feasting, and swoops down beside the bait. He first walks suspiciously around and around the coyote, and at last steps over upon the branches and begins to eat. I then push my hands through the branches and, grasping him firmly, first by one leg and then by the other, I pull him quickly down into the hole, and kill him by breaking his back with my foot. In this way the wings fall to either side, and the feathers are uninjured. After sunset, my wife comes to the pit with food. She uncovers the top and helps me out. I desire most to catch the Peta (Golden Eagle), because its feathers are the most valuable. Its head and breast are light brown, with white beneath the wings. Its tail feathers are also white, with black tips. We never use Black Eagles, and White Heads (Bald Eagles) are very scarce, as well as dangerous. They are so strong, they have almost lifted me out of the pit.

" In former days, when grizzly bears were plentiful, eagle-catching was very dangerous. I remember one Indian, who was in his pit, when a big grizzly came to the bait, and started to drag it away. The man foolishly held to his bait, and the bear turned to investigate. He scratched off the branches and, seeing a man in the hole, dragged him out and, in a rage, tore him to pieces. His friends found nothing but his bones. There are now so many white men in the country, it is difficult to find a locality wild enough to catch eagles. At present I go to a place on the other side of the Porcupine Mountains."

Pointing towards the north, Brings-down-the-Sun said : " You can see from here the highest peak of the Porcupine Mountains. It is surrounded by a thick forest and no trail leads to that peak. Its summit is precipitous and covered with scrub pines. You will notice that our most severe storms come from the direction of that peak. When my eldest son died, I felt his loss so deeply, that I climbed to its summit and lay there fasting, for ten days and ten nights. During that time I had a dream, in which the Spirit of the Mountain appeared and gave me a Medicine Robe [1] with a song. He instructed me how to make the robe, and said that, if I used it in doctoring, or when I appeared before the assembled people, I would be endowed with wisdom and supernatural power.

"The Spirit of the Mountain warned me never to enter the sweat lodge at the Sun-dance, lest my children should die; nor to use it even for purification, but to wash daily in the river instead, and afterwards, to purify my body in the sweet smoke of the incense. Since that time, I have bathed in the river every morning, even in winter, when it is necessary to break the ice. When I am in the water, I call to my sons to come in, that they might be clean. After the men have finished bathing, the women also go into the water. I believe that, by keeping the body clean, and by using the sweet smoke as incense for purification, sickness may be warded off. I am convinced that the reason O-mis-tai-po-kah and Running Crane lost so many members of their families by death was because of their continued use of the sweat lodge. O-mis-tai-po-kah lost a wife, three sons and a daughter, while Running Crane lost one of his wives and four children."

Brings-down-the-Sun remained in our camp for the evening meal. He took his seat at a little distance from the rest, where he waited in dignified silence,

[1] See Appendix.

apparently paying no heed to the ceaseless chatter of the women, who were busily engaged around the outside fire preparing the food. Instead of allowing his plate to rest upon the bare ground like the rest, he produced a clean piece of paper, which he smoothed out and then placed his plate upon it. While the women were removing the food, he filled his everyday pipe for a smoke. When we were again seated around the fire, Menake was surrounded by a group of children, eagerly watching her making toy lodges out of leaves of the balsam poplar. She formed the two ears by cutting out the top of the leaf, then, winding it around her fingers, in the form of a lodge, she fastened it together by means of an inserted twig. After making several of these remarkable little lodges, she grouped them into a miniature camp, to the great delight of the children. Nitana was making whistles for Yellow Mink and Walks Underneath, by means of two pieces of cotton-wood bark, with a leaf between. Long Hair, seated near Brings-down-the-Sun, held in her arms Feather Woman, her granddaughter, but a few months old, of whom she was evidently very proud. Its little buck-skin dress was trimmed across the front with many kernels of corn. Long Hair was pleased at my notice of the baby, for she held it out towards me, and said to it, "Show A-pe-ech-eken how the good children look." I was surprised at seeing the little thing turn its diminutive face towards me and wrinkle up its nose (one of her baby tricks).

When I inquired of Brings-down-the-Sun as to the number of his children,[1] he said, "There are nine living, four sons and five daughters; Running Wolf (named as directed by the Medicine Wolf), Iron Shirt (after his

[1] See Appendix.

grandfather), Double Walker and Three Eagles. The daughters are : Long Hair (because of her un-usually long hair when a young girl), Turns-back-the-whole-herd-alone (I once performed this feat in buffalo days), Whistling-all-night (she was born in January, the time the jack rabbit, like the bull elk, whistles at night, when calling his mate), also Good Kill and Double-Gun-Woman." At this point, Bird joined the circle, and Menake, pointing towards me, said, to frighten her, " Look out ! Did you not notice your son-in-law sitting there ? " The old woman turned to run, but, when she saw it was only intended as a joke, she laughed, saying, " A-pe-ech-eken, you should give me a good horse, even if you are not my son-in-law, because you gave me such a fright."

Brings-down-the-Sun, who had been smoking in silence, said : " This is the third summer since the heavy rain. It came during the moon of High Water, (June). At that time, I was in the country of the South Piegans, disposing of eagle feathers, and visiting my daughter Pretty Blanket. I also intended to remain for the Sun-dance, but a messenger came from the north with the news that the Crow Lodge River had overflowed its banks and my camp was washed away. I hastened back and found, that there had been such a storm that, in a few hours, the river came out from its banks. My son, Running Wolf, was here with our family. The river rose so suddenly in the night that, before they could realise it, they were upon an island, cut off from the mainland by the swift current. The water continued to rise so fast, that Running Wolf made the women and children climb into a big tree. There was no other way of escape. When daylight came, and the women felt the swaying of the tree, and could see the swift current, they became so dizzy and frightened, that Running Wolf had to tie them to the branches. They saw the carcasses of many horses and cattle floating past. One of my daughters had a young baby, which she held all the time in her arms. They were two days and two nights in the tree without food. When they were finally rescued, they were exhausted from exposure and lack of food."

CHAPTER XXXIII

THE OLD NORTH TRAIL

Brings-down-the-Sun comments on his boyhood name Running Wolf.—
He tells about the Old North Trail formerly used by Indian tribes.
—The Lone Pine Tree land-mark.—A former Blackfoot expedition
into Mexico along the Old North Trail.—It returns with the
Dancing Pipe.—Blackfeet names for rivers, mountains and other
land-marks along the trail.

THE long silence following Brings-down-the-Sun's talk
was broken by the mournful, long-drawn howl of a
wolf from among the hills to the north. The sound
suggested another topic to the old chief and he
continued, "We consider the wolf a friend of man, and
do not believe it is right to shoot him. We have
a saying, 'the gun that fires upon a coyote or wolf will
never again shoot straight.' Did you ever know of a
wolf that did not wander? They never stay long in
one locality. They raise their young in one place and
then go to another. They are continually roving over
the country and are always on the move. My father
named me Running Wolf, and I believe that, by nature,
I am like the wolf, for I love to roam over the prairies
and among the mountains. I cannot stay still very
long, I, too, have always kept moving.

"There is a well known trail we call the Old North
Trail. It runs north and south along the Rocky
Mountains. No one knows how long it has been used
by the Indians. My father told me it originated in the

migration of a great tribe of Indians from the distant north to the south, and all the tribes have, ever since, continued to follow in their tracks. The Old North Trail is now becoming overgrown with moss and grass, but it was worn so deeply, by many generations of travellers, that the travois tracks and horse trail are still plainly visible.

"On Crow Lodge River, just across from our present camp, a lone pine tree once stood. It was a land-mark for people travelling north and south along the Old North Trail, because it stood upon the plain and could be seen from a long distance. Finally the Lone Tree fell, but two children took its place. They have grown large and now they mark the former course of the North Trail. The Indians still speak of the spot as the Lone Tree. In many places the white man's roads and towns have obliterated the Old Trail. It forked where the city of Calgary now stands. The right fork ran north into the Barren Lands as far as people live. The main trail ran south along the eastern side of the Rockies, at a uniform distance from the mountains, keeping clear of the forest, and outside of the foothills. It ran close to where the city of Helena now stands, and extended south into the country, inhabited by a people with dark skins, and long hair falling over their faces (Mexico). In former times, when the Indian tribes were at war, there was constant fighting along the North Trail. In those days, Indians, who wanted to travel in peace, avoided it and took to the forest. My father once told me of an expedition from the Blackfeet, that went south by the Old Trail, to visit the people with dark skins. Elk Tongue and his wife, Natoya, were of this expedition, also Arrow Top and Pemmican, who was a boy of twelve at that time. He died only a few years ago at the age of ninety-five. They were absent four years. It took them twelve moons of steady travelling to reach the country of the dark skinned people, and eighteen moons to come north again. They returned by a longer route through the 'High Trees' or Bitter Root country, where they could travel without danger of being seen. They feared going along the North Trail because it was frequented by their enemies, the Crows, Sioux, and Cheyennes. Elk Tongue brought back the Dancing Pipe. He bought it nearly one hundred years ago and it was then very old. The South Man, who gave it to him, warned him to use it only upon important occasions, for the fulfilment of a vow, or the recovery of the sick. Whenever anyone was starting on a war, or hunting expedition, a safe return could be secured by vowing to give a feast to the Dancing Pipe. In the Medicine Bundle that went with it, were the skins of animals and birds. The otter and lynx were the largest, the otter belonging to the head man and the lynx to the woman. The South Man also told Elk Tongue that, it had been their custom, in giving the Pipe ceremonial, to cut open a badger, and to place inside a preparation mixed with paint. Everyone who attended the ceremonial looked into the badger, trying to see themselves. If their reflection looked black, or wrinkled, it was a sign of death, but, if they looked gray haired, they would live to be old. The South Man advised discontinuing this part of the ceremonial, saying it was not well to try to read the future, because people were made unhappy by it. When the Pipe was unrolled, it was shaken, and, if any of the skins, or feathers fell, misfortune would be sure to overtake the man who made the vow.

" I have followed the Old North Trail so often, that I know every mountain stream and river far to the south, as well as towards the distant north. We call the Three Tetons in the the south (Wyoming), Teat Buttes, because of their shape. North of the Mud Head Creek is a stream along whose banks many berries grow, so we named it Sweet Creek. North of it is another stream we call the Ghost Piskun [1] Creek. On its shore is a miniature cliff about three feet high. At the base of the cliff are small circles of stones, similar to those made by the Indians for their lodge fires. It looks to us as if, at one time, there must have been a miniature Indian camp there. If you visit the place early in the morning you will see many mice. We believe these mice are the ghosts of buffalo, which take the forms of mice, whenever people look at them. North of the Ghost Piskun Creek is a place called ' Where-war-parties-meet.' Many years ago, a Blackfoot war party was travelling north by the Old Trail. The chief's name was Koko-nút-stokè (Owl), so called because of his large eyes. One day, when Owl was in advance of the others, he discovered a war party of Crow Indians coming south by the same trail. Owl ambushed himself in a thicket. The Crow war party had secured plunder and the chief was in advance, carrying in his arms the sacrifices he was about to make to the Sun. He happened to enter the same thicket and was preparing to fasten his gifts in a tree when Owl killed him and took his scalp. Ever since that time we have called that spot, and the stream near by, ' Where-war-parties-meet.' Farther south is Mosquito Creek. Anyone who is foolish enough to camp there, will be almost eaten up by mosquitoes. Just beyond is low

[1] See Appendix.

ground which we have named 'Big Timber,' because
trees grow very large there.   Birch Creek was named
because of the groves of birches along its shores;
Badger Creek, on account of the many large badgers
seen along its banks; Black Tail, because of the
quantity of black tail deer in the thickets near that
stream.   Mud Head River was named, because of the

PISKUN NEAR TWO MEDICINE RIVER.
(Top of cliff.)

piskun we had there.   When we ran a herd of buffalo
over the cliff they fell into the mud which was so soft
it covered their heads.   Two Medicine River was named,
because we once had a double piskun there.   We drove
the buffalo over one, or the other, as we chose.   Lee's
Creek is called 'Banks-roped-together' by our people.
An Indian when on a hunt killed a buffalo there,
marking the spot by cutting the raw hide into strips

and making them into a rope, which he fastened to
stakes on both sides of the stream.   When the Indians
saw the rope they named the place ' Where-the-
banks-are-roped-together.'   The stream finally became
known by that name.

" In the mountains, at the head of the Green Banks
(St. Mary's), are two lakes.   We call them the In Lakes,

PISKUN NEAR TWO MEDICINE RIVER.
(Base of cliff.)

because they run so far into the mountains.   At the
head of Swift Current River, is another lake, surrounded
by thick forests and high peaks, and with falls at the
outlet.   We have named it Moose Lake.   When some
of our people were once hunting there, a moose dived
into the lake and escaped.

" At the place, where the Kootenai River flows out of
the mountains, there is an old trail leading past some

large rocks, which we have named the Rockies. It
leads up to a pass over the Big Mountains (Rocky
Mountains), which a large war party named Bad Luck
Fat Pass. When they were crossing the summit, they
were caught in a storm so severe, that they were forced
to camp there. The snow was very deep and they spent
their time hunting. They killed so many elk and
moose, that it was very difficult to pack out the fat
meat and hides, so they called the pass, 'Bad Luck
Fat.'

"There is a high peak in the Rockies, where this
river rises, which we call Crow Lodge Mountain,
because it is the home for enormous flocks of crows.
They gather every evening, and roost in the trees on
the mountain side during the night, but they always
leave in the morning. An Indian secured there the
dream for the Crow Lodge, and we have given the river
the same name, because he made the lodge in a ravine,
not far from this camp. A short distance up the river,
is a high cliff, called the Women's Piskun. It is the
place where a large band of women once camped.
They supported themselves by running buffalo and
antelope over their piskun. We have a tradition, that
men and women have not always lived separated into
families, but ran in bands like the animals. Napi
(Old Man) is said to have started our living together
in families."

CHAPTER XXXIV

BLACKFEET SOCIETIES

A practical joke at my expense.—Irregularity in time of meals.—How women bake camass roots.—Brings-down-the-Sun receives present of medicinal plants.— He asks for my family history.—In return he gives the origins of the Blackfeet Societies.—The Sinopaix (Kit-foxes) and their society dance.—He describes Tsin-ksi-six (Mosquitoes). —Kuko (Doves).—Muto-ka-iks (Buffaloes).—Knut-some-taix (Mad Dogs).

OUR camping ground had once been the old bed of the river and was covered with a plentiful deposit of loamy sand. When the grass and undergrowth were tramped down, the ground became very dusty and the fine sand, carried by the wind, penetrated our food and everything we had. The South Piegans noticed that I was frequently scratching myself and seized the opportunity for a joke at my expense. Menake said to Onesta, so that I could overhear, " During the past few days I have been feeling itchy. I believe we have become lousy from sitting on the blankets and robes of the North Piegans." Onesta replied without a smile, " I have had the same trouble, but got rid of them by bathing in the river." I had had my own suspicions of the cause of our discomfort, but, after this conversation, I imagined that lice were crawling in my hair and all over my body. To the great amusement of the entire camp, I hastened to the river, where I soon discovered that sand was the real cause of my affliction. Onesta told me afterwards, that few of the Blackfeet were troubled with vermin, but, that it was a common thing among the Crees, Gros Ventres and Assinniboines. The Blackfeet say that this fact made them feel uncomfortable, even to go near the Crees, or Assinniboines and because of it they disliked to fight with them, or use their spoils.

It is the custom of the Blackfeet to cook but two meals a day; one in the morning and the other late in the afternoon. The hours are very irregular, meal time coming when the women happened to feel hungry, or thought it convenient. When we were travelling, the morning meal was eaten very early, generally before sunrise. But, in a permanent camp, it sometimes did not come until noon, and if the women were not in the mood for cooking, they omitted it entirely. The evening meal varied from five o'clock until nine. Sometimes almost a day elapsed between meals, and I became so ravenously hungry that I resorted to the dried meats and pemmican, which the Indians ate at all times of the day, and which I finally acquired a liking for.

For baking the Mississa (camass roots, Camassia esculenta), Menake and Nitana dug a hole about three feet deep. They placed hot stones at the bottom of the hole, covering them over with long grass and leaves of the A-pono-kauki (Paper Leaves), Balsamorrhiza sagittata. The camass roots were placed in layers, with the grass and leaves between each layer. When the hole was filled, it was covered over and a fire built on the top. In this way the camass was thoroughly baked. Menake said that it required two days and two nights to prepare it properly for food. In former times, when the women were baking camass, it was contrary to their custom for men to come near the place. The camass roots, that Menake dug, were in size like a small potato, and had a very delicate sweet flavour. The women generally secured them in the mountains, where they grew in great abundance. It was at its best for eating after the blossoms had fallen.

Menake chose a day, when Brings-down-the-Sun came alone to our camp, to present him with a supply of roots she had brought from the south. The old chief was a doctor with much skill and reputation. Very few of her medicinal plants grew along the Crow Lodge River, so that Menake's collection was of great value to him. She first handed him a large plant called Eksisoke (Sharp Vine) by the Blackfeet (Bear Grass or Yucca glauca), which she had found when travelling along Sun River, 250 miles to the south. Brings-down-the-Sun was greatly pleased by this rare plant and, as he took it, uttered a prayer and chanted a sacred song. He said to Menake, "I am glad to get the Sharp Vine, because of its great healing properties. I prefer it above all other remedies for fractures, or sprains. I first grind the root up and then put it in boiling water. For a broken leg, or arm, or sprain I use it with thin willow sticks for splints and then hold the part in the rising steam to allay the inflammation."

Brings-down-the-Sun having carefully stowed the precious gift of roots in his medicine sack, came over to the big log and sat down by my side. He smoked awhile in silence, as was his custom, and then addressed me,

"From the time when you first came into my camp, I have been doing all the talking, while you have listened. I do not as yet know very much about you, but I want to know you better, and to come closer to you, because you are now my son. I now ask that you will talk to me. Tell me your age, and in what moon you were born, the ages of your father and mother, and what the country is

like where you live." When I told him my age and that of my
father and mother, he looked at me in surprise, saying, " You look
like a mere youth, and have the voice of a young man. You were
born in the year of the last great scourge of small-pox (Apicksosin,
Great Sickness, 1869–70). It came during the winter, while you
arrived in the spring. I have recorded three of these Great
Sicknesses. The first was sixty years ago (1845). Twelve years
intervened until the second (in 1857). The third and last came
during the winter of 1870. I hope there will never be another.
Your father was born in the year when Big Lodge, head chief of
the Blackfeet, was killed. Your mother during the hard winter,
when the snows lay so deep that many of our horses perished."

He inquired if I lived beyond the Big River
(Mississippi). I endeavoured in my reply to use
words and ideas he could easily understand, and said,

" My home (Pittsburg) is far away toward the rising Sun. It
is beyond the Big River and not far from the Great Water (Ocean).
There are many people where I live, more than the leaves on these
trees. The sun seldom shines clearly there, for it is hidden by
heavy clouds of smoke, like that from a great prairie fire. Great
fire-places light up the night skies like a burning forest. We make
the trails for the Iron Horse (Locomotive) in these fires. When
the iron trails come first from the fires, they are red hot and glide
around like huge snakes. The houses are built of stone, and some
of them are so large and high they look like the peaks of the
Rocky Mountains. My father lives down there now, and his heart
feels warm towards the Indians."

During my talk, Brings-down-the-Sun sat, closely
watching my every movement. My remarks brought
forth exclamations of surprise and wonder, and, when I
had finished, he said simply, " I would like to go to
your home, that I may meet that new friend of mine,
your father. If you can arrange it for me, I will go
back with you." Then slowly shaking his head he
said, " The white man does very wonderful things and
does not seem to realise it." He sat smoking and
musing, until I broke the long silence by asking that
he would tell me about their different societies, or
brotherhoods, which he described as follows :

Sinopaix (Society of Kit-foxes).

" None of the dances of this society have been given in the last twenty-five years. It was one of our old societies and had this origin : The Blackfeet once went on a war expedition against the Snakes. When they reached the Yellowstone country a man named Elk Tongue decided to turn back. After he left the expedition, he came to a prairie-dog village, where he saw two Kit-foxes run ahead of him for a short distance and then disappear in a hole. He sat down near the hole to rest, for he was very tired after his long, hard journey, and fell asleep. He dreamed that a Kit-fox came out and invited him to go inside. In his vision, he followed the little fox into a den, where he found the chief of the foxes with his mate seated beside him. They were kind to him, and finally explained to him their dance, and showed him how to dress for it. They instructed him to get a fox-skin and to carry it with him as his medicine, always wearing it on his back. On the right side of their lodge, Elk Tongue saw two spears covered with other skins and fringed with feathers, while on the left side, were two spears decorated with white swan's down, and fringed with bells and plumes, and bent into a circle at one end. Before Elk Tongue left the hole, the Fox Chief said : ' When you return to your people, gather some of the young men together, and form the society of Kit-foxes. Instruct the members to dress and to dance, just as we have taught you. If you will do these things, and not kill any more foxes, all of your members will have good fortune and long life. If any of you should harm a fox, it will surely bring misfortune.' When Elk Tongue returned to camp, he did just as the fox had directed. He wore the fox-skin for his medicine, and founded the society of Kit-foxes. He was the only one, who could explain the mysteries of the society. He directed the other members, but they did not understand the significance of the dances. When he died, the Fox-skin Medicine and the story were given to his son. From that time, they have been handed down from father to son. The Blackfeet used to trap foxes, but after this society was formed, the members did not allow their children to injure a fox."

Dance of the Sinopaix.

" When the Kit-foxes gave a dance, they opened up two large lodges and made them into one. For four days and four nights they sat inside, painting and dressing themselves, singing and making ready for the dance, only appearing at night, outside of the dance lodge. On the fifth day they marched through the camp. Their chief wore the fox-skin, with the head made into the form of a hood. The nose was in front, the ears on the top and the skin, with bells fastened to the tail, hung down his back. The face of the leader was painted green to look as frightful as possible and inspire the spectators with awe. The second in rank, called the White-Circle-Man, carried a spear, with one end bent into a circle. It had bells attached, and was covered with white swan's down and white plumes. The third held a spear of the same shape, covered with white feathers, but fringed with black and red plumes. The rest of the members carried pointed spears, covered with otter skins ornamented with feathers and bells.

The Kit-foxes all painted their faces. They wore, for garters around their legs, wide bands of otter skins, with bells attached, and an eagle feather, decorated with red, green and yellow, in their back hair. White weasel-skins were also attached to either end of this feather, while a strip of otter skin was suspended from its centre. When they marched through the camp they formed in the shape of a fox head. The chief went first standing for the nose. Behind him were the second and third men for the eyes, and then came the rest of the society in a group, all together representing a fox head. The two second-men, as the eyes, watched the chief, who was the nose, or leader, and acted just as he directed, the rest following after. When they were ready to dance, they sat in lines. In the first line were the regular members. If there were men withdrawing from the society, or giving their spears to new candidates, they sat in the second line, while the wives of the members sat behind. As soon as the drum began, the chief started the dance. The two circle men with the white spears followed. After them came the other members, with otter spears. They danced in pairs,—the same way that Kit-foxes run together. They gave short regular jumps with their feet close together, imitating the movements of a fox, barking and moving about, first in one direction, and then in another, just as a fox does. The two second-men (eyes) danced between the two lines, barking and swinging their spears. They did not move in straight lines, because the fox never goes straight. His tail always seems to guide him. When the white-circle men shouted, ' That is enough,' the dance ceased and they all seated themselves. After a short rest the dance was continued."

Tsin-ksi-six (Society of Mosquitoes)

" There was once a man who was thickly surrounded by mosquitoes. They stung him so badly that he wondered if they could kill him. Removing his clothes he lay upon the ground. The mosquitoes quickly covered him and bit him so severely, that he lost all feeling. In this condition, he dreamed that a mosquito came to him saying, ' because you have been generous and have allowed us to drink our fill from your body, we give you the Mosquito society and dance, and we make you its chief.' The Mosquito society wore bracelets of eagle-claws, and also buffalo robes, with the hair-side out. They painted themselves, and tied a plume in their back hair. When they danced, they sat in a circle, with the drummers in the centre. They jumped up, waving their robes like wings, dancing in a stooping posture, hovering close together and pushing each other, imitating the movements of mosquitoes. Whenever they were making ready to light, or sit down, they made a singing noise, like a mosquito. They danced four times. After the fourth dance, they scattered throughout the camp, some going on foot, others on horseback. Anyone whom they met, whether a chief, or Medicine Pipe man, they attacked and scratched with their eagle-claws. They were always specially delighted to catch a man without clothes. If anyone resisted, or ran away, the Mosquitoes followed, even into the lodges, just as real mosquitoes do, and scratched them hard. But, if a man bared himself and offered himself freely, they did not wound him, but passed on. If they caught a woman on the way to the river for water, and she held forth her hand saying, ' It is yours, fill yourselves up,' they did not hurt her, because, if you let a mosquito alone, until he fills up, the sting does not pain. If the Mosquitoes came to a lodge and decided to enter, one of their members, who had at some time entered the lodge of an enemy, opened the door, saying, ' I come in, because I was brave and once entered the lodge of an enemy.' If the women, and even the children, endeavoured to hide under the robes, or behind the lodge lining, he scratched them with his eagle-claws. If they resisted, the entire society followed, and all scratched them, until they yielded."

Kuko (Society of Doves).

" This society was originated in recent years among the South Piegans. When an expedition of our people went to visit them, they brought it back and started the dance over here. The Bloods afterwards borrowed it from us. There is a high hill, just north of here, where the society once went to feast and prepare for their dance. It was then named Dove Hill. The society originated in the dream of an old man named Change Camp. When the doves gave him the dance, they said to him : ' Gather together a band of people of all sizes, both young men and boys, that have no power in the tribe. If they band together, they will become strong and every one else will fear them.' They carried bows and arrows made of sarvis berry wood. Their quivers were made of the yellow skins of buffalo calves. They stripped and painted their bodies for their dance. The doves did many mean and cowardly acts and had no regard for anyone. They molested no one who obeyed their orders. If a prominent chief did not do as they said, they continually annoyed him. They played many mean tricks. In those days we did not have buckets, but used buffalo paunches for water bags. Sometimes the Doves lay in ambush, and, when they saw a woman returning from the river with her water bags filled, they shot their arrows into them and let the water run out. If she became angry, or if they could not pierce the skin, they sometimes destroyed the bags. If a woman was starting off to pick berries, and they ordered her not to go, and she disobeyed, they awaited her return and spilled her berries, or they took long willow sticks and beat the berries from the bushes where she was picking. They always took one woman into their society, who liked to dig roots and to pick berries, so that they could have an abundance for their feasts. She always followed them through the camp, carrying a bow and arrow just as they did, calling out, ' the Doves are now out. It will be better for everyone to stay inside.' All feared them. The head chief, and even the powerful societies, overlooked their mean actions and excused them, saying : ' the Doves are young and foolish and will go to any extreme to have their own way. It is dangerous to oppose them ' '

Muto ka-iks (Buffalo Society).

" The Muto-ka-iks is composed entirely of women. Their dances are continued even to this day among the Bloods. A large lodge is erected, having a centre pole, to which is tied the sacred ' root digger,' as a cross piece. The women assemble clothed in the costumes of their society. They wear robes and headdresses of soft tanned buckskin. There are four leaders, called ' Snake Medicine Hats,' with bonnets of eagle feathers. One of these, ' Lodge-Pole ' by

name, is chief. Four more, wearing bonnets of hawk
feathers, are called 'Hawk Medicine Hats.' Two
others, called 'Old Bulls,' wear head-dresses with
red plumes fastened to the horns. Old women and
young children come before them and are painted on
their foreheads with a red cross, symbolical of the
'centre pole' and the 'root digger.' A young boy,
son of a prominent chief, is chosen to take part in
the ceremonies. He is elaborately dressed and rides
a horse to the lodge of the society, followed by his
father and mother bearing presents in return for the
honour conferred upon their son. When the dancers
come forth from their main lodge, they walk slowly
to a lake, or stream, like a herd of buffalo going to
water. They lie down upon the shore and wait for
the two bulls which follow slowly. When they too
lie down, the boy rides to windward with a lighted
buffalo chip, allowing the smoke to blow towards the
dancers. They rise slowly to their feet. After
sniffing at the wind and tossing their heads, in
imitation of buffaloes, they start towards their lodge.
The boy on horseback follows, imitating the call
formerly used by Indians in driving buffalo. When
the women reach the lodge, they run about the centre
pole, until they fall exhausted. The old bulls do
not join in the stampede, but walk slowly and
deliberately, with heavy tread and bellowing, sometimes lowering their heads and running at each other
like bulls fighting. Finally, they too enter the lodge
and join those about the pole. The actions of the
dancers, after smelling the smoke, are in imitation of
buffalo driven by Indians to a piskun. When they
enter the lodge, they are supposed to be driven over
a cliff. When they run around the pole, their

motions are in imitation of buffalo wounded by their
fall, and caught in the corral at the bottom of the
cliff."

KNUT-SOME-TAIX (SOCIETY OF MAD DOGS).

"This society is sometimes also called Crazy Dogs.
Two prominent Gros Ventre chiefs, Big Road and

MAD DOG SOCIETY WAITING FOR EXPECTED FEAST.

Wolf-skin-around-his-neck, who killed enemies in
battle, by riding over them with their horses, were
the founders. The society of Mad Dogs was secured
from the Gros Ventres by the Blackfeet, through
O-mis-tai-po-kah. One of the most influential of the
Gros Ventre societies had refused to accept Wolf-skin-
around-his-neck as a member, and he was so angry with
them that, in retaliation, he disclosed the secrets and

mysteries of the Mad Dog society, of which he was one of the founders, to O-mis-tai-po-kah, head chief of the Blackfeet. Many members of the Mad Dog society are living to-day, and they still give their dances in our big camps. They dress and prepare for their ceremonial together, in a large lodge. Before beginning to dance, they notify the camp of their readiness, by first marching around and singing their society song. There

MAD DOGS MARCHING THROUGH CAMP.

are two head men, or leaders on horseback, who are said to be braver than the other members, and represent the two Gros Ventre chiefs, founders of the society. The two leaders must see that the big dance lodge is erected, and their wives must cook food for the society feast. While marching through camp, the Mad Dogs stop beside the lodges of chiefs, who are under obligations to them for favours, and dance until they are given a feast, or suitable reward. If there should be no response, the society seat themselves in a circle and wait, attracting the attention of the entire camp, by drumming and by singing their songs. The mounted leaders move slowly along the line, riding in opposite directions, and making the others rise when it is time to begin the dance. The Mad Dogs formerly had great power, because they were composed of chiefs who had earned a reputation for bravery and everyone feared to act in opposition to them."

CHAPTER XXXV

THE MUTSAIX (SOCIETY OF BRAVE DOGS)

Brings-down-the-Sun tells of its origin.—Weapons and characteristic dress of members.—Their society dance and customs.—A courageous mother saves the life of a Brave Dog.—Usefulness of Blackfeet Societies.

" I MYSELF am a member of the Mutsaix, which has the reputation of being the most exacting of the Blackfeet societies. We have even been known to kill men, who refused to obey our orders. It was started by Red Blanket and his wife, Generous Woman, who died of old age many years ago. She became so old, that she lost all of her teeth, and, before she died, it became necessary to move her everywhere on a travois. Their graves are close together on the summit of a high ridge, near the entrance to Cutbank Canyon, overlooking the river and the plains.

" When the Blackfeet were once travelling across the plains, Generous Woman told her husband, Red Blanket, that one of her dogs was missing with a loaded travois. Red Blanket turned back, but could find no trace of the dog. When he came to their former camping ground, it was dark and he lay down to sleep. During the night he heard a strange voice calling, ' Lone Chief invites you to prepare for the dance.' Then a drum began to beat and Red Blanket, supposing he was in a camp, looked around, but saw no lodges, nor people ;

THREE LODGES OF BRAVE DOG SOCIETY NEAR THE CENTRE OF ENCAMPMENT.

there was no sign of life,—nothing but the barren plains. When he lay down, he again heard a drum and the same voice calling, saying : ' Lone Chief invites you to come and eat, for he is ready to give a dance.' This time Red Blanket jumped to his feet, thinking he must be dreaming. While walking around the old camp, he found some dried meat that had been left behind. A

INTERIOR OF SOCIETY LODGE SHOWING MANNER OF HANGING CLOTHES AND HEADDRESSES.

female dog ran out from a thicket of willows and stood gazing at him. He supposed that this dog must have been doing the mysterious talking, so he threw her the meat, which she ate and immediately returned to the bushes. When Red Blanket lay down again, he went to sleep and the spirit of his lost dog came to him, saying : ' I am giving this dance here to-night, in behalf of a poor mother and her six little boy dogs.

They were left behind, when the camp moved, and I am trying to help them. If you feel sorry for this unfortunate mother and her children, carry them with you and save their lives. We will show you our dance and, when you return again to camp, you can make use of it to found a dog society.' In his dream, Red Blanket followed the dog spirit into the bushes, where he saw

BUCKSKIN SHIRT OF MAD DOG SOCIETY.
(Decorated with beads and trimmed with ermine.)

many dogs dancing. One of their chiefs wore a long black robe, dragging behind like a tail, while others wore decorations and streamers, trailing behind for tails. In the morning, when Red Blanket awoke, he found the dog family among the willows. He took up the pups and, placing them in his shirt, carried them back to camp, followed by their mother. He then started the society of Brave Dogs, taking members as the dog spirit had instructed, and teaching them to dance, just as he had seen the dogs dancing. Red Blanket, as the founder, wore a small rattle tied through the flesh of his wrist, the medicine of the Brave Dogs. He first took in three prominent chiefs, Many Eagles, Lost Feather,

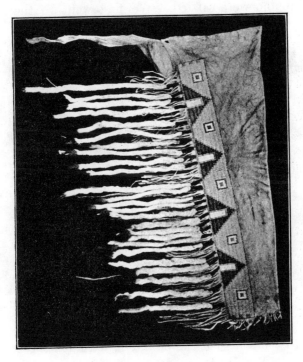

BUCKSKIN LEGGING.

and Lone Chief. They together selected other members. We formerly gave our dance, when the camp was to be moved. We first marched around, beating drums, and singing our society songs, and then we went to the centre of the camp, where we lay on the ground, curled up like dogs sleeping. We wore no clothes, but painted our bodies all over. Our moccasins were decorated with porcupine quills, but had no ankle-tops. Each man carried a knife, bow and a big quiver filled with arrows. Next morning, when camp was broken, we went around the deserted circle, and ate food that was left behind, just like dogs. Then we followed the tribe slowly, always coming in after the people had their lodges pitched and were settled. We first went to the head chief's tipi, where we danced four times, and then we

BUCKSKIN SHIRT FRINGED AND DECORATED WITH COLOURED PORCUPINE QUILLS.

went to the centre of camp, and curled upon the ground to sleep. We did this for four successive nights. On the fourth morning, all of the Brave Dogs returned to their own lodges, where we painted, dressed in our best clothes, ate good food, and acted like dogs no more, until our next dance. While we were giving our dance, we stole anything we wanted, even food, while it was cooking, just as dogs do. Sometimes we danced at the lodges of prosperous chiefs. If they gave us clothes as presents, we could not wear them until after our dance, so we gave them meanwhile into the care of our wives.

" We placed stones in a circle, near the centre of a new camp ground, where we intended pitching our big dancing tipi. We always entered it early in the morning of the day of our dance. We carried long sticks as spears, with the bark peeled off and wrapped with red and black cloth. Feathers, with small bells attached, were fastened at intervals along the staff and a spear point tied to the end. The leader was called Wolf-Skin-Man. He wore a coyote skin, with the head in front, and tail hanging behind. To the left of the chief sat two men, with white spears driven into the ground before them. Their bodies were painted white and they had yellow stripes across the nose and eyes. This was their distinguishing mark, because the others had red and black stripes over the nose and eyes. Another man, holding a long willow stick, wore a blanket made from an old lodge top, well browned with smoke. To his blanket were tied many buffalo hoofs, so that they would rattle when he moved. Two other men, called " Water Braves," painted black over their bodies, carried on their backs pieces of old lodges made into small bags, which were filled with back-fat and pemmican. They also carried water-bottles.

" There were two dancers representing Grizzly Bears. They were stripped, wearing only a waist band of bear skin. They always painted as hideously as possible to inspire the spectators with awe. They covered their faces with thick red paint, and made black streaks downward across their eyes. They made their front hair stand erect with thickened paint. They carried bows and arrows with large points, and wore head-dresses made from grizzly bears' heads, with the ears on,

and two buffalo horns added, to make them look like
double ears.   The bears were separated from the other
dancers, lying in a hole for a den, and covering themselves over with robes.   Wolf-Skin-Man, the leader,
arose first to dance, the entire circle following him.   All
wore blankets and carried spears.   They also held
whistles in their mouths, which were blown while
dancing.   The two white-painted dancers pushed into
the circle, driving the others away with their spears.
When the black-painted water carriers passed the white
dancers in the circle, they stopped.   Then the man with
the willow stick entered, but he could not sit down,
until after the bears had stopped dancing.   Every time
these five leaders arose, the entire society must dance,
with the exception of the bears.   They always did as
they pleased, lying lazily in their den, covered with
robes.   When the spectators, eager to see them dance,
threw things at them, they pretended four times that
they were going to begin.   After the fourth feint, they
stood up, holding their hands hanging down, just as
bears hold their paws.   While dancing, they carried
their bows and arrows, pretending to aim at the dancers.
The Brave Dogs kept going around in a circle, just like
a dog looking for a place to lie down.   When we had
danced four times, the bears held the sharp pointed
arrows ready to shoot, but, changing them quickly to
two painted arrows without points, they took aim at the
crowd, as if to shoot them, but the arrows were sent
high over their heads.   The rest of us ran off over the
prairie, following in the direction the arrows flew, and
throwing our moccasins into the air as we ran.   Many
boys followed us to pick them up, for we wore finely
decorated dance-moccasins, but no one was allowed to
pick up the two painted arrows, which the Grizzly Bears

followed to recover. When the bears again returned to our ranks, we formed into line and marched through camp, singing our society song. If any of our members held back, the bears shot at them, or at any people, who might interfere with us. When we had completed the camp circle, we announced the events that would take place on the following day, and then entered our society tipi and feasted. After the feast, we went off on a hunt and killed two buffalo bulls. Each member took two pieces of the meat. One he left in the society tipi, the other he took back to his family. The Brave Dogs always said the opposite of what they really meant. The people understood this custom. If we announced that camp was not to be moved in the morning, we really meant that camp was to be moved. If we returned from a scouting expedition for game, and reported that there were no buffalo in sight, and that there was no need of their sharpening their knives and arrows, they felt glad and started at once to prepare for a hunt, for they knew well that buffalo were near at hand. If one of our members stepped into a hole and fell, when we were running and throwing away our moccasins, he could not get up by himself. He had to lie there and wait, until the society came back, when we lifted him up with our spears.

" A Brave Dog must always face the enemy, no matter how much he feared them. We were once camped near Chief Mountain, when the Pend d'Oreilles attacked us. It happened that one of our number, named ' Nose,' walked out alone and faced the enemy. According to the rules of our society, he could not turn back, unless one of his relatives drove him back like a dog, so he stood there in plain sight, chanting and shaking his rattle. His mother, Red Flower, realising her son's danger, ran through camp, imploring someone to drive her son back, but no one was willing. When the Pend d'Oreilles caught sight of him and began shooting, she ran out herself. She had to run in front of him, and strike him four times in the face with a switch, before he could turn. After her fourth blow, he ran for the brush like a dog, and they both escaped in safety. Because of this brave deed, the Piegans changed his name from 'Nose' to 'Brave Dog.'

"Whenever it became necessary to move camp, the Mad Dogs always prepared a feast, and sent a messenger to the head chief, inviting him to eat in our society lodge. After we had finished eating, and were seated, talking and smoking together, he would enquire :

"'My children! Why have you asked me to come here? What is it that you desire?' Our leader would then say, 'It is now the time for the tribe to move. The camp ground has become foul, the water supply is no longer good, and it has become necessary to drive our horses a long distance to secure good grass.' The chief would reply, 'It is too late for us to move to-day. Have your herald announce that we will break camp early to-morrow morning. Instruct everyone to bring in their horses before dark, and to picket them close to their lodges, that we may not be delayed in the morning. We shall start before sunrise.'

"Men did not join the Blackfeet societies for pleasure, but to fulfil vows, generally made because of sickness, or for some remarkable escape from danger. The leading societies ruled the camp, and helped the chiefs to administer public discipline. They protected the tribes' sources of food and secured equal opportunities for all. They strictly enforced the rule that private advantages must be surrendered to the public good. Under the exercise of such police regulations [1] and the enjoyment by all of equal rights and a joint ownership of game and lands, no individual could claim or enjoy special privileges. The roaming herds of buffalo, a gift from the Great Spirit in the Sun, and their chief source of food and materials for shelter, were owned in common. The society-men alone had authority to decide when and how they should be hunted. If an Indian disregarded their authority, and hunted for himself alone, they followed him, forced him to return, and took away his horse and weapons. If his selfish hunting scared away the buffaloes, they punished him severely, destroying his saddle and tipi, stripping him of his clothes, and even whipping him. Sometimes, when several Indians started for a hunt, without their knowledge, the society-men took a position on a hill and waited, watching the direction the hunters had taken. If, in returning, the hunters sought to avoid them, the society-men followed them, and seized their meat and horses.

" If they had given an order against picking berries, and a woman disobeyed, they spilled all she gathered. If a husband and wife fought, and their quarrels disturbed other people, one of the societies would punish them, by cutting their lodge to pieces, or by destroying their saddles and parfleches. The societies compelled everyone to submit to their rule, but they never annoyed or interfered with people who obeyed their commands."

[1] See Appendix.

CHAPTER XXXVI

LEGENDS OF THE FRIENDLY MEDICINE GRIZZLY AND THE FRIENDLY MEDICINE WOLF

The North Piegans gather their winter supply of berries.—Brings-down the-Sun tells the legend of Nis-ta-e and the Medicine Grizzly.—A sole survivor and wounded after a fight with the Snakes, faces death in the mountains.—A supernatural grizzly feeds him and carries him back home.—Legend of Itsa-pich-kaupe and the Medicine Wolf.—The community of spirit between animals and men.—Some animals can read the future.—Coyote barks an omen of death.—Owls are dreaded because they are the unhappy spirits of evil doers.

DURING my visit at Brings-down-the-Sun's camp, the women were gathering their winter supply of sarvis berries. The bushes, which the old chief so carefully guarded, were loaded down with ripe fruit. Their method was to strike the bushes with sticks, catching the berries in blankets, and then spreading them in the sun to dry. Berry-bags for carrying them were made of small skins from deer legs, wolf-pups or unborn calves of large animals such as the elk, or deer, or, most often, of the buffalo. I saw a beautiful berry-bag made of a spotted fawn skin and ornamented with coloured porcupine quills. Sarvis berries are a favourite article of diet with all the plains-tribes. They are eaten raw or cooked in soups and stews. My Indian friends warned me that the berries sometimes make people very ill, who are not accustomed to eating them. Large quantities are dried for winter use. The dried berries, strung together in necklaces of many strands, are worn by women for ornament. They are also much used as sacred food in ceremonials. While in Brings-down-the-Sun's camp, I secured a quantity of them to take back with me to Montana for my friend Wolf Plume. I knew that they would be an acceptable present, as he owned a Beaver Bundle, which required in its ceremonial sarvis berries for the feast. One evening, while finishing our supper, a crowd of sarvis berry pickers, consisting entirely of women and children, filed past our camp, with bags and parfleches filled with the fruit. No man was allowed to accompany them, because they had to cross the river by wading. The children were in the lead, then followed the women in bright coloured dresses, some carrying babies on their backs, wrapped in blankets after the Indian fashion. Last of all came Kops-ksis-e (Swell-nosed-pup), Brings-down-the-Sun's faithful old watch dog, who brought up the rear with his canine followers. I was interested in watching the women dividing up the fruit, before separating to their tipis. Each woman seemed to know exactly the amount she had gathered, and there was no bickering.

Brings-down-the-Sun had noticed his wife, Bird, in the company, hurrying past our camp with a large sack of berries. Turning to Menake he said, "There goes Sis-tse (Bird), she is tired I know, and hungry after her hard day's work. I would be pleased if you could carry to her some tea and a little food." He then hastened to her side to tell her that he was being well cared for and that she need not cook for him. Menake soon carried a bountiful repast to the old woman and, on her return, reported to me, that she had overheard the chief say to his wife : " My white son in yonder camp will soon leave us to start for the south. I must go over this evening to talk to him, for he will want to hear more of my stories. I will not return, until the Last Brother points downward towards the prairie" (very late).

When he had taken his accustomed seat at our camp fire, I enquired about Calf Robe's (Nis-ta-e) expedition against the Snake Indians (Shoshones). Brings-down-the-Sun said, "I remember it well, and have seen the picture writings of the expedition among the records of my father. More than fifty marks represent the years that have elapsed since the battle; four symbols stood for the four leaders; a kettle on a tripod by a solitary pine tree indicated the location of the camp, and many tracks, leading up to it, told the story of the attack by the enemy: three red marks represented the three chiefs, Brave Breast, Lone Cutter and Poor Robe, who were killed; a circle enclosing arrows, pointing in every direction, told of the surrounding, the desperate fighting and wounding of Nis-ta-e, who was left alone to die."

LEGEND OF THE FRIENDLY MEDICINE GRIZZLY

"One morning, in the early spring, Nis-ta-e, a young chief, entered his father's lodge, saying, 'After the sun sets this evening, I will start on a long war expedition.' 'Where will you go?' inquired the old man. 'I intend to go with three other chiefs against the Snakes, for I hear they have many fine horses.' His father warned him that it would be a dangerous journey, but Nis-ta-e replied: 'I am not afraid. If I do not come back before the first big snow-storm in the autumn (November), do not be anxious, but if I do not come before the snow grows deep in winter (December), I will never return.' ' Go,' said his father, ' and I wish you good luck. Bring back both horses and scalps, for through brave deeds you will become a great chief.' Nis-ta-e and his companions travelled southward along the Rocky Mountains. One morning, after crossing the Yellowstone River, they came upon a fresh trail. Nis-ta-e said, ' These are the tracks we have been looking for. We are now in the country of the Snakes.' They followed the trail for several days, until one evening they saw from the summit of a high ridge, the camp of the enemy in the distance. ' To-night,' said Nis-ta-e, ' we will get some horses.' They drew near the camp, and lay in ambush, for the moon was bright. After midnight, when the moon had set, Nis-ta-e said, ' Wait here for me, I will go alone into the camp and drive out some horses.' When he returned driving a herd, his companions said, ' Let us run with what we have, for day will soon break.' Nis-ta-e replied, ' We have come a long distance and must have more horses.' He again entered the Snake camp, but this time the three waiting chiefs heard the barking of dogs, and at once realised their danger. Nis-ta-e came out on the run, shouting, ' Ride for your lives; the Snakes are after us.' He took the lead, directing the others to follow with the stolen horses. As they rode away in the gray light of the early dawn, they saw the sun's rays already touching the distant mountain peaks. Morning soon broke over the plains, and as the sun rose, Nis-ta-e saw in the distance a cloud of dust made by the Snakes in hot pursuit. He signed to the other three chiefs to drop some of the horses. When a shower of arrows flew by them, Nis-ta-e shouted, ' Hurry, let us get to shelter, for we will have a hard time to-day.'

They made for a solitary pine, distant on the plain and surrounded by a thicket of poplars and underbrush. Jumping from their horses they sought shelter in the bushes. The Snakes surrounded them and shot arrows into the thicket. The Blackfeet dug a pit in which they lay and defended themselves as best they could. During the day, Brave Breast, Lone Cutter and Poor Robe were killed, while Nis-ta-e was shot through the knee. When night came on, the Snakes built fires around the thicket to prevent their escape. As he lay in the pit wounded, not daring to leave the cover of the bushes in the bright firelight, Nis-ta-e thought his time to die had come. There was small chance of escape, for the night was clear with no sign of rain. Knowing it would be sure death to remain in the bushes until daylight, Nis-ta-e took off his Otter Medicine, and kneeling, prayed to the Great Mystery in the Sun, that a heavy rain might come and put out the fires. Then, holding his Medicine in turn towards the north, south, east and west, and swaying his body to and fro, he chanted the sacred song,

> " ' The Otter is my medicine,
> His power is very strong.
> The Thunder is my medicine,
> He will help his children,
> He will help his children.'

" Nis-ta-e drew the Medicine to his breast and, holding it towards the sky, continued his song. While chanting, he felt upon his face the rising of a gentle breeze from the east. He then made a vow to the Sun saying :

" ' Pity me, O Sun ! Give me help that I may escape from my enemies. If I may return in safety to my people, I promise that I will torture myself at the next Sun-dance.'

" A bank of clouds appeared in the north and the sky became overcast. Nis-ta-e knew that his Medicine was prevailing and his life would be saved. A light rain soon began to fall, gradually increasing into a heavy shower and making the fires of the Snakes burn low. He then crawled through the bushes and safely reached the open prairie. He travelled all that night, and, when daylight came, found himself close to the mountains. His leg was badly swollen from the wound and he felt he could go no farther. Stopping in the thick pine forest, he gathered a few poles and made a brush lodge by covering them with pine boughs. He lay under this shelter, and when he was thirsty crawled to a small stream nearby. He also gathered and ate a few roots. A coyote came to the lodge and made friends with him. In a few days Nis-ta-e became so weak from lack of food, that he was unable to crawl to the stream. One day, as he lay expecting death, and dreaming of his home far to the north, and his old father waiting for him in vain, he heard the sound of heavy footsteps back of the lodge. Nis-ta-e wondered if an enemy had found him. The footsteps approached and stopped. A huge form appeared suddenly in the entrance. Instead of an Indian, it was a grizzly bear. He stood there snuffing, grunting, moving his head from side to side and gazing steadily at Nis-ta-e, who thought his end had now surely come. He raised himself feebly and said, ' I suppose you have come to eat me. If you intend to kill me, do it quickly, that I may have no pain.' The grizzly walked in and smelled him from head to foot. Nis-ta-e was wondering which part he would eat first, when the grizzly began to smell his wounded leg. He concluded it would go first, but, to his surprise, the bear only licked the wound.

'Bear,' said Nis-ta-e, 'you had something in mind when you came in here. Are you going to kill me, or help me?' The bear answered, 'Yes, I will help you. I have come to take you home, that you may again see your people. In four days we will start.' 'If you wait that long,' said Nis-ta-e, 'I will be too weak to travel, for I am starving.' 'You will not starve,' replied the bear, 'for I will hunt.' He went off and soon returned with a grouse. Every day the bear and the coyote hunted, always bringing in some game. Nis-ta-e became stronger, and, on the morning of the fourth day, the bear said, 'To-day we must start. Get upon my back. Hold tight to my hair and I will carry you safely.' Nis-ta-e stretched himself upon the grizzly's broad back, and held on to the long hair. The bear started towards the north, closely followed by the coyote. They travelled at a swinging trot until Nis-ta-e, becoming exhausted, said, 'Rest awhile my brother, for I can hold on no longer.' They stopped and, while Nis-ta-e lay upon the grass, the bear followed the trail of some elk. He soon returned with a bloody mouth, and carried Nis-ta-e to the place where he had killed a bull elk. The three friends feasted together and camped there for the night. Next day, while passing through a narrow defile in the mountains, they met another grizzly. The stranger raised upon his legs and was prepared to fight, but the Medicine Grizzly also stood erect, towering above the other bear. The coyote came next and behind him stood Nis-ta-e. The strange grizzly quickly made off and there was no fight. Again they started, travelling steadily, until, one evening from the top of a high ridge, Nis-ta-e looked down upon the camp of the Blackfeet on the Marias River. The bear said, 'You will now soon see your relatives.' He carried Nis-ta-e to the river and said he must leave him there. Nis-ta-e was sorry to part with his two faithful friends, the Medicine Grizzly and the coyote. He invited them to come and live with him, but the Grizzly refused, saying, ' The moon is now nearly past when the leaves fall off. It is time I should find a den, for the heavy snows of winter will soon come. The only favour I ask of you in return is, that you will never kill a bear that has holed itself up for the winter.' The Medicine Grizzly then turned toward the mountains, followed by the coyote, while Nis-ta-e signalled to some young men not far distant, who were trying their race horses. They swam their horses across the river, and carried him safely to camp.

" For the sake of the Medicine Grizzly, that saved the life of Nis-ta-e, the Blackfeet will not kill a hibernating bear."

Legend of the Friendly Medicine Wolf.

" The events, which I will now relate, happened many years ago. The Blackfeet were moving camp. They travelled slowly and, when stretched out on the plains, their line extended so far, it was hard for those in front to see the people in the rear. As a protection against hostile war parties, the warriors were divided into two bands, one riding in front and the other in the rear. Between these two bands of warriors were the old men, the women and children. While passing through a hill country, a large party of Crow Indians, which had been hiding in ambush, attacked the line in the middle. Before the Blackfeet warriors came to their defence, the Crows had killed many women and children, and carried away some women prisoners. One of the captured was a young woman named Itsa-pich-kaupe (Sits-by-the-door), the mother of Calf Looking and grandmother of Ap-ai-kai-koa (Little Skunk). She was carried on horseback by the warrior who took her prisoner, over two hundred miles to the Crow camp on the Yellowstone River. There she was presented to one of his friends, who took her to his lodge and gave her into the care of his wife, an older woman. Itsa-pich-kaupe was so closely watched she could find no chance of escape. Every night the Crow man hobbled her feet, so that she could not walk. He also tied a rope around her waist, and fastened the other end to his wife. One day, when the Crow man was away, and the two women were together in the lodge, the Crow woman conversed with Itsa-pich-kaupe in the sign language, saying, 'I overheard my husband say last night that they intended to kill you. I feel sorry and will help you to escape to-night when it is dark.' That evening the Crow man hobbled Itsa-pich-kaupe as usual and tied her to his wife. When the lodge fire burned low, and the Crow woman knew from his heavy breathing that her husband was asleep, she crawled over to Itsa-pich-kaupe and unfastened the ropes. She then tied the loose end of the waist-rope to a lodge pole, so that if her husband should waken and pull upon the rope, he would not suspect her escape. She loosened the bottom of the lodge covering from the pegs and, giving Itsa-pich-kaupe a pair of moccasins, a flint and a small sack filled with pemmican, pushed her outside. Itsa-pich-kaupe travelled all that night as fast as she could go, away from the Crow camp. When daylight came she hid in some underbrush. The Crows tried to follow her but they could find no tracks and gave up the chase. When she had walked for four nights, and was a long distance from the Crow camp, she began travelling by day also, but her supply of pemmican soon gave out, and there were large holes in her moccasins. One day, when her feet were bruised and bleeding, she saw a large wolf following her. At first she was frightened and tried to run, but her strength was gone, and she sank down exhausted. The wolf stood watching her, and then crept nearer and nearer until he lay at her feet. When Itsa-pich-kaupe arose to walk, the wolf followed, and when she sat down again to rest, he lay down by her side. She then besought his aid, saying:

" ' Pity me, brother wolf! I am so weak for food that I must soon die. I pray for the sake of my young children that you will help me.'

When she finished her prayer, the wolf trotted to the summit of a high butte, where he sat watching. He disappeared, but soon came back, dragging a buffalo calf he had just killed. With the flint the Crow woman had given her, she built a fire. After roasting and eating some of the meat, she felt stronger and started on, but her feet were so bruised and torn she could scarcely walk. When the wolf drew near, she placed her hand on his broad back, and he seemed glad to bear her weight. In this way the wolf helped Itsa-pich-kaupe, hunting every day and keeping her supplied with food, until he brought her safely home. When they entered camp together, Itsa-pich-kaupe led the friendly wolf to her lodge, where she related to her family the story of her escape from the Crow camp. She besought the people to be kind to the wolf, and to give him food. But she became very sick, after her return, and, as there was no one to look out for the wolf, the Indian dogs attacked him, and drove him into the hills. They would not allow him to remain in camp. The faithful wolf waited for a long time, watching in vain for Itsa-pich-kaupe. He came every evening to the summit of a high butte, where he sat gazing down at the lodge where she lay. Her relatives continued to feed him, until he disappeared, never to return. The Blackfeet never shoot at a wolf, or coyote, believing them to be good medicine. We have a saying, 'The gun that shoots at a wolf or coyote will never again shoot straight.'"

Brings-down-the-Sun continued : "At one time animals and men were able to understand each other. We can still talk to the animals, just as we do to people, but they now seldom reply, excepting in dreams. We are then obedient to them and do whatever they tell us. Whenever we are in danger, or distress, we pray to them and they often help us. Many of the animals are friendly to man. They are able to read the future and give us warning of what will happen.

"If a coyote comes near the lodge, and barks in front of a door, it is an omen that one of the family will soon die. I can remember, many years ago, observing a band of coyotes on a ridge overlooking our camp. Every one of them, one after the other, barked directly toward our lodge. The very same day, when I came suddenly upon a coyote among the willows, it turned and barked toward me. They were omens of death, for my sister died within a few days."

The camp fire was now burning low. Every one sat gazing silently into the glowing bed of coals. From the depths of the woods came the mournful hooting of an owl, called because of his appearance, Ko-ko-nút-stòke (Ears-far-apart). The Indians listened in silent awe, believing it was a ghost. The Blackfeet have a superstitious dread of owls and say that "their ways are evil, because they dread the sun-light and travel only at night." They believe they are the restless and unhappy spirits of people long dead, who were transformed into owls because of their evil deeds. Being dissatisfied with their abode in the spirit world, they continue revisiting their old haunts, crying dolefully through the night, and seeking to bring misfortune to the living. When the hooting came nearer, and was joined by the voice of another owl, the people became uneasy. When he finally settled in a big tree, close to the camp, some of the women became greatly alarmed. Brings-down-the-Sun said, "Listen! he calls his own name, Ko-ko-nút-stòke; Ko-ko-nút-stòke; Ko-ko-nút-stòke (Ears-far-apart; Ears-far-apart; Ears-far-apart). You can easily distinguish the different voices in a family of owls: the deep notes of the father, the higher tones of the mother, and the small voices of the children." Nitana declared that, shortly before her sister died, an owl had been seen looking in at the door of her lodge. When Spotted Eagle, the medicine man, was told of the incident, he warned her sister that it was an evil omen and gave her a charm to use, if the owl ever returned.

In order to satisfy the women of our camp, and to effectually ward off any injury from the owl, Brings-down-the-Sun called back, " Noks-sto-mo-au (You are my relative)." The Blackfeet believed that an owl will do no harm to a company, if he thinks one of his relatives is present.

The old chief then arose, saying: " I see the Last

Brother is pointing downwards toward the prairie, and it is time for us to sleep. The nights are now short and the light of day will come again quickly. When the sun rises, and is high in the sky, I will return to continue my talk."

CHAPTER XXXVII

BRINGS-DOWN-THE-SUN TALKS ABOUT BIRDS AND THE STARS

Variety of song-birds in the Blackfoot Country.—Brings-down-the-Sun
tells of the habits of the birds and explains their songs.—He gives
the Blackfeet names for the moons.—How to read the signs in the
skies.—He tells the ancient star-legends of The Seven Brothers
(Great Bear), and The Lost Children (Pleiades).

In the morning, I was awakened by the musical song of
the western lark sparrow. I lay watching him seated
on the tip top of a lodge pole, enjoying himself in the
bright warm rays of the rising sun. Every few minutes
he raised his crown, and throwing back his head, burst
into his plaintive song, " Che-che-che-wée-che," the
fourth syllable with a rising, and the last with a falling
inflection. The Blackfeet call him the Gros Ventre bird,
because they are unable to understand his song, which
they say sounds like the Gros Ventre language.

The wonderful song of the western meadow lark, with
its loud clear notes, was frequently heard both in the
morning and at twilight. He closely resembles the
meadow lark of the eastern states, although his song is
very different, resembling more that of the hermit
thrush.

One of the most interesting of the song birds of the
Blackfoot country, is the chestnut collared longspur,
called black breast by the Indians. He sang at all times,
through the heat of midday and even during the night.

When riding across the plains, I saw him along old
trails and abandoned wagon roads, running swiftly
ahead of my horse, or springing from the ground and
mounting to a height of about fifty feet, when he
extended his wings and fluttered slowly to the ground,
always against the wind, and singing a cheerful, rippling

MEDICINE WEASEL'S CAMP NEAR THE ROCKIES.

song. I do not recall hearing a longspur singing while
mounting into the air, but only when descending. His
song reminded me of that of the English linnet.

During hot days in early summer, I often heard over
Indian camps "pallid horned larks," singing so high up in
the air, as to be entirely out of sight. But, if I watched
closely, they would re-appear and sing, while floating
downwards. From their continuous singing, while at a

lofty height, it seemed as if they must be rejoicing in a cool breeze, discovered high above the sun-heated earth.

A few days before the formation of a large Blackfeet camp, while walking a half mile from the camp, I found a nest with five eggs, which a western lark sparrow had made in a moist meadow, where the grass and wild flowers grew luxuriantly. The grazing Indian horses soon stripped the ground of all vegetation as closely as. if cut with a scythe. Visiting the place a week later, I found three nearly fledged young larks in the nest. Their hatching and nurture had proceeded without interruption, notwithstanding the horses had tramped all around them, and had eaten away their protective covering, leaving them exposed and in plain view. Other birds that I had found on the Blackfeet plains, were the vesper sparrow, white-throated sparrow, chicadee, goldfinch, king bird, kingfisher, cat bird, raven, Brewer blackbird, long-billed curlew, Wilson snipe, herring gull, and yellow warbler.

When Brings-down-the-Sun had taken his seat on the log, and was placidly smoking his everyday pipe, I asked him to tell me the Blackfeet names for the different birds and to explain the meanings of their songs. The old chief said, " The birds that you see making so much disturbance near the camp, chattering while flying from tree to tree, and looking eagerly for scraps, are called Ma-mi-as-ich-imi (long tails or magpies). I look upon them as my friends because they always come first to my coyote bait, when I am catching eagles. They say to each other, ' Long tails fly on ahead and fasten your provision bag to another tree.' If you take notice you will see them flying ahead of each other, continually in search of food. The old women often sing these words as a slumber song to children."

A large woodpecker with red wings lighted on a dead tree near by. He hammered diligently with his bill on the hollow trunk, making a loud noise, but suddenly stopped to give his cry. Pointing up to him, Brings-down-the-Sun said : " That fellow was saying, in the Blackfeet tongue, to the worms and bugs in the old tree, ' Stick your heads out now for I want to eat you.'

" The O-toch-koki (yellow breast, meadow lark, or prairie robin) is called big-stern bird, because he is so broad across the back. He is one of the first birds to come in the spring. We are always glad to see him, because we know that summer is near. He has many songs and sings in different tongues. All of the Indian tribes understand the songs of the yellow breast. He sings in Blackfoot, ' Nat-sia-ke-oa-se-kim-aki,' ' Good Whistler (his wife) is a selfish woman,' also ' Kit-o-kin-tsit-o-tsin-aicht,' ' The fat is part of his liver,' and another one, which we consider very impudent, ' Kitaki-ma-siks-a-stoki,' ' Your sister has a black skin.'

" When the Isik-o-ka-e (black breast, or chestnut collared longspur) is flying, he sings, ' Kiowa-kinix-apis-is-tsis-ta-kits-itope,' ' Spread out your blanket and I will light upon it.'

" The Nepe-e, Summer bringers (white-throated sparrows), sing, ' The leaves are budding and summer is coming.' They also sing, ' It-sis-oks-is-taki,' ' Crushed inside.' Goldfinches are called grease birds, because they have the yellow colour of grease, or tallow. The cat bird is ' Pokaup ' (the baby), because he cries so like a baby." When a king bird alighted among some berry bushes and began a loud chattering, Brings-down-the-Sun said, " There is the Si-kim-e-newan (stingy-with-his-berries). The Blackfeet women gave him this name, for the reason that, when they are gathering berries and disturb him, he flies about, fussing and chattering, as if angry, because they are gathering his berries. There are some small dark coloured birds, which live in winter close to the springs that never freeze. Whenever we call ' Meat ! Meat ! ' they begin to dance. The swallows are called fire birds, because there is a legend that they brought the first fire to the Indians.

" The Raven is very wise. He knows more than any of the birds. We have found that he always tells the truth, so we watch his actions very closely, that we may be able to look into the future. If we see a raven circling high in the air over camp, we know that a messenger will soon come from a distance bearing news. In former days, when we were on a buffalo hunt and found no game, if we saw ravens playing together on a ridge, we took our course in that direction, knowing we should soon secure meat. If we were on a war exped-ition, and saw ravens light in the trail ahead of us and two of them had their heads close together, as if whispering, we hurried to get into ambush, because the ravens knew an enemy was approaching, and were giving us warning.

" The kildeer is called Kit-se-pit-se-koye. They say that, if its nest is robbed of the eggs, or young birds, it grieves so deeply, and cries so hard, it will fall upon the ground. The Ma-pit-so-to-e, Brings-something from-the-water, is a little smaller than the kildeer, but of nearly the same colour.

" Snipe are called So-otak-skan, Shadow in the water, because they stand in shallow water, where they can see their own shadow. There is a bird a little larger than a snipe, with long legs and a black breast. The Stony Indians understand him and say he sings in their language, 'Buffalo! Buffalo!'

"The Rooster sings when he wakens in the morning, 'Nepó-akà. Get up!' The curlew is our Ma-ken-ima. If anyone kills a curlew, or steals its young, we believe a storm will arise. The Peta is the golden eagle. Se-ka-kin-eoa is the white headed eagle. Pekoke is the buzzard.

"The fish hawk is called Pa-tse-ksis-acom (Mistake Thunder), because he is so dangerous. It is said that an Indian once climbed to a fish hawk's nest, on a high cliff to secure the young birds. When he came to a dangerous place on the cliff, the old birds swooped down on him with such force, that he was thrown over the cliff and killed. Ever since that time, we have called them Mistake Thunder, meaning that they are as powerful and as dangerous as the Thunder (or lightning)" When a night hawk flew overhead, Brings-down-the-Sun, looking up, called out, " Pisto (Short face), shoot down now." I followed his gaze in time to see the night hawk fall like a flash, making the peculiar, rushing noise with his wings, which we call " booming," but the Blackfeet call it " tearing his wings off."

It was a very hot day, and the chief's head evidently pained him, for he placed his hand upon his forehead, saying, " I have a long scar here, just over the temple, where a wild horse kicked me, when I was a young man. Ever since that time, whenever the sun is hot, or the wind blows hard, the old scar becomes quite painful. You have heard the old saying, ' My dogs are scattered, and I must gather them together and go away, but,

when the sun is set, my dogs will come together again.' "
This was a Blackfoot figure of speech, by which he
meant that he was tired and must stop, but would
continue his talk in the cool of the evening.

A golden sunset was fading over the Rocky Mountains, when Brings-down-the-Sun returned to our
camp. With the night came a cool breeze from the
mountains, which made us draw closely together
around the outside fire. It was our last night in
camp, and many of the North Piegans came for a
farewell visit. At sunrise we were to start for the
south. The camp fire lighted up the tops of the green
cottonwoods, the swarthy faces of the Indians, with
their brightly coloured blankets and clothes decorated
with beads and porcupine quills, and the lodges, with
their picturesque tops and crowns of tapering poles.
Beyond the circle of the firelight was the black line of
the forest. Menake, Long Hair and Nitana were
roasting meat on long sticks. They also roasted over
the hot coals peeled stalks of Po-kint-somo (wild
rhubarb). The roasted stalk was sprinkled with salt
and eaten hot. In early summer wild rhubarb, prepared in this way, has a delicious and delicate flavour.
Menake also brewed from roots a refreshing drink,
tasting like root beer. It was made by boiling, in a
kettle, a mixture of the poch-coi-as-sukas (smell mouth,
Western sweet cicely) and siksocasim (Indian horehound).

Brings-down-the-Sun, as was his custom, sat apart.
He was quietly smoking, gazing dreamily into the fire.
Knowing that he would soon begin his talk, I was busy
preparing my writing materials and notebooks. The
old chief had noticed my movements, for he said
to Menake, "My white son over there reminds me of a

gopher (ground squirrel). He runs in one direction, as if about to steal something, and then he quickly jumps up again and darts in another. He never sits still for a moment." When he finally came into the circle of the camp fire, and took his customary seat on the big log, the Indians knew he was ready to talk and became silent. Knocking the ashes from his pipe, he laid it beside him on the log, and began to speak.

"My father used to lie beside the fire on long winter evenings, giving me instructions, and recounting the interesting events that happened during his life. He taught me how to look into the future, by observing the warnings of the animals, and how to know the different moons, which enabled him to keep his records, by watching the changes in the seasons, and by studying the habits of birds and wild animals."

Calendar of Moons.

"We call the moon of early winter,—'After the first snowfall' (November), or 'Time of the first Chinook'[1] (last of Dec. and early January).

"Midwinter,—'When the buffalo calves are black,' or, 'When the heavy snows come,' or, 'The time, when the jackrabbit whistles at night' (January).

"When we see the first signs of spring, we say, 'The home days are coming.'

"Early spring,—'The time for sore eyes' (snow blindness) (March), or, 'When the ice breaks up in the rivers' (April).

"We call spring,—'When the geese come,' or, 'The time when the leaves are budding,' or, 'When the buffalo plant is in flower,' or, 'When the buffalo calves are yellow,' or, 'When the grass becomes green.'

[1] A warm wind from the Pacific Ocean.

" Late spring,— ' Time of high water ' (June).

" Early summer,— ' The moon of flowers ' (late June and early July).

" Summer is,—' Home days ' (July and August).

" Autumn is,— ' When the leaves are yellow ' (September), ' Time of the first frost.'

" Late autumn,— ' After the leaves fall off ' (October), or, ' When the geese fly south ' (last of Oct. and first of Nov.)."

Foretelling Events by Signs in the Sky

" My father taught me to read the signs in the heavens : ' When the Akatsis (Lariat or Rain-Roper, *i.e.* Rainbow) appears in the sky I know the Thunder Chief is roping the rain and the storm will slow up.   When the fires of the Northmen (Aurora) [1] flash in the winter sky, it is a sign that a violent wind will arise.   When the Sun paints both his cheeks, that is, when two Sun Dogs [1] (Ickski) appear on both sides of the Sun, it is a warning that fierce storms, with violent winds and severe cold, are coming.   When the Sun paints his face on the forehead, chin and both cheeks (four Sun Dogs), it is a warning that a chief will soon die.

" When a heavy storm is raging, I can foretell whether the weather will clear up by a certain cloud formation in the south west, at the time of sunset. When I see ' a star-feeding ' (the Blackfeet name for Comet [1]), it is a sign of famine and sickness, and when the Sun hides his face (Eclipse [1]), I know that a great chief is about to die.'   That bright star (pointing overhead), we call the Day Star.[1]   Sometimes, if you look carefully, even while the Sun is in the sky, you can see the Day Star shining almost overhead.   My father

[1] See Appendix.

told me many stories about the stars of the night sky, explaining how they came there. There is one family of stars in the northern sky, which we call 'The Seven Brothers.'[1] When we wish to know the time at night, we say, 'How does the Last Brother point?'[1] I will tell you the story of

"The Seven Brothers (Great Bear).

" There was once a camp of ten lodges. In one of them there lived a family of nine children, seven boys and two girls. While the six older brothers were away on the war-path, the eldest girl, Bear-Skin-Woman, married a grizzly bear. Her father was so angered that, with the help of the others, he surrounded the grizzly's cave and killed him. When Bear-Skin-Woman knew of her husband's death, she took a piece of his skin and wore it for her medicine. One night, by means of her husband's supernatural power, she was changed into a huge grizzly bear, and attacked the camp, killing everyone, including her father and mother. She spared her youngest brother and sister, Okinai (Body Chief) and Sinopa (Kit-Fox). Bear-Skin-Woman then changed herself into her former shape and returned to the lodge, occupied by her brother and sister. Okinai and Sinopa were greatly frightened when they overheard her talking to herself, planning how she might kill them. One day, when Sinopa went to the river for water, she met her six brothers returning from the war-path. Having explained to them the danger, they planned to rescue her. Gathering many prickly pears, they directed Sinopa to place them

[1] See Appendix.

in front of the lodge in such a way, that the safe approach would be by a narrow path. At midnight the children quietly left the lodge, carefully avoiding the prickly pears, and safely passed out to their waiting brothers. But Bear-Skin-Woman, hearing them leave the lodge, followed, only to step on the prickly pears. Roaring with pain, she immediately changed herself into a bear and ran after her brothers. Okinai proved to be a medicine man, with supernatural power, even greater than his sister's. When Bear-Skin-Woman overtook them, he shot an arrow into the air. Immediately the brothers found themselves just as far in advance of their terrible sister as the arrow flew. When she again drew near, Okinai waved his Medicine Feather, which brought thick underbrush in her way. Then he made a lake to come between. Finally, for the fourth and last effort to escape, he made a large tree, into which the seven brothers and their little sister climbed. But the grizzly knocked the four lowest from the tree, and was about to kill them, when Okinai waved his Medicine Feather, and singing the song,

> " ' There is no place to be saved except in the sky,'

shot an arrow into the air. Immediately the little sister arose to the sky. He shot six arrows, and each time a brother went up. Finally, Okinai himself followed, and all of them together formed the family of the 'Seven Brothers.' They took the same position in the sky they had in the tree. The small star at one side (of the handle) is Sinopa, 'the little sister,' [1] while the four at the bottom are the brothers who had been knocked from the tree by their terrible sister ' The Grizzly.' "

[1] See Appendix.

LEGEND OF THE LOST CHILDREN.   (PLEIADES.)

"There is also a family of six small stars we call the
'Lost Children' (Pleiades).[1]   These children were lost
a great many years ago from a large camp of Blackfeet,
during the moon, when the buffalo calves are yellow
(spring).   The Indians had been running buffalo over a
piskun and had secured a large number, among them
many buffalo calves.   The little yellow hides were given
to the children, who played with them a game of buffalo.
There was a poor family of six children who were
unable to secure any of the yellow skins and went
naked.   One day, when many of the children were on
the prairie, playing buffalo together, putting the skins
over their heads and running after each other, they
made fun of the poor children, calling them 'scabby old
bulls,' and shouting derisively that 'their hair was old
and black and coming out.'   The six children did not
go home with the rest.   They were ashamed because
their parents gave them no yellow skins.   They
wandered off on the plains and were taken up to the
sky.   They are not seen during the moon, when the
buffalo calves are yellow (spring, the time of their
shame), but, every year, when the calves turn brown
(autumn), the lost children can be seen in the sky every
night."

[1] See Appendix.

CHAPTER XXXVIII

LEGEND OF POÏA, THE CHRIST STORY OF THE BLACKFEET

Brings-down-the-Sun tells the beautiful star-legend of Poïa, who was born in the sky as Star Boy, came down to earth, lived in poverty among the Blackfeet, and was called Poïa (Scarface) in derision.— Through his bravery he reached the home of the Sun, where his scar was removed.—The Sun God sent him back to earth to instruct the Blackfeet in Sun worship.—After establishing the ceremonial of the Sun-dance Poïa returned to the home of the Sun and became a Morning Star.—Brings-down-the-Sun explains the conjunction of two Morning Stars.—Tells about the constellations.—Sacred articles brought from the home of the Sun. His explanation of a brilliant meteor.—Interruptions to my slumber.—In early dawn on Lookout Butte I behold Venus and Jupiter in conjunction.— Sunrise on the plains.—An early start.—Farewell of Brings-down-the-Sun.

"THERE are two bright stars that sometimes rise together, just before the sun comes up, Morning Star and Young 'Morning Star or Star Boy (referring to the conjunction of the planets Venus and Jupiter before daybreak).[1] I will tell you the story of these two Morning Stars, as it was related to me by my father, having been handed down to him through many generations."

LEGEND OF STAR BOY (LATER, POÏA, SCARFACE)

" We know not when the Sun-dance had its origin. It was long ago, when the Blackfeet used dogs for

[1] See Appendix.

491

beasts of burden instead of horses; when they stretched the legs and bodies of their dogs on sticks to make them large, and when they used stones instead of wooden pegs to hold down their lodges. In those days, during the moon of flowers (early summer), our people were camped near the mountains. It was a cloudless night and a warm wind blew over the prairie. Two young girls were sleeping in the long grass outside the lodge. Before daybreak, the eldest sister, So-at-sa-ki (Feather Woman), awoke.

SUMMER CAMP OF THE BLACKFEET NEAR THE MOUNTAINS.

The Morning Star was just rising from the prairie. He was very beautiful, shining through the clear air of early morning. She lay gazing at this wonderful star, until he seemed very close to her, and she imagined that he was her lover. Finally she awoke her sister, exclaiming, 'Look at the Morning Star! He is beautiful and must be very wise. Many of the young men have wanted to marry me, but I love only the Morning Star.' When the leaves were turning yellow (autumn), So-at-sa-ki became very unhappy, finding herself with child. She was a pure maiden, although not knowing the father of her child.

When the people discovered her secret, they taunted and ridiculed her, until she wanted to die. One day while the geese were flying southward, So-at-sa-ki went alone to the river for water. As she was returning home, she beheld a young man standing before her in the trail. She modestly turned aside to pass, but he put forth his hand, as if to detain her, and she said angrily, 'Stand aside! None of the young men have ever before dared to stop me.' He replied, 'I am the Morning Star. One night, during the moon of flowers, I beheld you sleeping in the open and loved you. I have now come to ask you to return with me to the sky, to the lodge of my father, the Sun, where we will live together, and you will have no more trouble.'

"Then So-at-sa-ki remembered the night in spring, when she slept outside the lodge, and now realised that Morning Star was her husband. She saw in his hair a yellow plume, and in his hand a juniper branch with a spider web hanging from one end. He was tall and straight and his hair was long and shining. His beautiful clothes were of soft-tanned skins, and from them came a fragrance of pine and sweet grass. So-at-sa-ki replied hesitatingly, 'I must first say farewell to my father and mother.' But Morning Star allowed her to speak to no one. Fastening the feather in her hair and giving her the juniper branch to hold, he directed her to shut her eyes. She held the upper strand of the spider web in her hand and placed her feet upon the lower one. When he told her to open her eyes, she was in the sky. They were standing together before a large lodge. Morning Star said, 'This is the home of my father and mother, the Sun and the Moon,' and bade her enter. It was day-time and the Sun was away on his long journey, but the Moon was at home. Morning Star addressed his mother saying, ' One night I beheld this girl sleeping on the prairie. I loved her and she is now my wife.' The Moon welcomed So-at-sa-ki to their home. In the evening, when the Sun Chief came home, he also gladly received her. The Moon clothed So-at-sa-ki in a soft-tanned buckskin dress, trimmed with elk-teeth. She also presented her with wristlets of elk-teeth and an elk-skin robe, decorated with the sacred paint, saying, ' I give you these because you have married our son.' So-at-sa-ki lived happily in the sky with Morning Star, and learned many wonderful things. When her child was born, they called him Star Boy. The Moon then gave So-at-sa-ki a root digger, saying, ' This should be used only by pure women. You can dig all kinds of roots with it, but I warn you not to dig up the large turnip growing near the home of the Spider Man. You have now a child and it would bring unhappiness to us all.'

" Everywhere So-at-sa-ki went, she carried her baby and the root digger. She often saw the large turnip, but was afraid to touch it. One day, while passing the wonderful turnip, she thought of the mysterious warning of the Moon, and became curious to see what might be underneath. Laying her baby on the ground, she dug until her root digger stuck fast. Two large cranes came flying from the east. So-at-sa-ki besought them to help her. Thrice she called in vain, but upon the fourth call, they circled and lighted beside her. The chief crane sat upon one side of the turnip and his wife on the other. He took hold of the turnip with his long sharp bill, and moved it backwards and forwards, singing the medicine song,

" 'This root is sacred. Wherever I dig, my roots are sacred.'

" He repeated this song to the north, south, east and west. After the fourth song he pulled up the turnip. So-at-sa-ki looked through the hole and beheld the earth. Although she had not known it, the turnip had filled the same hole, through which Morning Star had brought her into the sky. Looking down, she saw the camp of the Blackfeet, where she had lived. She sat for a long while gazing at the old familiar scenes. The young men were playing games. The women were tanning hides and making lodges, gathering berries on the hills, and crossing the meadows to the river for water. When she turned to go home, she was crying, for she felt lonely, and longed to be back again upon the green prairies with her own people. When So-at-sa-ki arrived at the lodge, Morning Star and his mother were waiting. As soon as Morning Star looked at his wife, he exclaimed, ' You have dug up the sacred turnip !' When she did not reply, the Moon said, ' I warned you not to dig up the turnip, because I love Star Boy and do not wish to part with him.' Nothing more was said, because it was day-time and the great Sun Chief was still away on his long journey. In the evening, when he entered the lodge, he exclaimed, ' What is the matter with my daughter ? She looks sad and must be in trouble.' So-at-sa-ki replied, ' Yes, I am homesick, because I have to-day looked down upon my people.' Then the Sun Chief was angry and said to Morning Star, ' If she has disobeyed, you must send her home.' The Moon interceded for So-at-sa-ki, but the Sun answered, ' She can no longer be happy with us. It is better for her to return to her own people.' Morning Star led So-at-sa-ki to the home of the Spider Man, whose web had drawn her up to the sky. He placed on her head the sacred Medicine

Bonnet, which is worn only by pure women. He laid
Star Boy on her breast, and wrapping them both in the
elk-skin robe, bade her farewell, saying, 'We will let
you down into the centre of the Indian camp and the
people will behold you as you come from the sky.'
The Spider Man then carefully let them down through
the hole to the earth.

"It was an evening in midsummer, during the moon
when the berries are ripe, when So-at-sa-ki was let down
from the sky. Many of the people were outside their
lodges, when suddenly they beheld a bright light in the
northern sky. They saw it pass across the heavens and
watched, until it sank to the ground. When the
Indians reached the place, where the star had fallen,
they saw a strange looking bundle. When the elk-skin
cover was opened, they found a woman and her child.
So-at-sa-ki was recognised by her parents. She returned
to their lodge and lived with them, but never was happy.
She used to go with Star Boy to the summit of a high
ridge, where she sat and mourned for her husband. One
night she remained alone upon the ridge. Before daybreak, when Morning Star arose from the plains, she
begged him to take her back. Then he spoke to her,
'You disobeyed and therefore cannot return to the sky.
Your sin is the cause of your sorrow and has brought
trouble to you and your people.'

"Before So-at-sa-ki died, she told all these things to
her father and mother, just as I now tell them to you.
Star Boy's grandparents also died. Although born in
the home of the Sun, he was very poor. He had no
clothes, not even moccasins to wear. He was so timid
and shy that he never played with other children.
When the Blackfeet moved camp, he always followed
barefoot, far behind the rest of the tribe. He feared to

travel with the other people, because the other boys stoned and abused him. On his face was a mysterious scar, which became more marked as he grew older. He was ridiculed by everyone and in derision was called Poïa (Scarface).

" When Poïa became a young man, he loved a maiden of his own tribe. She was very beautiful and the daughter of a leading chief. Many of the young men wanted to marry her, but she refused them all. Poïa sent this maiden a present, with the message that he wanted to marry her, but she was proud and disdained his love. She scornfully told him, she would not accept him as her lover, until he would remove the scar from his face. Scarface was deeply grieved by the reply. He consulted with an old medicine woman, his only friend. She revealed to him, that the scar had been placed on his face by the Sun God, and that only the Sun himself could remove it. Poïa resolved to go to the home of the Sun God. The medicine woman made moccasins for him and gave him a supply of pemmican.

" Poïa journeyed alone across the plains and through the mountains, enduring many hardships and great dangers. Finally he came to the Big Water (Pacific Ocean). For three days and three nights he lay upon the shore, fasting and praying to the Sun God. On the evening of the fourth day, he beheld a bright trail leading across the water. He travelled this path until he drew near the home of the Sun, when he hid himself and waited. In the morning, the great Sun Chief came from his lodge, ready for his daily journey. He did not recognise Poïa. Angered at beholding a creature from the earth, he said to the Moon, his wife, ' I will kill him, for he comes from a good-for-nothing-race,' but she interceded and saved his life. Morning Star, their only son, a young man with a handsome face and beautifully dressed, came forth from the lodge. He brought with him dried sweet grass, which he burned as incense. He first placed Poïa in the sacred smoke, and then led him into the presence of his father and mother, the Sun and the Moon. Poïa related the story of his long journey, because of his rejection by the girl he loved. Morning Star then saw how sad and worn he looked. He felt sorry for him and promised to help him.

" Poïa lived in the lodge of the Sun and Moon with Morning Star. Once, when they were hunting together, Poïa killed seven enormous birds, which had threatened the life of Morning Star. He presented four of the dead birds to the Sun and three to the Moon. The Sun rejoiced, when he knew that the dangerous birds were killed, and the Moon felt so grateful, that she besought her husband to repay him. On the intercession of Morning Star, the Sun God consented to remove the scar. He also appointed Poïa as his messenger to the Blackfeet, promising, if they would give a festival (Sun-dance) in his honour, once every year, he would restore their sick to health. He taught Poïa the secrets of the Sun-dance, and instructed him in the prayers and songs to be used. He gave him two raven feathers to wear as a sign that he came from the Sun, and a robe of soft-tanned elk-skin, with the warning that it must be worn only by a virtuous woman. She can then give the Sun-dance and the sick will recover. Morning Star gave him a magic flute and a wonderful song, with which he would be able to charm the heart of the girl he loved.

" Poïa returned to the earth and the Blackfeet camp by the Wolf Trail (Milky Way), the short path to the earth. When he had fully instructed his people con-

cerning the Sun-dance, the Sun God took him back to
the sky with the girl he loved.   When Poïa returned
to the home of the Sun, the Sun God made him bright
and beautiful, just like his father, Morning Star.[1]   In
those days Morning Star and his son could be seen
together in the east.   Because Poïa appears first in the
sky, the Blackfeet often mistake him for his father,
and he is therefore sometimes called Poks-o-piks-o-aks,
Mistake Morning Star.

"I remember," continued Brings-down-the-Sun,
"when I was a young man, seeing these two bright
stars rising, one after the other, before the Sun.
Then, if we were going on a war, or hunting expedition, my father would awake me, saying, 'My son, I
see Morning Star and Young Morning Star in the sky
above the prairie.   Day will soon break and it is time
we were started.'   For many years these stars have
travelled apart.   I have also seen them together in the
evening sky.   They went down after the sun.   This
summer, Morning Star and Poïa are again travelling
together.   I see them in the eastern sky, rising together over the prairie before dawn.   Poïa comes up
first.   His father, Morning Star, rises soon afterwards,
and then his grandfather, the Sun.

"Morning Star was given to us as a sign to herald
the coming of the Sun.   When he appears above the
horizon, we know a new day is about to dawn.   Many
medicine men have dreamed of the Sun, and of the
Moon, but I have never yet heard of one so powerful as
to dream of Morning Star, because he shows himself in
the sky for such a short time.

"The 'Star that stands still'[1] (North Star) is
different from other stars, because it never moves.   All

[1] See Appendix.

the other stars walk round it.   It is a hole in the sky,
the same hole through which So-at-sa-ki was first drawn
up to the sky and then let down again to earth.   It is
the hole, through which she gazed upon the earth, after
digging up the forbidden turnip.   Its light is the
radiance from the home of the Sun God shining through.
The half circle of stars to the east (Northern Crown)
is the lodge of the Spider Man, and the five bright stars
just beyond (in the constellation of Hercules) are his
five fingers, with which he spun the web, upon which
So-at-sa-ki was let down from the sky.   Whenever you
see the half-buried and overgrown circles, or clusters of
stones on the plains, marking the sites of Blackfeet
camps in the ancient days, when they used stones to
hold down the sides of their lodges, you will know why
the half-circle of stars was called by our fathers, ' The
Lodge of the Spider Man.'

" When So-at-sa-ki came back to earth from the lodge
of the Sun, she brought with her the sacred Medicine
Bonnet and dress trimmed with elk teeth, the Turnip
Digger, Sweet Grass (incense), and the Prongs for lifting hot coals from the fire.   Ever since those days,
these sacred articles have been used in the Sun-dance
by the woman who makes the vow.   The Turnip
Digger is always tied to the Medicine Case, containing
the Medicine Bonnet, and it now hangs from the tripod
behind my lodge."

Brings-down-the-Sun then arose saying, " The Last
Brother is now pointing towards the horizon.   Day will
soon dawn and it is time for us to sleep."   As we
turned to gaze at the constellation of the Great Bear,
a ball of fire suddenly appeared high in the northern
sky.   It flashed across the heavens, leaving in its wake
a beautiful light, and burst into a shower of sparks. as

it vanished in the southern sky. The Indians were filled with awe and broke out in exclamations of wonder and of fear. Some said it was a Dusty Star (Meteor), others that it was too large for a Dusty Star, which is always small and looks like a star changing its place in the sky. Those, who were filled with dread, spoke of it in subdued whispers as Is-tsi,—" The Fire " ; and said it was an omen of bad luck.

Brings-down-the-Sun had been silent. When I asked his explanation of the strange sign, he said, " The Sun God is all powerful, he watches over every one and sees everything. The Great Mystery may have sent this wonderful star as a warning, that there will be much sickness during the coming winter, or, it may be a sign that a great chief has just died. By a great chief I mean a man who had a good heart and has lived a straight life." When Brings-down-the-Sun had finished speaking, the North Piegans quietly withdrew to their lodges.

When I laid down on my blankets, beneath the big cottonwood, the moon had risen over Lookout Butte, and was shining upon my bed, through an opening in the trees. My mind was filled with thoughts of the poetical beauty of the legends I had just heard from Brings-down-the-Sun ; of the wonderful imagination of the ancient Blackfeet medicine men who originated them ; of the brilliant beauty of the night skies, which had inspired them, and of the scrupulous care with which they had been handed down from father to son.

These inspiring thoughts about the heavens were rudely interrupted by my old enemy, Kops-ksis-e, the North Piegan watch dog. He came prowling through the trees, as if in search of lurking enemies. But he was really on a thieving expedition to our camp for food. creeping stealthily along, like a moving shadow in the moonlight. When he came very suddenly and unexpectedly on my bed, covered with white canvas, he was at first startled, and stood with half-suppressed growls, but when he discovered that it belonged to the white man, whom he had, from the first, hated and distrusted, his fear quickly changed to anger. With fierce barks and bristling hair, he advanced to drive me out. Fortunately, I understood the ways of Indian dogs. If I had shown any sign of fear, he would have attacked me with a sudden rush. But I seized a big stick, and went so quickly into action, that the thoroughly frightened Kops-ksis-e gave a series of frightened yelps and fled into the forest.

Returning to my blankets, I had no sooner fallen into a light sleep, than I was again aroused, by the sound of an Indian riding furiously down the steep embankment from the plain. When I heard him enter the woods, the thought at once flashed through my mind, that it was Bull Plume, the defeated medicine man, coming to make me the victim of some vindictive purpose, before I could leave his country. My bed was near a small path, a short cut from the main trail, which ran around our camp. I heard the rider coming down the trail, until he had turned into the side path, which would bring him directly to my bed. Jumping from my blankets, I hid in the thick underbrush. When his horse came to my canvas, shining in the moonlight, it reared and with a snort plunged to one side. For a moment, the rider lost his balance and swayed, as if to fall, but, quickly recovering himself, he tried to force his horse across my bed. But the frightened animal went crashing aside into the underbrush and, to my

great relief, disappeared in the forest, his rider singing
a Wolf song until lost in the distance.

When the moon was high, I fell asleep. It seemed
but a brief interval, until I was aroused, before daybreak,
by Menake and Nitana preparing our morning meal. I
rolled from my warm blankets into the chill air, with a
" tired feeling." I was soon refreshed by a cold bath in
the river and by the fresh air of the woods in the early
dawn. Taking my lariat, I hurried past the silent
white lodges of the North Piegans to the hills, where
our horses were feeding. Passing from the shadows of
the big trees to the open prairie, I was met by a gentle
breeze, coming from the mountains, fragrant with the
sweet odour of wild flowers and growing grass. I
climbed Lookout Butte and, from its summit, saw the
shadowy forms of our horses in a meadow nearby. On
the eastern horizon I beheld the two magnificent
planets, Venus and Jupiter, now in conjunction. Jupiter
had risen first, and I realised that he was Poïa
(Scarface), and that the other planet was his father,
Morning Star.

While driving the horses back to camp, I heard the
distant cries of wolves and coyotes. The Rockies were
beginning to flush with a soft rosy light, reflected from
the eastern sky. Then the higher summits were
touched by the first direct rays of the sun. The red
glow crept slowly down, lighting up in turn the dark
timbered slopes below, until, at length, the sun rose
majestically above the plains, and the whole landscape
was flooded with the brilliant and glorious light of a
new day. Directly, there burst forth, on all sides, a
bird chorus of wonderful harmony and gladness, as if
all nature joined in welcoming the Sun-God's coming.
I recognised the bird notes of thrushes, white-crowned

sparrows and Maryland yellow-throats, from the willows and cottonwoods of the river valley, and of prairie larks, Savanna sparrows and horned larks, from the near-by ridges of the plains.

The camp had been dismantled and the morning meal was ready, when I returned. When our outfit was packed, and we were prepared to start, Brings-down-the-Sun and his family came to say farewell. We wondered at seeing the old chief leading his favourite saddle horse, Soks-kinne (Loud Voice). Soks-kinne, with his beautiful head and long silvery mane and tail, was a familiar friend with all the tribe. Although a noted race-horse, he was intelligent, docile and reliable, and a child could safely ride him. Brings-down-the-Sun was greatly attached to him, as to an old and faithful friend. To our astonishment, he presented the horse to Menake, saying : " I now give you Soks-kinne, because I have felt grateful to you, ever since you cared for the dead bodies of my daughter, Pretty Blanket, and her three children. I know that your heart is good, because you alone, of all your people, were not afraid to go to them, when they were murdered in your country by Wakes-up-last, when he was crazed by the white man's fire water." [1] But Menake refused to take Soks-kinne, explaining that she knew how highly he valued the horse, and she wanted no reward. Brings-down-the-Sun laid his hand affectionately on Soks-kinne's head, saying, " I prize this horse more than anything else that I possess. I resolved to give him to you, because you were kind to my dead children, but I am glad that you have refused to take him, and now I know that your heart is good. Whenever any of your friends or relatives may come to visit in our

[1] See Appendix.

SUNRISE FROM LOOKOUT BUTTE

By Walter McClintock

country, they will always be well cared for in my camp."

I shook hands with all of my Indian brothers and sisters. When I came to say farewell to the old chief, he presented me with his stone pipe, explaining that it was his "everyday pipe," which he had smoked for many years. He said in his farewell talk, "My children, I have never before gone into any camp to sit and talk, day after day, with strangers, as I have done with you. My heart will be heavy after you have gone, and I will feel lonely every time I look at your camping ground."

When I mounted my horse, the old chief gazed towards the rising sun and, lifting his hand impressively, prayed,

> "Hear, Oh Sun! May he go safely while travelling afar!
> May we live long and continue to be friends!
> May we both meet and be happy again!"

In Blackfeet :

> Haiyu! Haiyu! Natosin! Nach-ki-tach-sa-po-au
>   ach-kach-pinna
> Acksi-sam-a-ik-so-ko
> Ita-ma-tau-tat-si-sinna.

As we rode slowly away towards the open plains, I turned in my saddle for a last look, and saw Brings-down-the-Sun walking with bowed head, along the wooded trail toward his camp, leading his favourite horse, Soks-kinne, and followed by his faithful old dog, Kops-ksis-e.

CHAPTER XXXIX

THE PRESENT AND FUTURE OF THE BLACKFEET

Appalling inroads of death upon the Blackfeet chiefs.—Decline in the
tribal spirit and religion.—Pathetic appeal of an old chief to the
young men to "keep up their old religion."—A government agent's
prohibition of the annual Sun-dance causes de-pondency and
indignation.—I attend a council of the Chiefs.—Stock-stchi's speech
in behalf of the Sun-dance.—Challenges me to name anything
harmful in its observance.—My reply.—Changed conditions bring
to an end the development of the noble line of unselfish and
patriotic Blackfeet Chiefs.—The passing of the buffalo gave the
death-blow to their tribal organisation and brought poverty,
government relief, pauperisation and moral decline.—The government passes remedial legislation.—President Roosevelt and Indian
Commissioner Leupp give new impetus to the progressive policy.—
The medical and practical missionary both needed.—The Blackfeet a
promising field for Christian Missions.

FOURTEEN years have passed since I first went among
the Blackfeet. In the meantime death has made appalling inroads upon the ranks of their leading chiefs
and medicine men, and but few of my friends are left.
There have passed over the " Wolf Trail " O-mis-tai-po-
kah, the head chief ; Mad Wolf, their greatest orator and
leader of the Sun-dance ; Running Crane, leader of the
southern division ; Sik-si-ka-koan, the scout ; Double
Runner ; Elk Horn ; Little Plume ; Flat Tail ; Drags-his-
robe ; Morning Plume and Running Rabbit; the
doctors Ear Rings and Awunna ; and the medicine men
Spotted Eagle and Bull Child, and many others.

At the last Sun-dance of the Blackfeet, I could not
suppress a feeling of sadness, because of the absence of

the familiar and inspiring figures of so many of their leaders and because of the visible indifference of the people towards the old chiefs, who were still living.

I found the once noted chief and medicine man, Brings-down-the-Sun, in a small poor lodge on the outskirts of the camp, unnoticed and seemingly unknown by the younger generation of the Blackfeet. He had come from his home in Alberta to attend their tribal festival, and to lead in the ceremonials of the Sun-lodge. I saw him standing in his customary position before the sacred booth, praying and waiting. But, instead of having the people come before him for his blessing, as in former days, they were thronging the horse races and social dances, and the young men were engaged in a base ball game by the side of the Sun-lodge.

I heard the sorrowful entreaty of an elderly chief, made to the younger men, exhorting them to keep up the religion of their fathers.   He said :

"Young men, come forth and help us!   You now have homes of your own and should do your share in keeping up the worship of the Sun.   You no longer are helpers, but sit idly by and seem willing to abandon all of our old religious customs.   While we live, we should keep up our religion.   You now seem to care only for whisky, gambling, and horse racing."

I was present when the Blackfoot agent permitted the tribe to assemble in their annual summer encampment, but his arbitrary interference prevented the religious ceremonies of the Sun-dance.   Much preparation had already been made to fulfil the vow made by a woman to give the Sun-dance to secure the recovery of her sick son.   The subsequent death of the boy and the prevalence of sickness and mourning for deceased relatives, during the encampment, filled the people with gloom and despondency.   They very naturally attributed

their misfortunes to their inability to fulfil the vow. At
that time a council of chiefs, to which I was invited, was
held beside the unfinished Sun-lodge. While I was
seated in their midst, Stock-stchi, an old friend of Mad
Wolf's, arose and addressing me said :

"You have been among us for many years, and have attended
many of our ceremonials. Have you ever seen a disturbance, or
anything harmful, that has been caused by our Sun-dance ? "

Then turning towards the council he continued very
earnestly,

"We know that there is nothing injurious to our people in the
Sun-dance. On the other hand, we have seen much that is bad at
the dances of the white people. It has been our custom, during
many years, to assemble once every summer for this festival, in
honour of the Sun God. We fast and pray, that we may be able
to lead good lives and to act more kindly towards each other. I
do not understand why the white men desire to put an end to our
religious ceremonials. What harm can they do to our people ? If
they deprive us of our religion, we will have nothing left, for we
know of no other that can take its place. We do not understand
the white man's religion. The Black Robes (Catholic Priests)
teach us one thing and the Men-with-white-neckties (Protestant
Missionaries) teach us another ; so we are confused. We believe
that the Sun God is all powerful, for every spring he makes the
trees to bud and the grass to grow. We see these things with our
own eyes, and, therefore, know that all life comes from him."

Then, turning again towards me, Stock-stchi said,

"If the Indians should go to a church, where the white men
were holding their religious ceremonials, and would order them to
stop, what would they do ? "

The attention of the council was fixed upon me, and
they waited in dignified silence for my reply. After
considering for a moment, I said,

"The white men, where I live, know nothing about your religion.
Many things have been told to them about you that are not true.
I have come to live among you, that I might learn the truth from
you, and then tell the truth to the white people. The hearts of
many of the white men feel warm towards their red brothers, and
when they know the truth about you, they may act more wisely."

With these words, I arose to depart and the council broke up.

These incidents in my recent experience indicate the drift of events and the changed conditions of the Blackfeet, which have brought to an end the development of such illustrious chiefs as O-mis-tai-po-kah, Mad Wolf, Brings-down-the-Sun and Running Crane. The growth of such strong and noble characters, out of the seemingly unfavourable moral soil of Sun Worship seems unaccountable. Their unselfish and patriotic lives, devoted to the welfare of their tribe, rise before me in strange and painful contrast with the selfish and sordid lives of many of the rich and powerful of my race. The latter's wealth and power, notwithstanding the advantages of education and Christianity, are not devoted to the amelioration, but tend rather to increase the suffering and degradation of their fellow men.

The constantly increasing migration of white settlers, like the rising tide of the sea, meant the inevitable extinction of the herds of buffalo, which had formerly sustained the Blackfeet, and the other plains-tribes, with food and shelter. The extermination, in 1883, of the last of these great herds, gave the final death-blow to their tribal organisation and suddenly cut off their food supply, necessitating governmental relief to prevent their perishing of starvation. Then followed the governmental policy of herding the Indian tribes on reservations, and supporting them on a ration-system, which included blankets, clothing and food supplies, conditioned upon their remaining upon their reservations and refraining from acts of violence. The gratuitous support of the government and an enforced life of idleness inevitably tended to pauperise and degrade them.

And, as if to doubly seal their fate, their contact with the white race was chiefly with its worst representatives, who had gathered along the frontier to seek their fortunes. These looked upon the Indian as only an obstacle to their personal advantage, a hindrance to the progress of civilisation and of necessity to be exterminated. No race, civilised, or uncivilised, could long withstand such adverse conditions. Moral decline was the swift and sure result. Then came the economic necessity of cutting down the Blackfeet Reservation limits, through selling their lands to the government by treaty, and the investment of the proceeds in cattle and supplies, with a view to making them self supporting. But, because of the inability of the Indians, from lack of experience, to adapt themselves to the new conditions, and because of the incompetency of government agents to properly handle their interests, their resources were wasted. Their cattle perished in large numbers, and their rich grazing lands, which had long been a coveted prize to the cattle-men, were depleted through over-grazing and the machinations of the cattle kings. Their condition and the similar condition of other Indian tribes simultaneously reached an acute stage. Dispossessed of their ancestral domains, their armed resistance overcome, their source of subsistence destroyed, they had become the helpless dependents of the American nation, requiring immediate action and the highest statesmanship and constructive philanthropy for their redemption.

The accession of Theodore Roosevelt to the presidency in 1905 and of Francis E. Leupp, as Commissioner of Indian Affairs, gave great impetus to the humane and progressive Indian policy of the government. This new policy, in general, seeks to dissolve the tribal organisation, to individualise the Indian, to make him a self-supporting citizen, and to ultimately assimilate him with the white race. Under it the Indian receives full recognition of his rights and, at the same time, protection for his interests. Under it, the Commissioner of Indian Affairs cuts up the reservations, giving to all Indians a generous farm-allotment, and selling the remaining, or surplus Indian lands to the public for settlement. The proceeds of such sales are set aside as tribal funds, to be used for their general benefit by the government under a wise and provident trusteeship, which safeguards their interests.

In pursuance of this policy, the House of Representatives, in 1906, passed a bill to survey and open for settlement lands formerly included in the Blackfeet Reservation in Montana, comprising about one and a half million acres. The disposal of these lands is now well under way. Irrigation systems are also being constructed at the expense of the tribal funds, which will give increased value to land heretofore unavailable for agriculture.

Under the passing of the old conditions and the coming in of the new policy, the younger generation of Blackfeet is already responding, and manifesting a capacity for improvement. They are becoming the owners of real estate, and are developing thrift and an ability to provide for the future. A visitor to-day, in the Blackfeet country, unless he should happen to come at a time when they have quit work and have assembled for a few days' recreation in their tribal camp, would not know that he was among Indians. He would now see a marked advance towards civilised conditions, and a striking contrast between the older generation of Indians, who, because of their fixed habits of hereditary savagery, are incapable of work, or a settled occupation, and their children, who are being educated and trained to work and to industrial pursuits. The industrious are rapidly becoming self-supporting. Some of them live in well-made and comfortable houses, and own ranches, with large herds of cattle and horses. They wear white men's clothes, purchased from the trading stores, own high priced wagons and buggies and make use of modern farming implements.

The mental and spiritual slavery of the Blackfeet, under their "Medicine" superstitions, and the unchecked ravages of tuberculosis and other diseases, which have come with the white men, offer a promising field of usefulness for the medical missionary. There is also a great opportunity for the practical missionary, who will not only teach the Blackfeet Christianity, but also by personal contact and personal example teach them how to live, in respect to hygiene, industry and thrift, how to become self-supporting and make the most out of their environment.

The whole question of lifting up the Indian is one of economical, educational, and moral difficulty to both state and church. They are together responsible for its solution, the work of each supplementing the other.

Christian missions among the Blackfeet have not yet made equal progress with the government. Nevertheless, the virility of the Blackfeet character, and the robustness of their physical manhood, under the old conditions of barbarism, give assurance of what should be forthcoming under Christianity, rightly applied. The Blackfeet stock is endowed with as favourable qualities for grafting upon it the fruits of our Christian Civilisation, as was the Anglo-Saxon before its conversion to Christianity.

APPENDIX I

BLACKFEET INDIAN SONGS

Copyright in the United States by Walter McClintock

LOVE SONG

Page 242. - *Andante*

WOLF SONG

Page 243.
Allegro

Wolf howl.

Blackfeet songs are generally sung without words.

SIOUX DANCE

Page 243.

WAR SONG

Page 277.

War cry.

SIOUX CELEBRATION SONG

Page 280 and 282.

Yell!

RIDING SONG

Page 281.

Yell!

NIGHT SONG

Page 281.

TRIBAL HYMN, "RAISING THE POLE"

Page 308.

CHILDREN'S GAME SONG

Page 391.

A - pe koi - ya so - ma - tia - ka - ke - kin - na.

APPENDIX II

Page 15.—"This region should be reserved as a National Park and Game Preserve."

There is a Bill before Congress which proposes to create this tract of mountain country into a National Park. The Public Lands Committee of the Senate in reporting the Bill to the Sixtieth Congress said :

"This Bill proposes to create a National Park which will be fittingly called 'Glacier National Park.' The territory embraced contains about 1,400 square miles with approximately equal areas on the east and west of the summit of the main range of the Rocky Mountains and immediately south of the International Boundary line.

"The park will embrace more than 60 glaciers, 250 lakes and many streams. From this area waters flow to the Hudson Bay, Gulf of Mexico, and the Pacific Ocean. The mountain scenery is of unparalleled grandeur and beauty. Mt. Cleveland, the highest peak, has an elevation of 10,434 feet and there are numerous other rugged peaks and mountains varying in heights from 6,000 to 10,000 feet above the sea level. Mountain goats, mountain sheep (Bighorn), grizzly and black bears, deer, wapiti, and moose are still to be found, as well as a great variety of birds, and it is believed these game animals and birds will increase in numbers, if protected by law, to such an extent as to furnish in the overflow from the park a tempting supply to sportsmen for all time to come."

The following Editorial concerning the proposed National Park is from the *Outlook*, New York, April 16, 1910.

"In North-western Montana, fronting on the Canadian boundary line, lies a tract of mountainous country which it is proposed in a Bill now before Congress to turn into a National Park. It is not a large tract—from south to north it covers approximately sixty miles. Yet within its limits is comprised the most beautiful portion of the range of the Rocky Mountains lying within the limits of the United States. The range there is narrow. The great grass-covered northern prairies sweep up to within twenty miles of the Continental Divide. There is no intervening mass of foothills to break in upon and tone down the abruptness of the approach. From out on the prairies can be seen, within easy distance, the precipitous crags and the hanging glaciers of a typical Alpine region ; and, on the other hand, from the summit of Chief Mountain on a clear morning one may look out on an ocean of prairie in which the Sweet Grass Hills, over a hundred miles away, appear to twinkle in the very foreground. The tract contains also an apex of the continent. In its centre rises the Blackfoot Mountain, with the great Blackfoot Glacier, containing almost as much ice as the Gorner Glacier at Zermatt, descending from its eastern slope. The water from this glacier forms the St. Mary's River, which, running north-westward, joins the Saskatchewan and ultimately finds its way into Hudson Bay. Near another slope of the mountain rises Cutbank Creek, flowing south-westerly into the Marias, the Missouri, the Mississippi, and ultimately the Gulf of Mexico ; while on the western slope of the mountain is found one of the sources of the Flathead, a tributary of the Columbia, flowing westward into the Pacific.

.   .   .   .

" The proposed park would make a wonderful recreation ground for the American people. The summer and autumn climate is cold and bracing. The mountains and glaciers offer the only chance for mountaineering of real Alpine character (except that afforded by the Coast Range and Alaska) to be found within the limits of the United States. The trout of the cold St. Mary waters fight with a vigour that is seldom seen even in the famous streams of eastern Canada. And the mountains still shelter a sufficient number of our game animals (including our three most splendid species, the mountain sheep and goat and the grizzly bear) to enable the tract to become in time an important animal refuge. If by the action of Congress the pending Bill becomes a law and the Glacier National Park is established we shall have added to our system of National parks one which in many features is unlike, and which in its beauty and opportunities for wholesome pleasure will fitly supplement those which we already have."

Page 29, 30, 35.—" Sacred bundle of the Beaver Medicine "— " Medicine Pipe " and " Medicine Bonnet."

The word " medicine," when used as a noun by itself, means something endowed with supernatural power ; but, when used as an adjective-prefix, it also means sacred, or set apart for use in religious ceremonials. " The sacred bundle of the Beaver Medicine " is a bundle containing many skins of birds and animals thus set apart. It was believed to have been given originally to the Blackfeet by the Beavers, and to have been handed down from generation to generation. (See legend of its origin in Chapter 6.) It was only opened upon an important religious occasion, acccompanied by a ceremonial. For more extended comments on the significance and use of the word "Medicine" see Chapter XI.

Page 50.—"Parfleches." A raw-hide case used for packing in horse transportation and also as a trunk or receptacle for use inside the tipi. The "parfleches" and "pemmican bags" were a necessity for a nomadic people. Both were favourite objects for decoration to gratify their sense of the beautiful. They ordinarily used conventional designs of triangles combined in quadrangular forms and painted in red, blue and yellow.

Page 53.—"Their lodge poles were worn too short." When changing camp, the small ends of the lodge poles were fastened to the horses' sides, the large ends dragging behind upon the ground. The Blackfeet changed camp so frequently that their poles were soon worn too short for the lodges, requiring a new set of lodge poles every year.

Page 152, 504.—"When Wakes-up-last murdered all of his children." The murder of Brings-down-the-Sun's daughter (Pretty Blanket) and her three children, and Wakes-up-last's suicide, was the result of the sale of bad whiskey, consisting largely of wood alcohol, to Blackfeet Indians by white saloon-keepers in the town of Cutbank, Montana. Their bodies lay for some time uncared for, because of the superstitious dread of touching the dead, until Menake prepared them for burial. Although the sale of whiskey to Indians is prohibited by United States Law the saloon-keepers escaped punishment.

Page 157.—Father De Smet was a Jesuit priest noted in his day for his influence with the Indian tribes in the North-West. His diary records that in 1841 he secured 30 brave Pend d'Oreilles to accompany him through the country of the Blackfeet, because the latter were so hostile to the whites that they never gave them any quarter. Later, in 1846, while living among the Blackfeet, he reported them equal in hospitality with other Indian tribes.

Page 137, 193.—"Travois." A horse litter made of poles. Two poles were fastened like shafts to the sides of a horse, the small ends crossing above and in front of the horse's head, while the large ends dragged behind on the ground. A cross-framing supported a network of raw-hide strips. Upon this simple but ingenious device young children, the aged and sick were transported, also provisions and camp equipage. Sometimes a canopy, constructed of bent branches and a skin covering, was used for protection from sun and rain.

Page 283.—"Indian music should be preserved."

Deeply impressed with the great possibilities of Indian music, I persuaded Arthur Nevin, an American composer, to go with me to the camps of the Blackfeet. During his stay in my Indian tipi, I proposed his composing an opera founded on the story of Poïa (page 491), the most ancient tradition of the Blackfeet, using an Indian environment and Indian musical themes. The opera, which was named " Poïa," was completed by Mr. Nevin in the spring of 1906. Mr. Randolph Hartley of New York wrote the libretto. The music was played for the first time in concert form by the Pittsburg Orchestra, January 16th, 1907. Poïa was accepted for production by the Berlin Royal Opera House in June, 1909. The premier performance took place April 23, 1910, and was followed by three other performances. The opera was superbly staged, both as to scenery and costumes, and was sung by a strong cast of the Berlin Royal Opera. The second performance was attended by the Crown Prince and Crown Princess and other members of the Royal Family.

Page 307.—" Counting Coups."

To " count coups " is to narrate deeds of valour. The bravest coup was to strike, or even touch an enemy before killing him. It was also counted as a coup to capture a weapon or article of clothing such as a shield, war shirt, or war bonnet.

Page 312.—" Bull Child wore a robe famous among the Blackfeet." This robe was purchased by Dr. Clark Wissler for the American Museum of Natural History, New York City, and is exhibited in their collection from the Blackfeet. Its design and the instructions as to how it should be made, were given to Brings-Down-the Sun in a dream (page 430).

Page 425.—" We call the thunder Isis-a-kummi (Thunder-bird)."

Nearly all of the widely spread tribes of the Algonquian stock, as well as other ethnical divisions of the Red Indians, had a myth concerning the awe-inspiring mystery of nature we call thunder and lightning. They personified this mysterious and supernatural power in the Thunder-bird, which they worshipped and to which they made propitiatory sacrifices. We find it among the Micmacs of Nova Scotia, the Passamaquoddies of Maine ; the Hurons, Ottawas, and Mississiquas of Lake Ontario ; the Ojibways of Lake Superior, the Crees of Hudson Bay ; the Athabascan tribes of Northern Canada, the Illinois of the middle west, the Comanches of the southwest, the Moquis of Arizona, all the plains-tribes and those of the north-western Pacific Coast.

The Blackfeet have a tradition that the Thunder-bird was once overcome by a snowstorm and descended into their camp. It was taken to the lodge of the head chief, where many of the tribe assembled. Its feathers had many colours like the rainbow and its claws were long and green. When it suddenly flew from the lodge, the Indians rushed out and saw it disappearing among the storm clouds.

The Indian belief made the storm cloud the Thunder-bird's vehicle, behind which he moved through the air, making peals of thunder by flapping his wings, and shooting forth lightning flashes by the blinking of his all-penetrating eyes.

The legendary habitation of the Thunder-bird was usually in a high mountain, or inaccessible crag in the tribe's vicinity. The Blackfeet believed its home to be in a great cavern near the summit of Chief Mountain, one of the most precipitous peaks of the Rocky Mountains. The family of Thunderers of the Passamaquoddies of Maine were said to dwell in the great cavern of Mount Katahdin. The Pottawotomies located the Thunder-bird in one of the high mountain peaks of Thunder Bay on Lake Superior. The Ojibways assigned their Thunder-bird to a high mountain west of them. The Illinois, now almost extinct, had a legend about the "Paieusen" or "Man-Devouring-Bird," which dwelt among the high cliffs on the Mississippi River, near the present town of Alton. Its effigy was carved and painted in large dimensions on the face of a perpendicular cliff overlooking the Mississippi River. Father Marquette gives a vivid description of it in the narrative of his voyage down that river in 1673. The Makah Indians of Cape Flattery named the mountain back of Clyoquot on Vancouver Island as his dwelling place, where, "on the shores of a small lake are quantities of whales' bones, which the Thunder-bird had killed." The Thlinkeets (Esquimaux) of Alaska have a tradition of a mythical person named Chethl, "who, in the form of a great bird, frequented the crater of Mount Edgecumbe, near Sitka, feeding upon whales, which he carried there in his talons."

The Thunder-bird was frequently represented in Blackfeet religious ceremonials. Its symbol was also painted on shields, weapons and war clothes for inspiring courage, and on tipis for invoking protection in behalf of the family.

Page 437.—"Piskun : " A natural trap, usually a perpendicular cliff or cut-bank, used for capturing game on a large scale and requiring the co-operation of many Indians. This method of killing buffalo by frightening and rushing them over a cliff to their death, was used by the Blackfeet in ancient times, when the buffalo were plentiful and their weapons primitive, but was abandoned after the introduction of horses and fire-arms. The approaches to the piskun were fenced to guide the frightened animals to the verge of the cliff. This hunting device for securing by wholesale their winter supplies of meat resembles the "deer-fences," which formerly the Chippewa Indians constructed with much ingenuity and labour, extending for miles through the unbroken forests of Michigan, and across the general direction of the deer-migration, bringing them within the range of the Indians' weapons in ambush. The

Blackfeet also built a corral about the foot of the cliff, to prevent the escape of any buffalo, which were not killed outright by the fall. The locations of piskuns are still easily recognised by the darker green of the grass, showing the soil-enrichment from animal slaughter. Numerous flint arrowheads and other relics of the chase are also found there.

Page 465.—Tribal regulations for hunting buffalo were not characteristic of the Blackfeet alone, but were used by the other plains-tribes as a necessary protection for their common interests. According to the journal of Alexander Henry (a partner in the North-Western Company of Montreal, 1806), the tribal policy of the Mandans, in the matter of hunting buffalo, was one of comity towards neighbouring tribes at peace with them, of provident conservation in hunting them, and of humane consideration of the poorest and helpless in the distribution of the meat. The exercise of police power to prevent private exploitation of the natural resources owned in common, fell into disuse with the advent of the whites. The Blackfeet, together with the other plains-tribes, finally joined with the white hunter in a blind and reckless slaughter of the vast herds of buffalo, until they became practically extinct in 1883.

Page 478.—"I see the Last Brother is pointing downwards towards the prairie." The pointing of the "Last Brother" furnished the Blackfeet with their night-sky clock. This method of telling time in the night is well known to shepherds and cattle herders, whose night occupation keeps them continually in the open. Observation soon teaches them that the "Last Brother" or end star of the handle of the Great Dipper, describes a great circle around the North Star once in twenty-four hours and therefore, that its pointing or relative position with the horizon would mark the time, as on a great dial-face.

It should be noted, however, that "star time gains three minutes and fifty nine seconds on solar time every twenty-four hours. If, therefore the 'Last Brother' occupied a certain position in the sky at midnight of June 1st, on September 1st it would have the same position at 6 p.m. This variation would not affect the Indians' use of this method, for they never had need for other than an approximate record of time, that being the one thing they had more of than they knew what to do with." (Dr. J. A. Brashear.)

Page 487.—"When the Akatsis (Lariat, or Rainbow) appears in the sky." The rainbow symbol is sometimes used in Indian decoration to represent the Thunder-bird. Other tribes call it "The Rain's Hat," "The Great Spirit's Fish Line," and "Strong-medicine-to-drive-away-rain."

Page 487.—"When the fires of the Northmen (Aurora Borealis) flash in the winter sky."

The Aurora Borealis is also called by the plains Indians, "The Light of the Northern Dancers," "Sacred Cloud," "The White Man's Fire," and "The Mysterious Fire of the North." The Indians of Vancouver Island believe that the light is caused by the fires of a tribe of Indian manikin, who live near the North Pole and boil out their blubber on the ice.

Page 487.—"When the sun paints both his cheeks, that is, when the Sun-dogs (Ick ski) appear." The concept, used in Indian sign-language to represent Sun-dogs, is "Fires to warm the Sun." The Shoshones' name for the phenomenon is "The Sun's Winter Ear-rings."

"When the parhelia, or Sun-dogs appear in very cold weather, the Sioux say that 'the Sun has kindled a fire.' When the Sun is eclipsed, they say it 'faints or dies.' The Sun 'travels' while the ground is motionless."   (Rev. J. O. Dorsey.)

Page 487.—"When I see a star feeding (Blackfeet name for comet)." "Comets have been regarded among all nations from the earliest ages as portents of evil. It is therefore not surprising that this superstition should be found among the Blackfeet. The appearance of several very bright comets during the 16th and 17th centuries caused universal alarm. Andrew Pare writes of the comet of 1528 : 'This comet was so horrible and so dreadful and inspired such terror in men's minds, that some died from fear alone, others by illness caused by fear.' Famine was generally supposed to follow the appearance of a comet. The recent return of Halley's Comet stirred up dormant superstition in the minds of multitudes of people, even those of intelligence, and from every part of Christendom, we have learned of the fear and dread associated with the comet's near approach to the sun and to the earth. It is true that the tail of the comet came in contact with the earth, as has occurred with other comets in the past, but it is known that it is built up of such tenuous matters, that it could have no effect upon the earth that could be detected with the most refined instruments. Sir Robert Ball has well said, 'The effect could not be greater than the contact of a rhinoceros with a cobweb.'"   (Dr. J. A. Brashear.)

Page 487.—"When the sun hides his face."

"A total eclipse of the sun is commonly regarded as the forerunner of war, disease and death among the nations of the earth. The writer of this note observed a total eclipse of the sun among a tribe of Winemucca Indians in Nevada, January 1st, 1900. They looked upon the phenomena in dread silence and yet with stolid bravery while, at the same time, a Chinese settlement near by made a dreadful noise by beating upon tin and other vessels to drive off the supposed dragon from the face of the sun."

(Dr. J. A. Brashear.)

Page 487.—"Day Star." In general the plains-tribes had more special names for stars and constellations than the mountains tribes. The Blackfeet called Mars the " Big-Fire-Star," and Venus " The Day Star " because visible in the daytime.

" When at its greatest brilliancy, the planet Venus can easily be seen overhead in a clear sky, even at midday. The period of visibility covers several weeks, but varies slightly from year to year."

(Dr. J. A. Brashear.)

Page 488.—" ' The Seven Brothers ' (Great Bear), also known in England as the ' Plough ' and ' Wain.' " According to a Sioux legend, " the four stars of the bowl of the dipper are called the ' bier.' It is borne by four men, behind whom comes the train of mourners. The second star in the handle has a very small one (the Little Sister) beside it. The Sioux say, ' it is she, who goes with her young one weeping ' " (following the bier).

(Rev. J. O. Dorsey.)

Page 489.—" The Little Sister " star is the smaller one of the two stars, at the bend in the handle of the dipper. In the older astronomy the brighter star is called " Mizar," and its companion " Alcor." Mizar itself is a double star, one of the most beautiful visible to the naked eye.

Page 490.—" There is also a family of six small stars we call the 'Lost Children' (Pleiades)." "This beautiful and brilliant group of seven stars, bringing its name Pleiades down from the ancients, has always been the central object in the astronomy of the world. It has been mentioned by many writers during the past ages. Job refers to them twice and the prophet Amos once. Only six stars are visible to the ordinary vision, but the seventh can readily be seen with a favouring atmosphere, and when the observer knows just where to look for it. Professor Langley has seen thirteen stars in the Pleiades in the clear sky of Mount Etna. The telescope shows many stars in the environs of this beautiful constellation. The photographic camera reveals to us the fact that the brighter stars are surrounded with vast fields of nebulous matter." (Dr. J. A. Brashear.)

Page 491.—" Morning Star and Young Morning Star or Legend of Star Boy (Later Scarface, or Poïa)." " The conjunction of two planets, that is their near approach to each other, has always been of deep significance to the untutored nations of the earth ; indeed to many of the learned it was considered a portent fraught with great good or evil. Even Bacon in his ' Astrologia Sana ' tells us that these phenomena are not to be rejected lightly.

"There can be conjunctions of any of the planets, but their importance seem to have been derived both from their near approach to each other, and from the increased brilliancy of their light. The degree of brilliance depends upon their distance from the earth at the time of conjunction.

"In July, 1905, the date when the Star Boy legend was narrated by Brings-down-the-Sun, Venus and Jupiter were in conjunction as Morning Stars. The Indians were doubtless attracted by the brilliant spectacle of the two planets ' travelling together,' but very probably recognised them by their characteristic colours.

"Because of the remarkably close approach of these two planets to each other, it was a rare and brilliant conjunction attracting the attention of astronomers all over the world. Between the 3rd and 4th of July they seemed to the naked eye to be almost in contact. They were both included in the field of the telescope at the same time, being separated by only a minute in right ascension, or about one-thirtieth of the diameter of the moon, and, north and south, by a little more than one-half of the diameter of the moon, *i.e.*, fifteen minutes. Jupiter (Star Boy) came up first, followed by Morning Star (Venus).

"Venus and Jupiter were in conjunction just before sunrise, October 14th, 1908. They were in conjunction again August 11th, 1909. The conjunction of Venus and Saturn on June 5th, 1910, will be very beautiful on account of their near approach to each other, which will be closest just before sunrise."

(Dr. J. A. Brashear.)

Page 499.—" The Star that stands still." "The North Star has a motion around the true pole at this epoch of one and one-third degrees, or in other words, it is nearly three times the diameter of the Moon away from the true pole of the heavens. This motion is so slow and so limited in extent that the unaided eye would not likely detect it. In fact, the Pole Star has been near enough to the true pole of the heavens for many generations to satisfy all demands of the tutored as well as the untutored observers." (Dr. J. A. Brashear.)

Page 364.—" My botanical collection."

This collection of herbs and plants, with a description of their Indian names, uses and methods of preparation by the Blackfeet, is deposited in the Carnegie Institute of Pittsburg. The specimens were identified by Mr. O. E. Jennings, Assistant Curator of Botany.

The same list was published by the Berlin Society for Anthropology, Ethnology and History (Zeitschrift für Ethnologie, Heft 2, 1909), after a lecture by the author in the Imperial Museum for Ethnography, March 6, 1909.

1. MATERIA MEDICA OF THE BLACKFEET.

KATOYA. Sweet Pine.—Balsam Fir. *Abies lasiocarpa*. Burned for incense in ceremonials. It was used in poultices for fevers and colds in the chest, also for hair oil by mixing with grease and for perfume. It is more fragrant than ordinary balsam. When it grows in dry places it has a more concentrated and sweet odour.

SE-PAT-SEMO. Sweet Grass. Vanilla Grass.—*Savastana odorata.* After drying, Sweet Grass was generally kept by plaiting several strands. It was burned for incense and used also for making hair tonic by soaking in water. In northern Europe and Sweden it is called Holy Grass, because, with other sweet scented grasses, it is strewn before the churches. It is found throughout the world in the cold north temperate zone, northern Europe, and Asia, Newfoundland to Alaska, south to New Jersey and Wisconsin to Colorado.

EK-SISO-KE. Sharp Vine.—Bear Grass. *Yucca glauca.* The roots were boiled in water and used as a tonic for falling hair. The Blackfeet thought there was no better remedy than the Ek-siso-ke for breaks and sprains. The roots were grated and placed in boiling water. The inflammation was reduced by holding the injured member in the rising steam. The roots were also placed upon cuts to stop bleeding and to allay inflammation.

NITS-IK-OPA. Double Root.—Squaw Root. *Carum Gairdneri.* Used for sore throat and placed on swellings to draw out inflammation. It was also eaten raw or boiled as a vegetable and used for flavouring stews.

OKS-PI-POKU. Sticky Root, also called AP-AKS-IBOKU. Wide Leaves.—Tufted Primrose or Alkali Lily. *Pachylobus caespitosus.* The root was pounded up and applied wet to sores and swellings to allay inflammation. It grows in alkali soil and is generally found in gravel beds.

APOS-IPOCO. Tastes Dry.—Alum Root. *Heuchera parvifolia.* It was pounded up and used wet as an application for sores and swellings. It grows on gravel bottoms and alkali flats.

MATOA-KOA-KSI. Yellow Root or Swamp Root.—Willow Leaved Dock. *Rumex salicifolius.* It was boiled and used for many complaints but generally for swellings. It grows in swamps.

MAIS-TO-NATA. Crow Root.—Dotted Blazing Star, named because of the brilliant scarlet of its flowers. *Lacinaria punctata.* It was called Crow Root by the Blackfeet because it was eaten by crows and ravens in the autumn. The root was boiled and applied to swellings. A tea was also made with it for stomach-ache. It was sometimes eaten raw.

O-MUCK-KAS. Big Turnip.—Parsnip. *Leptotaenia multifida.* Belonging to the carrot family, the Big Turnip is found on the sides of hills, growing in sandy loamy soil. It was gathered in the fall. The root was used to make a hot drink as a tonic for people in a weakened condition, and to make them fat. The root was also pounded up and burned for incense. When horses had the distemper they were made to inhale smoke from this root. It was also mixed with brains and used in soft tanning.

PA-KITO-KI. Gray Leaves.—Double Bladder Pod. *Physaria didymocarpa*. It is to be found growing on gravel bottoms. The Blackfeet chewed the plant for sore throats, also for cramps and stomach trouble. It was also placed in water with hot stones and used to allay swelling.

A-SAT-CHIOT-AKE. Rattle Weed.—Purple Loco Weed, Crazy Weed. *Aragallus lagopus*. Some of the flowers are purple, others blue, yellow and white. It grows on gravel bottoms. The Blackfeet chewed it for sore throats to allay swellings.

A-SA-PO-PINATS. Looks-like-a-plume.—Windflower or Round Fruited Anemone. *Anemone globosa*. It is adapted for a windy place and is found growing on hillsides where the wind strikes it, either on the plains, or in the mountains. In midsummer the flower turns into cotton which the Blackfeet burn on a hot coal for head-ache.

ET-AWA-ASI. Makes-you-sneeze (Snuff). American White Hellebore. *Veratrum speciosum*. The plant grows to be about six feet high and is found in the mountain forests. The root is poison-ous for eating. It was gathered by the Blackfeet both in the fall and in the spring and was used for head-ache. They broke off a small piece of the root which was very dry and snuffed it up the nose.

SIXA-WA-KASIM. Black Root.—Red Bane Berry. *Actaea arguta*. The berries are both red and white. It is found near the mountains in the underbrush along rivers. The roots were boiled and used for coughs and colds.

SIXIMAS. Black Root.—White Bane Berry. *Actaea eburnea*. The root was boiled and used for coughs and colds.

SIX-OCASIM. (Indian Horehound). It is not found on the prairies but in the mountains along streams. It was generally used after compounding with other plants, for babies' colds.

KAKSAMIS. She Sage.—Sweet Sage, Old Man, Pasturage Sage Brush. *Artemisia frigida*. The roots or tops were boiled and used as a drink for mountain fever. It was also chewed for heart-burn. Sage was generally tied to articles that were offered as sacrifices to the Sun.

OTSQUE-EINA. Blue Berry.—Oregon Grape. *Berberis aqui-folium*. The roots were boiled and used for stomach trouble, also for hemorrhages. It grew in the forest on the mountains.

APOKS-IKIM. Smell Foot.—Northern Valerian. *Valeriana septentrionalis*. A hot drink was made from the roots for stomach trouble.

A-MUCH-KO-IYATSIS. Red Mouth Bush.— Paper Leaf Alder. *Alnus tenuifolia*. A hot drink was made of the bark and taken for scrofula. The bark split readily and was also used for making stirrups, which were covered with raw-hide. The Blackfeet name originated because the bark when chewed made their mouths red.

MA-NE-KA-PE. Young Man.—Horse Mint. *Monarda scabra.* An eye wash was made by placing the blossoms in warm water and was used to allay inflammation.

SO-YA-ITS. Lies-on-his-belly.—Long Plumed Avens. *Sieversia ciliata.* It grows on the plains and in the mountains. The Blackfeet boiled it in water and used for sore and inflamed eyes.

KINE. Rose Berries or APIS-IS-KITSA-WA.—Tomato Flower. Says Rose. *Rosa Sayi.* A drink was made of the root and given to children for diarrhoea. The berries were sometimes eaten raw.

OMAKA-KA-TANE-WAN. Gopher Berries.—Wild potato, Ground Cherry, Cut Leaved Night Shade. *Solanum triflorum.* The berries were boiled and given to children for diarrhoea. The plants grow on prairie-dog hills.

KITA-KOP-SIM. Garter Root or Pachsi, Dry Root.—Silver Weed. *Argentina anserina.* The root was used for diarrhoea.

NUXAPIST. Little Blanket.—Indian Kemp, Dog Bane. *Apocynum cannabinum.* A drink was made by boiling the root in water and taken for a laxative. It was also used as a wash to prevent hair falling out. It grows on high cliffs and was gathered at all times of year.

A-PO-PIK-A-TISS. Makes-your-hair-gray.—Pore Fungus. *Polyporus.* A small quantity was used as a purgative. It was said to make the hair gray if too large a dose was taken. It was also used for cleaning buckskin.

AT-SI-PO-KOA. Fire Taste.—Sharp Leaved Beard Tongue. *Pentstemon acuminatus.* The Blackfeet named it At-si-po-koa because of its biting flavour. It was boiled in water and taken internally for cramps and pains in the stomach. It was also used to stop vomiting.

SIX-IN-OKO. Juniper.—Red Cedar. *Juniperus scopulorum.* The berries were made into a tea to stop vomiting. The Juniper was used ceremonially on the altar of the sacred woman at the Sun-dance.

AKS-PEIS. Sticky Weed.—Gum Plant. *Grindelia squarrosa.* The root was boiled and taken internally for liver trouble. It grows on the prairies.

OPET-AT-SAPIA. *Gutierrezia diversifolia.* Grows on the prairies in the foothills to the mountains. The roots were used by medicine men in doctoring. They placed red hot stones in water with the roots and made the patient inhale the steam.

E-SIMATCH-SIS. Dye.—*Evernia vulpina.* A lichen that grows on pine trees. It was used as a yellow dye for porcupine quills.

The quills were placed with the dye in boiling water. It was also used for head-ache.

E-SIMATCH-SIS. Dye.—The Yellow Orthocarpus. *Orthocarpus luteus*. Used for dyeing gopher skins red. The plant was first pounded up and then pressed firmly upon the skin. It grows on the prairies.

ANA-WAWA-TOKS-TIMA. Buffalo Food.—Yellow Cancer Root. *Thalesia fasciculata*. Used by Buffalo medicine men in doctoring wounds. They chewed and blew it upon the wound.

SA-PO-TUN-A-KIO-TOI-YIS. Joint Grass.—Scouring Rush. *Equisetum hiemale*. The grass was boiled in water and used as a drink, for horse medicine.

PACH-CO-I-AU-SAUKAS. Smell Mouth.—Western Sweet Cicely. *Washingtonia divaricata*. It was given to mares in winter. The Blackfeet say that it put them in good condition for foaling. They placed it in the mares' mouths and made them chew it. A pleasant drink was made with a small piece of the Western Sweet Cicely root, a little more of the Sixocasim (Indian Horehound) to three cups of water. It was taken hot for colds or tickling in the throat.

TOBACCO.

KA-KA-SIN. Larb or Kinnekinick.—Bear Berry. *Arctostaphylus uva ursi*. The leaves which are thick and evergreen were dried and used for smoking. The berries were eaten raw and also used mashed in fat and fried. It grows in northern North America also northern Europe and Asia.

O-MAKSE-KA-KA-SIN. Big Larb.—Pipsissewa, Princess Pine. *Chimaphila umbellata*. It flourishes among decaying leaves in a sandy soil in the mountain forests of Northern North America. The dried leaves were used for tobacco by all the Mountain Indians. The Blackfeet had a special preference for the Big Larb in smoking.

2. PLANTS FOR CEREMONIALS.

PONO-KAU-SINNI. Turnip Elk Food.—Narrow Leaved Puccoon. *Lithospermum linearifolium*. The tops were dried and used for burning as incense in ceremonials.

SO-YO-TOI-YIS. Spring Grass or I-TA-PAT-ANIS, Cut-your-finger.—Slough Grass Sledge. *Carex nebrascensis praevia*. The Blackfeet said it was the favourite grass of the buffalo and for this reason the medicine men tied it around the horns of the sacred buffalo head used in the Sun-dance ceremonials. It grows in marshy places on the prairies.

A-PONO-KAUKI. Paper Leaves or O-TO-KAP-ATSIS. Yellow Flower. —Arrow Leaved Balsam Root. *Balsamorrhiza sagittata*. The large leaves were used in a ceremonial, while roasting Camass roots.

3. Berries and Wild Vegetables Used for Eating.

OK-KUN-OKIN. Berry.—Sarvis Berry, June Berry, Service Berry, Shad, May Cherry. *Amelanchier oblongifolia.* A tall shrub or small tree growing on the prairies, along side hills and in river bottoms. The berries ripen in midsummer generally about the middle of July. The Blackfeet used them in great quantities with stews, soups and meat. They also dried them for winter use. Violent pains often followed the eating of raw Sarvis Berries.

PUKKEEP. Choke Cherry.—Western Wild Cherry. *Prunus demissa.* The Blackfeet say it does not ripen till later than the Sarvis Berry, generally September or even October. They were used for soups, eaten raw, and pounded up and mixed with meat. The bark was boiled and used internally in combination with roots of the Western Sweet Cicely, Northern Valerian, and Sixocasim (Indian Horehound).

MISS-IS-A-MISOI. Stink Wood.—Buffalo Berry, Silver Berry. *Elaeagnus argentea.* The Blackfeet gave it the name of Stink Wood because of the bad smell of the smoke. In gathering firewood a person was ridiculed if he brought in Stink Wood. The berries were used for soup. The bark was very tough and made strong rope for tying skins and parfleches when raw-hide was not at hand.

IM-A-TOCH-KOT. Dog Feet.—*Disporum trachycarpum.* It bears yellow berries which are eaten raw.

PO-KINT-SOMO. Wild Rhubarb.—Cow Parsnip. *Heracleum lanatum.* In the spring the stalks were eaten after being roasted over hot coals. The Blackfeet say the stalks are of two kinds which they designate by Napim (He) and Skim (She). They peeled and split the stalk of the Skim before roasting but only peeled the Napim. A stalk of the PO-KINT-SOMO was placed on the altar of the Sun-dance ceremonial.

PACH-OP-IT-SKINNI. Lumpy Head.—Wild Potato, Spring Beauty. *Claytonia lanceolata.* The Wild Potato grew on the prairies and in the foothills of the mountains. The Blackfeet dug them in spring for eating, preparing them for eating by boiling.

EK-SIK-A-PATO-API. Looks Back.—Smart Weed. *Polygonum bistortoides.* The root was used in soups and stews.

PESAT-SE-NEKIM. Funny Vine.—Wild Onion. *Allium recurvatum.* Eaten raw and also used for flavouring.

KACH-A-TAN. Tender Root.—Carolina Milk Vetch. *Astragalus carolinianus.* The root was gathered in the spring or fall and eaten raw or cooked by boiling in water. It grows on the gravel bottoms, or side-hills of the prairies.

EKS-IX-IX. White Root.—Bitter Root, State Flower of Montana, Red Head Louisa. *Lewisia rediviva*. The Blackfeet believed it was healthy food. They prepared it by boiling in water. It grows plentifully in the mountains.

SAX-IKA-KITSIM. (Quick Smell).—American Wild Mint. *Mentha canadensis*. The leaves were placed in parfleches to flavour dried meat. It was also used to make tea.

MASS. Wild Turnip.—Elk Food. *Lithospermum linearifolium*. The roots were prepared for eating by boiling or roasting. It grows on the prairies.

O-MUCK-AI-IX-IXI. Big White Root.—Evening Primrose, Alkali Lily. *Musenium divaricatum*. The Blackfeet say the root has no flavour until dried. It was gathered in the fall and eaten raw. It grows on the prairies.

MISS-ISSA. Camass.—*Camassia esculenta*. The roots were generally dug in the fall after the blossoms had fallen. They were baked by placing in a deep hole with heated stones and a covering of leaves and grass. A fire was also kept burning on top of the ground. It was said to require two days and two nights to cook them thoroughly in this way.

4. PERFUMES.

AT-SINA-MO. Gros Ventre Scent.—Meadow Rue. *Thalictrum occidentale*. The berries were dried and placed in small buckskin bags.

KATOYA. Sweet Pine.—Balsam Fir. *Abies lasiocarpa*. The leaves had a delightful odour when confined in a buckskin bag. Sweet Pine was also mixed with grease in making hair oil to add fragrance.

MAT-O-AT-SIM. Perfumed Plant.—Rayless Camomile, Oregon Dog Root, Dog Fennel. *Matricaria matricarioides*. The blossoms were dried and used for perfumery.

SE-PAT-SEMO. Sweet Grass.—Vanilla Grass. *Sevastana odorata*. Sweet Grass was the most popular perfumery among the Blackfeet. It was made into braids and placed with their clothes or carried around in small bags. It was also used for a hair-wash and as incense.

Pieces of punk from the Cottonwood Tree, leaves of the Balsam Poplar, and the Ring-bone from a horse's leg were also used for perfumes.

5. Blackfeet Names for Flowers.

Sik-a-pis-chis.   White Flower.—*Aster commutatus.*

Ota-kap-is-chis-kit-sima.   Yellow   Flower. — Clasping-leaved Arnica.   *Arnica amplexifolia.*

A-pis-is-kit-sa-wa.   Tomato Flower.—Red Rose.   *Rosa Sayi.*

Ot-ska-a-pis-is-kit-sa.   Blue Flower.—Oblong Leaved Gentian. *Gentiana affinis.*

A-sa-po-pin-ats.   Looks-like-a-plume.—Round Fruited Anemone. *Anemone globosa.*   Its name was derived from the appearance of the flower when it turns into cotton and resembles a soft, downy feather.

A-po-no-kau-ki.   Paper Leaves.—Arrow-leaved Balsam Root. *Balsamorrhiza sagittata.*   In the hot weather its large leaves become very dry and resemble paper.

Sto-o-kat-sis.   Ghost's Lariat.—Columbian Virgins Bower. *Atragene columbiana.*   A vine, with a beautiful light blue flower that trails along the ground and also climbs trees.   The Blackfeet have named it Ghost's Lariat because it catches people and trips them up unexpectedly.

Page 431.—GENEALOGICAL TABLE OF BRINGS-DOWN-THE-SUN'S FAMILY.

Brings-down-the-Sun's grandparents.

Kina-ksi-taki (Little Mountain) ══ Natayo (Bob Cat).

Children of his grandparents with their wives and husbands.

Miks-kim-iks-okas=Napis-tapsi (Iron Shirt), (Eagle-white-on-both-ends).

Makapi-apotsi (Sitting-in-lodge-long-time).

Makaki-potka=Nana-nikki (Smart Child), (Killed-a-Chief).

Nista-sami =: Sita-ka-poki (Calf Looking), (Stays-in-different-lodges).

Nik-tis-is-tie (Got Wet).

Kis-ta-pina, Sapia-sinau (Took-a-good-gun-in-night).

Nato-kina (Two Guns).

Peta-paks-ina.

Nato-soko (Holy Robe).

Kik-si-papeta (Striped Eagle).

Omuckseta (Big Smoke).

Katatatsi (Not-very-brave).

Natosin-ne-pe-e =Bird (Brings-down-the-Sun).

Iron Shirt

Neoks-a-nama (Three Guns).

Sons of Brings-down-the-Sun and their wives.

Neoks-ama-peta=Anatoki (Three Eagles), (Pretty Head). Three children.

Apeso-mucca=Sit-soaki (Running Wolf), (Water Bird). Four children.

Iron Shirt=Poks-ki (Small Face). Three children.

Mak-sa-kitapi=Water-Spider-Woman (Riding-good-horse), Three children.

Daughters of Brings-down-the-Sun and their husbands.

Bear-Child=Long Hair. Eight children.

Born-with-teeth=Medicine Bonnet Woman. Four children.

Old Wolf Man=Whistling-all-night. Five children.

Daughters of Brings-down-the-Sun and their husbands (*continued*).

Sure Chief=Double Gun Woman. Three children.

Red Fox=Good Kill. Four children.

Heavy=Turns-the-whole-Runner | herd-back-alone. Three children.

Wakes-up-= Pretty last Blanket. (Mane), Three children.

Yellow=Owl-calling-Robe coming. Two children.

Double=Beaver. Spy Two children.

INDEX